MW00619017

ClipWords Promotion is the second in a series
of books based on the popular ClipWords CD-ROM.
Future releases will provide Clips on different topics,
such as Sports, Holidays, Education, Issues,
Government, Quick Laughs, Events, Industry,
People and Science & Technology.

Now available from Epigraphics:

ClipWords Motivation book
ClipWords CD-ROM for Windows™ and Macintosh™
ClipWords *Pro* CD-ROM for Windows™ and Macintosh™

ISBN 0-9727861-1-2

Cover designed by Gorski-Osterholdt, Inc., Hillside, IL
Printed in the United States of America

Published by
Epigraphics Software, Inc.
Book Division
4418 Roosevelt Road
Hillside, Illinois 60162
www.clipwords.com
Toll-free: 1-888-291-3883

*"The difference between the right word
and almost the right word
is the difference between lightning
and a lightning bug."*

Mark Twain

Now, You'll Never Have To Say...
"I Can't Think Of What To Say!"

The end of writer's block is at your fingertips. With ClipWords you can find instant inspiration when you're looking for just the right words to jump-start the thinking and writing process.

ClipWords are common and uncommon headlines, phrases and statements. You see them every day in newspapers, magazines, junk mail, annual reports, letters, movies and on billboards. You hear them at cocktail parties, in sermons, on the news, at sporting events, on talk radio, on TV, in business meetings and on the street. From everyday expressions to snappy attention-grabbers, ClipWords has thousands of ideas waiting to inspire you.

You might recognize a well-turned phrase when you hear one, but would you remember it six months later when you could really use it? Bob Gorski, a four-decade advertising veteran and founder of Chicago-based ad/promotion agency Gorski-Osterholdt, Inc., has taken the time to jot down those everyday gems of our American language and sort them into categories for easy access. He's done all the grunt work for you. ClipWords is the result of years of ongoing research and a veritable mountain of post-its and legal pads, which all add up to a unique resource book–the first of its kind!

If you're a professional copywriter, don't worry– this book won't put you out of business, but it will give your ideas a fresh twist and make your writing job easier. If you're not a professional copywriter, you can add a pro's touch to promotions, sale events, announcements, ads and a wide variety of other projects where just the right words can make all the difference. *Now you can make that difference with ClipWords. It's like having a copywriter in a book.*

Foreword

By Rick Segel

It all starts with a name.

Every sale or promotion has its own identity, its own unique brand in the mind of the public. From the colors that are used to fonts that are selected, these are all part of the mosaic of the sale or promotion. The foundation of that mosaic is the name or theme, which sets the tone for the promotion.

When you select a name, you must understand what the name will do. In order to do that we have to address three issues. The first is what the difference is between a sale and promotion. That's the easy one. Second is the purpose of the event, and lastly is where you want the sale to register on the Misery Meter, a gauge that measures the power or strength of a sale title in the eye of the customer.

Before we tackle these three issues, let's clarify the different terms we use when discussing a sale or promotion name. The word *name* is the most logical. However, the terms *title, theme,* and *handle* are also used. I can assure you they all mean the same thing. Think about the term *handle*, a term used by many professional promoters, which is powerful in its simplicity. A handle allows us to pick up things, and isn't that what a promotion or sale name is supposed to do? It allows us to get a handle on what we are trying to do. The name is our handle. It becomes our roadmap to follow, our mission and vision all rolled up in a few short words.

Remember, any fool can make their point when they have an unlimited amount of words, but it is the true genius who can generate action with just a few. *Remember the Alamo.*

The Difference between a Sale and a Promotion. Generally speaking, when the word *sale* is used, that means that there is a price incentive added to the mix. Both terms, sale and *promotion*, attract attention and generate some form of action—usually participation.

The Purpose of the Event. Every event has a reason for its existence, and there is a great range of purposes, from just creating excitement in a business because things are getting routine or mundane to the cash-raising sale that means the business needs money to continue. Some of the other more popular reasons for sales and promotions are expansion, moves, making room for new merchandise, adding names to your database, marketing to a new geographical area, overbuying, retirement, opening a new department, seasonal events and clearances, anniversaries, and of course, going out of business. Just by listing those reasons for a promotion, it helps to define the goals.

If your goal is to raise cash, and you know how much cash you need, then you know how to determine the success of the promotion. If your goal is to add 100 names to a database and you reach 110, then you know that you have exceeded your goal. What the promotion name is doing is telling you where you want to go. Once you know where you want to go, it is always much easier to get there. That's why determining the reason or purpose of the event is such a critical step. It makes all the other steps that much easier.

The Misery Meter. As strange as it may sound, the more miserable the customer believes the retailer to be, the stronger the event will be. On one end of the Misery Meter is the softest of sale titles—the 5%-10% off sale. On the opposite end is the Going Out of Business Sale. This sale title is so powerful that every state in the Union has laws regulating its use. We have all seen fly-by-night businesses that are constantly "going out of business" just to capitalize on the power of that handle. Of course, there are those unscrupulous businesses that try to run the Going Out of Business Sale just to try to fool the public. Following lower on the Misery Meter, but still powerful, is the Store Closing Sale, and a little less powerful is the Liquidation Sale. The Misery Meter registers the level of misery perceived in the mind of the customer and dictates how deep the perceived discounts should be. When naming your sales, keep the Misery Meter in mind.

The Misery Meter focuses on the price of the merchandise in the mind of the customer. In today's competitive environment, many businesses have been very successful in focusing on the Excitement Meter. This highlights how much entertainment or fun the event can be. Titles like Back Room Sale, 72-Hour Sale, and Sidewalk Sale focus on the shopping experience, as opposed to the price.

People like Sidewalk Sales not only because the prices are low, but because of the way merchandise is displayed. The same holds true with the Back Room Sale. So, being strong on the Misery Meter or strong on the Excitement Meter will make for a good sale. If you are able to combine these two meters, the results can be sensational.

ClipWords has become an integral part of my idea-generation and brainstorming processes. All the different Clips in this book are categorized for ease of use. Although its purpose is to supply ideas for sale and promotional names, *it can be used to promote products and services too.* ClipWords inspires more sales, promotions, store themes and even layouts and designs by taking us down a path that we never would have followed without this direction!

I am excited to be able to recommend this new book to my clients and audiences. It's the first collection of its type, and I know it will be a valuable tool for anyone who uses it for years to come! Try it once and you'll never be without it for your brainstorming sessions!

Rick Segel is a seasoned retailer and the author of several books, including "Laugh and Get Rich" and the best-selling "Retail Business Kit for Dummies". He is also a Certified Speaking Professional who has delivered over 1,400 presentations worldwide.

How to Get More Value out of ClipWords™

Purchasing this book (and we thank you) gives you a unique new resource with thousands of user-friendly phrases and statements to help recharge your creative batteries. Here are some helpful hints that will give you the most bang for your buck!

Do... check out the 169 topics listed in the table of contents. List several topics that might apply to the task at hand, and take a glance through them. **It's a great starting place for ideas!**

Don't... stop if you find a good clip right away. Dig a little deeper and you might find a better one. They can even give you ideas for other aspects to address in whatever it is you're promoting! **ClipWords is a definite cure for writer's block!**

Do... check out unrelated topics if you want to try a different approach. The best ideas sometimes come from the most unexpected places. If you're promoting tennis bracelets and looking for a new angle, open the book to, say, Furniture. The phrase "Designed to complement your finest furnishings" can become "Designed to complement your finest eveningwear". **It's all about sparking your creativity!**

Don't... forget, none of these Clips are set in stone. "Cabin Fever Sale" can become "We treat cabin fever depression… with fantastic savings!" or "No need to suffer from cabin fever with these super savings!" or "Chase away cabin fever with our red-hot deals!" Sometimes you can create the perfect Clip by mixing two or more ClipWords phrases. If you have a St. Patrick's Day promotion, you can combine "A hearty toast to St. Patrick's Day!" and "A salute to the Irish" to get "A hearty salute to the Irish on St. Patrick's Day!" **ClipWords makes it easy to find the right words to get your project on paper quickly and easily!**

The whole point of ClipWords is to help you find interesting ways to get your message across to your customers. Whether these Clips give you the phrases or help you come up with your own, it's a valuable resource to get you through that brain-drain syndrome crisis. **All you have to do is open the book and let ClipWords open your mind!**

Table of Contents

Table of Contents

Alcohol / Spirits

250 social values of drinking

A beer a day may be the way to keep the doctor away

A bounty of glorious, thirst-quenching beers!

A good drink never goes out of style

A good place to hoist a few

A good place to slam down a couple beers

A great bar where you can see and be seen

A great treat for beer lovers

A perfect after-dinner drink

A perfect hangout for honeys who want to go hog wild

A place where you want to hang out

A rare find for wine aficionados

A refreshing drink for any occasion

A selection of fine wines are available at our...

A six-pack of joy!

A special time that calls for a special wine

A taste above the rest

A thirst quencher that will drive you mad

A unique taste at the price of an ordinary wine

A white wine that will make your meal special

An old-fashioned tavern with a great jukebox and pool tables

And be sure to stop in for a beer

Any time is margarita time!

Anyone for a good old-fashioned?

Ask an Irishman where to find a good pub

Attention! Martini drinkers

Barstool sale!

Beer drinking isn't the only game in town

Beer lovers of America

But it doesn't taste like beer

But what is the right wine?

Certainly quenches your thirst

Champagne taste for a beer budget

Cocktails just for you

Come alive after 5

Does your drink match your mood?

Drinks and hors d'oeuvres are free!

Easy to drink and so very pleasant

Elegant and classy, with character

Featuring the best wine values

For a true tequila experience...

For beer belly customers only!

For hot times and cool cocktails

For your cocktail-party conversation

For your next cocktail party

Free beer brewed on site daily

Free beer night!

From the finest wine country in the world

Get ready for a cold one

Get your paws on our bar

Get yourself a beer... you earned it

Good times and great beer are always brewing at...

Great for beer bellies

Great taste is worth repeating

Guaranteed lowest prices on every wine... everyday!

Happiness is on tap

Happy hour comes but once a day, so make it count

Have a beer... you'll feel better

Hey, cold beer!!!

Hip, hip, hooray... nickel-beer night!

Holiday cheer served here

How about a nice wine for the weekend?

How do you take your gin?

How to brew beer at home

How to host a wine-tasting party

I'll drink to that

If it tastes good to you, it's good wine

If you are drinking to forget, please pay in advance

If you drink beer, you live

If you show up with a case of beer, you'll be invited back!

In pursuit of the perfect cocktail

In the bottle! In the mouth! In the price!

In the mood for saloon slumming?

Indulge your good taste in a...

It only takes one sip to know if it's a good bottle of wine

It's a beer blast!

It's a beer for Americans

It's a cocktail jungle in here

It's a great place to be

It's good for what ales you

It's ladies night, tonight!

It's the beer of choice

It's the finest alcoholic drink ever

It's the perfect place to end the night with a kick

It's the ultimate cocktail

It's time to pack the coolers

Join our beer festival

Join us for wine, hors d'oeuvres and a celebration

Just your friendly neighborhood pub

Let your taste buds choose the wine

Let's go bar-hopping

Lift your glass and let us drink to the future

Looking for a good beer bar?

May I offer you a tall, cool one?

May we suggest a wine with your dinner?

My kind of drink

No one under 21 admitted without a fake I.D.

Non-alcoholic drinks are not served here

Nothing so fine as wine

Now, this is what we call a sports bar

Octoberfest 12-pack sale!

One of the world's best dessert wines

Our wines speak for themselves

Pick up a bottle for dinner tonight

Please drink responsibly

Please, think before you drink and drive

Pop one open tonight

Pour yourself a tall one

Real men really do drink beer

Refresh your spirit with a...

Saturday night is Saturday night at...

Shake, stir, pour

Share the taste of a good wine

Show your hospitality with a bottle of wine

Simply add wine to any meal

Social drinkers... only!

Special meals require special wines

Stock up on gin for the party!

Take a nice bottle of white wine to your next dinner party

Take a sip... ahhhhh!

Tangy. Spicy. Zesty.

That's my drink!

The bar is now open!

The beer for beer lovers

The best beer on the beach

The best neighborhood bar in town!

The best wines you can find at...

The beverage of choice is champagne, of course

The cocktail hour!

The coldest beer in town... on tap!

The corner bar is a remarkable institution

The drink of the gods

The drink you'll tell your friends about

The Great Beer Festival!

The greatest bottle of wine ever!

The hip place to be!

The label you're most likely to see most often

The most famous red wine in the world

The perfect choice after a busy day

The perfect wine to pair with a special meal

The place is clean! The food is good! The beer is cold!

The right wine. The right price. The right place.

The see-and-be-seen spot

The ultimate destination for the "in" crowd

The wildest bar in town... bar none

The wine for everyday wine drinkers

There's an empty stool in the bar with your name on it

There's no such thing as a bad wine

There's nothing like a beer after a hard day's work

This drink is sure to satisfy any cocktail snob

This place is jammed on weekends!

Tropical flavor drinks that make you feel as if you're on a faraway island

Tuesday is martini night!

Want something more special than ordinary wine?

We offer a limited selection of interesting wines

We serve fabulously festive cocktails!

We stock the best wines in the world!

We'll set aside a cold beer for you!

What could possibly beat tequila?

What's your beverage of choice?

What's your pleasure?

When beer is your beverage of choice

When was the last time you bought a bottle of wine to take home?

Where drinking is encouraged

Where the beer flows like honey

Where there is great food, there is great wine

Where you feel like a regular even if you aren't

Where your 13th drink is free!

White Zinfandel and scotch on the rocks, both solid favorites

Why wait for a special occasion to buy a bottle of champagne?

Wines of personality and passion

With a twist of lemon or a splash of a lime

Work hard, play hard... have a beer

World's best cocktails... right here!

Would you care for a cocktail?

You can quench your thirst with this

You don't have to grow up on a vineyard to enjoy wine

You don't have to pay big bucks to get high-quality wine

You'll feel like you're in Mexico with our margaritas

You'll love our saloon atmosphere

Your guide to the art of cocktails

Your port of call for tropical drink

100-year-old legend... and a
100-year anniversary

10th Anniversary Red Tag
Clearance Event

150 years of bricks and mortar

1st Anniversary Savings!

25 Years is a lot to shout about...
Now roar for more in the next 25 years

25th Anniversary Super Sale!

50 years ago, we opened our first store...

50 years of excellence, of quality,
of customer loyalty

50th Anniversary Sell-A-Bration!

50th celebration: Prices from the past

55th anniversary celebration... Thank
you for 55 years of support!

A celebration 25 years in the making

A century of excellence

A proud milestone

A quarter of a century old celebration

A special anniversary offer

A successful first year celebration, our
First Annual Sales Event!

An anniversary celebration of
our success

An anniversary sales extravaganza!

An invitation to share the joy and share
the savings!

Anniversary Blowout!

Anniversary Celebration
Savings Spectacular!

Anniversary Sales Event of the Year!

Anniversary Sell-a-bration

Anniversary Special Values

As we celebrate our 30th anniversary

Available only during our
anniversary sale!

Celebrate our 35th anniversary with
35% savings

Celebrate our 50th with great items for
only 5 bucks!

Celebrate that special event at...

Celebrate with us, our first anniversary

Celebrate your anniversary in style

Celebrating 100 years means you have
been around for a long time

Celebrating 100 years of
academic excellence

Celebrating 100 years of achievements

Celebrating 100 years of innovation

Celebrating 150 years of quality

Celebrating 25 years of savings

Celebrating 50 amazing years

Celebrating 50 years in business

Celebrating a century of service

Celebrating our 16th Anniversary Sale
with bargains, values and deals!

Celebrating our first year as the...

Celebrating the 150th anniversary of
our founding

Chalking up 100 years is
an accomplishment

Check out our money-saving
anniversary sale offer!

Congratulations on 25 years of excellence

Congratulations on 50 years
of innovation

Congratulations on 75 years of success

Don't miss our 90th anniversary
sale celebration!

Fifty bloomin' years... Everything is
50% off, today only!

Fifty great years... thank you

Fifty years old and still growing strong

Happy Anniversary Time

Help us celebrate our 65th anniversary

Here's to your next 25 years

In celebration of our 40th anniversary, we're giving away the store!

In honor of our anniversary

It is a time of celebration. 25 years of success

It was 30 years ago today

It's a marquee event

It's nice to be remembered on special occasions

It's our 10th anniversary... so we're giving away the store

It's our 1st Anniversary Sale!

Join us for our anniversary celebration

Just our anniversary sale for our customers!

Last chance! Anniversary sale!

Make it an extra-special anniversary

Make this anniversary a memorable one

Make your anniversary an event

Mark your calendar for this gala event

One hundred years and still growing

Our 100-year heritage of excellence and value

Our 50 years in business calls for one big celebration

Our anniversary has been 15 years in the making

Our gala anniversary savings celebration

Proud to have served you for the last 65 years. Looking forward to the next 65 years

Silver anniversary sale! 25% off all purchases!!!

Storewide Anniversary Sale!

Sweet 16 Anniversary Celebration

Thank you for 25 wonderful years

Thanks a million anniversary

Thanks for helping us reach our 50th anniversary

The anniversary event of the year

The biggest event in 10 million years

The celebration of a dream come true

The sesquicentennial celebration

This anniversary commemorates our...

This anniversary is worth celebrating

This is one anniversary you don't want to miss

This is what we'd call a golden anniversary

Three cheers for 30 years... Celebrating 30 Days Sales Event!

Twenty-five glorious years... we thank you for your loyalty!

We are celebrating a century of service and achievement

We are proud to congratulate you on 50 years of great leadership

We have 25 reasons to celebrate our 25th anniversary

We invite you to come help us celebrate our anniversary

We invite you to share in our anniversary... with exceptional savings

We salute five fabulous decades of success

We salute you on 50 years of excellence

We turn 150 today... Thank You!

We're 100 years old and we're celebrating...

We're 50 years new

We're celebrating 25 years in business

We're celebrating our 100th anniversary with a spectacular...

We're celebrating our 25th anniversary by reducing our prices 25%

We're kicking off our 25th year with...

We're making our 50th an extra-special anniversary

We're preserving the memories of this special day... One Big Sales Event!

13

Assisted Living

A community designed for adults who desire comfortable living

A complete lifestyle for mature adults

A full range of health care services are available

A healthy approach to aging

A life-care approach to healthcare

A lifestyle of vibrancy, fullness and spirit

A lifestyle you'll love... as well as your loved ones

A maintenance-free lifestyle

A new kind of assisted living residence

A place you want to call home

A premier life care community

A self-contained independent living retirement community

A senior living alternative, beautiful beyond your expectations

A supportive and encouraging environment that allows you to be independent

A warm, loving environment that makes it a real home

An environment where you would not be lonely

An innovative living arrangement

And now you can call it home

As a resident, you will enjoy a full array of activities, events, amenities and services

Assisted living... ageless attitudes

But is it right for you?

Carefree. Secure. Comfortable. Active.

Caring for an aging family member?

Come to a place that can make your life even better

Comforts, convenience and all the necessities of life

Committed to serving the needs of our residents

Creating a better quality of life for all seniors

Enjoy easy living

Experience a new way of living

Faith-based independent living and assisted living for older adults

For people who recognize the conveniences and security of lifecare

From assisted living to skilled nursing

Fulfilling, wellness-oriented lifestyle sought by so many of today's seniors

Gracious living at an affordable price

Helping seniors maintain their independence

I enjoy it here for a thousand reasons

Independent living or assisted living?

It all comes down to who will take care of the elderly

It isn't about where you live... it's about how you live

It's a good way to live and enrich life

It's a new sense of freedom

It's all here... assisted living that makes you feel at home

It's not just a home; it's a lifestyle

It's the right approach to assisted living

Learning to build a new way of life

Let us know how we can help you meet the care need of a senior in your life

Live a maintenance-free lifestyle

Live better. Feel better. Look better.

Live happier, healthier, and as independently as possible

Live your life in a caring style

Living in a community within a community

Looking for the right assisted-living facility?

My life's been wonderful since I moved here

Not just assisted living, but better living

Prepare for assisted living before it's needed

Spend your golden years surrounded by companionship and friendship

Spiritual, emotional, social and physical care

Tailored to individual needs and preferences

Take advantage of the concept of independent living

Talk about a great place to live

The choice of an assisted-living community is an important one

The finest in assisted living services

The focus is on quality of life

The good life made affordable

The life of exceptional living

The perfect community. You'll call it home

The place designed for happy living

The search for a good nursing home can add a few gray hairs to anyone's head

The solution is to purchase long-term care insurance

This is where the people come who want to get away from people like you

Value-added care to meet your healthcare needs

We are committed to improving the quality of life

We are more than just a great place to live

We bring your vision of better living to life

We cater to independent living for seniors

We give them the care they deserve

We go out of our way to make you feel at home

We make life a little easier and a lot more fun

We offer a full spectrum of services from light support to daily comprehensive care

We offer an abundance of activities

We offer the comforts of home without the hassles

We offer you an environment that puts you at ease

We provide health, independence and active lifestyles

We provide the quality care you desire and they deserve

We treat all residents with the compassion, respect and dignity they rightfully deserve

We would like to introduce you to our friendly, family-oriented community

We're committed to taking that extra step to provide you with the quality lifestyle you deserve

We're here to answer your questions about senior care service

What a peaceful place to be! What a wonderful way to live!

Where caring is our No. 1 concern in growing old

Where independence and assistance go hand in hand

Where individual privacy is respected and social interaction is relished

Where visitors are always welcome

Where your loved one can live life to the fullest

You make the choice, we will make you happy you did

You'll have peace of mind knowing assisted living is available

Your individuality and independence will be preserved

Your quality of life is our main concern

A big-league auto racing sale event!

A daredevil of a sale!

A full day of sales excitement!

A Race to the Grill Sale!

A run for championship savings!

A sale event for race fans of all ages

A salute to stock-car racing

A Victory Lap Sale Celebration!

All revved up and ready for sales action!

Another clutch sales performance

Auto racing at full speed

Auto racing's May Madness is in full force

Bargains for race fans of all ages!

Bargains from the starting line to the finish line!

Before you rev up your engine...

Blaze down the track for drastically slashed prices!

Bringing racing excitement to you

Burning Rubber Bargain Days!

Catch the bug for auto racing

Committed to the racing enthusiasts

Crank up the savings!

Deals are hitting on all cylinders

Don't pass up these bargains!

Dragsters are ready to roar for fired-up savings!

Drive in for spectacular savings!

Driving its way onto the local sports scene

Engines Screaming, Brakes Glowing, Tires Smoking Sale Event!

Feel the engine revving with unheard-of deals!

For fast-lane deals, call...

Fuel up with fantastic savings!

Get a head start on savings!

Get on the clutch and throttle for quick savings!

Get on the fast track to amazing deals!

Get on track to explosive savings!

Get your engines fired up for winning savings!

Get your ticket to the thrills, chills and spills of auto racing!

Go for the big race sale!

Grab the green flag to checkered flag savings!

Hear the roar for more savings!

Here's how to turbo-charge your savings at...

High-octane savings!

If you love road racing, this is the place to be

Is your car ready for the big sale?

It's a deal from start to finish

It's big league auto racing at its finest

It's Demolition Derby Savings Time!

It's the Super Bowl of stock-car racing

Jump Start Savings Event!

Keep your motor running in high gear with...

Last on the brakes... first in the savings circle!

Lay down some traction for real savings!

Let the sale begin!

Let's go, and hurry up, the sale is starting!

Let's really hear them roar

Make tracks for big savings!

Meet us in the Winner's Circle of Savings!

Motor sports take the green flag

On the American racing scene

On the right track for savings!

One of the best racing facilities
in America

Our annual Demolition Derby Sale
Event!

Put the Pedal to the Metal Sale Event!

Puts you over the finish line,
again and again

Race Day Savings! Only today!

Race in and race out with big savings!

Race in today and try a...

Race ready... sale ready!

Race to the finish line for...

Race to the savings!

Racing pros' choice for racing fans

Racing revs its engines at...

Rev up for real savings!

Rev-up for some head-to-head
sales competition

Rev-up incredible savings at...

Savings too hot to pass up

Slamming on the Brake Sale Event!

Some of the hairiest, bare-knuckled
racing in the world

Start 'Em Up Sale!

Start up the engines and let the fun
begin

Start your engines and dash in
for savings!

Taking the checkered flag for
more savings!

The action is hot, but the savings
are hotter!

The Big Race Day Sale Event!

The greatest place in American motor
sports history

The green flag drops at noon

The more you race, the more you save at...

The power! The speed! The sale!

The premier motor sports sale event
in the world!

The race is on to smashing savings!

The Race to Saving Sale!

The savings never make a pit stop

The thrill of victory! The thrill of savings!

The trip down Victory Lane is brought
to you by...

The ultimate race... the ultimate
sale event!

The winning team... week after week

There is more great racing to come

There's no "Start your engines" at
this sale!

This deal takes the checkered flag!

This is your race to win... this is your
sale to save!

Today is Pole Day for the first
200 customers

Virtually unbeatable savings!

We are ready to roar with savings!

We look forward to seeing you at
the race

We'll put you back in the driver's seat
with...

Welcome race fans to the biggest sale
event ever!

What a finish... what a sale!

What a great race! What a great sale!

Where the people behind the wheel...

You don't have to be a race car driver to
shop and save at...

You won't run out of gas at this sale event!

You'll drive home a winner...

You'll love the excitement of auto racing

You'll save big bucks on tires during our
Pit Stop Sale Event!

You're clicking on all cylinders with
these prices!

You're in the driver's seat for
fantastic savings!

Your savings pit stop!

1st time buyer's program!
We'll finance you!

A car you could live with every day of the week

A cream puff of a car

A driver's dream

A lean, mean running machine

A lease that's as exciting as the car

A load of standard equipment for the price

A pure driver's car

A ride you'll never forget

A Super Duper Car Sale Event!

A tip from the old gas cap

Afraid to get ripped off?

Ah yes, you've got the bug to buy a new car!

Air included with every airbag

All new cars and trucks sold at $200 under invoice!

All pre-driven priced below Blue Book

All the bells and whistles anyone could want

All you have to do is jump in and take off!

America's best selling car!

An auto extravaganza!

An enjoyable driving experience

An offer you can't refuse!

Anything less is just a car

Are you ready for winter driving?

At a price that won't break the bank!

At prices that say "take me home!"

Bet you'll find your next car here!

Bumper-to-bumper maintenance service

But under the hood, you have a very fuel-efficient engine

Buy a new car at a fleet price!

Buy an extraordinary car for an ordinary price!

Buy now during our Great Zero Event!

Buy or lease... you save!

Buying a car elsewhere can be hazardous to your pocket book

Buying a used car is buying someone else's trouble

Call it mint condition

Cars on the go!

Check out our service department

Congratulations... you're the proud owner of a brand new payment book

Depend on us to take care of your car

Do you come with the car?

Does anybody know how to drive a stick shift?

Does your car make a statement about you?

Don't you love that new-car smell?

Donate your car for a tax deduction

Drive home today!

Drive in for value

Drive into our world of deals!

Drive it before you buy it!

Drive them to school in style

Drive your dream car... today!

Every bit a family vehicle

Everybody drives regardless of credit

Everybody likes a new car

Fill up the tank for a high-octane drive

For anyone who enjoys driving

For car nuts only!

For Sunday drivers only!

For the true driving enthusiasts

Full trade-in value

Fully loaded and ready to go

Fun with the top down

Get charged up during our battery jamboree!

Get the most mileage when selling your car

Getting a grip on auto repairs

Getting the most for your used car

Go ahead... drive a gas guzzler

Go-anywhere, do-anything vehicle

Great cars... no lemons!

Have car will travel

Hop in! Buckle up! Take off!

Hot deals on summer wheels!

How much motor do you really need?

How to get going when your car won't start

How'd you like to buy a late-model used car?

If you could drive one car to your high school reunion, this would be it!

If you don't know cars... Know your mechanic

If you don't like lots of attention, stay away from these cars

If you think it looks different, wait until you drive it

If you think you can't afford a new car... think again!

In the market for a new car?

In the market for a new set of wheels?

Includes everything but the gas tank

Is your car on its last leg?

Is your car ready for a vacation?

Is your car still under warranty?

Is your car winter-ready?

It can hold its own on today's roads

It helps to have a nice set of wheels

It is a lot of car for the money!

It should work like a horse, not ride like one

It'll drive you wild!

It's a cold winter day when your battery fails

It's a darn good time to buy a car!

It's a driver's market

It's a smart car worth shouting about

It's for car buffs

It's fun to drive

It's got plenty of get-up-and-go

It's got road comfort

It's more than a car, it's an adventure!

It's our number-one seller!

It's rugged. It's macho. It's individualistic.

It's the automotive experience of a lifetime

It's time for a new car!

It's today's time machine

It's trade-in time!

It's very wrenching to find a good mechanic

Just peel off the window sticker!

Last chance to buy a new car at prices this low!

Let our professionals assist you in financing your new car or truck

Let the credit wizards put a car in your future

Let's talk cars!

Lifetime oil and filter change with every new car

Lift up the hood and you'll see a whole new world in there

Look what we've got under the hood

Looking for ways to stretch your dollars at the fuel pump?

Love it... then lease it!

Makes driving enjoyable and safe

My car is broke... where do I take it?

No bull! Just straight talk! Great deals...
A whole new attitude!

No reasonable offer refused!

Nobody beats our prices... nobody!

Nobody walks... everybody drives

No-haggle pricing

No-hassle clearance!

Now is the best time to drive a bargain!

Now it's time to move into the
driver's seat

Now that's a smart car!

Now's the time to get your car in shape
for summer

Now... put the pedal to the metal

Off-road fun and on-road fun

One dollar under invoice!

One-stop service on all your
automotive needs

Our cars will change the way you look at
other cars

Our prices are making everybody talk

Over 200 in stock and we're ready to deal!

Overstock sell-offs!

Performance and power

Pick your price!

Please, don't drool on the car

Pre-Auto Show Sales Event!

Pre-driven bonanza!

Price-buster tire sale!

Priced so that you'll have cash left to
buy gas

Priced to go, go, go!!!

Prices reduced! Payments reduced!

Prices so low, it's almost like giving
them away!

Put a new car in your garage, today!

Put this baby in your driveway

Put your car in the winner's circle with...

Quality used vehicles

Ready for winter? Now make sure your
car is

Reliable car care

Right car... Right deal... Right now...
Right here!

Right cars... Right prices!

Safety, economy and outstanding
performance

Save on car repairs... now!

Sell your old car in the obituaries

Service, parts, body shop and sales open
six days every week!

Show off your manhood

So what's it like to get a sports car
as a gift?

So you want to buy a new car?

Spring car care savings!

Steel this car!

Stop and smell the new car

Stop dreaming! Start driving!

Stop here and drive a terrific deal!

Super savings for used-car shoppers only!

Sure they're fast, but at these prices...

Take a couple of months off...
from car payments!

Take a risk-free test drive today!

Take care of your vehicle if you care for
your life

Take it for a spin and let us know what
you think

Take one for a drive and you'll
understand

Talk about your trade-in value

Test drive and see for yourself

Test-drive the future!

The best dealer... the best deal!

The best thing on wheels

The car you want to be seen in

The car you're dreaming about

The cheapest car to buy is not the cheapest car to own

The flip side of sticker shock

The hottest deals on wheels!

The most beautiful thing about the car is the price

The most imitated car on the road

The previous owner of these cars was the manufacturer!

The rougher the road... The tougher the car

The sales crown in luxury automobiles

The world's best-selling car ever!

There's never been a better time to lease

They even gave me a free loaner...

This baby can really roll!

This car is you all the way

This car needs a home too

This car says... have a nice day!

This is the ride you've been waiting for

This is why we sell more cars

This winter, tell your car you love it

Tires looking a bit bald?

To say this car is a beauty is an understatement

Truly enjoyable to drive

Unbeatable selection. More for your trade. Great finance rates. Guaranteed savings.

Used car save-a-thon!

Used car savings center!

Walk in... Drive out!

Want an economic ride?

We brake for low prices!

We can put you behind the wheel

We can see a new car in your future!

We have these cars! These are not come-on prices!

We help keep your engine in great shape

We make driving easier, safer and more comfortable

We put you in the driver's seat

We sell technology with our cars

We stand in front of our brake repairs

We will meet or beat any advertised price!

We're dealing!!!

We're keeping the driver's seat warm

We're not just selling a car but a lifestyle moment

We're overstocked with tons of cars to move!

We're talking wheels!

What a deal! I nearly fell out of the car

What a perfect time to get a new car

What an automotive entertainment system!

What kind of car would you like to drive to your mother-in-law's?

When was the last time your car was serviced?

Who says 4 doors are boring?

Why buy used when you can buy brand new?

Win a lifetime oil change for your car!

Women love this car!

Yes, the car comes with seats, steering wheel and tires

You can sell an old man a young man's car but you never can sell a young man an old man's car

You name it, this car's got it!

You now have the edge in car-buying

You'll just feel good when you drive it

Your key to low payments

Your tax refund is your down payment!

Zero down! Zero payment! Zero interest! Zero over invoice!

"Wow" prices you'll really love

A level of wow satisfaction: guaranteed!

A sale with a great WOW to it

A totally awesome offer

Absolutely fabulous, most incredibly awesome...

After the savings you're going to say "Wow!"

Amazing prices...awesome stuff!

An amazingly awesome sale event!

An awesome spectacle of savings!

Awesome bargains for every shopper

Awesome buys: Buy now!

Awesome deals! Start now!

Awesome deals! Wow prices! Easy credit!

Awesome doesn't begin to cover this sale!

Awesome nightlife that never stops

Awesome savings on all merchandise

Awesome values that'll rock your world

Awesome values!!! On every item!!!

Awesomely attractive prices!

Bargains that will make you go wow!!!

Bet you're going to say, "Wow!"

Big Wow Sale of the Year

Colossal savings! Stupendous deals! Awesome sale!

Come and see the wow!

Crunch! Whack! Zoom! Wow!

Do I hear a "Wow"?

Don't miss these incredibly awesome savings!

Downright awesome value time!

Electrifying. Amazing. Awesome.

Everyone together now, woooooow, what a sale!!!

Everything about the deal is a wow!

Fabulous savings! Thrilling bargains! Awesome deals!

Flat-out awesome deals!

Get wowed at the sale event of the century!

Great! Fabulous! Awesome deals!

Have we got awesome bargains for you

Here's why everybody is getting wowed by...

How to create the "wow"

Isn't this an amazingly awesome sale?

It all adds up to awesome savings!

It all comes out to... awesome

It moves! It jumps! It bends! It's awesome!

It never fails to get a wow!

It will save you money... wow!

It would be putting it mildly to say the savings are awesome!

It'll make your customer say... wow!

It's exactly what you can expect from awesome savings!

It's just like, wow!

It's sensational! It's an awesome sale event!

Just awesome savings!

Just awesome to know how big the savings are!

Keeps you smiling with awesome buys!

Let us wow you with our annual sale!

Like totally awesome savings!

No sweat! No haggling! Just awesome deals!

Nothing short of awesome deals!

Now... there's a "wow" of a sale!

Ooh! Ahh! Wow savings!

Put some wow in your life with awesome savings!

Put the awesome in your pocket of savings

Really? Wow! That's an awesome sale!

Savings that will make you go Wow!

Scoop up an awesome deal... today!

Still the awesomest sale of the year!

Stupendous! Smashing! Awesome sales event!

The "wow" sales event of the year!

The awesome power of a great sale!

The Big Wow Sale Event of the Season!

The name of the sale is awesome!

The sale says it all... awesome!

The savings add up to awesome!

The savings will make you say, "Wow"

This is just amazingly wow!

This is our amazingly wow... sale event of the season!

This sale is just awesome!

This sale never fails to get a wow!

To say it's an awesome sale is an understatement

Unbelievably awesome bargains

We put the awesome in our sale!

We put the wow in savings!

We're going to wow you with amazing savings!

What an awesome place to hang out

When was the last time you were wowed?

Wow buys in store for you

Wow plus wow equals awesome savings!

Wow your honey with...

Wow! All this and more

Wow! Check out these hot deals

Wow! Gotta have it

Wow! I won! You won! We won!

Wow! Incredible savings for a limited time

Wow! Look at all the cool bargains

Wow! Now we're cooking with outstanding deals!

Wow! That's what I've been looking for... sale event!

Wow! The deals are the greatest...

Wow! This sale is just incredible!

Wow! What a deal!

Wow! What a fantastic sale!

Wow! What a great, great sale!

Wow! What a weekend sale

Wow! What an offer

Wow! Wow! Wow! Fantastic savings!

Wow! You'll feel special with these awesome buys!

Wow! You'll love the savings

Wow!!! What a bargain!!!

Wow!!! That's a great bargain!!!

Wow, are they ever great deals

Wow, I want to get one of those

Wow, super size it

Wow, this sale is awesome

Wow, this stuff is unreal

Wow, what a place for hangin' out

Wow, you ate the whole thing

Wow, you really did hit us with your best buys!

Wow. What fantastic savings and service!

Wowhoo!

You are entering the awesome zone

You will love our awesome service

You'll be wowed in new and different ways with awesome savings!

You'll get wowed at our sale event!

You'll take one look and say, "Wow!"

You're in the circle of awesome savings!

Your smile says it all... awesome!!!

23

A Baby Boom Sales Event!

A Big Bundle of Joy Sale!

A gift to make your baby drool

A star is born

After I have a baby, will I...

All babies start life 100% pure

All baby cribs safety certified by...

All your needs for baby's first wardrobe

Anyone who has ever been to a baby shower knows...

Are breast-fed babies smarter?

Are you ready... most babies go through 8 to 10 diapers a day!

Ask your baby doctor about...

Babies don't come with instruction manuals

Baby bonus days!

Baby Boom Sale Event!

Baby registry "must-haves"

Baby-rock-a-buys!

Big Baby Day Sale!

Big savings for growing babies!

Born in the U.S.A.

Can you afford to have a baby?

Celebrate baby week at...

Celebrate the birth of your baby with a...

Countdown to B-day!

Diaper like a pro with...

Do you know how to change diapers?

Don't forget the diaper bag

Drive-thru baby delivery

Every baby needs attention, warmth and love

Everything starts when the child is born

Expecting a baby?

Facts you should know about your baby's booster seat

Feeding your baby comes naturally with...

Find babies' necessities all in this store!

For anyone who has ever changed a diaper...

For new moms and smart moms

For Your Baby's Sake... Sale Event!

For your baby's sensitive skin

For your little baby

Free! Your guide to raising a genius

From Bibs to Cribs... Sale Event!

From diapers to dollars!

From the crib to college

From the most trusted name in cribs and strollers

Furniture that grows with your baby!

Get the care your baby needs and deserves

Get to the bottom of diaper rash with...

Getting your body back after the baby

Giving birth is the original do-it-yourself project

Growing up with a rattle in one hand and a mouse in the other

Happy babies make for happy moms

Have you hugged your baby today?

Healthy moms deliver healthy babies

Hello world. I'm here!

Helps your baby grow from head to toe

Here's a cuddly little friend to keep baby company

Here's the truth about teething

How to clear up diaper rash fast

If you buy diapers, we know you have a baby

If you're pregnant, see a doctor

Is there anything more special than reading to your baby?

Is there anything softer than a baby's skin?

It's the number one choice of pediatricians

Join In the Diaper Derby Sale Event!

Join us in welcoming the latest addition to our family

Keep your baby healthy and happy with...

Keeping your baby comfortable, content and cheerful

Keeps baby warm and cozy

Let's talk, baby

Making the switch between bottle and breast easier on you and baby

Moms love having babies at...

My Baby Just Cares For Me... Sale Event!

No other diaper can stop leaks better

Now that your baby has arrived

Now you can prevent diaper rash

Only 65 years until retirement!

Our toughest customers are babies

Pamper your baby with...

Pediatricians recommend it

Save a bundle on any baby gift

Saving on car seats for babies on the move!

Savings for you and baby!

Soft as a baby's bottom

Start your baby out right with...

That bundle of joy will cost a bundle... are you financially prepared?

That's My Baby Sale Event!

The baby bottle battle between parents

The best moms buy at...

The largest selection of baby needs at guaranteed low prices!

The perfect gift for every proud parent

Thinking about having a baby?

This bib's for you!

Throw it in your diaper bag and go!

Tips to a new mom

Tuck your baby into our cozy...

We deliver humans

We do not serve alcohol to pregnant ladies!

We have someone we want you to meet

We make really good baby food

We sell only baby-approved products

We specialize in motherhood

We take the bite out of teething

We're mom's place to shop for baby!

We're tough on diaper rash!

What are you craving for?

What do you get for the baby who has everything?

What you should know before you get pregnant

What your baby and you can expect

What's it like today, to have a baby?

What's the best way to have a baby?

When shopping for your baby, your first stop begins here!

Who's the most important baby in the whole wide world?

With a new baby, who has time for...

Wrap your bundle of joy in warmth and love

You know about the shots your baby needs...

You really have to send the baby something cutesy

You're in charge of your baby's safety

Your baby's first step begins here!

Your baby's skin will look and feel beautiful with...

A crunch course for back-to-school values!

A lesson in back-to-school savings!

A mind-expanding back-to-school sale!

All the back-to-school essentials kids need

All the tools for school in stock right now!

At The Head Of The Class Sale Event!

Awesome back-to-school savings on all computers and accessories!

Back 2 School Sale!

Back to class with everyday-low prices!

Back to class with fantastic savings!

Back to school... Everything's now on sale!

Back to school, back to savings!

Back to the basics sale!

Back-to-campus headquarters for your computer needs

Back-To-Campus Super Sale!

Back-To-School Bonanza!

Back-to-school coupon savings!

Back-to-school essentials on sale!

Back-to-school is always easier at...

Back-to-school is coming: be prepared

Back-to-school lunch-box favorites

Back-to-School Sale. The first lesson is, "wow"!

Back-to-school savings are the rule at...

Back-to-school shopping = back-to-school skimping

Back-to-school shopping tips

Back-to-school supplies with back-to-school savings!

Balance your budget for back-to-school shopping!

Beautiful prices on school fashions!

Before you bury your nose in the books, bury it in our...

Before you hit the books, hit the savings!

Caught up in the back-to-school madness?

Chalk up big back-to-school savings!

College clean-up savings!

Cool stuff... school stuff

Cool supplies for cool back-to-school kids

Cool tools for e-school

Don't be tardy! Get insurance protection before kids go back to school

Don't forget to send them to school with...

For all your back-to-school computer needs, start here

For back-to-school shopaholics

For the college-bound

Gear up for back-to-school values!

Get a cool class start with...

Get all your school stuff here

Get the back-to-school stuff your kids want

Get the money you need for back-to-school

Get the right tools for back-to-school

Getting wired for e-school

Give them the back-to-school stuff they'll love

Going-back-to-college savings!

Great storewide sale for back-to-school!

Hassled by back-to-school frazzles?

Have you ever said... Someday, I'm going back to school?

Head back to school with style, quality and value!

High tech stuff for back-to-school high school students

Hit the desks with back-to-school savings!

Hot back-to-school fashions!

How to furnish your dorm room

How to get your kids started before school does

Incredible back-to-school savings!

It's time to get a back-to-school haircut

It's the best back-to-school sale in its class!

Kick off the school year with us!

Learn your first lesson of the new school year... big savings!

Let us help you get ready for back-to-school days

Make sure you have a No. 2 pencil with a good eraser

Make this school year everyone's best ever

Must-haves for this school year!

New books! New pencils! New book bags!

Official back-to-school headquarters!

Our back-to-school prices make the grade

Our back-to-school sale is one for the books!

Pack up for school and save!

Putting the value in back-to-school shopping!

Savings is our favorite subject!

Savings that earn an A+

School supplies for home and school!

School-supplies sale!

Shop early for the best selection of school supplies

Shopping for back-to-school supplies can be expensive

Sign up for a lesson in savings!

Sizzling back-to-school values!

Strictly back-to-school stuff

Study those back-to-school savings!

Stuff your kid's backpacks with our back-to-school savings!

Sure beats the old back-to-school sale!

Take care! Take stock! Take to school!

Take note of these back-to-school savings!

Team up with back-to-school values!

That's what we call a back-to-school advantage

The ABC's of back to school shopping

The annual pilgrimage to buy school supplies

The latest and greatest for back-to-school

The wise choice for back-to-school

Things you need for back-to-school

Time for bake sales, raffles and saving labels

Time for new back-to-school clothes

Time is slipping by... school is just around the corner

Time to shop for back-to-school for all the kids in your house

Top of the class savings... Now on sale!

Unbelievable school savings!

Values that travel back to school

Wanted: School bus drivers!

We have everything your student needs to make the move, so relax!

We offer one-stop shopping for students!

We've got a lot of back-to-school cool stuff!

We've got all the back-to-school essentials you'll ever need!

What to put in a child's school lunch?

Where you get the best deals for back-to-school computer needs

Wise buys for the college-bound wise guys

Ya Gotta Go Back to School Sale Event!

Your back-to-school budget gets you an A+

Banking

A bank that works with you

A commitment to superior banking services

A community-owned bank

A great way to get instant cash

A home equity loan... of little interest

A savings account is all about saving you money

A sure way to make your money grow!

A truly one-of-a-kind bank

Add up the savings with us

Ahhhhhhh savings!

Are checking fees throwing you a curve?

Bank from home or on the road

Bank on us!

Choosing an online banker isn't easy

Come to us for great rates

Dedicated to saving your money

Do you need a private banker?

Does your bank see the future?

Does your banker understand you?

Don't let your money go down the drain

Don't put off until tomorrow what you can save today!

Easier, faster banking... Anywhere, anytime!

Enjoy affordable financing with our home improvement loan

Everything is coming up savings for you!

Expect the unexpected at our bank!

Experienced, trustworthy service that our customers have come to expect

First, go shop for your home, then see us for your loan

For a more intimate and personalized experience

Friendship banking is more than... Let's do lunch!

From the Vault Department

Get a great mortgage deal and a great deal more!

Give your money a beautiful home and it will stay longer

Have cash... will lend

High performance banking is here!

High-quality service for all your banking needs

Home sweet loan

How safe is your bank?

If all our customers were alike, we'd only offer one savings program

If anybody knows time is money, it's your bank!

If you need money, we'll loan you some

Instant savings... as in right now!

Is your bank's approach a currency-exchange approach?

Isn't it time you put your money to work for you?

It is better to put your money into the bank than to take money out

It's not the money, it's the principle

It's our way of helping you save

It's your money... save it

Let us show you how much better banking can be

Live for today. Save for tomorrow!

Looking for a safe place to store your money?

Making you more money

Money isn't the only perk we offer

Money-saving tips!

No two banks are alike

Now... Bank on your own hours!

Old-fashioned banking is what we do!

One-stop banking

Our 6-month CD... is not to be fiddled around with

Our success is tied to your interest

People come here just to do their banking

Put your money in our mattress!

Save a few bucks with us!

Saving for the peace of mind

Saving your money isn't the only thing we do!

Savings really do grow on trees!

Secure way to grow your savings!

Serious about saving money?

Service that can't be measured in dollars and cents

Should you expect any less from your bank?

Take advantage of our savings plan now!

Thank you for banking with us!

That's the difference between us and some other bank!

The bank of great rates!

The bank that fits in your future

The cutest piggy bank in town

The kind of bank you deserve!

The leader in technology banking

The neighborhood bank you won't outgrow!

The new frontier in banking

The safest place for your money is in our bank

There's nothing like money in the bank

This bank's for you!

This should pique your interest

Time to stop and smell the interest

Understanding the banking needs of our customers

Watch savings grow... and grow... and grow!

We are the right bank for you!

We don't give away stuffed animals, we give better rates

We don't think like other banks

We get your first home mortgage... your second and third

We have the solutions for all your banking needs!

We have ways to make your money grow!

We have your best interest at our bank

We keep your bank account sound

We loan dreams!

We make banking easier for you!

We make saving money a piece of cake

We offer business-banking services... in your office

We understand your financial and business needs

We're a 24-hour bank-by-phone

We're an Internet bank only!

We're big with small business

We're the kind of bank that's for you!

We're your technology banking team

What to do with $10,000?

What's the best way to save for college?

When is a 12% return better than a 12% return?

When was the last time you smiled in your bank?

Who needs a bank, anyway?

Who's watching your money?

You'll fall for our rates!

You'll like our banker's hours

You'll love the way we say... NO points, NO application fee, NO appraisal fee!

You've come to the right bank!

Your banker should be a step ahead of you, not a mile behind you

Zero in on our home equity loan sale!

Bargain

A bargain hunter's dream

A bargain hunter's paradise

A good, old-fashioned bargain

A makeover at a bargain

A real antique at bargain prices

A rousing day of bargain shopping

A sale for bargain-seekers

Absolutely... everything must be sold at bargain prices!

Act fast... when they're gone, they're gone

All are nifty bargains

All hard-to-find items are bargains!

All sales final on bargain items!

All your favorite stuff at great bargain prices

Americans love a bargain

And who are we to pass up a bargain?

Are you really getting a bargain?

As long as the price is right... it's a bargain

At real bargain prices

Attention: All bargain hunters, bag the big savings!

Awesome bargain blast!

Bargain excitement starts today!

Bargain hunters sale!

Bargain prices are not always the answer

Bargain specials and a lot more

Bargain-basement conformity

Bargaining is encouraged

Bargains and a lot more!

Bargains at dirt-cheap prices

Bargains at fantastic prices

Bargains by the bushel

Bargains can become treasures

Bargains don't get any bigger than this

Bargains Going! Going! Gone!

Bargains on all sky-high prices!

Bargains or bummers

Bargains that rock your world

Bargains that will leave change in your pocket

Bargains that will make you go wow!!!

Bargains that will make your hair stand up

Bargains to snap up in a heartbeat

Bargains worth shouting about!

Bargains you can put your arms around!

Bargains you can't pass up!

Bargains you will love!

Bazaar bargains!!!

Best bargain in town

Best bargains ever!

Blast off to bargains when you shop at...

Bountiful bargains

Brand names at a bargain

Break open your wallet for one heck of a bargain

Bronc-bustin' bargains

Browse! Bargain! Buy!

Budget stretcher bargains!

Bushels of bargains

Calling all bargain hunters

Cheap but good bargains

Clean up with these bargain prices!

Closeouts priced to move

Come early, beat the rush, get the best bargain

Do it the bargain way and save!

Dollary Day! Dollary Day!
Dollary Day Bargains!

Don't just take our word for it...
it's a bargain

Don't pass up these bargains!

Driving a hard bargain

Even at dirt-cheap prices... it's still
a bargain!

Even at the bargain price of...

Even our rummage is on sale!

Everybody Loves a Bargain Sale!

Everything is bargain-priced

Explosive bargain blowout!

Extreme bargains!

Fabulous bargain days are here again!

Fantastic bargains you can't pass up

Get 'em before they're gone!

Get a bargain for your money at...

Get something for nothing

Getting a bargain is always a good feeling

Getting more than you bargained for

Good, old-fashioned bargains!

Great bargain buys!

Great bargains for exceptional gifts

Hard-to-find bargains are really bargains!

Have we got a bargain for you!

Hey, bargain shoppers!!!

Hungry for bargains?

Hunt wisely for bargains

Hunting for the best bargain?

I bought it at an estate sale!

I just can't pass up a bargain

If it's not a bargain, I don't buy it!

If you're fishing for a bargain...

If you've been looking for a bargain,
don't miss this one!

It ain't a bargain if it isn't 70% off the
sale price!

It's a bargain!!!

It's a deal... big bargains!

It's a genuine bargain... guaranteed!

It's bargain time all the time!

It's bargain-basement shopping time

It's better than a bargain

It's not just a bargain;
it's something more!

It's one heck of a bargain!

It's worth it!!!

It's worth the price

Learn how to find a bargain

Let the bargains begin

Looking for bargains?

Lots of neat bargains... now on sale!

Lots of summer bargains in store

Magnificent bargains too good to miss!

Maybe the thing's a bargain

Monstrous bargain bonanza!

Monstrous bargains for your home

No sales pitch, only bargains!

Nobody can compare to our bargains...
nobody!

No-haggle, take-it-or-leave-it price

Now that's a bargain... pure and simple

Now that's an outstanding bargain!

Old-fashioned bargain days are
here again!

One can never have too much of a
great bargain!

One of the hottest bargains around

Our bargain prices are making
everybody talk

Our loss is your gain

Out bargain hunting?

Outrageous bargains like this can't
last forever

Outrageous bargains! Unheard-of
bargains! Incredible bargains!

Outstanding Bargain Buy Sale!

Bargain

Real antiques at real bargain prices

Relax and enjoy the great bargains

Sale for bargain-seekers!

Save big bucks in the bargain!

Savings for bargain-seekers!

Scoop up some bargains... today!

Seems like a bargain to me

She who gets the most bargains... wins!

Show me the bargains!

Some bargain, huh?

Sometimes a bargain isn't a good deal

Spectacular bargains throughout the store!

Spring Break Bargain Specials!

Strike up a great bargain

Super bargain days to save!

Take a look at these bargain prices!

Take in great bargains at...

Terrific Bargain of the Day Sale!

Terrific bargains for your browsing pleasure!

The bargain corner

The bargain-basement sale is on!

The bargains are bigger at...

The best is still a bargain

The early bird gets the biggest bargain-hunter sale... ever!

The no-haggle, take-it-or-leave-it price

The one and only bargain store in town

There's a sale item to make any bargain hunter happy

These bargains will be gone before you know it

These bargains won't last forever

This garage sale has unreal bargains!

This place is hoppin' with great bargains

This week only... Old-Fashioned Bargain Days!

Thrilling bargains for every shopper!

Today is bargain day!

Today only! Outrageous bargains!

Treasures and bargains you'll love!

Unbelievable bargains galore

Unique bargains at thrilling prices

We couldn't pass up a great bargain... neither should you

We'll have you swinging from the rafters with these bargains!

We're almost giving it away!

We're giving you what you want, bargains, bargains and more bargains!

We're looking for all bargain hunters

We've got bargains galore!

We've got the biggest and best bargains!

Welcome to a whole new world of bargains

What a bargain!!! What a value!!!

When we say bargains... we mean it!

Worthwhile bargains... worthwhile savings!

Wow! What a bargain!

Wow... it's bargain time!

You don't need a real eye for these bargains!

You know where the bargains are

You won't believe the price!

You'd be nuts to miss our inventory of bargains!

You'll get more than you bargained for at...

You'll get the best bargains for your money

You'll never see real bargains like this again!

You're going to love the bargains

You're too smart to pass up a bargain!

Your search for a bargain is over!

Baseball

25% off all baseballs, bats and gloves

A baseball glove can be a child's most important gift!

A big league savings celebration!

A Field of Dreams Sale Event!

A grand slam sales extravaganza!

A great double-play savings combination!

A major league sales pitch

A salute to all the old-time ballplayers

A Spectacular, Over the Fence Sale Event!

A strike is a strike, a ball is a ball and a bargain is a bargain!

A wild pitch! A wild finish! A wild sale!

All roads lead to a big win when you team up with...

All-star deals, all week long!

All-star savings!

Always keep your eye on the savings!

Anyone for peanuts?

Bargains... right down the middle!

Baseball isn't the only game in town during our sale!

Bases-clearing saving winner!

Before the first pitch is thrown... c'mon over to the first sale of the season

Big League savings... Little League prices!

Big league values!

Catch a great sale for baseball fanatics!

Catch big savings with...

Check out our super lineup of savings!

Coming soon to a ballpark near you

Doubleheader of savings!

Ever sat in a ballpark and wished your lawn looked as good as center field?

Five-Time Gold Glove Sale Event!

Get in the swing with Home Run Deals!

Get ready for some major league exciting deals!

Go for the double play with these bargains!

Go up to the plate and take three good swings at our deals!

Going... going... gone deals!

Grand slam savings going on now!

Hard-hitting baseball deals!

Help us knock the cover off high prices

Here's the inside pitch on fabulous deals!

Here's the pitch, here's the catch and here's the sale!

Hey batter, hey batter, hey batter... swing into our sale!

Hit a game-winning home run with savings at...

Hit a home run for your kids... all kids summerwear is on sale!

Home run values!

How to put more saving bucks in your lineup

It might be... it could be... it is our big sale celebration!

It's absolutely a home run of a deal!

It's our Home Run Sale Event!

Join the home run derby... today!

Let us be your designated hitter

Make a clean sweep on savings!

Nine innings of entertainment

No runs. No hits. No payments until...

Now here's the windup, and the pitch

Opening day exciting sale!

Baseball

Our bullpen won't let you down with these savings!

Our lineup is full of super savings!

Our Rock-Bottom-of-the-Ninth Sale Event!

Our sale events are always a hit!

Our winning lineup saves you money

Outlandish savings. Big league deals!

Play ball. It's our opening day sale!

Put more power in your lineup with fantastic savings!

Rounding home and heading for big savings at...

Season opener sale!

Spring training savings at...

Spring training savings for shopping enthusiasts

Steal a deal sale!

Step up to bat for big savings!

Step up to the plate with gusto

Stretch your budget with our Seventh Inning Stretch of Savings!

Strike up the sale!

Support your minor-league team

Swing big into savings!

Swing for the Fence Sale Event!

Swing into a sale... slide into savings!

Swing into spring with these home run deals!

Take a big swing into big savings!

Take a swing at our prices!

Take me out to the Opening Day Sale!

The bases are loaded with big savings at...

The big game savings pitch!

The crack of the bat... the roar for savings!

The first sign of spring is opening day of our sale!

The Seventh Inning Stretch Sale Event!

The windup and here's the sale!

These deals are one-hit wonders

This is a big-league sale event!

This is no squeeze play of a deal!

This sale is one for the record books!

This season we've got great bargains for all baseball fans!

Time to plaaaaay ball and time to saaaaave!

Up for a big inning and up for a big deal!

We don't throw brushback pitches with our deals!

We go to bat for you with great savings!

We'll give you our best pitch of a deal!

We'll put you in the right ballpark with great values!

We're pitching great deals here!

We've got all the bases covered for a winning sale!

What a catch! What a sale!!!

Whoever heard of a nine-inning sale?

You Can't Beat Fun at the Old Ballpark Savings Event!

You won't lose the ball in the sun with our summer closeouts!

You won't strike out with these savings!

You'll be a Hall of Famer with these bargains, values and deals!

You'll go crazy over our Wild Card Race to Savings!

You'll hit a home run with these savings!

You'll knock the cover off with our deals!

You'll score with these savings!

You're batting 1.000 at our annual Clean-Up Sale Event!

You're really out in left field if you don't buy now!!!

You're talking baseball and we're talking savings!

Your savings scoreboard for unbelievable values!

Basketball

A big rebound! A big assist! A big sale event!

A real barn-burner of a sale!

A Season Of Madness Sales Event!

A slam-dunk of a deal!

Above the Rim Deals!

Basketball crazy day sale!

Big plays! Big shots! Big game savings!

Big savings for the home team!

Break In The Action Sale Event!

Buzzer-beating deals!

Celebrate a slam-dunk weekend with us!

Celebrate the basketball season with big savings!

Celebrate this basketball season by breaking away from...

Courtside countdown to outstanding savings!

Courtside seats are now on sale!

Double dribble bargains!

Down to the last shot savings!

Enjoy a little one-on-one action at...

Even before the game begins, you know where the savings are

Follow the Bouncing Ball Sale Event!

Follow the sale for road game savings!

Free basketball with every...

Free throws are free!

Get a jump on the basketball season with your favorite...

Get all your halftime favorites here!

Get ready for the basketball sale of the season!

Get ready to hoop it up during our Festival of Savings!

Get the fast break from the all-pro team

Get there for the tip-off of our Amazing Annual Sale Event!

Give yourself two points for...

Good to the last rebound

Grab a rebound... grab a deal!

Great shot! Incredible savings!

Halftime sensational savings!

Hit the big shot with fantastic values!

Hoops Fever Sale!

How to take advantage of the home-court advantage

If your ball don't got air, you don't got game

It's a Full-Court Press Sales Event!

It's Basketball 101 Savings!

It's our Final Four Sale of the Season!

It's slam-dunking time!

It's tip-off time, and here's the tip...

Last-second savings throughout the store!

Let's slam-dunk the competition with...

Lots of momentum! Lots of scoring! Lots of savings!

Make a fast break to our Super Spectacular Sale Event!

Make your first slam-dunk of the season at...

March insanity! March crazy! March savings!

March Madness Deals going on now!

March Madness Sale! Anything and everything goes!

March Mania Savings!!!

Nothing But Net Sales Event!

Our March Madness of Savings!

Our Season Opener Slam Dunk Sale!

Outscore 'em... out-jump 'em

Basketball

Playing above the rim

Put points on the board with big savings!

Put the ball in your basket of savings!

Race up the court with outrageous savings!

Rim-rattling savings!

Run up the score by saving at...

Saving is a slam-dunk here!

Savings right from the tip-off!

Savings that we pass on to you!

Score big during our March Madness Sale Event!

Score big savings on all discounted items!

Score by saving at...

Score with great savings during...

Slam jam savings event!

Slam, dunk and score with great deals!

Slam... Jam... Savings!

Slam-Dunk Days! Slam-Dunk Savings!

Stick it to the hoops

Sure-shot savings!

Take it to the basket

Take time out to save!

Take your last shot on these deals!

Takin' it down to the final tick... drastically slashed prices!

The best of the best buzzer-beating deals!

The Big Shootout Sales Event!

The ins and outs of basketball

The sale for lifelong basketball fanatics!

The shot of the game... the sale of the season!

The Tip-Off to the Final Buzzer Savings!

This is what great basketball is all about

This three-point play will get you to the big sale

Three-point buzzer-beater deals!

Three-point specialist... bargains, values and deals!

Time out for great savings!

Tip-Off Sale Time!

Tournament time savings!

Travel the road to the sale of the season!

We got fever! We got savings!

We'll jump through hoops for you during our Wild, Incredible Sale Event!

We'll out-slam the competition with super spectacular savings!

We're dunking the competition with unheard-of savings!

We're hoopin' it up with awesome savings!

We're hooping!

We're promoting women's basketball

We're putting a full-court press behind these discounted items!

What a crowd-pleaser, what a deal!

When the ball stops bouncing, the sales start hopping!

When you've got the home court advantage... you can't miss the savings!

Win On the Court, Win Off the Court Sales Event!

Women's Slam Dunk Sale!

You call the shots on price!

You shoot for show... You play defense for dough

You'll be the top scorer with these savings!

You'll get a free throw bonus with every purchase!

You'll get savings at both ends of the court

You'll get the home-court edge with our terrific deals!

You'll score big with these savings!

Your slam-dunk starts here

Best

10 steps to look and feel your best

A cut above the best

Accept only the best offer

Ain't none better

All the best brands, at the best price!

Are you ready for the very best?

Best of what's new!

Best prices of the year!

Best quality, best service, best price!

Best! Better! Great! Greatest!

Better than the best

Bring home the best in...

Buy the best you can afford

Check out our best sellers

Considered one of the best, if not the best

Definitely the best!

Demand the best!

Do not settle for second best

Dollar for dollar, we're the best buy!

Don't just settle for the best...
get the best!

Don't you deserve the best?

Expect the best

Experience the best

First with the best

For those who demand the very best

For you, only the best

Forget the rest. It's time for the best!

Get the best for less

Get the best, pay the least

Go for the best

Heads and shoulders above the best

I'm proud to say we are the best

In a class by itself

Invest in the best

It is one of the best in the world

It is, quite simply, the best there is

It takes a lot to be the best

It's even better than best

It's not enough to be the best, today!

It's our business to bring you the very best

It's so easy to give the very best!

It's super duper! The best!

It's the best time to buy!

It's time you had the best

It's your money... demand the best!

Making the best even better

More than a bit better

Naturally the best

Never settle for less then the best

No one was ever sorry they bought
the best

Nobody else comes close

Now the best is even better

Now you can expect the best for less

One of America's best

One of the best... if not the best!

One of the year's best

Only the best wear our label

Only the best... you deserve it!

Our best just got better

Ours is the best

Positively the best

Shop early for best selections

Shop the best... buy for less!

Simply the best buy!

Best

Stacks up with the best of 'em

Step up to the best with...

The Best For Less Sale Event!

The best is waiting for you at...

The best money can buy!

The best name in town

The best of the best... is not double talk

The best stuff on earth

The best stuff... right here... right now

The best thing since sliced bread

The best things in life... can still
be affordable

The best we've ever made

The best you've never seen

The best! The first! The winner!

The best, bar none

The best, hands down

The big. The bigger. The biggest.

The biggest and best in...

The biggest! The brightest! The best!

The cheapest is not important...
the best is

The cheapest price isn't always the
best price

The original, the best

The real thing vs. the best thing

The ten best...

There's no such thing as second-best

This week's best buys!

Top of the line

Treat yourself to the best!

Undisputedly the best

Visit the rest, come see the best

Want the best? Choose the best!

We accept nothing but the best

We all want the best

We aren't the cheapest... just the best!

We carry only the best!

We demand the best and nothing less

We do big best

We hand-picked the best for you!

We offer you the best buys!

We only accept the best, and so should you

We only sell the best!

We only want the best

We saved the best for last

We sell the best!

We won't stand for anything less than
the best

We'll give you our best shot

We're committed to giving you our
very best

We're heads and tails above the best

We're not just different, we're better

We're not saying we're the best... we are
the best!

We're the best of the best!

We're the best. Now let us prove it!

Welcome home to the world's best...

What you do well, we do best!

When only the best will do

When you want the best... Call the best!

Where the best deals make the best friends

Why not the best?

Why waste your valuable time on
anything less than the best

You can trust the best

You deserve only the best!

You don't have to spend the most to get
the best

You have the best of everything here!

You only want the best

You shouldn't have to do without the best

You've tried the rest, now try the best!

Your family deserves the best

Biking

A bicycle adventure is on your horizon

A bicycle built for you!

A bike tune-up sale!

A bike worth sacrificing for

A friendly place for the biking folk

A godsend for biking enthusiasts

A marvelous way to promote cycling

A once-in-a-lifetime cycling experience

A top bike for bottom dollar

All Thrills, No Spills Sale Event!

All you need is a bike and a willingness to get dirty

America is the home of bikers

America's best bikes, now on sale!

America's best cyclists shop here!

Are you a kamikaze cyclist?

Bicycling is one of the most popular forms of recreational activities

Big savings on all boys' and girls' bikes!

Bike and buy!

Bike it... like it!

Bike owners: beware

Bike-buying advice

Bikes and all

Bikes for the entire family

Bikes for the rugged at heart!

Biking for transportation can be fun

Biking is a great aerobic exercise

Biking is a whole different experience when the bike fits

Biking through the good life

Born to ride

Breaking Away Sale Event!

Bring the bikes!

Buying the perfect bike

Calling all bike riders

Concerned about bicycle safety

Crazy about biking

Cycle madness

Cycling is a family affair

Cycling is a good type of exercise

Cycling is more than just high-tech gear

Deals for all bike-aholics!

Did you know bicycling is great exercise?

Do you have a passion for cycling?

Enjoy the support of a great bike shop

Every bike on sale!

Exceptional savings on high-tech, lightweight road racers!

Exclusively for bike lovers

Favored by cyclists

Feel the overwhelming desire to ride

Fellow biking junkies

Follow the bike path to...

For All Bike Riders, Young and Old Sale Event!

For bike enthusiasts

For bike-seat drivers

Free assembly on all bikes

Free safety bike inspection!

Full-service bike shop

Get a handle on defensive biking

Get on your bike and roll

Get on your bikes and riiiiiiide

Great bike deals going on now!

Happy cycling

Have a great cycling weekend

Biking

Have bike, will travel

Here's how to get rolling

How many gears do you have on your bike?

How to power pedal like a pro

I love cycling

I'm going shopping for a bike

It can go anywhere... do anything

It's a bike tour for everyone

It's not like riding a bicycle, believe me

It's time to get out and enjoy your bicycle

It's time to saddle up and step into the toe clips

It's your bike, so why not treat it right

It's your dream bike!

Jump into summer with awesome bike bargains!

Jump on your bicycle and pump those pedals

Just me, the bike, and the road

Keep on biking

Keep riding and stay healthy

Keep your bicycle running smoothly

Make sure your bike is as ready as you are

Mountain bike adventure

Nothing beats the fun of cycling

Now it's time for you to ride!

Now, anyone can have that bike you always wanted!

On a roll for bike week

Our bikes are not all nuts and bolts!

Pedal for power

Peddle your bike today!

Put more power behind your pedaling

Racing with the big boys

Register your bike

Ride any bike before you buy... free!

Riding for fun, fitness or competition

Saving for cycling lovers only!

Savings for all cycling enthusiasts!

Sexiest looking bike you'll ever see

Shift your biking skills into high gear with...

So don't settle for just any bike

So, bike in for a check-up and then hit the trail

Special deals on all high-tech, lightweight road racers!

State-of-the-art bike shop!

Take a hike or a bike

The bike for bike enthusiasts!

The bike trail starts here

The bike you'll never outgrow

The boldest, brightest, freshest bike in town

The exciting world of competitive cycling

The lucky winner will receive a new bike!

The perfect bike for you

The power to go the distance

The ultimate cycling workout

The value of a pro cycling shop

The Wheel Thing Sale Event!

This is not just another $500 bike

This is one bike you'll want to ride forever

This one-day bike tour is for you

Time for biking

Walk in, ride out!

Ways to improve bike performance

We want biking to be safe, efficient and fun

We're looking for bikers

Welcome to the world of biking

Whatever your cycling passion

Wheelistic deals on all...

Where do you want to ride today?

Birthday

100th birthday extravaganza!

50 or better? Join the club!

75th birthday bash to benefit...

A belated Happy Birthday Sale Event!

A birthday gift that takes the cake

A colossal birthday sale event!

A vacuum cleaner for a birthday gift? You've got to be kidding!!!

All right... who put us up to this? It's a birthday saving celebration!

Almost forgot, didn't you? Our 10th Annual Birthday Sale Gala!

An "in" spot for birthday celebrations

Anyone who wants to send me a birthday greeting can send a contribution to...

Are you buying your mother-in-law a birthday gift?

Be a Birthday Club member and win...

Before your birthday, give your best friend a...

Begin a new birthday tradition with us!

Big-bucks birthday bash!

Birthday celebrants are free at...

Birthday gifts to be savored

Catch the fun at our annual birthday party!

Celebrate it with a night on the town... it's on us!

Celebrating our 25th birthday with a 25% off sale

Do you buy a birthday present for your pet?

Don't you just love surprises?

For that perfect birthday gift...

For that special birthday

Forgetting can be forgivable with a gift from...

Happy birthday! You deserve it!

Have a fantastic birthday at...

Honor a loved one's special day with...

How are you planning to spend your birthday?

How to survive a child's birthday party

Humor a loved one's special day with a...

I'm happy... we're happy... even you're happy... happy birthday!

If it rains on your birthday... the meal's on us!

If it's your birthday, the lunch is on us!

If you can sing "Happy Birthday" you could win a...

In celebration of your birthday... we're giving you a free dinner!

Isn't it nice to still be surprised? It's our annual Happy Birthday Bargains Day!

It's a stress-free birthday party... no gifts

It's easy to become a Birthday Club member

It's easy to say happy birthday with a gift from...

It's our 25th year, big birthday bash!

It's our birthday sale celebration and the party's just begun!

It's our birthday... So we're giving away the store

It's our birthday... today... and everything is on sale!

It's our fabulous birthday celebration!

It's our hundredth birthday... and we're having an awesome day of exciting savings!

It's our Mad, Mad, Mad Birthday Sale!

It's shaping up as a happy birthday sale event!

41

Birthday

It's the biggest birthday party in the world!

Join the Happy Birthday Club and receive a...

Join the Senior Birthday Club and your dinner is free!

Kicking off a birthday salute to bargains, deals and savings!

Live at 65 Birthday Sale Celebration for seniors!

Long live our birthday values day!

Make her birthday the most delicious celebration of the year with...

Not just a birthday, but a celebration of savings!

Nothing says happy birthday like a gift from...

On to the birthday celebration

Only ten shopping days left till your birthday

Oops, it's that time again!

Our 10th Annual Birthday Sales Celebration!

Our birthday sale celebration comes every year!

Our birthday gift for you!

Plan your birthday party with us!

Savings is our birthday gift to you!

Say it's your birthday and we'll give you a 20% discount on your purchase!

Show your love with a birthday card

So you'll never forget our birthday, we're having a sale!

Spend your birthday with the one you love at...

Tell us it's your birthday and receive a free gift!

The big birthday sales celebration of the year!

The birthday extravaganza of the year! Everything is on sale!

The birthday party not to be missed

This birthday sale is all about you!

This is your lucky day! It's our birthday celebration of surprising savings!!!

Three cheers for our exciting birthday sales event!

Throwing a birthday party can be a piece of cake! Call today for details

To celebrate our first birthday, we're cutting a lot more than cake! We're cutting our prices!

We have the best birthday presents for that special person in your life

We just made your birthday a little easier to celebrate

We make birthdays special!

We supply the gifts... you supply the birthday cake

We'll take the cake, you take an extra 10% off on any sale item!

We'll treat you like a princess on your birthday

We're celebrating our 100th birthday with a spectacular sales event!

We've just made 65 a little easier to celebrate! No taxes on any purchase!!!

Welcome to birthday land!

You can't sing Happy Birthday without a cake

You don't need a reason to party at our birthday bash!

You'll feel like a kid, no matter how many birthdays you've had

You'll have a great birthday party with us!

You'll have a hee-haw happy birthday time at...

You'll have a rip-roaring time at our birthday celebration

You'll keep the savings during our birthday celebration!

You'll never forget her birthday again!

Your birthday must be on or before today's date to receive...

Bits of Wit

A bargain is not a bargain unless you can make use of it

A box without a gift is a box

A doctor who takes credit cards is a plastic surgeon

A lower price on something is better than a higher price on nothing

An action plan is just another form of inaction

Are latchkey children something you buy at a hardware store?

Ask ten people and you're likely to get 11 different answers

Bad breath is contributing to global warming

Banks are robbed because that's where the money is

Brought to you by interesting people in an interesting way

But generally speaking, big is better than small

By the time you realize a trend's a trend, it's almost over

Can something be both valuable and inexpensive?

Computers work or they don't

Diamonds are forever, but the girlfriend may not be

Do bottled water sales suffer when it rains? Or is that theory all wet?

Do only Pilgrims enjoy Thanksgiving?

Does a throwaway camera take throwaway pictures?

Don't buy a treadmill if you don't like to walk

Don't spend a small fortune to borrow one

Education is a good thing. So are bobble-head dolls

Even a short line is too long

Ever wonder what a winning recipe tastes like?

Have it your way... go somewhere else

He has a tough time convincing his wife that even a bargain costs money

He made his money the old fashioned way... he inherited it

He needs a hand, but he doesn't want to pay an arm and a leg

How can you teach what comes naturally?

How to make better use of your time while meditating

How to sell anyone anything without selling everyone everything

I was so moved I couldn't move

I would rather have nothing than settle for less

I'm too busy to be saving this much time

If he says something doesn't belong in the newspaper, it belongs in the paper

If it's sugar-free, why do they call them sweets?

If success is 10% inspiration and 90% perspiration, you'd better use plenty of deodorant

If you're wearing matching socks, consider yourself lucky

Is it a lot easier to buy a new house instead of trying to clean up the old house?

It's cheaper to buy new socks than get them done at the laundry

It's like driving a luxury car without enough power

It's like wearing the same pair of pants every day: You'll wear them out

It's the sour truth about the lemons you buy

Laughing is nothing to laugh about

Make your words sweet in case you have to eat them

Mother's Day comes around every year

Never buy a car where the service department has a different area code

Never give a party if you're the most interesting person there

Never look at automobile ads after you just bought one

Never order anything you can't pronounce

Never pay full price to get your oil changed

Never steam-clean your body

New and improved isn't necessarily better

One-size-fits-all no longer fits all

Paying more is the American way

People go shopping more than they care to admit

People have been using the Web for as long as the Web has been around

Some games are better rained out

Sometimes new and improved don't go together

Stuffed animals do not require feeding

Talk isn't free... it's cheap

The average size person doesn't exist anymore

The first cup and the last cup come from the same pot

The only dessert a Thai restaurant offers is a fan

The only thing you can count on today is that you can't count on anything

The savings fit you like an expensive suit

Their products have been around longer than most marriages

There are no free lunches or breakfasts or dinners

There's never a good time to lose your shirt

This product is so new, it doesn't even have a use

Times Square is just a theme park

Today, if you look like a million bucks, it doesn't mean anything

Unless you're getting full undivided attention, you're being ignored

We all spend our money differently

We are brought to you by you

We do not cash checks. Not even our own.

We're giving you ten bucks for your two cents

What do you call a deal no one buys?

What we have to sell is what we have to sell

What's the point of being the same

When in doubt, overdress

When the bananas turn soft and brown, who you gonna call?

When there is a stampede, the safest place is a tall tree

Where do you hide a white elephant?

Wherever the buck stops, so do we

Why deal with anyone who is crazy enough to accept the deal?

Why is it my favorite store... the one I go to all the time?

Why limit happy to an hour

Years back, handmade soap was the norm... today it is a luxury

You are what you don't wear

You can only drive one Rolls Royce at a time

You can't go very fast on the treadmill if you don't turn it on

You can't have a party with one person

You cannot spend a dollar if you only have 50 cents

You only get better at playing the game when you play the game

Book / Library

A book is a gift you can open again and again

A book you can sink your teeth into

A bookstore is more than just a place to buy books

A great pace to grow: the library

A library card is your best credit card

A person who reads is prepared for a wonderful future

An evening of book reading is relaxing

Are you passionate about books?

Be a bookworm!

Book lovers are book givers

Books can change your future

Books for book addicts

Books for days at the beach. Please return without the sand!

Books make personal gifts

Books that reflect your taste and sensibility

Books that will be read again and again

Books to brighten young minds

Books, books, and more books

Building a community of readers, one book at a time

Catch the reading habit

Caution: Reading can be contagious

Celebrate "Reading is Fun" week

Come in and support our library

Discover the fun of reading

Dive into a good book this weekend

Do you love to curl up with a good book?

Don't just read a book... be part of it

Encourage your children to read everyday

Enjoy a good book tonight

Enjoy a summer full of learning, discovery and reading

Expand your vocabulary... read!

Find time to enjoy a book

Follow the road to the bookshelves

For your summer reading enjoyment

Friends of the library

Get a kid to read a book

Get a library card... today!

Get connected with your library

Get hooked on books this fall

Get into the reading habit

Go to a library and read a good book

Good books are best friends

Hard-to-put-down books

Have we got books!

Have you read any good books lately?

Hello, young readers

How to start your own bookstore

How to use your library

Hungry for a good book?

If a book is worth reading, it is worth buying

If you don't know what to do... read a book

If you read, you won't regret it

Imagine a world without books

Is the book you're reading overdue?

It's a book you will treasure forever

It's burning up the best sellers list

It's not how much you read. It's what you read

It's Visit a Library Day!

Love your library

45

Book / Library

Meet the author

Motivate kids to read

Never buy a book you don't love

Now available on E-books

Open a book and you may never find your way out

Our books are always open to the public

Pick up a book, any book, and read it

Put a book in the hands of a child

Rattle your brain... read a book

Rave reads for rainy days

Read any good books lately?

Read for fun... read for success

Read the summer away

Read to learn... learn to read!

Read today for a great future for tomorrow

Reading is a love that lasts a lifetime

Reading is the most precious gift you can give your children

Recycle your books

Remember, the library is here for everyone

See you at the book fair!

Share the love of books with others

So take a trip to your library... and check out the world

Stuff your beach bag with lots of good books

Support your library; read books

Take a look at our paperless books!

Take time to read a book

Teaching a child to read is a responsibility

The book you've been longing for

The books you'd like to become friends with

The borrowing power of your library card

The joy of audio books

The library is a gem of the community

The library is your ultimate lending center

The summer reading game begins on...

There's always a friend for you at the library

There's bound to be a book in your future

There's no telling where a love of reading will take you!

There's nothing like having a good book to read on a long trip

They're books you can't put down once you start reading them

This free book could save you money!

Today's most sensational bestsellers

Turn the TV off and hit your library

Visit your bookstore today!

Watch what happens when reading is fun!

We are a used book store with plenty of charm

We only sell books that deserve to be read!

We put our heart and soul into books

We spread the joy of reading

We've got lots of books and great reading spots

Welcome to the last chapter

What are tomorrow's adults reading today?

When was the last time you sat down with a good book?

Where can you find a needle in a book stack?

Where great readers meet great writers

Wherever books are sold!

Why not join a book club?

Without question, a book worth reading

You can't beat the price of a paperback

You're always welcome at the library

You're welcome to our Annual Book Fair!

You've got to read it!

Bowling

3 strikes and you're a turkey

A glow-in-the-dark good time

A great place to get your own bowling ball and bowling accessories

America's favorite leisure sport

America's love for bowling

Are you sure bowling is your game?

Ask your league secretary or bowling proprietor for details

Be a bowler or be an alley cat

Be the new age bowler!

Beat the Champ Bowling Contest

Bowl mania

Bowl one, get one free!

Bowl with us this fall

Bowl-a-thon

Bowlers with the highest combined scores win

Bowling action is happening here!

Bowling alone can be fun

Bowling brings friends together

Bowling buys in the fast lane!

Bowling for beginners

Bowling for bucks!

Bowling has a clean-cut family image

Bowling is a great way to spend an evening with friends

Bowling is on a roll again!

Bowling is on a roll at...

Bowling is part of the family's recreational life

Bowling is right up your alley

Bowling is the world's largest participation sport

Bowling season is here again

Bowling Strikes and Spares Sales Event!

Bowling takes center stage

Bowling. Beers. Pizza.

Can't come up with five for a team?

Catch the excitement of a strike!

Enjoy the sport of bowling, and it is a sport!

Everything you need to bowl your best

Family bowling fun

For average and hotshot bowlers

For fast-action bowling fun!

For serious bowlers! For super-serious bowlers! For die-hard bowlers only!

Get in it with the spin

Get in the right "frame" of mind... Go bowling!

Get into bowling

Get rolling! Go bowling!

Glow in the dark bowling is pure excitement

Go bowling!

Good luck, and we'll see you on the lanes

Happy Hour Ladies' League... Join today!

Headpin hunting

Hey, whaddaya say we go bowling?

Hitting the lanes and throwing a few balls

Home on the lanes

How about a few frames of bowling?

How to add pins to your average

I am a bowlaholic

I love bowling

I won a bowling ball and a bag!

I'm having a ball

47

Bowling

Includes two games, shoe rental and a beer

Individuals bringing in a full team bowl free all season!

It took a striking performance to...

It's a striking performance

It's always bowling night at our lanes

It's family! It's fun! It's friends! It's affordable!

Just aim for the head pin

Just go up there and throw the ball

Keep knockin' 'em down

King of the lanes

Knock 'em down... rack 'em up

Let us bowl you over with...

Let's get ready to roll

Let's get the ball rolling

Let's go bowling... shall we?

Let's put the zing in bowling

Mow 'em down

Nothing beats bowling

Old people can still bowl... here!

Open bowling every day!

Rack 'em up and knock 'em down

Ready to roll

Recreational bowling is a lot of fun

Right up your bowling alley

Roll 'em

Rolling out the dough

Scratch bowlers bowl and bowl and bowl

Strike it up!

Super savings to recreational bowlers... league bowlers!

Ten pins... ten frames

The charity bowling event of the year!

The excitement of a bowling alley

The future of bowling fun is right here!

The plane truth about bowling

The Super Bowl of bowling!

There's not only great bowling, but a lot of fun things to do

Time to go bowling

To bowl or not to bowl

Tournament time!

Traditional fun for family and friends

Wanna go bowling?

We all have time to roll a few!

We are a proud sponsor of a bowling team

We are going bowling!

We bowl to win!

We don't need more golfers. We need more bowlers!

We invite you to go bowling with your family and friends!

We just keep rolling in bowling

We'd say that's a strike

We're going to bowl you over

We've got everything you need to bowl your best

What a bowling center!

What could be more American?

Where spin and speed tell the score

Who's in your alley?

Why not just rent a ball?

Win free game with strike on red head pin!

Yep, we've got cosmic bowling!

You can hear a pin drop

You don't have to be a pro bowler to enjoy bowling

You don't need to be a scratch bowler to win

You take it one ball at a time

You're on a roll

Your source for balls, bags, shoes and accessories!

Boxing

10 rounds of knockdown deals!

A double-right-hook combination... sensational bargains... smashing deals!

A hell of a fight and a hell of a bargain!

A knockout combination of values!

A man who knows the ropes

A one-two punch sale!

A one-two-three combination of savings!

A sale event that packs a powerful punch!!!

A sale that delivers a big punch!

A sale that packs a powerful punch!

A sale that will knock you cold!

A sale that will knock your socks off!

A solo punch that will knock you cold with savings!

A spectacular first-round knockout

A ten-round sales event everyone has been waiting for!

Add punch to your profits!

Aim for the knockout blow

An incredible 10-round sale!

And the winner is...

Answering the bell

Are you ready for the next round of savings?

At knockout prices!

Bare-knuckle slugfest of savings!

Beat the 10 Count Sales Blitz!

Beat Us to the Punch Sale Event!

Boxing gloves make a knockout gift

Browbeating over the price

C'mon, hit me harder... with outrageous old-fashioned prices!

Come out fighting with these deals!

Come Out Swinging Sale Event!

Don't let our sale knock you out!

Don't let the savings knock you out!

Don't Wait for the Bell Sale Event!

Duking it out with savings!

Feel the power of the punch during our KO Sale Event!

Feel the Power of the Punch Sale Event!

Fight Night for fight fans

Fighting back with great savings!

Fighting Tooth-and-Nail Savings!

First we lowered the price, now we're throwing in the towel!

First-round knockout bargains!

From bare-knuckle savings to knockout values!

Get Down to Your Fighting Weight Fitness Sale!

Give Me Your Best Shot Sale!

Great savings for great fight fans!

Here is a sale you will want to fight for!

Here's a great one-two punch of values!

Here's a knockout punch of a sale!

Here's an offer you will literally knock yourself out for!

Hit 'em early and hit often with great bargains!

How to fight back on high prices!

It takes a smart fighter to save at a sale!

It's a First-Round Knockout Sale Event!

It's a great deal for boxing fans!

It's a knockout of savings!

It's a scoring punch with our service

It's Winner-Take-All Deals!

Boxing

Jump on the bargains and start throwing a few punches yourself!

Knockdown prices!

Knocked out cold bargains!

Knockout combination of values!

Let's duke it out with super spectacular savings!

Let's Put On The Gloves And Let's Go At It Deals!

Letting the Punches Fly Sale Event!

May the best buyer win

Meet me outside in the parking lot and we'll settle it!

Never underestimate the slugging power of a great sale!

Now for the main event!

Off the canvas prices

OK, we're dropping the gloves on everything... including prices!

One-punch knockout of a deal!

Our sale prices beat their sale prices!

Packs a Punch Buy of the Week!

Pound-for-pound, the world's best sale!

Prepare to be dazzled by this amazing sale!

Put a winner in your corner

Put some punch into your workout

Put-up-or-shut-up deals!

Savings that pack a mighty wallop!

Savings that pack a punch!

Savings that'll knock you silly

Slugging it out deals

Solutions that will knock you out

Take a swing at big savings!

Ten rounds of bashing savings!

The Gloves Are Off Sale Event!

The heavyweight champion of all sales!

The last round of hard-hitting savings!

The main event of spectacular savings!

The opening bell and the sale is on!

The referee won't stop this sale event!

The sales fight has started

The Winner... and Still Champ Sale Event!

There's nobody out there who can beat our savings!

This sale packs a mighty wallop!

Time to Take Off the Gloves Deals!

Toe-to-Toe Savings!

We decked out our competition with these fantastic savings!

We KO the middleman so you can save!

We never pull any punches with our deals!

We put the punch in our sale!

We'll beat the pants off anybody's price!

We'll give you our best shot at our savings!

We're always in your corner

We're dropping the gloves on all our prices!

We're duking it out with our values!

We're fighting mad with deals!

We're going for a knockout punch with our closeout merchandise!

We're throwing in the towel with big price cuts!

Where you'll save a fistful of dollars!

Will knock out any challenger

You won't be against the ropes with these values!

You won't get your teeth knocked out with these deals!

You won't go through fighting a tough steak here!

You'll be at ringside for all the action

You'll get knocked silly with savings!

You'll knock yourself out with these bargains!

You're on the savings end of a unanimous decision

Budget

A budget with stretch marks

A great sale for budget-minded customers!

A lesson in budget management

A sale perfect for any budget

Are you a budget-buster?

Are you on top of your bills?

Balancing the budget

Bargain prices for people who are on a tight budget!

Be a thrifty budget maker

Be buck smart

Break out the budget hatchet

Budget cut backlash

Budget-friendly deals!

Budgeting. Bill-paying. Investing.

Calling this a budget war is no exaggeration

Cost-saving advice

Count your pennies before you spend another dime

Don't be afraid to be frugal

Due to budget constraints...

Facing a pile of bills?

For those on tight budgets...

Get a grip on the purse strings

Get into the budget frame of mind

Good for you if your budget is in the black

Good news for your pocketbook

Got the budget blues after the holiday season?

Here's a sure-fire way to save money: stay home!

Here's budget-soothing news

Here's how to get the most mileage out of a dollar

How can we make ends meet?

How dangerous is it to get yourself buried in debt?

How do you spend your money?

How to drink champagne on a beer budget

How to perfect the art of spending

How to stretch the dollar

I can stay within my budget

I'm a member of the Open Wallet Club

I'm on a budget

If the budget allows...

If the budget doesn't get cut...

If you're on a budget...

In addition to saving money...

It won't take a big bite out of the family budget

It works with everything... including your budget

It's bill-paying time

It's the budget-challenged economy

It's time to splurge

Its not what you spend, but how you spend it that counts

Juggling the family budget

Just because you're on a budget doesn't mean you have to live on a budget

Keeping your wallet shut

Know what a dollar means

Learn to budget the money you have

Learn to live on a budget

Live cheap and avoid debt

Living cheap and paying down your debt

Budget

Long on fun, short on cash

Make every dollar you spend... count!

Managing your budget

Minimize spending all of your budget

Money is too hard to earn to waste

No budget? No problem!

Nobody likes paying bills

Now that's a real budget crisis

Only a few dollars... can add up over the course of a year

Overburdened by debt

Overspending is a contagious disease

Paying the bills makes the world go 'round

Pinched by everyday expenses; saving any money?

Prices to stretch your budget

Review your budget, and find ways to save money

Save For A Rainy Day... Sale Event!

Save money by paying cash

Savings for people on a shoestring budget

Savings for people who are on a tight budget

Savings to help your household budget!

Screw the Budget Sale Event!

Seeing red... as in red ink

Sharpen that pencil

Short on cash between paydays?

Show me the budget!

Slam the brakes on cost

Snowed under by your bills?

Speaking of that unbalanced budget

Spend now, save later!

Spend wisely; extravagance won't solve anything

Spend your money wisely

Stay on time... stay on budget!

Staying right on budget

Stick to your budget

Stretch your last dollar as far as it will go

The all-important budget

The budget may be tight, but...

The old way is to balance the budget

The piper must be paid

The right way to baby your budget

The tighter your budget, the better it fits

There's no such thing as enough money

Think before you spend

Tight on cash?

Tipping the scale of your budget

Trouble paying bills?

Try to set a budget before going shopping

Unfreeze the budget

Was it money well spent?

We all know trimming costs is a fact of life these days

We baby your budget

We won't blow your budget

We're keeping our prices in line with your budget

We're very easy on your budget

What happened to the budget?

What you don't know about money can cost you

What's the effect on your budget?

What's your budget?

Where you're most likely to blow your budget

Why you should be on a budget

You can cut the cost on just about every deal!

You'll keep your budget in shape with these savings!

You'll stay on budget with these super deals!

Buy

10,000 fantastic reasons to buy here

3 ways to buy...

5 unbelievable reasons to buy at...

7-day bonus buys

A big event! Big buys!!!

A day that's made for you! 30% off everything you buy!

A good day to buy stuff at half-price

A great bonus buy!

A hoot of a sale for wise buyers

A must-buy!

All the more reasons to buy... now!

Always buy in bulk

Always in stock or it's on us!

An outrageous time to buy!

And guess what? Even you can afford it

Are you a smart buyer?

At event special buys

Attention: First-time buyers!

Awesome buys... guaranteed!

Be a wise buyer and save!

Be careful what you buy: You could be complicating your life

Be the first to buy!

Beautiful buys to look your very best

Before you buy! Check out these values!

Best buys for you!

Best Buys in America Sale!

Best Time to Buy Sale!

Better go out and buy some

Better yet, buy it today!

Biggest and best buys of the year!

Bonus Buys!

But if you build it, will they buy it?

But look what you can buy for only...

Buy 2 or more and save 50%

Buy a lot in one stop!

Buy all you need at prices you can afford

Buy any of these, get all this free!

Buy anywhere else and you'll pay for it

Buy better and buy less

Buy big! Save big!

Buy it and buy some more

Buy it! Hate it! Return it!

Buy more! Save more!

Buy now! Pay later!

Buy now! Save $50 to $100 instantly!

Buy now! Today's the final day!

Buy on impulse and still get a great deal!

Buy one entrée, get one free!

Buy one, get one free!

Buy our stuff at unreal savings!

Buy out the store with these ridiculous savings!

Buy today... save today!

Buy where there is the lowest price!

Buy with confidence at...

Buy! Buy! Buy! Sale Event!

Buyers alert

Buying impulsively is not recommended here!

Can I get it wholesale?

Clean up with great buys

Come prepared to buy

Count all the ways you can buy

Does impulse buying make sense?

Does that really make you want to buy?

Don't buy 'em until you try 'em

Don't buy anything unless you have the option of exchanging it

Don't buy anywhere before you read this ad!

Don't empty your wallet buying full-price merchandise

Doorbuster Buy of the Week!

Eager shoppers are ready to buy, buy, buy

Earn five extra bucks when you buy...

Empowering you with outrageous buys!

Extra savings with bonus buys!

Fantastic buys under $10

Forget the rest. Buy from the best!

Get cookin' with these sizzlin' buys

Get our low-price guarantee before you buy

Get what you need today!

Get yours before they're gone!

Go ahead. Get carried away

Good Buy Sale of the Year!

Got anything I can buy?

Great buys come to those who get here first

Great buys to see you through the season

Great buys... guaranteed!

Hey, it's an impulse buy

Hey, look what a buck buys!

Hot buy savings!

How to buy and not get sold

How to buy on impulse and still be ridiculously responsible

I don't buy it... I sell it!

If it's good, people will buy it

If it's not on sale, I don't buy it!

If money is your excuse, think up another one

If not now, when?

If they don't see an 'on sale' sign, they don't buy

If you don't plan to use it, don't buy it!

In stock! Guaranteed!

In the throes of buy-it-now!

Incredible buys!

It's a good buy!

It's a good day to buy stuff at half-price

It's an outstanding buy!

It's buy, buy, buy!

It's easy to buy with these savings!

It's never too late... or too early to buy...

It's the best time to buy!

It's the next best thing to buying wholesale!

Just about everything is a terrific buy!

Just great buys, period!

Just look what you can buy for only...

Keeps you smiling with today's best buys!

Learn the value of buying on sale

Like we've said for 65 years... shop for it anywhere, you'll buy it at...

Limited time offer! Power buys!

Look what $1.00 buys!

Look what one buck buys at...

Make your dreams a reality with these great buys

Maybe I'll just buy one!

Need to buy or upgrade your...

Never has there been a better time to buy! It's now or never!

No money down! Buy now and save!

No one will ask you to buy anything

Not a buyer, just a browser? Welcome!

Not in a buying mood??? You're still welcome to browse!

Now awesome buys for under $10

Now is the time to do it!

Now's the time to buy! Don't wait!!!

Now's your best time to buy!

Oh, what fun it is to buy

On a buying spree?

Over 100 buy-one-get-one-free items

Power buying is the key to this sale!

Power home some sweet buys!

Save when you buy two or more

Say hello to good buy$!

Sensational buys on today's hottest...

Shop early for the best buys

Shop for it anywhere, you'll still buy it here

Shop here for the best buys!

Shop locally, it's where the buys are

Simply the best buy!

Simply the easiest and most economical way to owning a magnificent...

Smart buys! Shop now!

So what are people buying these days?

So you're ready to buy, right?

Something to buy... just to play with

Spend a little, get a lot!

Stock up and save on bell-ringer buys!

Super Buy Sale!

Super low prices! Fantastic buys!

Super-bonus buys!

Take the buying challenge!

Terrific buys on the brands you trust!

The Best Time To Buy Savings Event!

The dark side of buy now, pay later!

The good buy sale of the year

The place to save... things to buy... money to save!

The time is now to buy!

There's no better time to buy than right now!

There's nothing more to buy, ever!

They say money will buy more at...

Things to buy... money to save!

This might be the best time to buy

This week's best buys!

Buy

Three big reasons to buy now

Top 10 reasons you should buy from...

Truckload buyout!

Try it! Get it! Buy it!

Turn to us for great buys!

Unbelievable buys in store for you

Unbelievable buys throughout the store!

Unleash your uninhibited individuality... buy today!

Warning: May cause sudden urge to buy

We buy right... you buy right

We know if you try it, you'll buy it

We stack 'em deep so you can buy 'em cheap

We'll bet you buy it all!

We're still the next-best thing to buying wholesale

We've got what buyers really want!

When times are good, people buy, and when times are bad, people still buy

When you know the score, you'll buy from the all-pro team at...

Where people come to buy, not to shop

Where to buy? What to buy? How much to pay?

Why buy anywhere else?

Why buy new?

Why just buy one when you can buy them all?

Why not buy both?

Wise buys!

Wow... a buying bonanza!

Yep! This one's the best buy!

You can buy what you need... when you need it!

You want it? We got it!

You'll come out ahead when you buy at...

You're a victim if you buy retail

A must for camping

A new view of camping

A sale event for outdoor enthusiasts such as campers!

A true wilderness savings experience!

A-camping we will go

Ahh, just like the great outdoors

And the outdoors beckons

Be prepared for the great outdoors

Before you break camp...

Bring the indoor living outside

Calling all campers

Camping trips exclusively for women

Camping with kids can be fun for all

Chances are there's a campground not far from home

Dear camping enthusiast:

Discover the nature of the great outdoors

Do you need all this stuff to camp out?

Don't forget the essentials... a cell phone and insect repellent

Eager to go camping?

Everything is on sale for all summer campers!

Experience the outdoors like never before

Extend the camping season year-round with...

Feel like camping out?

For a rustic camping-style experience

For outdoor adventure seekers

For people who love the great outdoors

For the outdoor enthusiast

For the rugged individual in all of us

Forgo the luxuries of a modern campground

Full service hook-ups

Gear up for a camping adventure

Gear up for a good time

Get in Touch with the Outdoors Sale Event

Get more out of the outdoors! Get more out of the savings!

Get the itch without the bites with...

Get the wants and need for camping at...

Go camping... and see what you're missing

Got the itch to go camping?

Great adventures start with camping

Great camping in the great outdoors

Great ideas for outdoor fun

Great outdoor deals for all campers!

Had it with the roughing it thing?

Have an exciting day in the wilderness

Having a good time in the great outdoors is easy

Head for the great outdoors

Heed the call of camping and you will be rewarded

Here's how to make your campsite a cool oasis

Hey dude, do yourself a favor and head on over to the Great Outdoor Sale Event!

How to ease into camping

How to keep bears from visiting your camp

If you want an outdoor activity, go camping

If you're a camper, cut loose this summer

Improving your camping skills

Is camping ready for you?

It's a wonderful way to really know the outdoors

It's about time you go camping, isn't it?

It's camp cooking bargain days!

Just where is the great outdoors?

Lace up your hiking boots. It's time to explore our mountain of savings!

Let's go winter camping

Load up those backpacks and fill your canteen during our Sale Camp-A-Rama!

Looking for some outdoor fun?

Make it an outdoor adventure

Make your next camping outing a little easier with our Outdoors Sale Event!

Our summer camping sale!

Outdoor living at its best

Outstanding equipment for all your camping needs

Pack it up with loads of savings!

Pack up the savings!

Perfect for those outdoor family adventures

Ready for the great outdoors?

Roughing it was never so comfy and convenient

Saving money is a good reason to go camping

Set up camp with the lowest prices ever

Speaking of roughing it

Stake out your site with all your camping needs at…

Taking your outdoor adventure to the next level

The camper of the year

The fun and relaxation of summer camp

The Great Outdoor Sale Event!

The wilderness awaits you

There's nothing like being in the great outdoors

There's outdoor fun for the whole family

Think outdoors! Think savings!

This outdoor adventure may be for you

This sale takes the rough out of roughing it

Unreal savings on all camping gear!

Want to go on an outdoor adventure?

We are a family campground

We are very big on the great outdoors savings!

We can all be happy campers with fantastic savings!

We have all wants and needs for campers

We make absolutely sure you're a happy camper

We make camping an enjoyable experience for everyone

We offer camping trips exclusively for women

We specialize in outdoor adventure

We supply everything for the outdoor life

We take the mystery out of camping

We take the rough out of roughing it

We're giving away free marshmallows during our Campfire Sale Event!

What to know before you go camping

When the outdoors beckon

Why not plan a vacation in the outdoors today!

Wingin' It in the Wild Sale Event!

You can be a happy camper with values like these!

You can set up your tent anywhere you like during our Happy Camper Sale Event!

You couldn't find a better excuse to get outdoors than camping

You won't find a better selection of outdoor living accessories anywhere

You'll be a happy camper with our wild bargains!

You'll be ready for the big outdoors with these savings!

Your one-stop headquarters for the outdoor gear families need

Celebration

A cause to celebrate with deals and bargains that add up to colossal savings!

A celebration that will make you want to dance

A celebration that's filled with bargains galore!

A grand celebration during our Grand Opening Days!

A jubilee celebration

A night just for you

A night you'll never forget

A rock 'n' roll extravaganza!

A sale that's something to celebrate!

A special occasion to celebrate again and again

A truly extraordinary event will take place this year

A year-long celebration for...

Add a fresh touch to your celebration

As we celebrate our victory...

As we honor the past and celebrate the present

Be part of the celebration! Be part of the savings!

But first, here's a little about what we're celebrating

Calls for one big wingding

Can you afford to miss our celebration of savings?

Catch the deals before the celebration begins

Celebrate da occasion wit us in style

Celebrate each day this year with...

Celebrate Friendship Day... today!

Celebrate that special day with us!

Celebrate the joy of birth with a gift of...

Celebrate the season with us

Celebrate this grand occasion with exciting savings!

Celebrating 25 successful years...

Celebrating 50 years of excellence

Celebrating 70 years of fun

Celebrating a decade of excellence

Celebrating a lifetime of memories

Celebrating a new beginning

Celebrating three decades of success

Celebrating without spending a fortune

Celebrations made easy with us!

Check out the celebration

Come and celebrate the future

Come celebrate the biggest and best event of the year

Come celebrate what's new at...

Come help us celebrate

Come join a fabulous celebration!

Come rain or shine, it's time to start celebrating

Do you need a reason to celebrate?

Don't fight it... celebrate it!

Every day is a celebration

Everyone loves a celebration... everyone loves a deal!

Family celebrations are our specialty

Fifty things to celebrate

For an exuberant celebration on any occasion, call...

For gracious gatherings and celebrations...

Gala celebration of terrific savings!

Get a jump on the celebration

Give them a celebration to remember

Got something to celebrate?

Here's another great reason to celebrate this holiday season

How would you like to celebrate your...

It's a savings celebration you won't want to miss!

It's our kickoff celebration

It's time to celebrate in style

Join the celebration

Let the festivities begin!

Let the Oooohing and Aaaahing begin

Let us help you create the perfect celebration

Let's celebrate the grand opening together

Let's liven up the celebration with...

Let's make the experience one to celebrate

Make your celebration super with...

Now here's something to celebrate

One celebration you'll never forget

Plan your celebration now!

Sizzling savings celebration!

So celebrate the season in style

So come celebrate

So how are you going to celebrate?

Something worth celebrating

Start celebrating now!

Stompin' Good Time Sales Event!

Tasty way to top off your celebration

The best place to celebrate anything

The celebration continues at...

The greatest sale celebration of all time!

The parties. The hoopla. The celebration. All at our place!

The perfect way to celebrate any special occasion

The sale celebration is here

The time is ripe to celebrate

There is a reason for us to sing and celebrate

There's always something to celebrate

This is the place for the young and hip to celebrate

Time to celebrate the sales event of the season

To celebrate and to remember, let us help you every step of the way!

Today... let's celebrate!

Trillion reasons to celebrate

Truly a day of celebration

We can help you do something memorable to celebrate your...

We do joyous weddings. Momentous celebrations. Jubilant festivals. Gala events.

We look forward to celebrating with you

We look forward to seeing you at the centennial celebration

We make every celebration special

We're celebrating with markdowns on everything in the store

We're celebrating with terrific, tremendous, incredible savings!

We're going to celebrate tonight at...

What a celebration! What a sale!

What a spectacular sale celebration!

What a way to celebrate! Fantastic bargains! Amazing deals! Exceptional savings!

What better way to celebrate than with 30 to 50% off on all merchandise!

What better way to celebrate with family and friends

Where the celebrating never stops

Where there's always something to celebrate

Words of celebration... fabulous, magnificent and outstanding!

You're invited to a fantastic celebration

You're invited to join the savings celebration!

You've got an excuse to celebrate with these awesome savings!

A Cause for Applause Annual Charity Benefit

A cause to believe in

A Charity Bizarre Bazaar

A generous heart

A New Century of Service Benefit

A Night of Fashion Charity Gala

A salute to our contributors

A Spring Fantasy Charity Ball

A time to share

A Very Merry Bazaar for Charity

All are invited for A Night Of Delight

All personal charitable contributions are tax-deductible

An Evening of Appreciation Gala

Annual Bunny Boutique Spring Craft Charity Show

Annual Green Tie Ball

Annual Shipboard Benefit Charity Concert

Architectural Walking Tour Benefit

Arts and Crafts Charity Fair

Be generous in giving

Beau of the Charity Ball

Blue Note Charity Ball

Calico Cottage Craft Charity Show

Care to share?

Cause for a Celebration Charity Ball

Charity Masquerade Charity Ball

Christmas Express Annual Charity Dinner Dance

Christmas in November Charity Jazz Festival

Did you call in your pledge?

Dinner Dance and Silent Auction for Charity

Donate it to charity

Donating to a poverty-fighting group of your choice

Fantasy of the Opera Gala to help the needed

Generosity is never forgotten

Generosity speaks for itself

Get Into Giving... Charity Ball

Give from the heart

Give until it feels good

Giving never goes out of style

Giving satisfies a profound human need

God bless your generosity to this very worthy cause

Gold Coast Charity Gala

Grand night for a gala to help the poor

Hats off to our Annual St. Charity Ball

Heartfelt smiles and gracious support

Helping hands to help the cause

Hey, big spender, how about our charity?

Hey, kick in a donation

Holiday Craft Fair for your favorite charity

Holiday Glitter Craft Charity Show

Holiday Happenings Craft Show

Holiday Market Bazaar for Charity

Holiday Open House For The Homeless

It couldn't be easier for you to give

It is in giving that we receive

It's a special relationship between you and the charity

It's for a worthy cause

It's for charity and it's a fun time

It's so much easier to give, y' know!

It's time for sharing

Join the fight for...

Join us for a charitable
star-studded event

Kick In for Charity Ball

Make a difference in somebody's life

Make a donation to your favorite charity

Mid-Winter Gala for the homeless

Operation Care Benefit

Our Annual Charity Raffle

Our Annual Christmas Charity Bazaar

Out on the Town Charity Fashion Show

Please be generous

Please patronize our sponsors...
thank you!

Proceeds from the event will be used to...

Pulling together for a cause

Responding to the needs of others

Rise to the occasion

Scents of Spring Fashion Charity Review

Share your treasure

Show how much you care

Silver Bells Charity Bazaar

Silver Moments. Silver Memories.
25th Annual Charity Benefit.

Snowflakes Charity Frolic

Spirit of St. Nick Charity Ball

Spread your generosity throughout
the year

Spring Fever Charity Ball

Standing tall with charity

Take a swing for a good cause

Tee it up for charity

The 50th Annual Benefit Luncheon
Fashion Charity Show

The Annual Charity Raffle

The Annual Christmas Charity Walk

The Annual Summer Charity Ball

The Belle of a Garden Charity Ball

The Blue Note Charity Ball

The Butler's Charity Ball

The Butterfly Charity Ball

The Candlelight Charity Ball

The Charity Ball of the Year

The Gingerbread Factory Charity Fair

The goodness of the human heart

The greatest satisfaction is
helping people

The Helping Hands Ball

The Local Fashion Shows for Charity

The Monday Night Charity Ball

The more you acquire, the more
important it is to give

The People Who Need People
Foundation Ball

The Princess Charity Ball

The season of charitable giving

The Tax Auditor's Charity Ball

Those who have been blessed with more
are asked to give

Through your generosity, we...

True generosity is giving what you
cherish most

We couldn't have done it without
your support

We depend on you!

We take the guesswork out of giving

What God has given must be shared

What the heck, the money goes for a
good cause

What would you give to end poverty?

When you give you shall receive

You can help make a difference

You'll feel good giving

Young at Heart Winter Charity Ball

Your donation is like no other

Your support will make a difference

A Christmas extravaganza sale like no other!

A few tips on what to give someone for Christmas

A reminder that the Christmas shopping season isn't far off

A very merry after-Christmas sale!

A warm welcome to great Christmas values!

After Christmas Sale... starts today!

All I want for Christmas is on sale at...

All the trimmings to warm your home... And heart

Are you singing the jingle bell blues?

At these savings even Scrooge would give gold and silver

Beat the December rush!

Book your Christmas party now!

Box It Up After-Christmas Sale!

Bring home the magic of Christmas

Buy yourself a gift this Christmas!

Call Santa's helpers for all your holiday needs!

Christmas is a wrap at...

Create a memorable holiday for your special someone

Dash in for Christmas specials!

Dashing through the values!

Deck the halls with holiday deals!

Did you buy everything your family wanted for Christmas?

Do you hear what I hear? Savings on all gift ideas!

Do your Christmas dreaming with us!

Do your Christmas shopping in your PJs

Don't be a Scrooge this Christmas

Don't lose sleep over what to get

Don't wait for Christmas to start the holiday season

Eager to make your holiday shopping a breeze

Even Santa can't deliver prices this low!

Even Santa saves at...

Even Santa shops here!

Every Christmas needs a wise man

Everything Yule need for the holidays!

Eye-popping shopping makes holidays sparkle

Fill your entire gift list in minutes at...

Folks, it's that time of year!

For everyone on Santa's list

From Santa's elves to our shelves... fabulous Christmas gifts!

Get all your Christmas treasures here!

Get decked out for the holiday season

Get your taste buds ready for the holidays

Gifts that are right up Santa's alley

Gifts that have the elves' seal of approval

Give a memory this season...

Give the holiday spirit

Glistening buys!

Great stocking stuffers!

Guaranteed delivery before Christmas!

Have your photo taken with Santa

He's making a list and checking it twice. How about you?

He's making a list... and checking the savings!

Here's a real family value for this holiday season!

Hey Santa! Our sale is bigger than your list!

Ho! Ho! Ho! Only 365 more shopping days till Christmas!

Ho, ho, ho! Our prices are low-low-low

Holiday gear... Holiday cheer...

Holiday sensations with all the bells and whistles

Home for the Holiday Sale, I'm on my way!

If your employees live all over, give them a gift certificate that's good all over

Imagine this under your tree!

In December, you'll be glad you thought of it now!

In the spirit, let us help you get started with your early holiday shopping

It is Christmas, after all... so, just do it!

It's also the season for getting yourself a gift, too!

It's Christmas in July at...

It's Christmas wrap-up time!

It's more Christmassy if you wait until the last minute

It's our kickoff to the holiday season!

It's time to get serious about holiday shopping

It's toy time... Are you ready?

Kick off of the holiday shopping season at...

Last call for Christmas!

Last-minute "must-haves"

Last-minute Christmas buys!

Layaway for Christmas... Now!

Leave the wrapping to us

Let the Christmas shopping begin!

Let us bring joy to your family and friends this holiday season... perfect gifts for less

Let us stuff your Christmas stocking this season

Light up the holidays with savings!

Make it a cool Yule with...

Make the most of your Christmas dollars

Make this a Christmas to remember... Rent a Santa suit!

Make your list, check it twice and take 30% off regular-priced items!

Make your list, check it twice, so Santa doesn't forget to...

Merry extras... Need we say more?

My true love gave to me

Need a little Christmas?

Nobody does Christmas better than us

Not even Santa can beat our kind of service!

Now is the time to start a Christmas club savings account!

Oh, what fun it is to buy!

Our business has the spirit for your holiday entertaining needs

Our Christmas elves will warm your heart

Our savings make the season merrier!

Our Very Merry After-Christmas Sale!

Play it safe... shop early!

Pre-Christmas selection... After-Christmas prices!

Priced so your pocketbook can take a holiday, too!

Prices so low they'll fit under your tree

Rev-up for holiday giving

Santa isn't the only one who delivers in time

Santa knows where the savings are!

Santa's cleared for takeoff

Santa's Super Savings Specials!

Save Like The Dickens Sale!

Savings can make wishes come true!

Savings that can make a Scrooge merry!

Savings that will help you wrap up the holidays!

Savings wonderland!

Savings Yule love!

Christmas

Shop and save at our "Christmas in March" sale!

Shop for Christmas year-round!

Sleighful of savings!

Sparkles that put savings in your holidays!

Start your holidays on our front door

Stuff their stockings with...

Stuff these in your stocking!

The 12 days of savings! You have only 4 days left

The Christmas countdown sale!

The hectic gift-buying season has arrived

The perfect way to wrap up the holidays

The ultimate Merry Christmas shopping destination

There's still time to give the best

These gifts are ready to give

They always made Christmas special for you. Make it special for them!

This holiday, Santa's not the only one running around

This holiday, there's no better price on the globe

This is an announcement regarding Christmas gift-giving

This is your final chance to get your last-minute shopping done

This season make it easier on yourself

This way to visit Santa

This year's hottest holiday gift

Tie up your last-minute gift-giving with us

Time to act fast for the holidays

'Tis the season and here's the reason to shop at our store

'Tis the season to be saving!

Traditional holiday fare your family will love

Trim-a-tree buys!

Trying to avoid the last-minute holiday rush?

'Twas the sale before Christmas

Twelve Days of Christmas Sale!

We created a solution to dull holiday shopping

We help you grab holiday shopping by the Claus

We make happier holidays!

We warned you, 59 shopping days 'til Christmas

We wish you big savings on...

We're making Christmas a little more wonderful

We're your Santa's helper

We've got the holiday all wrapped up for you!

We've got what's on your list at Santa's sidewalk sale!

What Santa Forgot To Give You... Sale Event!

What the wise men are giving this Christmas?

What's on your wish list?

When do you start shopping for Christmas?

When it comes to holiday savings, we're really gifted!

When they open it, they'll say thank you!

When you're ready to mingle... we're ready to jingle!

Where great Christmases begin

Where smart Santa saves!

Whether it's a big bash or a small soiree, we make holiday entertaining so easy!

Wrap up big "ho, ho, ho" holiday savings!

Wrap up your Christmas shopping in just one call

You can save like Scrooge at...

You can't wrap it up tomorrow!

You'd better watch out... Time's running out!

Circus

A big sale and the circus were made for each other

A big sale in the Big Top!

A circus atmosphere of unbelievable savings!

A circus is born! A celebration of savings!

A circus of savings!

A delightful mix of laughs and thrills for the young and old

A fun-filled night under the Big Top

A great evening for the family

A real-life, non-stop circus of magnificent savings

A sale that's all the fun of the circus

A sale that's sure to bring a smile to your face!

A super circus celebration!

A three-ring sales extravaganza!

A truly big show... and a truly big sale!

Ah, the circus

All ages love a circus... and all ages love a sale!

An Old American Tradition Sales Event!

An old fashioned circus of values!

Be like a kid again

Be part of our circus of savings!

Be ready for the Circus of Amazing Savings!

Big deals under the big top!

Big price cuts under the big top!

Buffalo Bob's Wild West Show of exciting savings

Circus thrills! Circus smiles! Circus deals!

Close your eyes, smile and relive your circus memories

Come to be entertained... come to the savings!

Come to see the greatest sale on earth

Deals that are the talk of the town

Designed to bring the circus to life

Enjoy an old-fashioned summer circus

Every circus needs a great clown

Everybody loves the circus

Exciting! Astounding! Unbelievable!

Experience the magic and romance of the circus

Feel the thrill and excitement of a circus of savings!

Fun under the Big Top!

Get ready for circus entertainment

Get ready to experience the savings of a lifetime

Get your circus tickets... now!

Get your three rings of big savings! 3-Day Sale!

Good evening ladies, gentlemen and children of all ages

Good old-fashioned circus fun

Hey, let's go to the circus

Hurry, hurry, step right up for exciting values!

If you love circuses, you'll love this sale!

It's Big Top Savings Time!

It's going to be a circus at our grand opening

It's like the circus coming to town

It's lions, tigers, elephants and much more

It's stuff that sticks with kids

It's sure to delight children of all ages

Join the circus parade of sensational savings!

Let the circus begin

Circus

Let the Oohing and Ahhing
Sale Event begin!

Look at the faces of young children in
the crowd

Make the circus memories last

May everyday be a circus day

More savings than a three-ring circus

Now! That's a circus

Old-fashioned, but always entertaining

One-ring circus spectacular!

Our tent sale is the greatest sale event
on earth!

Raising the Big Top!

Real entertainment... real savings!

Real horses, real lions... this is a real sale!

See the circus again and again and again

See the circus while it's in town

Send in the clowns

Share the magic of the circus with
the family

So step right up and bring the entire
family to a grand opening spectacular!

Step right up! Step right into
super savings!

Strictly a PG performance for all to enjoy

Strike up the band for big savings at...

Take your place in the potentate's box

Tent-A-Thon Big Top Sale!

The biggest circus of all

The biggest savings treat on earth!

The circus must go on before the sale!

The classic American circus of saving!

The excitement! The pageantry! The sale!

The greatest circus sale event in any
tent, anywhere!

The greatest parade of values on earth!

The greatest sale performance on
any planet!

The Main Tent Sale Event is
going up now!

The most famous, spectacular and
intriguing circus ever

The most magnificent and greatest sale
event ever seen!

The old-time circus comes to town

The smallest show on earth is at...

The smell of the greasepaint deals!

The splendor and majesty at the circus

The tent with good will

There is nothing else like it in the world

This ain't no circus... just real deals!

This is a wholesome family
entertainment for young and old alike

This way to the big sale event!

Turn your three-ring circus into a
well-managed business

Want to get paid for clowning around?

We make people laugh

We'll jump through hoops for you

We're not clowning around during our
Value Days Sale!

We've got more clowns at our store than
they have at the circus

We've taken circus entertainment to a
whole new level

What a circus of a sale!

What's more fun than a circus?

When it comes to the circus, it's all fun
and savings!

When the tent goes up, our prices go down

Where dreams of savings come true

Will surely bring smiles to both young
and old

You really must see the circus

You won't clown around with
these savings!

You'll be fascinated by our circus of
unbelievable savings!

Classifieds

20 words for 2 weeks for 20 bucks

Advertise for free in the meeting place

All classified ads are subject to the newspaper standards

Buying or selling, classified is the place for you

Check out our help wanted classified section

Classified ads make it easy to buy and sell

Classified is the place to advertise

Classified marketplace

Do you have something you'd like to sell?

Don't hide it; sell it in the classifieds

Find it fast in the classifieds

Find your home in the classifieds

For as low as 75¢ per day

For greater efficiency, advertise in the classifieds

For once, go to the classifieds first

Free advice on how to write the most effective classified ad

Get real results!

Got too much stuff? Sell it! Need more stuff? Buy it!

Have you tried our classified ads online?

How do you classify today?

If you really want to see results, advertise in the classified

It gets results! That's why we're in the classified

It's a classified clearance sale!

It's do-it-yourself advertising!

It's easy to sell your old car fast with a classified ad

Let the classifieds sell for you

Look what I found in the classifieds!

Looking to sell your car, stereo, snow blower?

Make room for the new by selling the old... with an ad in the classifieds

Need it quick? Find it fast in the classifieds

Need to hire? Start with the want ads

Now aren't you glad you read the classifieds

Online recruiting vs. classified ad recruiting

Placing a classified ad is easy

Put a little extra money in your pocket. Sell items in the classified

Put your ad in every day to reach thousands of customers

Puts your message right in front of the people you want to have see it

Sell it quick... advertise in the classifieds

Sell it! Find it! Buy it!

Sell your stuff in the classifieds

The people's marketplace

Thousands of people are seeing this ad... but we're only selling one home

Turn to today's classifieds for great buys

Want ads are reasonably priced

Want ads get results, not promises

Watch the classifieds for buried treasure

When you advertise in the classified, it's like money in the bank

When you have something to sell, sell it fast with an ad in the classified

When you want to sell anything, use the classifieds

Why not advertise your service in the classifieds?

Your marketplace of opportunity

67

Columbus Day

A brilliant discovery of an unbelievable sale!

A dino-mite discovery! A dino-mite sale!

A new world is waiting to be discovered

A salute to Columbus

A voyage of discovery

A world of savings is waiting to be discovered

And you'll discover it's a holiday sale!

Be willing to explore the...

Before Columbus landed, he already knew what makes the business world go 'round

Buy one Columbus Day item at regular price and get a second item for just one cent

Celebrate Columbus Day by discovering our sale!

Celebrate Columbus Day with us!

Celebrating the discovery of America

Columbus Day is not only for shopping day sales!

Columbus Day one-cent sale event. You'll find it very rewarding!

Columbus Day sailing savings sale!

Columbus Day sale... Sea what we've got!

Columbus Day savings celebration!

Columbus Day values... We'll get you there

Columbus Day weekend spectacular!

Columbus did discover our savings spectacular!

Columbus had a great eye for real estate and an eye for a great sale!

Did you ever discover something?

Discover a Columbus Day extravaganza!

Discover a delicious new world of your own

Discover a new way to save on everything for your...

Discover a whole new world for your...

Discover a world of beautiful savings!

Discover America one dollar at a time

Discover great savings on all sale merchandise!

Discover it all! Discover it here!

Discover our low prices... Discover our quality... And discover our service!

Discover phenomenal savings on all...

Discover savings of 30 to 70% on all special purchase...

Discover the great Columbus Day sale!

Discover the way to super spectacular savings!

Discover unheard-of savings at...

Discover utterly unbelievable savings for everyone

Discover what a little wind in your sales can do for your best customers

Discover what you can do for America

Discovery Day Sale Event!

Don't miss the boat on this Columbus Day Sale!

Don't skip the Columbus Day parade

Everything is priced at $14.92 in this department

Explore the celebration of Columbus Day

Fill your sails with Columbus Day sales!

First, discover our Columbus Day values, then go out and celebrate!

Get in step at our Columbus Day Parade of Fashion

Get set for a great Columbus Day Sale!

Get set for Columbus Day fun!

Have a Columbus Day brunch on us!

How many times can Columbus discover America?

It opens the door of discovery to a...

It's an honor to celebrate Columbus Day

It's Columbus Day, discover a new country

It's not goodbye Columbus, it's hello to oceans and oceans of savings!

It's our annual Columbus Day weekend sale!

It's the day to discover the best prices in town!

It's time to discover, or rediscover, a great sale!

It's worth celebrating... Christopher Columbus Day!

It's your day of discovery!

Let us help you discover the new you!

Make today your day of discovery

Now here's a real discovery

Now thru Columbus Day!

On Columbus Day, you'll find out what you've been looking for!

Only today, you can double your savings!

Our discovery is a salute to Columbus

Our great Columbus Day sale... Starts today!

People were buying here even before there were places to stay

Please take time and join our Columbus Day festivities

Pre-Columbus Day sale... What timing!!!

Really big Columbus Day closeout!

Rediscover America's values... That's all it takes

Sail in for our Columbus Day sale... And we'll ship it out free!

Sail with our Colossal Columbus Day Sale!

Scan the horizon with Christopher for quality, value and price

Seizes the opportunity to explore our discounted items!

Ship to shore Columbus Day savings!

So exactly when do you celebrate Columbus Day?

Some Americans go through life without discovering our Columbus Day sale!

Start your journey with us

Thank You Columbus Day Sale!

The adventure of a lifetime awaits you at...

The day Columbus discovered America is the day to discover our amazing deals!

The Eggsplorers, Santa Maria Scramble, Pinta Pancakes are being served!

The urge to explore! The urge to shop! The urge to save!

There's a great sale out there to explore

This Columbus Day discover the tradition of...

This Columbus Day, discover great savings at...

This sale is a dino-mite discovery

Today is a Columbus Day Holiday and we're celebrating with fabulous old-fashioned prices!

Today, you'll find what you've been looking for all along

We all remember Christopher Columbus, don't we?

You can rediscover the world at...

You never know what you'll discover! Bargains!!! Values!!! Deals!!!

You won't sail off the edge at our Columbus Day Sale Event!

You'll be celebrating the discovery of drastically slashed prices!

You'll discover a whole new world at our store!

Your discovery days are here again!

Your ship has come in with Columbus Day values!

Communications

A failure to communicate... no more!

Adaptable to any environment on the communication horizon

Anytime, anywhere communication

Applying old ways of thinking with new communication tools

Are we communicating?

Are you totally outside the communications revolution?

Better to communicate too much than too little

Bridge the communication gap with...

Business is all about communication

Changing the way businesses communicate

Closing the communication gap

Communication is an age-old thing

Communication starts here

Communications are simple... the possibilities are endless

Communications at work

Communications beyond all boundaries

Communications solutions for e-business

Communications without boundaries

Doing business in a competitive communications environment

Effective communication in the info-glut age

Even when you're not talking, you're communicating

Exaggeration is a way to communicate

Expert communicators needed!

Face to face communicating is the best

Failure to communicate means failure

Finding new ways of thinking and communicating

For really clear communication...

Forget everything you learned about communications, because it's about to change

Fostering effective communications

From communication central

Get on the cutting edge of the evolving communications industry

Global communications

Good communicating skills start with learning to listen

Good communications create good business!

Have you realized your full communications potential?

Having communication problems?

How do you communicate with your customers?

How to communicate much better

How to use voicemail more effectively

If you don't communicate like a winner, you won't be a winner

I'm just a communications executive

I'm used to straightforward communication

Information technology has stimulated communication

Is instant communication throughout the world necessary?

Is verbal communication dead?

It's an alternate way to communicate

It's not what you communicate; it's what gets communicated

It's the holy grail of communications

It's the worst communications service I've ever had

It's a new form of communications

It's all about communications! It's all about miscommunication!

It's just a different way of communicating

It's mind-boggling to think how much communication has changed

Keeping the channels of communication open

Learn patience and yearn for communication

Leaving the information age, moving into the communication age

Looking for other ways to communicate?

Looking to enhance communication?

Make a commitment to communications

Meeting the world's growing communications needs

More opportunity to communicate with people in different ways

More ways to stay connected

Now communicating can be all you imagined

Now you'll communicate like never before!

Overcoming communication barriers

Poor communications has a new twist

Problems communicating with others?

Put your communications on the right track

Putting yourself out of touch, rather than choosing to be in touch

Quality in telecommunications

Real time communication

Remember when communication was very simple?

Sharpening your communication skills

Sound confusing?

Struggling to communicate

That's how communication is being done

The age of instant communication

The dynamic world of communications

The future of your communication depends on...

The job of communicating accurately becomes more and more important

The marvel of communications

The power of communication

The solution to meet every communication challenge

The string just isn't long enough

The world of communications

Think and communicate

To know how to communicate is a virtue

Today, everything depends on communication

Today, there are more ways to communicate a message than there ever were before

Tools for communication

We are truly sorry we have not been able to communicate with you

We are without a doubt a communications-centric society

We do business communications!

We keep the lines of communication open

We need people who communicate well

We offer a comprehensive communication solution

We pay for communications

We understand the telecommunications business as a whole

We're all about communication

We're communicators... let's communicate

What tools do you use to communicate?

What would we do without e-mail communications?

When it comes to communicating an idea...

When it comes to communication, less is more

When you communicate, we're with you

Worldwide cellular communications

You need a site that communicates effectively

You'll be living in tomorrow's communication world with...

9 out of 10 mice prefer...

A computer is a terrible thing to waste

A computer works or it doesn't

A mouse that really clicks

And now a word from your computer

Anybody can buy a computer, but the trick is making it work

Are you a product of the computer age?

Are you an upgrade junkie?

Are you frustrated by your computer?

Are you living in our totally PC world?

Are you up-to-date on your computer skills?

Burning the midnight modem

Buy your computer a gift... this Valentine's Day!

Computer crashes got you crazed?

Computer learning free!

Computers don't care if you throw a tantrum

Create with your computer instead of just using it

Customers are not buying just a computer. They are buying what the computer will do for them

Customers don't care about bits and bytes, they care about outcome

Cutting-edge savings on all computer supplies for home or office

Did you ever want to punch your computer in the nose?

Do you have a love-hate relationship with your computer?

Do you live with a laptop all day and all night?

Does your computer recognize you?

Don't be afraid, just upgrade

Don't forget your computer... this holiday season!

Don't leave home without your laptop

Don't worry, I'm a Macintosh man

Ever wish you could chuck your PC out the window?

Everyone's talking about our computers

Fire Up the Computer Sale Event!

For computer buffs

For people who are computer-driven

For technical support press "1"

Free combo drive upgrade!

Gentlemen, start your PC's

Get a fast, big-screen notebook at a great price from...

Get all the extra power and accessories your PC needs!

Give us your old, your unwanted, your tired computers

Give your computer a break today!

Have you maxed out with the PC?

Have you taken a look behind your computer lately?

Here's a computer that operates in real time, not behind the times!

High-tech savings on computer accessories

Home is where the laptop is

How to become computer-savvy

I don't want to upgrade, I'm happy with what I've got

I'm your computer today, tomorrow and forever!

If you want to make money, think computers

Is that a computer you're holding?

Is the mouse mightier than the pen?

Is your computer after your job?

It's easy to be a savvy computer user

It's not a luxury anymore;
it's a necessity

It's time to upgrade the computer again

Just when you thought it was safe to go
back to your computer

Let our computers do your dirty work

Let us upgrade your PC with more
memory, more graphics and a new drive

Lights! Camera! Computer!

Looking beyond the PC

My computer is a piece of cake

Never ask a man what computer he uses

Next window please!

Nine out of ten mouse pads prefer us

No upgrades, please!

Not just for geeks anymore

Now everybody can afford a computer

On the road with your laptop

Our computers are idiot-proof

Our computers are very polite to
our customers

Out-of-the-box, ready to go!

Protect your PC for up to three years
with our service plan

Pure power solutions for any PC

Put your money into hardware,
not houseware

Read the user manual

Remember when they laughed...
when you said "I don't do Windows!"

Rx for computer viruses

Savings with the click of a button!

Take your mouse shopping, today!

The three golden rules for computer
safeguarding: backup, backup, backup

The computer survival checklist

The computer that revolutionized
the world

The mouse has roared for ferocious
savings on all computers!

The world's most powerful computer

Think outside the computer

This computer can do it all

This computer is as easy to use as
your telephone

This computer will have changed the
way you live!

This offer is for computer-smart seniors

This sale is not all computer jargon!

Turn to your computer... turn to
the savings!

Unleash the power of your PC with...

Warning: Your computer may be
hazardous to your family

We don't give you all that computer
mumbo jumbo

We fix schizophrenic computers

We speak in plain English, not computer
gobbledygook

We'll get your computer talking!

We'll help get your computer up to speed

We'll show you how easy it is to get a PC
that's just what you need

Welcome to my hard drive!

What do people really want a computer
to do these days?

What if Columbus had a computer?

Why not just buy a new computer?

Where's my laptop? On sale at...

Which computer is right for you?

Why can't buying a computer be like
buying an appliance?

You too can be smarter than
your computer

You won't get carpal tunnel syndrome
with these savings!

You'll be spoiled by this PC

You're Pulling My Mouse... Sales Event!

Your computer will be buzzing with
these awesome savings!

Contest

A Big Cash Windfall Contest

A Ladies' Night Out Contest

A Night on the Town Contest

An Over the Top Blast Contest

April Showers Bring May Flowers Contest

Back-to-School Photo Contest

Be a Clown for a Day Contest

Beat the Clock Contest

Beat the Pro Contest

Belly Up to the Bar Contest

Best Shot Digital Photo Contest

Block the Shot Contest

Breakfast in Bed Contest

Bring a Smile to Your Face Contest

Catch a Cool Breeze Contest

Catch the Taste of Spring Contest

Color Your Way to College Contest

Count the Bunnies contest

Craziest Idea Contest

Cutest Baby Contest

Dash for Cash Contest

Deal Yourself a Winner Contest

Dialing for Dollars Contest

Diamond in the Rough Contest

Dishing Out Dollars Contest

Draw Your Mom's Picture Contest

Everyone Loves a Winner Contest

Fairy Tales Do Come True Contest

Fall in Love with Fall Contest

Fill Your Shopping Cart Contest

Friday Night Madness Contest

Get a Free Lunch for Life Contest

Get Into the Spring of Things Contest

Get Lost in the Maze Contest

Get Your Share of the Loot Contest

Give it the Ol' College Try Contest

Give-Me-A-Break Weekend Contest

Good Old Greenbacks Contest

Goof Off of the Year Contest

Great Cash Giveaway Contest

Guess the Jellybeans Contest

Have a Crazy Day Contest

Having the Time of Your Life Contest

Here Comes the Bride Contest

Hit a Home Run Contest

Hit the Jackpot of Fame and
Fortune Contest

Ho-Ho-Ho Christmas Cash Contest

How Many Seeds Does This Watermelon
Have Contest

I Love You Valentine Contest

I'm Going for the Dough Contest

Join in on our Beer Chuggers Contest

Lasso the Moon Contest

Laugh and Get Rich Contest

Let's All Scream for Spring Contest

Let's Go Skiing Contest

Let's Play Ball Contest

Look-Alike Contest

Lucky Number Contest

Made in the Shade Contest

Make a Monster Contest

Make a Witch Smile Contest

Match 'Em Cowboy Contest

May the Fastest Eater Win Contest

Millionaire Madness Contest

Mom of the Year Contest

My Christmas Fantasy Contest

My Opinion Matters Contest

Mystery Photo Contest

Name that Site Contest

Name the Restaurant Contest

Okay, Knock My Socks Off Contest

On the Road to Success Contest

Pet of the Month Contest

Pigskin Picks Contest

Pumpkin Patch Full of Cash Contest

Punt-Pass-Kick Contest

Queen for a Day Contest

Rake In the Sales Contest

Run With the Best Contest

Search for the Hidden Treasure Contest

Springtime Big Bucks Contest

Stars' Night Out Contest

Strike it Rich Contest

Super Match for Cash Contest

Take Aim and Win Contest

Tell Us Your Story Contest

The Annual Tug-Of-War Contest

The Best Recipe Contest

The Best-Dressed Person Wins Contest

The Big Payback Contest

The Country Fair Annual Pie Contest

The Dash for Cash Contest

The Fourth Quarter Scoring Drive
Sales Contest

The Good Neighbor Contest

The Goose That Laid the
Golden Egg Contest

The Great Grocery Giveaway Contest

The Great Home Giveaway

The Great Rainbow Contest

The Great Steak Roundup Contest

The Messiest House Contest

The Midnight Oasis Contest

The Million-Dollar Smile Contest

The Most Original Costume Contest

The Perfect Father Contest

The Stupidest Thing Said Contest

The Ugliest Couch Contest

The Wearin' o' the Green Contest

This One's a Gem Contest

Thrill of the Hunt Contest

Thumb's Up Contest

Valentine's Day Baby Contest

Watch the Birdie Contest

What's Your Favorite Time of
the Day Contest

Who Can Moo the Loudest Contest

Who Has the Biggest Beer Belly Contest

Why My Teacher is Tops Contest

Win a Dude Ranch Vacation Contest

Win a Front Row Seat to the
World Contest

Win a Hollywood Getaway Contest

Win a Pizza Party Contest

Win a Year of Chocolate Contest

Win All This Stuff Contest

Win an Experience of a Lifetime Contest

Win an Extravagant Shopping
Spree Contest

Win an Ocean of Cash Contest

Win Free Groceries for a Year Contest

Win the Time of Your Life Contest

Win the Ultimate Summer Vacation
Contest

Win the Vacation of Your Dreams Contest

Win Your Weight in Gold Contest

Winter Wonderland Contest

You Could Be Worth Millions Contest

You've Hit Pay Dirt Contest

Your Dream House Contest

Your Favorite Great Moment
in Sports Contest

Coupon

$2,500 Shopping Spree Coupon

10% off your entire store purchase with this coupon

25% off all meals with this coupon

30% Off Everything Coupon

32 Money-saving coupons inside

A family value coupon

A fax-back coupon

A triple coupon weekend

Add this $250 coupon to these already terrific offers

After Thanksgiving Sale Coupon!

An exceptional coupon with great savings!

Are you a coupon saver?

At last, a coupon you can't live without

Back-To-School Coupon Savings!

Before you can cut your shopping costs, you've got to cut these coupons

Big savings for coupon people

Bonus coupon savings storewide!

Bring in your coupon... let's make a deal!

Cannot be redeemed for cash. Period!

Check out our bag full of coupons

Clip and save with Cabin-Fever Coupons!

Clip and save with these extra savings coupons

Clip once and save!

Clip our coupons for extra savings

Clip our Cupid Coupons for sweet savings!

Clip out and cash in

Clip the savings in the bud

Clip these coupons and save big!

Clip-and-save or tear-and-burn

Clipping coupons will not dull your scissors

Coupon days are here again!

Coupon good for $25 toward any purchase of $50 or more

Coupon sale! One day left!

Coupon savings spectacular!

Coupons to clip... coupons to save!

Coupons to save even more

Cut out a great deal!

Cut yourself a deal... Koupon Daze!

Don't miss the bonus coupon savings!

Doorbuster coupons

Double the savings... double coupon day!

Enjoy savings with these coupons!

Every coupon redeemed earns money for...

Every day is coupon day at...

Extra Savings Coupon for you

Factory-authorized coupon sale!

Find great coupon savings at...

Follow that coupon to...

For veteran coupon shoppers only

Free coupon book worth over $300!

Free Money Saving Coupons!

Free valuable coupon

Get more coupons online

Get your scissors; we'll clip together

Great savings with these coupons

Here's a coupon to help get you started

Here's how you'll save with your bonus coupons

Hey... Coupon users!!!

Hey... Look what these coupons buy!

Holiday Coupon Sale!

Hurry! These special coupons expire soon

It's a mystery coupon for you!

Jingle Bell Bonus Coupon!

Look for our money-saving coupon in...

Look inside for valuable coupons

Loyalty coupon madness

Manufacturer-authorized coupon sale!

Money-saving coupons inside

More coupons online – to print out

Not to be used with any other coupons or discounts

One Christmas Buck Coupon!

One super coupon is all you need

Online coupon service now available

Only for committed discount coupon clippers

Our coupon is not a ripoff... just clip and save

Please fill out, clip and mail this coupon

Plus... use this coupon to save even more

Preferred Customer VIP Coupon

Pre-holiday Savings Coupons!

Present this coupon and receive...

Quick! Grab all the coupons!!!

Rip it, snip it, clip it

Save your coupons for the turkey

Season Coupon Sale!

Senior coupons for seniors only

Spring Coupon Days!

Storewide Coupon Sale!

Summer savings can start with these coupons

Super Summer Coupon Sale!

Super value coupon

Tear out this coupon instead of your hair

The 25% off everything coupon

The 3-day Coupon Sale!

The Any Day Coupon Sale!

The Great Pumpkin Coupon!

There's no penalty for clipping here

These coupons have no fillers, salt, sugar or corn syrup

This Breakfast Coupon is worth $25

This coupon doesn't expire until we do

This coupon entitles you to thousands of free...

This coupon is as good as cash

This coupon is good on any product in the store except the one you want

This coupon may be combined with other coupons

This coupon will self-destruct on...

This is your lucky coupon

This super coupon is all you need

Tomorrow is Double Coupon Day!

Use our coupons for extra savings storewide!

Use our drive-thru coupon

Use the attached coupons to help you with your food budget

Use these money saving coupons for real values!

Use your coupons on these sale items!

Valuable money-saving coupons

We honor all competitors' coupons

We would be honored to accept your clipped coupons

We've included coupons so you and your friends can try it

With this coupon you automatically get an extra 10% off everything!

You clip it... We'll beat it!

You'd have to clip a lot of coupons to get savings like this!

You're sure to save with our coupons

Your coupon to big savings!

Your next coupon promotion will be on...

A bargain that feeds your inner cowboy!

A boot-scootin', rockin' sale event!

A great roundup of...

A Kickin' Boot Sale Event!

A shootout sale of all sales!

A Stampin' Stampede Sale Event!

A Western sales extravaganza!

Ask anyone wearing a cowboy hat... where's the sale?

Be a cowboy for at least a day and you'll save big!

Be part of the stampede to super spectacular savings!

Booth shootin' bucks

Boot-slappin', bushwhackin' deals!

Buckaroo bonanza!

Calling all cowboys and cowgirls

Capture the Old West in every way imaginable

Chuck Wagon Sale Days!

Come along on a ride as we take you to...

Come on in for an old, Wild West hoedown

Corral these bargains, quick!

Corral your kids and treat them to...

Country Jamboree Sale Event!

Cow-punching memorabilia... now on sale!

Deals as wild as the Old West!

Deals straight as a gun barrel!

Don't let us get the "drop" on you!

Don't wait for the dust to settle for incredible savings!

Dressed for western fun and adventure

Eat No One's Dust Sale Event!

End-of-Year Sales Roundup!

Everybody Wants To Be A Cowboy Sale Event!

Exceptional savings on lingerie for cowgirls!

First Annual Cowboy Ball

Follow the trail to outstanding savings!

For a real taste of the Old West...

For midnight cowboys

Free cowboy hat to all buckaroos

Free horse-drawn hayrides

Frontier days are a-comin'

Galloping high-adventure fun is waiting for you!

Get a charge out of the bull-riding circuit

Get ready for a shootout of a sale!

Go west... pay less

Good 'till the last roundup

Gotta Move 'Em Out Sale Event!

Hang on to your saddle horns, folks

Hats off to Wild West style

Head for the last roundup during our Annual Clearance Sale!

Hey partners, mosey on down to...

Hit the trail with a saddlebag full of savings!

Howdy pardner, how about roundin' up a...

If you're going to be a cowboy, you need to dress the part

It's circle-the-wagons time

It's rootin' tootin' dealin' time!

It's the awesome savings, buckaroo!

Join us for a 10-gallon salute to...

Join us for an exciting Friday night hoedown in the old barn

Let the hootin' and hollerin' begin

Mooove 'em out

Mosey on down to the biggest sale of the season!

Out of the Wild West and into your home comes the real deal

Outfit your bunkhouse at...

Outstanding savings for rough ridin' cowpokes!

Put on the cowboy boots and get ready to horse around

Real cowboys and cowgirls buy our clothes!

Rope yourself a deal at...

Round up one of our bargains for your corral

Round up some rootin', tootin' fun

Roundup rally!

Rustle up your young-uns and mosey on out to a rootin' tootin' Wild West Sale Celebration!

Saddle up for old-fashioned fun at...

Saddle up for the biggest, friendliest roundup of the season!

Saving stampede

Sensational savings for cowgirls and city girls alike

Shoot your way to the best deal in town

Stake your claim on these deals!

Sure as shootin', you'll get the best price... anywhere

Sure-as-shootin' fun for the cowpoke in ya

The best prices this side of the Pecos!

The best selection of boots, hats and western wear... anywhere!

The sale for young cowboys and cowgirls

The sale starts at high noon!

The sales stampede begins on...

There's a load of bargains comin' in

Wagons of bargains and deals loaded with outstanding values!

Wash down some trail dust with...

We give you the West... and the rest

We put the wild into our Old West Bargain Days Celebration

We'll give you 'till sundown to make a deal!

We'll have you holding onto your cowboy hats with these bargains!

We'll put the spurs to your boots with tremendous savings!

We're kicking up a little dust with 50% off all sale items!

We're not horsing around with these prices!

We've decided to bite the bullet... prices slashed on every item!

We've got more brands on sale than a cattle auction

Wear your boots and jeans, and bring your roping gear

Welcome to the New West Sale Event!

Western boot blast! All footwear now on sale!

When you're ready to stake your claim, we're ready to deal!

Wild West Extravaganza Sale!

Wrangler days are here again... big price cuts on all merchandise

Y'all ain't never seen a sale event like this!

Yeahhhhhhh, 30% to 50% off during our Westward Ho Days!

Yew fixin' tuh wrangle up them savings?

You can bet your boots on the savings!

You won't get bushwhacked with these deals!

You'll be riding tall in the saddle with unbelievable savings!

You'll get a kick out of our blazing boot sale

You'll have to cowboy up to keep up with our sale celebration!

You'll round up some great deals at…

You're never too old to buy cowboy boots!

A Fool and His Money Are Soon Parted... Super Savings Days!

A sale that borders on the wild side!

A sight for sore eyes... all jewelry 50% to 70% off

A store you shouldn't be caught dead in

A wackazany festival of savings!

A Walk on the Wild Side Sale Event!

A Wild Weekend Wipeout Sales Event!

A wild, wild night of savings!

A wild, wild, wild week of savings

Absolutely nutty deals!

All Right, Let's Get Crazy Sale Event!

As crazy as it sounds... it's on sale!

Bargains galore... about-to-expire cold cuts!

Bargains that drive people crazy

Bargains that wouldn't make that good a doorstop after all

Be a disgusting slob... eat here!

Be crazy... it's free!

Beyond Your Wildest Expectations Sale Event!

Blame It On the Economy Savings Event!

Bloomin' crazy savings!

But That's as Crazy as it Gets Sale Event!

Call me crazy, but it sounds like a sale!

Can't We Just Be Friends Sales Event!

Color Me Wild Bargain Days!

Crazy 'Bout You Sale Event!

Crazy Like a Fox Savings!

Dare to Be Crazy Sale Event!

Don't be a schmuck! Go for the deal!

Don't believe us, you say? Then take a gander at these bargains

Don't spend your hard-earned savings on inferior imitations when you can get the inferior original at the same price!

Don't Wait 'Till Next Year Sales Event!

Even if you don't want it or need it... shop here first!!!

Every item is overpriced! Today only!!!

Everything about this sale was intended to amaze you!

Find out why America's crazy about our savings!

Get wacky! Get crazy! Get savings!

Go a little crazy with...

Go hog-wild during this sale event!

Go wild, it's on sale!

Here's a crazy deal!

How did you ever live without our spectacular sale?

I'm crazy about your sale!

If such a sale should ever come into being... we'll let you know!

If this isn't enough of an incentive to buy, we don't know what is!

If you can't swim, we won't float you a loan

If you don't believe the savings, don't shop here!

If you have the guts to enter... you can save big-time!

If you're prone to fantasy... check out these savings!

It Does Pay to Be a Little Crazy Sale Event!

It'll never rain on this truckload sale!

It's a hunger strike... we're raising all our food prices!

It's a sale guaranteed to drive people crazy!

It's a total bargain mentality gone wild

It's a Totally Wild Sale Event!

It's a wacky sales event, where the madness never stops!

It's Absolutely Insane Sale!

It's all over for you! You're surrounded by tremendous savings!

It's as Crazy as it Gets Sale Event!

It's gonna be crazy with these savings!

It's hard to get things on sale... but at least you know you're in the right store

It's Just Another Sale... Savings Event!

It's Just Bonkers, Absolutely Crazy Sales Event!

It's like totally wild!

It's Not as Crazy as it Sounds Sale Event!

It's Wild, Not Mild Sale Event!

Join the rat race with unbelievable and unreal savings!

Just let us be outrageous with these deals!

Just pretend what you're doing is normal

Krazy, wacky sale of the season!

Let us show you something wild

Let Your Imagination Run Wild Sale Event!

Let's Go Crazy Sale Event!

Let's See Who Cries Uncle Deals!

Let's whoop it up!

Magnificent savings for families with disposable income

Mundane to insane savings!

No One Understands a Crazy Sale Like a Crazy Man Sale!

No reasonable person would argue with these deals!

Nothing will cost much... here!!!

Off the wall savings!

Off-beat! Whacked out! Oddball deals!

One crazy cool sale!

Only an idiot would have a sale like this!

Outrageous savings on holiday treats that were over six months go!

Ride With the Wild Bunch... Sale Event!

Ridiculous if not downright crazy savings!

Savings as crazy as it may sound

Savings coming to a shelf near you!

Savings enough to drive you insane!

Savings on the chintzy, badly-painted knick-knacks you love!

Savings on the crazy side!

Savings that add up to absolutely nothing!

Savings that take all the fun out of shopping

Savings that will make you crazy!

Say goodbye to silly sales events!

Since we can't unload these dogs to anyone... we put them on sale!

Something Really Wild is About to Happen Sale Event!

Special purchase items to go nuts over!

Spending spree... going on right now!

Stop driving yourself... crazy! Just buy it!

Take Our Word For It... Savings Event!

That'll Be the Day... Sales Event!

The craziest deal you'll ever try to run away from

The only woman you're going to impress with these phenomenal gifts is your mother

The sale that has everyone going crazy!

The sillier, the better deals!

There is always a wild side to a wild sale!

These bargains are not available in any store

Things Are Tough All Over Closeout Sale!

Things can only get loonier

This is a pretty wild sale!

This sale doesn't have a slogan... just great savings!

Crazy/Wild

This sale is a bust... but the savings are fantastic!

This sale is crazy!

This store is really different... no deals, no bargains, no sales!

Totally insane savings!

Two Can Live as Cheaply as One... 2 For 1 Sale!

Unaffordable items... now on sale!

Unleash your uninhibited individuality... buy today!

Unwanted music... unheard-of savings!

Wacky, weird and downright bizarre savings!

Want a non-buying experience? Come in and browse!

We all love the hum of a bargain!

We are in the business of keeping people crazy!

We never sell junk!

We really screwed up... Great deals! Terrific bargains! Super savings!

We really want you to go crazy with savings!

We're not completely crazy, but it's our Annual Sale Event!

We're Not Really Nuts... We're Just Plain Crazy... Storewide Clearance Sale!!!

We're out to baffle you with savings like never before

We're Outta Our Minds... Bargain Days!

We're positive... there's not a bad deal in this store!

We're talkin' crazy deals... here!

We've gone ballistic with savings!

Wet and wacky savings!

What an idiot of a sale!

What sale are they talkin' about?

What You See Is What You Get... Sales Event!

What's with us??? Storewide clearance! Outrageous savings!

Where crazy deals run wild!

Where lower quality means lower prices!

Who's the Craziest of Them All Sale Event!?!

Wild Hysteria Sale Event!

Wild Wednesday Savings!

You ain't seen nothing yet! Explosive savings!

You can just go nuts over the savings!

You don't have to buy anything you don't want to... during our savings days!

You either shop here or you shop there!

You Gotta Be Kidding... Sales Event!

You have every right to these exceptional deals!

You have two kinds of savings to take, small or large

You Must Be Crazy Once in a While Sale Event!

You'll be a raving loony with incredible deals!

You'll flip over our super special savings!

You'll go ballistic over... drastically slashed prices!

You'll go bonkers with these savings!

You'll go nuts over the savings!

You're going to keep your mouth a-flappin' with deals like this!

You're making me crazy with monstrous savings!

You're not crazy as long as you shop here for savings!

You're Only Old Once... Senior Savings Days!

Your state attorney general backs up these deals!

Credit

A credit card that saves you money

A long credit history is required

A special promotion to credit account holders

All credit cards will be honored during the sale!

All credit sins forgiven

All major credit cards accepted

Another credit card is the last thing you need

Are you a credit risk?

Are you a deadbeat?

Are you credit worthy or not?

Are you hiding your credit-card debt from him?

Are you taking advantage of these credit opportunities?

Avoiding the credit-card trap

Bad credit holding you back?

Bad credit! Slow credit! No way to get credit!

Buried in debt?

Check your credit report periodically

Climb out of debt... today!

Could you qualify for a credit card?

Credit card bills got you singin' the blues?

Credit cards can be hazardous to your financial health

Credit cards... Spend! Spend! Spend!

Credit power!

Credit problems? No problems!

Credit solutions that work

Cut up those credit cards!

Deferred billing for credit card purchases

Do you have a fear of credit card fraud?

Do you know the score on your credit history?

Do you know where your credit cards are?

Do you need more credit?

Does your credit-card debt look like the national debt?

Don't forget you have to pay back what you charged

Don't cry over bad credit

Frustrated with your credit?

Gaining control of your spending

Get credit today!

Get out of debt fast

Give us your credit poor

Good credit? Bad credit? No credit?

Got your credit in a big mess?

Have credit card, will shop

Have your credit card ready when the operator comes on

How far can you go without over-extending yourself?

How high is your credit-card limit?

How to avoid the credit treadmill

How to ease the credit pain

I'm the credit doctor

If you are denied credit...

If you're fishing for easy credit with fast approval, contact...

In the market for a credit card?

Instant credit for everyone

Is your credit all messed up?

It's like shopping with cash

It's the only card!

It's time to give your credit card a rest

Credit

Just one word: plastic!

Just pull out your credit card and start shopping

Just Say Charge It Sales Event!

Keep a safeguard on credit

Keep a sharp eye on your credit card balances

Look for the best credit card deals

Looking to boost your credit rating?

No credit check needed

No credit refused

No credit, bad credit... no problem

No Credit... Good Credit... Savings Event

No monthly fee on credit card processing

Now with no-interest financing until...

Pay your taxes with this credit card!

Rebuild your credit with us

Remember when it was considered disgraceful to be in debt?

Robbing Peter to pay Paul

Scrambling to pay off your debt?

See us regardless of your credit history

Six months with zero interest and zero payments on all merchandise when you use your card

Smart ways to use credit wisely

Start a credit-card diet

Stop feeling like a credit card victim

Stop paying high-rate credit card balances

Strapped for cash?

Switch to our credit card

Take the plastic out of credit cards... Please

Taking control of your credit privileges

Taking credit for good credit

Taking the ugly out of credit

The Credit Bureau is your friend

The longer your credit history, the better

The power of credit

The right choice for credit now!

The road to the poorhouse is paved in plastic

There's no annual membership fee

Think of us as your credit exterminator

Think twice before mortgaging your credit-card bills

Thinking of switching credit cards?

Till debit do us part

To report card lost or stolen, call...

Toll Free Credit Hotline

Too many bills? Nowhere to turn?

Up to your eyeballs in debt?

Use your credit card and save on...

Use your credit card to establish a credit record

Use your credit power now!

We accept all major credit cards

We can get you approved regardless of your credit history

We can put cash in your pocket

We prefer payment by credit card

We understand your need for credit

What good is a credit card if you can't use it?

What is the credit expert's solution?

Will lend you money as long as your credit is good

With credit card in hand

You can expect more from our credit card

You can have it NOW!!!

You never know when you might need it

Your credit is good with us!

Your job! Your life! Your credit!

Customer

A complaining customer can become a satisfied customer

A customer is a terrible thing to waste

A real-world battle for the customers' hearts and minds

A savings event for only new customers!

A simple goal: please the customer

A special sale for dissatisfied and difficult customers

A special thanks to our customers

A special welcome for our first-time customers

Above and Beyond Customer Expectations Savings Event!

All customers are not created equal

An educated consumer is a good customer

And now a word from your customer

Are the customers really always right?

Are your customers satisfied?

Ask a happy customer

At prices customers will love!

At your service!

Bargains and deals that make the customer happy!

Bargains that are rocking the customers!

Bargains, deals and savings for our forgotten customers!

Based on customer comments...

Because our customers want it, we work very hard to get it

Best buys for all our best customers!

Best values! Best prices! For our best customers!

Butter up your customers

Can you spot the customer?

Capturing the imagination and loyalty of customers

Changing to meet customers' needs

Commitment to the best customer service

Communicate your enthusiasm to your customer

Connect with your customer

Create the repeat customer

Customer Appreciation Days!

Customer Cash Back Sale!

Customer Friendliness Sales Event!

Customer Privileges Day!

Customer service is a top priority with us!

Customer service pays off... big time!

Customer service with a human touch

Customer treasures! Our bargains!

Customers are not just customers; they are friends

Darn right, we're demanding

Deals that won't leave your customers broke!

Delivering value to the customer

Different customers have different tastes. So why are you treating them all the same?

Different customers... different needs

Discover the secrets of better customer service

Do we really treat our customers as customers?

Do you really put your customer first?

Driven to meet your customers' requirements

Earn your customers' trust

Every customer is an investment

Exciting bargains for our valued customers

Facing the challenge of new customers...
Every day!

For our best customers... the best deals!

Friendly no-pressure customer service

From customer satisfaction to
customer loyalty

From the customer's point of view

Give 'em what they never knew
they wanted

Go above and beyond customer
expectations

Great buys for you... our customer!

Helping customers help themselves

Here's the last word... Customerize

Here's what we'll do for our
best customers

Hot days! Cool deals for our
best customers!

How do you deal with a dissatisfied
customer?

How do you touch your customer?

How to handle difficult customers

How to show customers that you care

How's that for customer service?

Hurry in! The first 500 customers
will receive...

If they're not your partners, they won't
be your customers

If you don't treat customers the way
they want, someone else will

Incredible buys for all our
incredible customers!

It's a favorite with all our customers

It's old-fashioned customer service

It's the "Can Do" attitude that
attracts customers

It's the only fair way we treat our
customers... terrific values!

Keeps our customers smiling with
today's super buys!

Let's get one thing straight: I am the
customer!

Live customer service

Make every customer feel like they're
number one

Make me a satisfied customer!

Meet and exceed your customer service

More customers! More sales!
More benefits!

More ways to save everyday customers
on everyday essentials

Need more customers?

Never stop loving your customer

No one offers better ways to get closer to
your customers than we do!

No pushy sales associates...
just pushy customers

Now you can clone your best customers

One to a customer, please

Our aim is simple... Customer Satisfaction

Our commitment to our
customer's success

Our customer is always the boss

Our customers always come first

Our customers are our best customers

Our customers get more than they
bargain for

Our customers get special attention

Our customers know a great bargain

Our customers save time and money

Our customers, and their needs, always
come first

Our customers' success is our success

Our goal is to have you as a
lifetime customer

Our idea of success begins and ends with
your satisfaction

Our job is to make the customers look
good at any cost

Our prices speak to our valued customers!

Over 5 million satisfied customers

Painkillers for customer problems

People, as in customers

Price-sensitive customers

Put a smile on your customer's face

Raising the quality of customer service

Repeat business is one of the signs of a satisfied customer

Satisfied customers come back for more

Satisfying customers, one at a time

Savings for the just-browsing customer

Savings that get the customers' attention!

Savings that go above and beyond customer expectations

Savings the customer has never seen before

Savings with you in mind

See no customers! Hear no customers! Have no customers!

Sell the customer... don't fool the customer

Service excellence is our pledge to the customer!

Service is a main road to customer satisfaction

Smart customers ask questions

So, what's a cash-strapped consumer to do?

Start putting your customers first

Thank you for your business, dear customer

Thank You Sales Event for all our loyal customers!

Thanks a million to our 10 million customers

Thanks for being one of our best customers

The customer always chooses to buy here

The Customer Is Always Right Sales Event!

The customer speaks... we listen!

The customer wins... we're slashing all our prices!

The customer: know them or lose them

The customer's feedback

The focus is the customer

The golden rule: Know thy customer

The most valuable customer is the one that's in the store right now

The number one complaint of customers is...

The only thing that matters, after all, is the customer

The race for the customer

The solutions that keep customers coming back

The trick to retaining customers is easy

There has never been a better time to be a customer

There is no finish line in the race for customer service

There is only one type of customer... the truly satisfied

There's no limit on how much the customer can save!

There's no magic to great customer service

They treated me like a customer

They're out there!!!

Think of yourself as a customer

Today's kids are tomorrow's customers

Treat every customer like gold

Treat your customers like you would treat a guest

Tremendous savings... because our customers want it!

Unbelievable savings... we listened to our customers!

We "wow" our customer with "wow" savings!

We delight our customers, everyday!

We do whatever it takes to keep our customers

We give consumers a choice

We go above and beyond with
our customers

We go to bat for our customers

We know our customers

We Love Our Customers Sales Event!

We make happy customers

We make our customers feel like
they're No. 1

We pass the savings on to our customers

We please tough customers

We put our customers first

We save the customer time and money

We spoiled many of our customers

We stay in touch with the customer...
with savings you can't believe!

We talk to you

We thank our customers for their
constant support

We treat all our customers like VIPs

We treat small customers like big ones

We value our customers with
value pricing!

We want you on our backs

We want you to be our next
happy customer

We work for you

We work our buns off to satisfy
the customer

We would of course be happy to
accommodate your wishes

We're a first-class customer service team

We're awarding our loyal customers
with award-winning savings!

We're customer-driven

We're Going To Spoil The Customer
Sales Event!

We're ready when you are

We're the undisputed leader in
customer satisfaction

We're willing to go the extra mile...
every time!

We've got the ear of the customer like
nobody else

What do our customers have to look
forward to? Everything we've done over
the last 30 years

What do your customers really want?

What have you done for the
customer lately?

What is customer service?

What keeps customers coming back?

What's a customer worth to you?

What's going on with your customers?

What's it cost to keep a customer?

When it comes to customer service,
winning isn't everything, it's the
only thing

When the customers want to talk,
we listen

Where customers come first

Where the customer is always right

Who are your customers today?

Who will be your customers tomorrow?

Who's the customer?

Why millions of satisfied customers
can't be wrong

Winning back unhappy customers

Without happy customers we wither
and die

Work your best deal... with your best
customers!

You can never go too far in providing
customer service

You owe it to your customer

Your commitment to customer
satisfaction

Your customer is overflowing with
information. Are you harnessing it to
power your business?

Your customers are shopping... can they
find you?

Your customers depend on you!

Deal

A deal that's a steal

A deal you can't afford to pass by

A deal you can't walk away from

A great deal and a great deal more

A monstrously good deal

A real show-stopper of a deal

A winning deal... every time!

Absolutely sensational deals!

Amazing "No Catch" Deals

An offer with a great deal to it

An offer you can't refuse

And last, but not least, we'll cut you a great deal!

And that's the big deal!

Are you getting the best deal you can?

Assume the worst and make the best deal you can make

Award winning deals... every time!

Best buys and deals for you!

Best selection! Best service! Best deals!

Better Than Ever Deals!

Big deal... little money

Big, big, big deal!

Blockbuster deals!

Call today for a great deal. And a great deal of respect

Carve out a great deal at...

Cash-on-the-Barrel Deals... all day long!

Catch your best deal now!

Cleanest deals in town!

Cost-saving deals

Cut yourself a great deal... today!

Dazzling deals

Deal of the Week

Deals are cookin'

Deals too good to be true

Deals! Deals! Deals!

Don't be a victim of a bum deal

Don't let a good deal slip away

Don't let this deal pass you by

Don't miss these spectacular deals!

Don't wait to get your best deal!

Drive home the deal of a lifetime

Dynamite Dealin' Days!

Early-bird special deals

Easy deals! Easy prices! Easy credit!

Everybody loves a good deal

Experience the big deal. Very big deal!

Fabulous deals all day long!

Feast your eyes on these great deals

For a great sale! And a great deal of savings!

Get ready to wheel and deal

Get the scoop on all the latest deals

Good deal or bad? You make the call!

Grand Slam Dealin' Days!

Great deals everyday

Great deals you can take home today!

Have we got a deal for you!

Here's a deal that's just ducky

Here's a sweet deal

Here's the scoop... Here's the deal

Hot days! Cool deals!

How far would you go to get a great deal?

How to spot a real deal

Incredible deals!

Isn't it time you got the best of the deal? **89**

It isn't a deal if it isn't what you want

It's deal time

It's the real deal. The whole banana

Just the deal for you

Know a good deal when you see one!

Last chance deals

Let me tell you, it's a big deal

Let's make a deal right now!

Let's rustle up a real deal for you

Let's swing a deal

Look for more deals soon

Look inside for a real deal!

Looking for some pretty good deals?

March in for a roaring good deal

Nail the deal down today!

Naming your own price is part of the deal

No deal! Sweet deals!

No haggling! No sweat! Just dealing!

No more... no less... no haggling

No reasonable offer refused

No risk. No commitment. No small print.

No-hassle deals

Not a bad deal all around

Not a penny more!

Now let's get down to the brass tacks

Now THAT'S a really big deal

OK, so here's the deal

One big deal!

One sweet looking deal

Our deals are out of this world

Our eye-opening offer

Out of the park deals

Package deals

Price-crushing deals!

Read this before you accept that "red hot" deal

Real big deals! Real new deals! Real hot deals!

Real deals... real savings

Scoop up a deal... today!

See us for a great deal!

Sleep on it

So here's the deal

Sometimes the best deal is the one you've already got

Sounds like a super deal

Squeaky-clean deals!

Steal a Deal Sale Event!

Still the best deals around!

Such a Deal Sale!

Summer deals so hot, you better bring your sunscreen

Super Dollar Deals throughout the store!

Surely worth every cent

Swap 'N' Shop: You got a horse? I got a cow. Let's talk!

Sweet deals for young buyers

Sweetest deals of the year

The amazing no-catch offer

The best deal in town!

The best deal just got better

The big deal! The best deal! The greatest deal! That's the deal!

The deals won't get any better than this

The good deal you're getting now can't last forever

The only things hotter than the weather are the deals at...

The question is, "how much?"

The real deal!

There is a deal for everybody that is fair and equitable

There is no catch to this offer

These deals will go fast

They're all big deals!

This deal is profitable

This deal's going fast, so hurry down to...

This is absolutely, unequivocally the best deal!

This is an exceptionally big deal!

This is the deal of a lifetime!

This offer is nothing to sneeze at

This offer is too good to refuse

Treat yourself to the best deal in town!

Want a deal that won't leave you broke?

We are ready to make unbelievable deals!

We are the best deal-cutters in the business

We can make you a spectacular deal!

We do the deal!

We give you a great deal more than just a great deal

We make the deal work for you

We offer pretty good deals!

We only do fair and square deals

We sharpen our pencils on both ends!

We won't put the screws to you

We won't say no to any good deal

We won't string you along

We'll ante-up with the best deals

We'll cut you a deal like never before!

We'll hammer out a great deal just for you!

We'll say yes before you do

We're branding our herd with the best deals

We're cooking up sensational deals all day long

We're dealin' like never before

We're dealing big time!

We're dealing! You're dealing!

We're making a big deal out of absolutely nothing

We're making sacrifice deals on...

We're putting it all together for you

We're ready to ink the deal

We're your best deal, and we'll prove it

We've got a tremendous deal for you

We've got a unique deal for you

We've never seen a deal we could not beat

What a honey of a deal!

What could be a better deal than this?

What more could you ask for?

What's it going to take?

What's the catch? What's the deal?

Wheeling and dealing like crazy

Where the deals are

Where the deals get done

Which deal is right for you?

Windfall of excitement with fabulous deals!

With a deal like this, who can refuse?

Work your best deal... here!

Wow, what a deal!

Write your own deal

You always have the right to change your mind

You don't start with a clean piece of paper to get a good deal

You just can't beat this price!

You want it, you got it!

You won't find a deal sweeter than this

You won't get better deals anywhere

You'll feel good with these valuable deals!

You'll get a great deal during our Sale of Savings!

You're too smart to pass this deal up!

You've got yourself a deal!

Your best deals are now!

Your terms... your deal!

Diet

A diet even a food addict could love

A diet that's healthy and delicious

A good way to lose weight

It's your choice... A healthful diet. A high-fiber diet. A quick-fix diet.

A low-fat update

Adopt a lifelong eating plan for good health rather than a diet

America's war on weight

An all-you-can-eat diet

Another inch... is it worth it?

Are you cheating on your diet?

Are you happy with the way you look?

Are you on some kind of fad diet?

Are you tempting fate with a poor diet?

Are you the right weight?

Beware of quick diets

Calling all calorie counters

Can't curb your cravings?

Change the way you eat to lose weight

Choose a diet with plenty of fruits and vegetables

Diet right! Diet time!

Do it the healthy way

Do you consider yourself overweight?

Do you lie about your diet?

Do you occasionally look in the mirror?

Does eating make you fat?

Don't be discouraged if you splurge

Don't forget that a calorie is a calorie

Don't starve yourself

Dropping the pounds

Eat smart

Eat yourself silly

Embark on a healthy eating plan, not a diet

Ever go on a diet?

Everybody could stand to lose a few pounds

Fat-buster products on sale here!

Feeling like a beached whale?

Fight the flab

Fighting fat makes sense

Fighting the battle of too much bulge

First of all, never give up

For a chunkier, funkier body...

From fat to fabulous

Gaining a few pounds, losing a few pounds, gaining a few pounds

Get a better life by losing weight

Get moving on your weight-loss goal

Get serious about obesity

Get smart about eating

Get the pounds off fast

Getting straight answers about losing weight

Go with what works

Good luck on your diet

Have patience

Have we got a fast and easy diet for you!

Healthful meals are healthy eating

Here are a few simple suggestions to help you lose weight

Here's a quick weight-loss quiz

Here's two ways to lose weight... eat less and exercise more

How do you know if you're overweight?

How those calories add up

How to eat more and still lose weight

How to make a bunch of fat people jealous

How to win at losing weight

How's your diet going? We thought so!

I did it!

I got hooked on eating

I wish I could find a diet that really works

I'm on my diet. I'm off my diet. I'm on my diet.

If I look skinny today... did I look fat yesterday?

If you are ready to lose weight, call...

If you must diet you may as well enjoy a little happiness

If you think you need to lose weight, you probably do

It's a diet you can live with

It's a lifestyle, not a diet

It's never too late to start watching your weight

It's the one diet proven by science to work!

Just say no to food!

Keep dieting until your clothes get loose

Learning about what you are eating

Leave your fat forever

Lighten up, eat the food we're designed to eat, and you'll lighten up too

Look great! Feel good! Lose weight!

Looking for the easy way to quick weight loss?

Looking for ways to keep a healthy diet?

Lose weight, look great

Losing a little weight can make a big difference

Make moderation your motto

Managing your diet

No one diet works for everyone

No one will do it for you!

Overweight kids are likely to become overweight adults

Plan what goes in your mouth

Push yourself away from the bleepin' table!

Scales don't lie

Searching for the perfect diet?

Sensible dieting goes hand-in-hand with good eating habits

Sick of all that diet and exercise?

So push yourself away from the table

Sounds simple, doesn't it?

Starving yourself won't take weight off

Stop dieting... forever!

Stop kidding yourself

That bulging belly

That evil "F" word... fat

That's one of those things that's easy to say but hard to do

The best way to battle the bulge is to...

The best way to lose weight is to stay in shape

The healthy way to lose weight

The search for your perfect diet is over!

There is only one way to lose weight: eat less and exercise more

There's no such thing as cheating on this diet

Think and get thin

Think thin for life

This is for all the fat people

Time flies when you're losing weight

To eat or not to eat

Waist-saving tips

Weighing in on weight loss

What you need in an effective diet plan

What's the best diet for you?

Who do we know who hasn't been on a diet?

Why go on a diet?

Why wait... start now!

You can almost hear the pounds melting away

A bunch of bargains for do-it-yourselfers

A fix-it-upper super sale!

A good time for do-it-yourself winterizing projects

A lot of bang for your DIY bucks

A money-saving offer for do-it-yourselfers!

A terrific sale for the ultimate do-it-yourself procrastinator

Act now and save on all...

Are you caught up in the do-it-yourself rage?

Ask a pro!

At these savings you can fix up the entire house

Awesome savings for the jack of all trades

Bargain hunters... nail down big DIY savings!

Bargains for the serious do-it-yourselfers

Best buys for do-it-yourselfers

Build on these spectacular savings!

Call it Do-It-Yourself 101

Catch the do-it-yourself can-do spirit at...

Dealing days for do-it-yourself projects

DIY customers are our bread and butter

Do it right... not fast

Do it yourself and save big money

Do It Yourself Sales Event!

Do it yourself... or we can do it for you

Do you do it yourself or hire a pro?

Do yourself a favor: don't do it yourself

Doing it yourself can be hazardous to your health

Doing it yourself never paid off like this

Doing your own home repairs can save money

Do-It-Yourself Bargain Days!

Do-it-yourself can save big bucks

Do-It-Yourself Ideas

Do-it-yourselfers love a bargain

Every DIY customer has questions, every DIY customer needs help

Every Saturday morning, get tips from the pros

Everyday savings for do-it-yourselfers

Everything you need to build it yourself

Expert advice for the do-it-yourselfer

Fantastic buys for do-it-yourselfers!

Fixin' Up The Joint... A DIY Sales Event!

Get started... super savings on the stuff you need!

Get the things you need at unbelievable savings!

Go-for-it time for do-it-yourselfers

Going the do-it-yourself route? We're here to help!

Great buys for wise do-it-yourselfers!

Great deals for DIY weekend warriors

Great savings for do-it-yourself home fixer-uppers

Handyman specials for handymen

Here's everything you need short of a few friends

Home Fixer-Upper Smashing Savings!

How to avoid do-it-yourself mistakes

How to be your own do-it-yourselfer

I Did It Myself Sales Event!

If you can saw in a straight line and hammer a nail, this is a job you can do

If you can't do it... let the pros show you how

If you prefer not to do it yourself, we'll do it for you

In stock, a complete line of DIY products

Is it really worth it to do it yourself?

It ain't braggin' if you can do it!

It isn't expensive if you do it yourself with these savings!

It's a Fixer-Upper Savings Event!

It's so easy you can do it yourself

It's the ideal time for do-it-yourself projects around the house

Just do it yourself!

Kick-start your fixer-upper project with outrageous savings!

Lesson No. 1 for do-it-yourselfers...

Look for the red DIY arrow in-store and save

Need something done around the house? Call...

No payments until your job is completed!

Rent a husband to get the job done

Repairs any woman can do

Save a lot, save a bundle on all your DIY projects

Savings for all woodshop duffers

Savings to get fired up about DIY projects

Savings to get it done right!

Should you hire a pro or do it yourself?

Show us your plans and we'll show you the savings!

Sign up today for in-store do-it-yourself clinics

So where do I start? Start with us! Call...

Solutions for do-it-yourself projects

Special savings for do-it-herself projects!

Super Saturday savings for all DIYers!

Take advantage of our do-it-yourself sale!

Take the plunge, do it yourself!

Terrific buys for do-it-yourselfers!

The do-it-yourself bargain days are here again!

The do-it-yourself season of savings!

The pain, the pride, the popularity in DIY

The place to buy... from your all-pro team!

The place to shop for DIY'ers!

The sale that do-it-yourself dreams are made of

The Weekend Warrior Sales Event!

Think of the money you'll be saving on your next DIY project

This is a DIY store

Tools for serious do-it-yourselfers

Tremendous savings for do-it-yourself enthusiasts

We are dedicated to do-it-yourselfers

We can tell you everything you need to know about do-it-yourself projects

We do training for the do-it-yourselfer

We help our DIY customers load their cars

We help you do it yourself!

We provide the know-how and courage to do it yourself

We specialize in helping do-it-yourselfers

We take the time to know our DIY customer

We've just made it easier to do-it-yourself

We've sharpened our pencils at both ends for tremendous DIY savings!

Weekend to-do list... starts here!

Welcome to our DIY seminar on...

When do-it-yourself projects go wrong, call...

Why do it yourself?

You build, you fix, you save at...

You're invited to spring training for the do-it-yourselfer

A basket full of pre-Easter savings!

A tisket, a tasket, time to fill up the Easter basket

Accessorize your Easter basket with us

After Easter clearance starts today!

After Easter sale... Need we say more?

All Easter home decorations on sale!

An Easter basket guaranteed to hatch a smile

An Easter Bonus Basket Sale!

An Easter gift you won't want to hide

A-tisket, a-tasket, Easter treats for your basket

Be a bunny this Easter and hop on over to...

Be a good egg today!

Be a munchin' bunny at Easter brunch

Big savings on Easter buys for all the good eggs!

Bring all your bunnies and enjoy our Easter Sunday brunch

Bring Easter to someone special with...

Bring your basket and join the hunt

Bunnies and chicks for cheep!

Buy 'em by the basket!

Celebrate Easter at Bunnyville, USA

Celebrate great values on our Easter best

Chick out our Easter values

Come and meet the bunny

Come to our Easter Bunny Breakfast

Don't be a dumb bunny, bring the family over to...

Easter classics for your shopping basket

Easter entertaining made easy

Easter is early... So hop in for holiday savings now

Easter savings are hoppin'

Easter savings are just a hop, skip and jump away

Easter savings for all bargain hoppers!

Easter savings on all toys, and treats all over the store

Easter sweets 'n' treats

Easter time savings!

Easter traditions start here!

Easter values are springing up

Easter's best sale!

Easter's coming... be ready!

Easter's early this year... better get cracking

Egg-ceptional values! Egg-citing prizes!

Egg-stra savings this Easter

Egg-streme savings!

Enjoy an elegant Easter dinner with us

Everything for a memorable Easter table

Everything to fill your baskets

Fantastic after-Easter savings

Fill up your Easter baskets with these great buys!

Fill your Easter basket full of savings

For a sweet Easter treat...

For the perfect Easter dinner...

Get hopping on your Easter shopping

Get your Easter lilies here

Happy Easter savings

Happy Easter specials all week long

Have an Easter egg omelet... Only today!

Have we got an Easter gift for you!

Here's a great idea for an Easter gift

Here's egg-cellent Easter savings

Here's how to ham it up for Easter

Hippity-hop on over and save!

Hop in for Easter gifts

Hop on down for Easter savings!

Hop on in for Easter Bunny savings!

Hop on these Easter values

Hoppin' good eats... at our Easter
brunch roundup

Hopping down the sales trail

Hunting for a great Easter sale? You've
found it!

It's never been so easy to find the perfect
Easter egg

It's our Annual Easter Preview

Join Our Easter Morning Bunny Bash

Last-minute ideas for a great
Easter basket

Make your Easter dinner extra special
with this Easter savings

Make your Easter dinner quick as a
bunny with...

More Easter savings!

One-hop shopping for happy
Easter buys!

Our candy is so tempting, the Easter
bunnies can't wait to nibble

Our Easter brunch is just to dye for

Our Easter savings are multiplying
like rabbits

Pre-Easter savings coupons

Pulling out all the hops this
Easter with...

Put a new twist on an old Easter tradition

Put a smile on your Easter Bunny's face

Quack open your eggs to find out your
Easter savings

Ready for Easter?

Savings for every little bunny

Shop 'til you hop!

Shower of Easter values

Spread your Easter joy with us

Start an Easter family tradition at...

Start your Easter egg hunt at...

Super Easter values!

Sweet savings for every-bunny

Take the bunny trail that leads to
hoppin' Easter savings!

Terrific basket-stuffers every kid
will enjoy

The best-dressed bunny wins a...

The chance of getting your kids dressed
up this Easter just got 25% better

The Easter Bunny will be hopping
around on...

The Easter Bunny will hide eggs and
goodies for the kids during...

The Easter parade of savings!

The last 7 days of big Easter savings!

This Easter, our great brunch will have
you all ears

This Easter, stick with your
family's tradition

This Easter, we'll put more eggs in
your basket

Today is your Easter parade

Visit the Easter Bunny at...

We have the perfect Easter gift for
all ages

We'll fill your Easter basket with value

What a way to celebrate Easter

What Easter bunnies of all ages want to
find in their baskets

What the Easter Bunny doesn't bring,
you can find here

Why hunt all over town for your Easter...

You won't have to hunt for Easter values
here

You'll find all your Easter favorites at...

You're invited to our Hippity-Hoppity
Bunny Brunch

97

A day in the life of an e-commerce site

A quality shopping experience

A sales force you'll never outgrow

America's number one website

An e-commerce pioneer

And now a word from your Web page

Are you at the forefront of the e-commerce world?

Are you watching over your e-business?

Beyond bricks and mortar

Check us out at...

Coming soon to a computer near you

Customer service comes down to people, not technology

Customers who come to our site expect the best

Did Santa get stuck at your site?

Does your web site measure up?

Doing e-commerce is doing e-commerce

Done right, you can increase efficiencies and lower costs

Drive revenue. Reduce costs. Lock in customer relationships.

E-business for small businesses

E-business is "the Big," for small businesses

E-business is a true competitive advantage

E-business is our business and it will always be our business

E-business solutions that deliver real-life results

E-business strategy got you down?

E-commerce anytime and anywhere

E-commerce is a high-tech business... no kidding!

E-commerce you can count on

E-commerceable

End-to-end e-commerce solutions

Enjoy the sheer luxury of sitting at home and browsing through our site

Every new e-idea has its costs

Everybody is in love with e-business, except the customer

Faster and cheaper is better

Fighting for e-commerce sales

Firing up your web sales

For a complete cashless commerce solution

For e-commerce wannabe's

For internet shoppers only!

For those who live and die for email

Get $25 off any online order

Get ready for the next frontier

Get the right tools to build your e-business

Grab your share of the web market

Has e-commerce changed your company yet?

Holiday shopping made easier

Hot spots on the Web

How are your e-relationships with your e-customers?

How do you handle a customer you can't see?

How to succeed in e-business without trying

If anybody can give you an enjoyable e-commerce shopping experience, it's us!

Increase sales... lower costs

Increase your e-business value

Is your e-commerce business moving fast enough?

It can only be good for business

It's a button click away

It's a dot-com world after all

It's a smart way to do business

It's big! It's smart! It's fast!

It's cheap, global and quick

It's visibility, stupid!

Let the Web do your work

Let your mouse do the shopping

Make your site a winner with more sales

No salesperson will call

Nothing equals the potential of
e-business

Now you can really shop at home

Now you have one of the largest sales
forces in the world

Our business is e-business

Our e-business has a new B-team

Our stores stay open all night

Our website can tell you everything
you've ever wanted to know

Outstanding e-commerce is outstanding
customer service

Plug in and buy

Point! Click! Buy!

Point, click, and make the sale

Presenting to the world, 24 hours a day,
7 days a week

Realizing your e-business goals

Remember when shopping used to be
a hassle?

Rev up your business with e-business

Sales increase is just a click away

Shop around the clock

Shop the world

Shopping... all in a matter of minutes

Tech smart! Web smart! Business smart!

The click heard in every home in America

The kind of shopping experience you've
come to expect

The Net is a toy for teens... for business,
it's a tool

The Web is no substitute for good
customer service

There are only 25 more e-shopping days
until Christmas

There's more to being an e-business
than just an e-business

To e or not to e?

To save time, money and effort

Too busy to shop?

We are an e-business store

We make your e-business buzz

We mind your e-business

We turn day and night into hours
and minutes

We're more than just e-commerce

What are you saying to your
website visitor?

What is the value of your e-business?

What's your B-to-B customer
relationship?

What's behind button No. 3?

When you hear the term "e-commerce,"
you think...

When you're shopping on the line, we're
online too

Who are your online customers?

Who-owns-the-customer?

You saw it! You wanted it!
You ordered it!

You're only as good as your web page

Your best bet on the Internet

Your company can buy almost anything
over the net

Your customers are headed for a great
shopping experience

Your dot-com lifestyle is just a
click away

Your E-Business Service Team

You've got to do more than just put up
a website

Education

A big look at small schools

A college degree does not require a learner's permit

A college degree... with a major in life

A fountain of youth really does exist with a good education

A good education is one that really works

A graduate degree in psychology... Comes to mind?

A little school with a big attitude

A real education for the real world

A school for the mind

A school of great academic caliber

A simple solution... education

A world-class education

Accept the challenge of education

After all, isn't school supposed to be miserable?

All the world's a classroom

An education is better than no education

An education is for a career, but an education is also for life

An education is like a diamond... it lasts forever

An education is something that no one can take away from you

Are you giving your child the best education?

Believe in the value of education

Bold tactic: Quit job, go to school

Bright minds thrive here

Can you put a price on education?

College grads know the value of an education

Contemplating returning to school?

Do the smart thing... get an education

Education comes in a building with four walls... But it contains tomorrow's future

Education is cheaper than re-education

Education is our best investment

Education is the way out of poverty and discrimination

Feed your spirit and your mind

For an education in the real world... call today!

For the budget-conscious college student

Furthering your education is always a smart move

Gain the advantage of a good education

Get a jump on your education

Get an education... they can't take it away from you

Get smart with education

Get your degree at home

Give your brain something new to chew on

Going to school is a privilege

How to cope with college costs

How to improve America's education, one classroom at a time

Is a law degree right for you? You be the judge

Is there life for the mind after college

Is your child prepared for learning?

Isn't it time you get smart?

It costs a lot more to be stupid

It is never too late to finish your education

It pays to know your A, B, C's

It will pay your dividend for the rest of your life

It's just plain common sense... Education

It's more than an education, it's the way we teach it

Knowledge is free. Get all you can

Learn as you earn

Let's face it, you need an education

Life changes... open your mind

Make higher education your priority

Make room for education

Making the college dream come true

Meeting the needs of today's students

No child is left behind at our school

Park your brain... here!

Plant a seed and watch it grow

Pound our pages, not the pavement

Run a college on ethical and moral principles and see where it gets you

School days are for learning

School is a valuable educational experience

Shopping for a college?

Stay in school... It's your best move!

Success through education

Support our colleges: They provide our nation's greatest resource

Support the education of our youth

The classroom is ready when you are

The more you learn... the brighter you get

The only thing you can't question is the results

The place for progressive people

The road to success is paved with a good education

The school of hanging in there

The school that offers the best educational value for the money

The school where you are challenged academically

The spotlight is on education

There is no better way to be prepared for change than with an education

There's another life waiting for you

To earn more you have to learn more

We are known for academic seriousness

We are more than just a school

We are the future for today's students

We feed young, hungry minds

We have a master plan for you

We help build your brain power, not to mention your cash flow

We just hope education goes to your head

We make smart students

We make students of average intelligence look like geniuses

We offer an exceptional opportunity to learn

We stress the value of education

We teach more than the ABC's

We wrote the book on education... now if only they could read it

We're hip on reading

We're the school that no one has heard of

What it means to be educated

What's stopping you from getting a college degree?

When our students succeed, we succeeded

When we talk about our school, we're talking about tradition

When you educate a mind, you free it

Where every imagination has a chance to grow

Where great readers meet great writers

Whether you're 8 or 88... it's all about lifelong learning

Who says education isn't free?

Why go to school?

You'll always learn the most amazing things at...

You'll get the best education money can buy at...

Your degree is worth more than the paper it's printed on

Entertainment

A blazing bonanza of entertainment

A box-office hit

A dazzling 90-minute extravaganza of entertainment

A fabulous evening of fun, food and entertainment

A fantastic entertainment complex

A gem of a show

A good, juicy piece of entertainment

A howling good time awaits you!

A magnificent piece of entertainment

A music and costume extravaganza

A must-see event!

A new world of entertainment is open to you!

A thoroughly entertaining compendium

A thrill money can't buy!

A tribute to a great entertainer

After-dark entertainment

All-new must-see entertainment

An entertainment extravaganza!

An entertainment Mecca

An entire evening's worth of entertainment

An event not to be missed

An experience you can't afford to miss

And that's entertainment

Are you starved for entertainment?

Back by popular demand

Big entertainment! Big fun!

Blazing new trails in the amusement industry

Bring the show home

Broadway-style entertainment

Catch the home entertainment experience

Coming soon!

Completely enjoyable and vastly entertaining

Do we have a show for you!

Don't miss the hits

Don't touch that remote control...

Engaging! Touching! Entertaining!

Entertaining stuff for family fun

Entertainment at its best

Entertainment for all ages

Entertainment that really entertains

Escape! Fantasy! Entertainment!

Exhilarating entertainment

Eye-popping entertainment

For awesome weekend entertainment

For entertainment purposes only

For great live entertainment...

For sheer entertainment value

Front row seats at nosebleed prices

Get ready for some wild and funny entertainment

Get ready to "ooo" and "aah"

Get your money's worth of entertainment

Give them what they want

Go early... stay late

Grand slam entertainment!

Great entertainment the whole family will love

Happily-ever-after entertainment

Headliner entertainment!

Here's a chance to kick up your heels and clap your hands

Hey, this is where you want to be

High-quality, world-class entertainment

Inspiring. Entertaining. Unforgettable.

It is an experience out of the ordinary

It is not just entertainment; it's something more

It's family entertainment at family prices!

It's old-time entertainment at its best!

It's the cheapest form of entertainment

It's the time of year for TV entertainment

It's too good to miss

It's top-shelf entertainment

It's very lively, very alive

It's where the entertainment is

It's worth shouting about

Joy! Pleasure! Entertainment!

Let the screaming begin

Let us entertain you

Living in the wide world of entertainment

Looking for an experience that's out of the norm?

Make your next dinner party a night to remember

Miss 'em and it's your loss

Old-style entertainment still lives on

On with the show

Our entertainment is produced for escapism

Out of this world entertainment

People are looking for good entertainment in their homes

Prepare to have your mind blown

Pure entertainment

Quality entertainment at the right price

Qualms about entertaining at home?

Sensational home entertainment values!

So downright entertaining

Speaking of live entertainment...

Splendidly entertaining

Take in that great feeling

Terrifically entertaining

That's showbiz...

The best family show in town

The finest quality entertainers

The hippest spot in town

The hottest form of entertainment

The icon of family entertainment

The one, the only

The show must go on

The world's most exciting entertainment

There will be no charge for the entertainment

This is entertaining with a twist

This is the place for live entertainment!

Thoroughly entertaining

Thrills and chills for the kids

To be entertained! To be amused! To be enlightened!

Totally entertaining

Treat yourself to a whole new dimension of entertainment

Unbelievably entertaining

Up for a night on the town?

We are entertainment!

We turn entertainment into an art form

We've got the action you're craving for

What if your name is Letterman and you're not funny?

When you think of entertainment, you think of...

Why not go for the total experience?

You are in for an unforgettable experience

You'd be nuts to miss it

You'll be dazzled, thrilled, elated and chilled

You're in for a real treat

Your best entertainment value

Your complete entertainment headquarters

Your total entertainment destination

Environment

A bottomless pit of new ways to recycle

A cleaner planet today, for a better tomorrow!

A sensible alternative to a clean environment

Accept responsibility... pick it up!

An Earth Day challenge

An important global announcement

And do something for the environment while you're at it

And they call this environmental protection

Are you an environmental wacko?

Are you kind enough to the earth?

Are you the only one who cares about the environment?

Be a partaker for clean air

Be an active recycler

Be environmentally conscious with everything

Be part of the pollution solution

Best of all, picking up litter is free!

Buy products that are environmentally friendly

Children should be taught not to litter

Clean air is a big deal

Cleaning up the environment begins at home

Clean-the-parks day

Committed to the philosophy of "reduce, reuse, recycle"

Dear friends of the environment

Do something for the planet... get with litter!

Do your part to preserve the environment by recycling

Doing the right thing for the environment

Don't be a litterbug

Earth Day... Save the planet!

Environmental awareness is increasing

Environmental problems hit home for everyone

Environmentally responsible

Every day is Earth Day

Everybody has to do their own job in protecting the environment

Finding a way to recycle e-waste profitably yet responsibly

For a better tomorrow, don't litter!

Fuel efficiency helps save the environment

Garbage cans don't have hands... pick it up!

Garbage of today will be the garbage of tomorrow

Get involved in your community recycling program

Give the environment a break... recycle!

Happy Arbor Day

Help save endangered species

Help the environment stay healthy... stop littering

Here's a cause you can really get your arms around

How can the average person help?

How much difference can one person make? Tons!

If everyone pitches in, we can all accomplish great things

Is the air in your home clean?

It's about your world, your future

It's called imaginative recycling

It's everyone's environment... it's everyone's job to stop litter!

It's our new environmental reclamation program

It's time to open the window and let some fresh air in

It's time we put a stop to waste

It's your call... recycle!

It's your planet, folks

Join the crusade to save our planet... recycle!

Just plant a few hundred trees and call it a day

Keep America beautiful... recycle

Let's clean up the air!

Made entirely from recycled materials

Making the world a healthier place to live

One person's trash can make you some cash

Our world revolves around you

Pick it Up Today and Every Day!

Pitch in and be a friend

Plant a tree, save the earth

Please share our enthusiasm for recycling

Protect our beaches! Save the wetlands! Clean our rivers!

Reach out and touch the earth

Recycle today, save the world for tomorrow!

Recycling: Make it happen!

Refreshed. Repackaged. Recycled.

Save the earth, change the world

Show your concern for our environment

Simple things you can do to recycle

Sit on it... step on it... pick it up!

Speak out in defense of clean air, land and water

Spread the message of conservation

Start a good green habit

Stop treating recyclables like garbage

Take care of earth because it takes care of you

Take pride in America... don't litter!

Taking a leadership role in protecting our environment

Tell the truth about pesticides

Ten ways to improve your recycling efforts

Thank you for doing your part to help the environment

Thanks for picking it up!

The environment is everyone's business

The environment will thank you for not littering

The planet belongs to you

The real problem... is not too many people, but too many cars

The whole world is depending on you to clean up the environment

The world will be cleaner thanks to a simple process... recycling

Think conservation

Think green... blue... brown

Today is Pick Up a Broom Day!

Water, water everywhere, but which one should I drink?

We only have one... earth!

We'll change your view of litter

We're cleaning up America

What do you do with household hazardous waste?

What is the cost of clean air, clean soil and clean water?

What you can do! Dispose of it properly!

Where every day is Earth Day!

Where preservation of the environment is a high priority

Who's committed to the environment?

You and recycling can change the world

You are the answer to our environmental problems

You control the environment... you control the litter

You dropped it... you pick it up!

Excitement / Enthusiasm

A blowout sale of excitement!

A journey of excitement

A must for all who seek the ultimate thrill

A new road of excitement

A phenomenally exciting time

A sale of excitement!

A weekend jam-packed with excitement!

A world both marvelous and exciting at the same time

Ah, the enthusiasm

Ain't life exciting?

Ain't the savings exciting?

An attitude of unbridled enthusiasm

An electrified sensation

An endorphin high and an adrenaline rush

An exhilarating experience

And now for the exciting news...

Are you X-cited?

Be a real live wire during our...

Be part of the excitement

Big city excitement at a great value!

Blowout Sale of Excitement!

Bubbling with enthusiasm

Build the excitement

Catch the enthusiasm

Caution: May cause excitability

Come see for yourself what all the excitement is about

Coming... Grand-slam excitement!

Curious. Focused. Enthusiastic.

Deals for all non-sports enthusiasts

Deals that will send you through the roof

Do your clothes lead a more exciting life than you do?

Electrified sensational excitement!

Embrace it! Enjoy it! It only happens once!

Enthused beyond expectations

Enthusiasm that comes along once in a lifetime

Excitement is the name of the game

Excitement... that's what it takes to draw a crowd

Exciting savings? You better believe it!

Experience the Excitement Sales Event!

Experience the thrill and excitement

Eye-opening savings excitement!

Fire! Urgency! Enthusiasm!

Foot-stomping, heart-pounding deals!

For people who like the spectacular, we make it spectacular!

For year-round excitement... join us at...

Get enthused and celebrate the savings with us!

Get lost... and you'll find plenty of excitement at...

Get ready for some real excitement

Get with the latest craze!

Grab the excitement, grab the savings!

Heart-pounding sale excitement!

High-flying excitement!

How to make exciting times even more exciting

If you love a white-knuckle thrill, take this ride for a lifetime of excitement

If you're hungry for some excitement...

It all adds up to an exciting sales event!

It is exciting to bring excitement back to...

It's exciting! It's exhilarating!
It's savings time!

It's hip, it's happenin'!

It's mind-boggling savings excitement!

It's spontaneous pleasure

It's take-home excitement

Just add a dash of enthusiasm

Let the excitement begin

Let's make things happen

Lifetime worth of excitement

Loaded with savings excitement!

Look for the excitement to begin on...

Looking for weekend excitement?

Mind-blowing! Spine-tingling! Thrilling!

New and exciting!

Now here's something to whet
your whistle

Okay, now I'm excited

One hundred and ten percent
pure adrenaline

Our enthusiasm is contagious

Our excitement... customer enthusiasm

Over-the-top excitement

Passion! Adventure! Excitement!

Relive the thrill and excitement of...

Ride the road with enthusiasm

See what the buzz is all about

Share the excitement

Show your enthusiasm today!

Show-stopping excitement

Soak up the excitement at...

Something exciting is taking place

Spills! Thrills! Chills!

Stand by for some exciting action

Start your day with all-out enthusiasm

Stir the excitement

Tap into year-round excitement

Thank you for your enthusiastic support

The drama! The action! The excitement!

The most exciting thing that's
happened since...

The most unusual, hair-raising
experience in the world

The Sale Event of Excitement!

The savings excitement starts here!

These are exciting opportunities

Time to get excited about...

Want to add some enthusiasm to
your life?

Warning: Thrills and spills

We are pleased to welcome you to
our exciting...

We'll put you in the middle of all the fun
and excitement

We're drumming up fabulous, exciting
deals all week long

We're excited about our savings
excitement!

We've got the excitement you deserve!

What could be more exciting than...

Who said it couldn't get more exciting?

Wild West Excitement!

Windfall of excitement

You can expect the unexpected

You have the right to remain excited

You want excitement? We got it!

You'll be super-excited with the savings!

You'll get carried away by the
amazing savings!

You'll have a blast, 'cause you'll never
know what to expect

You'll have a whimsical and exciting time

You're sure to create exciting memories
when you...

You've got to experience the excitement!

Your countdown to excitement

Your search for fun and excitement
is over

Your ticket to a life of excitement!

Extreme Sports

A fine line between adventure and insanity

A sport that is x-tremely interesting

Adrenaline is the hook that keeps athletes in the sport

Adventure racing can take a few years off your life

Air it out

All the right stuff for action!

An element of danger is the foundation of extreme sports

An event like no other!

An extreme sport is an exciting non-traditional sport

Any of you daredevils ready for...

Athletic extremists

Be an extreme sportsman

Calling all thrill-seekers!!!

Catch the enthusiasm for a dangerous sport

Chaos is encouraged in extreme sports

Climb. Sprint. Skate.

Death-defying feats

Do you mind being asked to perform insane feats?

Don't get extreme with it

Dreaming up more outrageous exploits is extreme sports

Each one more daring than the next

Exciting! Thrilling! Breathtaking!

Extreme is cool

Extreme sport athletes keep pushing the envelope

Extreme sports are for high achievers

Extreme sports are limited by how daring people can be

Extreme sports can become very addictive

Extreme sports have arrived

Extreme sports have captured the public's eye

Extreme sports is an outlet

Extreme sports offer a venue that's ripe for extreme innovation

Extreme sports... extreme harm

Extreme-sports are x-tremely interesting

Feeling the urge

Fling your body into raging white-water rapids

For those who dare!

Fringe sports have been a wake-up call for the industry

From awesome to extreme and everything in between

Get out and give new sports a try!

Get up and do it again

Go for it!

Going beyond what most will not tolerate

Great for thrill-seekers

Having fun with physics

High adventure sports... for high adventure people

If you don't get killed, it's quite an experience

If you want to do it, you have to risk something

In true radical spirit

In-line skating is the fastest growing sport in America

It takes a different type of person to do these things

It was such a rush!

It's a fun sport, but it's also dangerous

It's a gravity sport

It's a sport for thrill seekers

It's a wonderful, exciting sport

It's beyond anything you've experienced

It's called mountainboarding

It's definitely the feeling of freedom

It's just you, the board and the vibe

It's pretty challenging

It's the big hype

It's the ultimate human experience

Let's hear it for the competition!

Looking for retro energy and new wave pep?

Making the impossible, possible

Multisport adventure

No athletic skill required. Just guts!

Once you go, all those funny feelings go away and you feel energized

Only the tough survive!

Out of the fringe and into the spotlight

Overcoming the fear, and responding to the challenge

Over-the-top excitement!

Prepare to make the jump

Pushing it is what extreme sports is all about

Ready to be daring!

Really extreme

Risk rather than reward

Riverboarding offers extreme sports junkies what they crave most

Save big on these in-line skates!

Seekers. Strivers. Dreamers.

Snowkiting is an intense, full-body workout

Speed! Metal! Punk!

Stare danger in the chops and smirk

Strap yourself to anything with wheels

Take it to the extreme

"Take No Prisoners" is the cry in extreme sports

Take the plunge into riverboarding

Taking it to the edge can get you in over your head

Talk about laughing in the face of danger

Testing your limits

That's one way to make a name for yourself

The allure of the X Games

The athleticism and reckless enthusiasm

The darlings of the mainstream world

The joy of physical exertion

The most over-the-top extreme sport ever

The most unusual and violent game ever played

The thrills and spills of skateboards

There are immense benefits offered by extreme sports

This is a ride you must take

Thrills and chills

We are now living in an X Games world

We dare you!

We're all adrenaline junkies

Widening the world of extreme sports

With extreme ease

X-treme idiocy

X-treme! X-citing! X-hilirating!

X-tremely cool fun for cool kids

You can do it... we dare you!

You can feel the adrenaline and energy pumping through you

You get one shot, that's it

You'll be doing things that you haven't done before

You'll get a reputation as a daredevil

You'll like the extremes!

You're not in control... the river is in control

You're not into taking uncalculated risks. You're into taking calculated risks!

You're not thinking what to do. You're just doing it!

A beautiful windfall of savings!

A bounty of fall specials!

A bounty of rich color awaits you

A bushel of fall savings!

A celebration of the changing of the season

A cornucopia of savings and selection is here!

A fall festival of savings you won't want to miss!

A fantastic fall festival of savings!

A feast for fall fans

A festive blaze of colorful deals!

A harvest of great tasting savings!

A new season to look and feel terrific

A preview of fall bargains!

A sale celebration of the autumn season!

Add a dash of color to your fall

All for fall... all for apple pickin'

All the color and splendor of a unique fall sale!

An autumn equinox sale!

An enchanting, exhilarating, exciting fall sale!

An October sale to remember!

Annual Fall Harvest Festival of Savings!

Another reason to welcome fall

Are we ready for fall? You bet!

Autumn accents sale!

Autumn attitudes... Energetic, exciting, exhilarating!

Autumn attractions... Catch 'em

Autumn bargains... Prices are falling!

Autumn color accent sale!

Autumn cornucopia of great savings!

Autumn is always in season at...

Autumn leaves are falling and so are the prices!

Autumn leaves priced to go!

Autumn savin' is the time to rake 'em in!

Autumn savings here!

Autumn savings never looked this good!

Autumn's Festival of Savings!

Autumn's Harvest of Values!

Awesome autumn savings!

Back-to-Fall Stock-Up Sale!

Beat the winter with these fall savings!

Best of Fall Sale!

Big ideas for fall fix-ups

Breeze into autumn with...

Bushels and bushels of buys!

Bye-bye summer... Hello fall savings!

Catch the autumn spirit with exceptional fall savings!

Caution: watch out for falling prices!

Celebrate the Arrival of Autumn Sales Event!

Celebrate the bounties of the season with sensational values

Check out our falling prices

Colorful buys during autumn daze

Come out to see our fall colors at the...

Coming this fall...

Cool weather essentials

Crisp fall savings are here

Discover the fall with us!

Don't fall around... Get it done with...

Don't fall for high prices

Don't wait for fall... get it today!

Dressing for a sensational fall

Drop in for fall savings

Duck in... duck out with fantastic fall ideas

Ease into the sweater weather

Enjoy a crisp fall afternoon of fabulous savings

Enjoy a great fall fling at...

Enjoy bountiful savings during the...

Enjoy the beauty of an early fall sale!

Everyday autumn savings for outside and inside

Everything for fall is on sale right now!

Exciting new colors for fall

Express yourself more colorfully!

Fall arrives officially at...

Fall bargain days!

Fall bonanza days are here again

Fall budget stretches

Fall Cleanup Sale!

Fall comes alive with bargains, deals and awesome savings!

Fall doesn't last forever... but the savings do!

Fall Fest Saving Days... going on now!

Fall Festival of Values

Fall Fix-Up Special Sale!

Fall for a great deal at...

Fall for more to buy, more to save, more to enjoy

Fall for the best

Fall forecast... hot deals!

Fall Harvest Days of Savings!

Fall home festival sale!

Fall in for fall savings!

Fall in love with incredible autumn savings!

Fall in with a winner!

Fall into a great sale!

Fall into a new look at...

Fall into autumn savings

Fall into our autumn promotion... everything is on sale!

Fall into real savings

Fall into September savings!

Fall into spectacular savings at your...

Fall into the latest fashions of the season

Fall is a great bargain at...

Fall is a great time to head for the great outdoors

Fall is an excellent time to plan for...

Fall is fun at the mall

Fall is the best time of the year to save!

Fall is the perfect time of year to enjoy...

Fall is the season of new clothes, school supplies and yellow buses

Fall kickoff days

Fall lawn and garden sale!

Fall maintenance pays off in winter

Fall parade of values!

Fall preview sale!

Fall price rollback savings!

Fall raking woes made easy and fun with...

Fall roundup of exceptional savings!

Fall sales explosion

Fall savings are piling up

Fall savings stock up sale!

Fall savings that don't burn a hole in your budget

Fall speed ahead with savings!

Fall starts here... With our super fall sale!

Fall value days... starting this Sunday!

Fall's falling prices

Fall's freshest picks

Falling leaves! Falling prices!

Favorite fall treats... apples, cider and caramel apples

First of fall sale!

Gear up for fall at...

Get a leg up on the fall season

Get a new start on fall

Get into the spirit of autumn with unbelievable savings!

Go ahead... fall for the sale of the season

Gorgeous fall buys!

Great outdoor projects for fall

Harvest incredible savings!

Harvest these great values at the right time and the right price!

Harvest time is savings time!

How to gather up the savings this fall

How to make sure you have a sensational fall!

Huge fall savings on...

Hurry, autumn savings are here!

If leaves can fall, so can our prices

If you want your husband to rake the leaves this fall, don't let him see this ad!

It happens every fall

It just wouldn't be fall without a cornucopia of savings!

It only happens once a year... our colorful Fall Sale!

It's a Harvest Moon Sale Event!

It's a new season of savings

It's fall furnace checkup time

It's time to get up for fall

Jump into our bushel of autumn savings!

Jump-start fall with August Best Buys!

Kickoff with fall values!

Last call for fall bargains, winter's on its way

Leaf on down to...

Leaf through these savings!

Leaves are falling and prices are falling

Let our savings of fall sweep you away

Let's hear it for outrageous autumn savings!

Look out for falling bucks

Looking for a short autumn getaway?

Looking for fall fun?

Make every fall day a celebration

More fall deals, more fall values for more fall savings!

Never mind the weather, the autumn sale is going on!

No need to wait for fall to enjoy the...

Nothing says "sale" like fall colors

Nothing starts the fall season like buying a new...

Now, here's a fall idea!

October leaves aren't the only things falling at...

October sales frenzy!

October's Last Hurrah Sale Days!

Oktoberfest savings days!

Our all fall sale... all across America

Our annual leaf-peeping sale!

Our best deals for fall

Our fall forecast calls for great bargains

Our fall sale spectacular!

Our savings show our true colors

Pile on the savings... big time!

Pre-season windfalls savings!

Prices are falling like leaves

Race your way through fall in our...

Rake in a real deal! With unbe-leaf-able sales!

Rake in big savings with full bushels of buys!

Rake in more savings... and even more savings!

Rake in the bucks

Rake in these values!

Rake in those autumn savings

Reap more savings!

Save a bundle with our falling prices!

Say goodbye to fall with these incredible savings!

Shop our barn of fall's bountiful harvest

Spectacular autumn sale!

Still time to rake up a pile of cash

Super autumn values are here!

Super autumn values to rake 'em in

Super weekend windfalls!

Sweater Days Are Here Again Sale Event!

Tackle these fall savings!

Ten great ways to welcome fall

The annual sale of autumn colors

The Fall Brawl Clearance Sale!

The fall season has arrived early at...

The forecast for fall is... unbelievable savings!

The four faces of fall... Cheerful, changeable, colorful and comfortable

The glow of the harvest moon will color your world

The sounds of falling prices

The taste of autumn

The Ultimate Fall Sale!

There's nothing quite like our fall sale!

There's something special about autumn savings days!

This fall is for you... this sale is for you!

This fall... Get a jump on winter!

This is the most enjoyable time of the year for a fall sale!

This weekend see a mix of gold, yellow and red and save a lot of green

Tidy-up fall values!

Time for fall cleanup!

Timely savings for your fall needs

Try a change of pace this fall

Turn a leaf into a windfall of savings!

Turn over a new leaf and save

Unique deals for diehard autumn lovers

Visit our pumpkin patch

Wake up to the fall season with awesome savings!

Watch prices fall now...

We bring fall to your door

We interrupt fall to bring you a special announcement...

We'll color your world!

We're celebrating autumn with falling prices!

We're dropping our fall prices!

We're showing our fall colors with sensational savings!

We've got it all for fall cleanup projects

Welcome to our new fall collection of savings!

Welcome to the fall season of savings!

Welcome to the spirit of fall

What's the new look in color for fall?

When the leaves are gone, so are the savings!

While the leaves are falling, our sales will be soaring!

Windfall pre-season savings!

With autumn getaways, good things come in fall packages

Wonder why they call it a fall sale?

You can bag a bundle!

You know autumn has arrived when the prices start falling from the trees!

You will fall for the best

You won't be-leaf these fall savings!

You'll fall for our prices!

You'll fall in love with savings when you step through our door!

You'll really fall for these savings!

Your autumn things-to-do list

Your Fall Cleanup Guide

Your home's fall checklist is full of savings!

113

A blue blazer can take you anywhere

A dash of southwestern flair

A delicate touch of comfort

A dress no one will forget

A dress you'll wear for the sheer love of it

A look that dazzles

A look that's as special as the occasion

A passion for fashion... a passion for savings!

A sense of independence and carefree style

A smart way for you to look good

A wardrobe of slick silk values

Absolutely perfect for special occasions

Add a touch of spice to your wardrobe

All the elements of a classic

Always sharp... always in style

An all-season wardrobe

An early preview of fall's fashions

An outrageous sale never goes out of style!

Are your clothes up to par?

As fashionable as it is functional

Bargains for style-conscious consumers!

Bright fashions have never been smarter

Brighten up your wardrobe!
Terrific savings!

Casual comfort with a sophisticated touch

Clothes that are a little offbeat

Clothes to suit any adventure

Comfortable yet chic-chic

Countless wardrobe possibilities

Create Your Own Look Sales Event!

Dare to be outrageous

Design your spring wardrobe with us

Do you ever think you have nothing to wear?

Dress well without dressing up

Dresses are what we know and dresses are what we sell

Elegance never goes out of style

Everyday to every-occasion dressing

Fall fashion will be down to earth

Family fashions all on sale!

Fancy these rags

Fashion and value at an unbelievable price!

Fashion must-haves

Fashion that commands a second look

Fashion, quality, value, service

Fashions for moms-to-be

Fashions for the girl who loves to dress up

Fashions with exceptional values!

Favorite fashions for every day of your life

For a perfect evening, the perfect dress

For people who want to express their individuality

For the fashion-minded woman

For the woman who is confident and doesn't mind being noticed

For weekdays, weekends and even special occasions

Fun, functional, affordable

Goofy clothes for men

Gracefully feminine

Great fashions with fantastic prices!

Great looking craftsmanship-quality clothing

Gussy up during our fabulous sales event!

Have fun with fashion values

High-fashion... high-quality

Hot prices on all cool looks

Hot teen fashions

How to buy underwear

How to look like a million for just peanuts

Isn't it time you update your wardrobe?

It Fits You to a "T" Sales Event!

It only looks expensive

It's A Fashion Statement Sales Event!

It's all the rage, fashion-wise

It's not in style, so it will never go out of style

It's so you

It's the look you're looking for

It's the smartest thing to wear this fall

It's value and fashion for the whole family

It's what America's fashion-conscious teenager really wants

It's your favorite, wear it every day, everywhere

Jazz up your wardrobe... today!

Just a shade of exotic

Just the right dress... at just the right price

Keeping up-to-date on fashion

Kickin' It In Style Sale Event!

Let us muddle your mind with simplicity

Life will be a bowl of cherries when you put on this red dress

Look and feel your best for less

Look beautiful! Spend smart! Dress with style!

Look like a million without breaking the bank

Look like a million, spend way less!

Look your best without spending a lot

Looking chic

Looking for something different?

Magnificent bargains for your career wardrobe!

Make a splash with exceptional savings!

Make room in your wardrobe for these sensational buys!

Making a statement from head to toe

More beauty. More fashion. More sleek. More chic. Never too dressy... never too casual!

More style! More striking! More savings!

Next season's hot new trend

Now, these aren't your ordinary denim duds

One-of-a-kind sales event!

Oodles of exciting clothes

Our basic black is anything but basic

Our clothes don't come to life on a hanger

Our fashions will make you blush

Our fashions will shake up your closet

Outlandish but outstanding

Perfect for day or evening

Perfect prices for fashion favorites

Planning to update your wardrobe?

Put some fashion into your clothes

Quality fashions cost less at our store

Refreshing fashion alternatives

Rev up your wardrobe

Round-the-clock fashions! Round-the-Clock Sale!

Savings that make you look terrific!

See it! Touch it! Try it on!

See our new look!

Simplicity with unstudied elegance

Simply beautiful, incredibly comfortable

Smart casual. Dressy casual. Friday casual.

Smart simplicity in spring colors

Smashing savings on all eveningwear!

Sophisticated, elegant, perpetually inviting

Special occasion dress sale of the year!

Spice Up Your Life... Sale Event!

Spring-fresh designs... all on sale!

Fashion

Stand Out and Be Noticed Sales Event!

Step into the perfect dress

Tailored with charming simplicity

Tailor-made just for you!

Take a fresh look at the fashion world

Take stock in your wardrobe

That's Totally You Sales Event!

The best spring fashions to wear now

The charming, casual look

The classics never go out of style

The dress to come home to

The easiest way to look great

The latest fashion with the "in" crowd

The look of success

The perfect touch of class

The pretty side of sporty

The right mix for today's fashions

The season's hottest styles

The streetwear young people wear

The wardrobe for your personality

The way to update your look

These fashions are for only the brave

Timeless fashions with a twist

Tips from the dressing room

Today's sophisticated casual

Top it off with a big straw hat!

Trends that will shape up your wardrobe

Tricks to looking great

Trying to figure out what to wear?

Turn of the century fashion

Undeniably alluring, subtle,
ultra-feminine is today's
current sophistication

Update your wardrobe from head to toe

Wait till you see the fall collection

We don't do fashion... we create fashion

We make getting dressed, no sweat

We've cruised the fashion runways of
today for fashions of tomorrow... just
for you!

Wearing nothing but the best!

Western wear with a city flair

What a fashionable woman wants to wear

What do you want to wear today?

What does your tie say about you?

What to wear... decisions,
decisions, decisions

What's in style for fall?

What's wrong with a nice piece
of cashmere?

When you go out, you want to stand out

When you want to look your very best...

When your living depends on your
appearance, you'd better look your best

Where elegance is down to earth

Where fabulous fashions
become irresistible

Where fashion, quality and value
come together

Who, what, and wear

Work clothes. Play clothes.
Going-out clothes.

You can be reassured to know that our
clothes won't be obsolete in six months

You deserve to dress your best

You will be comfortable in our fashions

You'll be flattered with
outstanding values!

You'll feel like a million bucks when you
look like it

You'll stand out from the rack with...

You're going to like the way you look!

Your clothes deserve nothing but
the best

Your nine-to-five wardrobe

Your summer wardrobe is now on sale!

Father's Day

A Father's Day event that's fit for a king

A Father's Day feast

A gift Dad will love

A good way to cap off Father's Day

A great day for great dads

After Father's Day sale!

All kinds of gifts for all kinds of dads

Are you ready for Father's Day? We are!

Are you stumped at the idea of buying Dad a gift?

Banner gifts for Dad

Bright ideas for dads and dads-to-be

C'mon, you know what Dad wants

Celebrate Father's Day... It hits home

Cool stuff for Dad

Dad gave you the shirt off his back... Now it's your turn!

Dad is the one, today!

Dad will flip over your gift

Dad, present this coupon at the pro shop

Dad's Day gifts for work or play

Dad's free... on Father's Day!

Dads are half-price on Father's Day!

Dads eat free... Today!

Don't just appreciate Dad. Overwhelm him.

Don't tie yourself in knots, buy Dad a great...

Doodads for Dad

Dress up Dad for Father's Day!

Fantastic Father's Day gifts for fantastic fathers!

Father's Day costs less at...

Father's Day fragrances, this will get his attention

Father's Day gift center

Father's Day gift spectacular

Father's Day is just another thing about fatherhood that ticks me off

Father's Day price break

Father's Day sale, go ahead, he deserves it

Father's Day... Pull out all the stops

Fathers Only Sale Event!

Finally, the gift Dad's been waiting for

For the sweetest dad of them all

For the world's greatest dad

Free Father's Day portrait

Fuss over your dad... today!

Get on course with great gifts for Dad

Gift ideas for Dad... So what's new?

Gifts for Dad you'd never think of

Gifts for golfing dads

Gifts for the Dad in your life

Gifts for your favorite dad

Gifts he'll remember

Gifts that fit Dad to a "tee"

Gifts to make your Father's Day

Give Dad something he'll really love for Father's Day

Give Dad something to grin about

Give Dad the recognition he deserves

Give the gift that pleases your dad

Give your dad a digital gift he'll love

Give your Dad the world, give him a gift of nature

Gone are the days when the only gift a father ever received was a tie

Great Dad's Day prices!

Great gifts for great dads

Father's Day

Great pre-Father's Day values

Happy Father's Day, Dad, you're the best

Happy Father's Day, Dad... And thanks!

Happy Father's Day to dads who support their family

Have a Fatheriffic Day!

Have a super Dad's Day at...

He's your dad: Handle with care

Here's to dads across the nation... Need we say more? You bet!

Honor thy father

How do you celebrate Father's Day?

How to top off Father's Day

How will you honor your father today?

In celebration of Dad, give him the royal treatment

In commemoration of Father's Day...

In honor of fathers, stepfathers and grandfathers

Incredible gifts for Dad at incredible prices!

Isn't it time to remember Dad?

It's a gift Dad will really appreciate

Just in time for Father's Day

Just what Dad needs

Let's all tie one on for Father's Day

Let's treat Dad to his favorite restaurant

Light up your dad's day with a...

Make Father's Day even more special at...

Make his day extra special with our Father's Day gifts

Make it a Father's Day he will always remember

My father is special to me because...

Nobody knows how to keep Dad in style like we do!

Not sure what to give Dad for Father's Day?

Our greatest savings for the greatest Dad!

Perfect for Father's Day!

Pick a gift to show Dad he's just as special

Pop for a priceless gift this Father's Day

Remembering Dad... Start Father's Day off right with...

Right on course for a great Father's Day

Right on time for Dad's Day

Saluting America's Dads

Scents for your sensational Dad

Shop early for Father's Day

Show off your fatherly wisdom and take advantage of this incredible value

Spoil your dad like never before

Super Dad deals!

Ten top reasons why Dad is the best

The 10 most wanted gifts for Father's Day!

The best gifts for the best Dads

The gift of all Father's day gifts

The gift that fits Dad's style of living

The gift your Dad really wants, at one unbelievably low price!

Time out savings for Dad

To the world's sweetest Dad

Toast Dad with a tasteful gift

Treat him to the great gifts he deserves...

Treat your Dad this Father's Day to some great food

We really know how to make Dad feel like a king

We saved our best values for Dad

We've got all you need for Father's Day

We've got Dad covered from head to toe

We've got the stuff fathers love

What do you give your favorite Dad for Father's Day?

What every man needs for Father's Day

Wouldn't Dad appreciate a gift he can use every day?

Your Dad = A great Father's Day!

Festivals

American Heritage Festival

Annual Bookfest

Annual Park Fest

Apple Butter Festival

Autumn Moon Festival

Autumn on Parade Festival

Bluegrass Pickin' Time

Blues Festival

Broom Corn Festival

Buckwheat Festival

Cherry Blossom Festival

Chilifest

Chowderfest

City of Lights Festival

Fall Festival of Gospel Music

Fall Fling Festival

Festival of Foods

Fishfest!

Food and Wine Festival

Freedom Festival

Funfest

Garden Harvest Festival

Ghostwalk Fest

Greetings, Festivalgoers

Harborfest

Harvest Days Celebration

Holly Jolly Festival

Indian Summerfest

It's an old-fashioned harvest fest

It's tomato festival time

Jazz Festival

Maine Lobster Festival

Mason-Dixon Festival

Missouri Mule Days

Molasses and Honey Festival

Mother Earth Festival

Multicultural Fest

Neighborhood festivals

Old Fashioned Apple Harvest Festival

Ozark Ham & Turkey Festival

Polkafest

Prairie Arts Festival

Railroad Days Festival

Ready your taste buds for the annual Food Festival

River Front Festival

Senior Fairfest

Snow and Ice Carving Festival

Southern Seafood Festival

Spring Festivals of Homes

Spring Funfest

Summer Kick-off Festival

Swing your partner at the Festival of Folk Dance

Taste of Spring Festival

The Annual Beachfest

The Annual Gardening Day Festival

The Empty Bottle Festival

The Festival of Foods

The Great Pumpkin Fest

The Holy Guacamole Fest

The Red Apple Harvest Fest

Tulip Festival

Turn of the Century Festival

Winter Shiverfest

Winter Wonder Festival

World's Largest Music Festival

Fire

A cozy fire is just a match away

A ferocious fire sale! Going on now!

A fireball of exciting savings!

A great way to light someone's fire

A spark! A flame! A torch!

Adding a little fuel to the Bigger-Is-Better Fire Sale!

All Fired Up Sales Event!

Are you ready to set the world on fire?

Baptism of fire deals!

Be ready to put out last-minute fires that flare up

Burning bargains going hot and fast

Candles ablaze with an incredible aroma of savings!

Caught on like wildfire

Deals to fuel your fire!

Enjoy a clean burning fire with...

Fan the fire with explosive savings!

Fanning the flames of hot deals!

Fire up the team for more sales!

Fire up your life with these fantastic bargains!

Fired up and ready to deal!

Get fired up for an adventure of a lifetime

Great Balls of Fire Sales Event!

Here's a deal that will light your fire

Hey, where's the fire sale?

How to get fired up about savings!

Ignite the fire of your imagination with explosive deals!

In case of fire... Please open!

It's a bonfire loaded with phenomenal deals!

It's an inferno of awesome savings!

It's easy to get fired up with these bargains!

Keep stoking the fire for hot deals!

Keep the fire burning with...

Keep the fires of passion burning with a gift of...

Keep the home fires burning during the Cold Days of Winter Savings!

On fire with red-hot deals!

Prices to get fired up about

Put out the fire with sizzling savings!

Savings that are hotter than a fire sale!

So go ahead, fire me up!

Sparks will fly with explosive savings!

Take advantage of this sure-fire offer

The torch is lit

This is no "fire" sale!

Too many irons in the fire?

We set the world on fire with Super Sensational Savings!

We're fighting fire with fire on these prices!

We're fired up with ready-to-go deals!

We're selling everything to fuel our fire

We've put a blowtorch to all our prices!

What's on fire for the weekend?

With deals like this, you'll see the fire in their eyes

Yeah, we're fired up!

You won't get burned with these explosive savings!

You'll need a fire hose to cool down the deals!

You're Playing With Fire... Sales Event!

You're the spark that lights the fire of...

Fishing

A jump-off point for anglers fishing

A rewarding place to wet your lines

All on sale, from boats to bait!

Angler of the Year!

Anyone fishing needs a license

Attention all anglers! All fishing gear now on sale!

Available to anglers only

Big bargains for fish fanciers!

Bragging is a part of fishing, and we're bragging about our deals!

Catch and Release Fishing Derby

Cooking up the catch! Cooking up great savings!

Don't let the big one get away during our Bargain Days!

Drop your hook at our fishing spot

Every tackle box should contain a...

Everything in our tackle box is for sale!

Fall prime-time fishing sale!

Fish-catching tips

Fishin' for savings?

Fishing buddies sale! Buy one get one free!

Fishing Derby Day!

Fishing for a good deal

Fishing for dollars

Fishing in a winter wonderland

Fishing special for special fishing people!

For the fishing trip of a lifetime, call...

Get hooked on fishing

Get hooked on our fish

Gone Fishin' Sale Event of the Year!

Got Fish on the Hook Deals!

Great savings for all fishing enthusiasts everywhere!

Here's a product that's on fire

Here's a quick-fishing fix

Here's what you need to reel in big sales!

How to catch the big ones

How to get hooked on fishing

I Jus' Wanna Go Fishin' Sales Event!

Ice fishing adventures for the whole family

It is the only fishing game in town

It's catfish time on the...

It's easy to get hooked on fishing

It's no fish story... it's our annual Closeout Sale of the Season!

It's not for men only... Rod and Reel Sale Event!

Join the Angler's Club

Let us show you how to catch fish

Let's go fishing!

Live bait sold here

Lookin' for some reel relaxation?

Lures of the North Woods

Make your fishing trip a rewarding one

National Catfish Month

No fishing license required

Nothing fishy about this sale!

Now you can fish with Big Fish Savings!

October is National Seafood Month

On the hook... off the hook deals!

Our fishing sale is gonna getcha!

Out here, you'll enjoy the days when they don't bite at all

Protecting our fishing resources is a must

Quality is our bait

Reap the rewards of fall fishing savings!

Fishing

Reel in whopping sales!

Reel life, reel fishermen and reel savings!

Relax... go fishing!

Savings for all fair-weather anglers!

See us for all your fishing needs

So you're ready to take the ice-fishing plunge?

Spring lure bonanza of savings!

Stop fishing around... the savings are staggering!

Summer conditions whet fishing appetites

Swim with the big fish... saving with the big sale!

Take a kid fishing... it's catching on!

Talk about the catch of the day

Ten percent of all anglers catch 90 percent of the fish

The best place to reel 'em in

The catch of a lifetime

The family outdoor event of the year

The fishing is awesome... the savings are fantastic!

The Fishing Report brought to you by...

The fishing's good... the savings are even better!

The greatest fishing area in the world

The hottest fishing destination in the world

The lure of fishing will reel you in

The most versatile rod ever

The new fast-action rod everyone should have!

The only thing better than eating catfish is catching 'em

There's nothing like eating a fish you caught

They've gotta be biting somewhere

To catch the Big Ones, you've got to go where the Big Ones live

Trade your gym shoes for waders

Unbelievable savings for the fishing enthusiast!

Want to catch fish?

We cater to an array of fishing experiences

We give free bait!

We offer a more comfortable fishing experience

We offer great guide service

We'll get you off the hook

We'll set you up with a crash course in fishing

We're ready to throw in a line of savings!

Whatever it takes to catch "the big one"

When was the last time you fished?

Where catching a fish is more than a wish

Where people get away, but the fish don't

Where the fish are tough, smart and fast

Where the fishing season never closes

Where you go and catch the limit every time

Who says fishing is a man's sport?

Wish you were fishing?

World's best fishing adventure

You catch them, you clean them!

You gotta catch 'em here

You'll be hooked at our Friday night fresh fish fry

You'll fall for these deals hook, line, and sinker!

You'll get hooked on our fish sale!

You'll hook the big one during our Early Morning Sale Event!

You'll never know what you might catch during our Spring Fishing Sale Event!

Your game warden wants you!

Fitness

A fantastic way to get fit

A great body starts here!

A great place to exercise the mind, the spirit and the body

A new body... in twelve weeks or less

A real gym for real people

A slimmer and healthier you for the holidays

A top-to-bottom fitness program

A workout for busy people with busy lives

A workout, not a wear-out

All fitness equipment sale event!

Almost as easy as gaining weight

An exercise in savings!

An expert view on getting fit

And everything else you need to make a whole new you!

Are you allergic to exercise?

Are you ready to invest in looking and feeling great?

At this price, they'll admire you for your brains as well as your body!

At your age you can't neglect the importance of exercise

Bend, twist, jump, stretch. It is easy to be in shape

Biggest muscle-fitness sale of the year!

Body-wise buys!

Break a sweat, get fit, stay in shape

Bring the health club home with you

Buy one year, get one year free deal... right now!

C'mon, it'll do you good to get some exercise

Call it Survival of the Fittest Sale Event!

Can you imagine feeling this way all the time?

Challenging yourself physically doesn't have to be unenjoyable

Choosing the right exercise program...

Come chew the fat with us!

Do I look fat? Am I fat? Do I feel fat?

Do it for 30 days, make it a habit for life

Do your health club fees make you sweat?

Don't buy a treadmill if you don't like to walk

Don't haggle with your body... get it fit!

Don't put your exercise cycle into the closet

Don't wait to feel good about yourself

Establish your own relationship with fitness

Exercise can be hazardous to your health

Exercise can be your connection to new social relationships

Exercise helps the body withstand the sands of time

Exercise is good medicine

Exercise is something you should do because you enjoy it

Exercise is the best investment you'll ever make!

Exercise is the prescription that's universal

Exercise should be fun, not drudgery

Exercise should enhance your life, not control it

Fall into fitness, a neat way to go

Feel fit and fabulous

Feel like yourself again!

Feel-good fitness

Feeling guilty won't get you to the gym

Fighting fatigue, going nowhere?

Find out how to feel better than good

Finding time to exercise isn't
an afterthought

Fit and hip, and that's just for starters

Fit for fun, fit for life

Fitness is a gift that requires
constant attention

Focus on fitness for lifelong health

For a healthy new you!

For people who want to
exercise conveniently

Get a kick out of fitness

Get another chance at your past years

Get fit your way, but don't be left
holding the fat!

Get fit! It matters!!!

Get in shape a fun way

Get moving, get in shape

Get off your duff and get in shape

Get on the fast track to fitness

Get ready, get set, get fit!

Getting more from your workout is
no sweat

Give your loved one the gift of fitness

Good for the body. Good for the mind.
Good for the spirit.

Help your body win the battle
against time

Here's good news for all the
fitness enthusiasts

Here's how to aspire to perspire

Hit the gym instead of the bar

Home-fitness sale!

How can a person stay thin and healthy?

How do you measure up?

How does your body feel at the end of
the day?

How to find a personal trainer

How to get fitter, stronger, better, faster

How to pump up your heart

If exercise doesn't excite you, you're
not living

If this sale doesn't excite you, check your
pulse, you might be dead!

If you don't turn your back on your
exercise, it will always be there

If you think our prices are reduced,
wait until you see your thighs in
three months!

If you want to be fit... then work out
with the rest of us

Ignore discomfort, ignore exercise,
ignore us

In your quest for health and fitness

Is thinking about getting fit driving
you crazy?

Is your body cheating you?

It won't cure insomnia, but it will cure
your weight problem

It's a time for feeling good

It's never too late to start exercising

It's never too late to take your physical
fitness seriously

It's not about looking young, it's about
looking great

It's shape-up savings time!

It's time to get in shape for your future

It's time to spring into shape

It's time you got serious about your body

Just wait until you see your body in
4 weeks

Just what your body needs

Let's get physical!

Look at yourself and say... it's now
or never

Look better. Feel better. Live better.

Look fitter! Feel younger! Live longer!

Looking tan, toned, fit and ready to go

Lose your gut for good

Losing weight isn't a fad, it's a goal

Make time for fitness

Muscle up and lean out

Need to get in shape but don't want to spend an arm and a leg?

New state-of-the-art health club

No butts about it. Lose weight now!

No gain! Some gain!

No gym membership required

Nothing tastes as good as being thin feels

Now's the time to take measures to shape up

Perfecting your body for maximum performance

Requires no additional outlay of sweat

Rev up your workout

Round-the-clock workout

Say goodbye to grueling, tedious workouts

So you want to get in shape?

Some call it work; we call it exercise

Spring Fitness Sale! This week only!

Stay in shape with our state-of-the-art fitness center

Stay young... stay healthy... join today!

Stretch your muscles and stretch your mind

Teaching our kids lifelong fitness

The All-American Workout

The benefit of exercise is improving your overall well-being

The best health club membership is the one you use!

The body of tomorrow... for today!

The fitness club you've been looking for

The fitness facility for the next century

The gift of life is a membership at...

The perfect way to burn off excess weight

The quick release from stress

The workout will make you sweat... The membership fee won't

There are a lot of muscles in your body you haven't used

Today, make it a habit for life

Too busy not to stay fit?

Walk this way to total body fitness

Want to look good and feel good?

We have the correct exercise prescription

We interrupt your daily work to bring you our exercise program

We keep you feeling fit

We know how difficult it is to get in shape

We make people feel terrific

We pump your body, not your wallet

We sell health and fitness!

We'll say it again: You need to exercise

We'll whip you into shape... if it doesn't kill you first

We're not offering a quick fix

What a week of work could do for a body

What do you want out of our exercise program?

What kind of shape would you like to be in?

Whatever it is... exercise for your heart's sake

When you're under the weather... work out

Work up a sweat and leave your worries behind

Workouts for couch potatoes, channel surfers and non-doers

Wouldn't a massage feel good right now?

You can't afford not to be in shape

You could have your 25-year-old body back for only $25 per month

You know you're in a gym when you join up

You say you're ready to step up your fitness program?

You're one step closer to fitness... sign up now!

A bunch of lunchbox values!

A great way to make a meal simply delicious

A hearty winter meal idea

Add some savings excitement to your meals!

America's favorite food on sale!

Any time's a good time for a good meal

Chew on these savings!

Chow down on scrumptious meal savings!

Come for the freshness. Leave with the savings!

Cookin' up special values!

Create a stir at dinner in ten minutes or less with...

Delicious-tasting food at unbelievable savings!

Dine in! Carry out! Food delivered!

Do you know what you're having for dinner tonight?

Do you like eating genetically-engineered foods?

Eat smart... eat healthy... savings-wise

Eggs are delicious morning, noon and night

Enjoy all-you-can-eat

Every bite is hot, juicy and delicious

Everybody loves Italian food... do you?

Exciting recipes for your enjoyment and savings too!

Feast on savings of 50% off!

Feel free to garnish your meal with exceptional savings!

Fine food is one of life's greatest pleasures

Flippin' for pancake savings!

Food and save are more than four-letter words!

Food, glorious food savings!

For dinner emergencies

Fresh ideas for your meal planning

Fun food facts

Good old spaghetti and meatballs savings!

Great value meals

Guess Who's Coming To Dinner Savings Event!

Guilt-free meals

Gussy up a casual meal with...

Homestyle meal goodness

Hot and ready to eat savings!

Hot meals warm the heart

Hot prices on frozen foods

How to select fresh seafood without feeling like a fish out of water

How's that brown bag lunch looking now?

I had no idea ravioli came in anything but a can

If you can't stand the heat, get out the chicken!

If you're fond of fondue, you'll be fond of the savings!

Incredible edibles, digestible comestibles savings!

It chops! It dices! It slices!

It costs no more to eat the best!

It makes a good companion on a picnic

It's chili roundup savings time!

It's for when your stomach says... feed me now!

It's Frozen Food Month

It's great food bargains... enjoy!

It's mashed potato savings time!

It's National Sandwich Week

It's one great hot dog sale!

It's the real meal deal

It's the yummiest sandwich in the world

Jazz up your meals with fabulous savings!

Kids eat free every day!

Let the eating begin

Let us soup you up with super savings!

Low-cost meals that look expensive

Make bread for less dough

Make your stomach sizzle with these savings!

Meal savings that really count

Meals for hungry people

Mmmmm, luscious savings!

More lunch... less lunch money

Mouth-watering values

Munch your bagel with great care

Need meal ideas?

New ways to feed the family

No apology needed when you serve these leftovers

No preservatives... plenty of savings!

Nothing fishy about a seafood sale!

Now that's good eating

Nutritious meals for your pocketbook

One of nature's best heart-healthy foods

One-stop shopping for the dinner table

Our food is time-tested

Our freshness shines through

Our variety brings endless pastabilities

Pamper your palate with sensational savings!

Perfectly prepared so you don't have to be

Pizza with pizzazz!!!

Put more bite into your meals

Put your money where your meatloaf is

Quality food at competitive prices

Quick and easy menu ideas

Real good food at a real good price

Roasted to juicy perfection

Sauce it up... super savings!

Savings just for the halibut

Savings that will blast your taste buds away

Savings that will surely make your mouth water

Savings to enhance your meals

Sink your claws into...

So creamy and rich, you'll almost feel guilty

Special meals made simple

Super delicious savings on all...

Supper in a snap, with appetizing savings!

Tackle your family's appetite with terrific savings!

Take a bite out of high prices

That's good eatin'

The best way to wrap a sandwich is finally out of the bag

The Great American Meal-Out Day

The proof is on the dinner table

The specialty of the house is now at your house

Think of us as a farmer's market with air conditioning

Time-saving dinner

Tonight's hamburger shouldn't taste like last year's chicken

Umm, that good-lookin' savings!

Unbelievably delicious... undeniably healthy

We make good food taste better

We make grocery shopping a breeze!

We put the deli in delicious

We've got food to satisfy every appetite!

Wholesome food for nutritional values

Yes, yes, yes... fresh, tasty and inexpensive

Football

A fall football tradition continues... our annual fall sale event!

A great football tailgate party needs a game plan

Action worth catching

Add some zing to your game plan

And now back to live action

And the fun doesn't end with the football game!

Are you ready for football?

As B-day draws near... are you ready to party?

At home or your next tailgate party

Big savings for anyone who loves football

Big-time catches... Big-time savings!

Bring on the Bowl... of chips!

Calling all football diehards

Can't Wait for the Kickoff Sale Event of the Season!

Catch the best gridiron action at...

Catch this insider deal!

Check the scoreboard for unbelievable savings!

Cheer-leading deals!

Count on us for all your Super Footbowl needs!

Don't drop the ball on these bargains!

Don't fumble around, tackle the sale and save big!

Don't let the savings pass you by

Don't worry; we're planning a comeback of a sale!

Enjoy our Super Footbowl Special!

Every deal is a sure touchdown

Everybody's All-American Sale Event!

Fired up on both sides of the ball for amazing savings!

Football specials that score big

Football's Big Bucks Saving Event!

From the coach's corner

From the opening kickoff to the final whistle... terrific savings!

Get in the game... get the deal!

Get ready for a great gridiron weekend at...

Get ready to kick off a winning season of savings!

Get the Super Sunday blitz here!

Get your halftime favorites here!

Go home with the football and with the savings!

Gut-Check Time Sales Event!

Having some friends over for the big game?

Here's your bonus blitz for...

Hey football fans! We've got the deals for you!

How to score big! Sale event!

Hut, hut, hut! You're calling the signals on these great deals!

I thought a quarterback was a big sale at...

In Your Face Sale Event!

Inside the Uprights Sale Event!

It's a Quarterback Sneak Sale Event!

It's a Super Spectacular Savings Sunday Sale Event!

It's football season once again

It's not every day you can save a game with a super spectacular sale!

It's time again for that annual gridiron spectacular

Kick off the season with our sale!

Kickoff countdown

Kickoff specials!

Let the tailgating begin

Let's hear it for football weekends

Line up with the pros

No fumbles! No penalties! No chokes! Just unheard-of savings!!!

Now's a perfect time to tackle your...

Once you know the score, you'll buy it at...

Perfect for a couch potato rooter...

Pick up the ball and run...

Put me in coach, I'm ready to buy the deal!

Savings from end zone to end zone

Score big with everyday low prices

Score big with super savings!

Score huge savings with us

Show me the tailgate feast!

Sink your cleats into the savings!

Stick it in the end zone

Tackle a tailgate spread

Tackle big-time savings at...

Tackle the halftime bunch

Tackle these smashing deals!

Tackle your family's appetite with...

Take the touchdown challenge

The biggest football game of the year!

The blitz is on with fabulous bargains, super deals and terrific values!

The No. 1 pick is our deal!

The perfect way to kick back and watch the game

The run to pay dirt

The savings start when the ball is snapped!

The savings will keep the drive alive

There are no delay-of-game penalties during the sale!

There are no heads or tails during Bargain Days!

This sale event is not over until the whistle blows!

This sale is bigger than three football fields

Throwing a tailgate party?

Touchdown to exciting savings!

Upon further review... the sale of 50% off stands as advertised

Watch football here!

We can tackle just about any deal!

We keep the chains moving with outstanding savings!

We put the foot in football

We'll get you in the end zone!

We're going the extra yard with super sensational savings!

We're going to move the chains... to 30% to 50% off all merchandise!

We're hitting 'em hard with unheard-of values!

We're kicking off the most fabulous sale event ever!

We've got all your halftime favorites

We've got the lineup you need to win

We've got the play that will score the best deal every time!

We've leveled the playing field with good old-fashioned prices!

What a night for football, folks

What's going on in the football world?

Why punt when you can score with super savings?!

You block! You shove! You shout! What an explosive sale!

You just scored a touchdown with this deal!

You make the call on these deals!

You'll be inside the huddle with these deals!

You'll have your own halftime show with these goodies!

You're our #1 draft choice for...

129

$10 worth of free...

30-day risk-free trial

A bonanza of Sunday freebies!

A fantastic free offer!

A free gift certificate to every...

A free service that can help you!

A place with so much fun, even the admission is free!

Absolutely free. There's no obligation whatsoever!

Absolutely risk free!

Act now! Get it free!!!

Admission is free! Of course!

All free for you!

All that glitters isn't free

Always free, always amazing!

An amazing free offer!

And it's all free!

And it's not going to cost you one penny!

And they're absolutely free!

And your spouse is included free

And, by the way, free means just that

Anything that's marked free will be sold until it's all gone

Ask for free samples!

Be leery of people willing to give you something free

Best of all, it's free!

Better-than-risk-free!

Beware of the word free

Bonus... first 50 customers receive a free gift!

Breakfast free with this ad

Bring a friend along... Free!

Buy 1 lunch... 2nd is free!

Buy one of these... get these free!

Buy one! The second one is free!

Buy one, get one free!

Buy one... get two free!

Call toll free for your free copy

Cheap is good... free is better!

Check the bottom of your receipt for a free gift!

Coming: More free advice

Did we mention it's free?

Did you say free?

Don't miss these free offers!

Eat free! Sleep free! Shop free!

Everybody loves the word... free!

Everyone loves getting something for free

Everything is free after rebates

Everything is free today!

Fast free facts

Feel free to call us!

Feel free to forget this offer

Few things in life are free

First month free

First we lowered the price. Now we're throwing in the free stuff!

For a free demonstration, call...

For more stress-free options, call...

Free admission for kids under 10

Free after combined purchase with mail-in rebate

Free cigar cutter when you purchase a box of cigars

Free cookies with a cup of coffee

Free doesn't mean no-cost

Free entertainment inside!

Free family portrait

Free for 90 days

Free for new homeowners!

Free for the taking

Free gift with every purchase!

Free grub for your kids!

Free installation comes with the price!

Free introductory issue

Free is a very good price

Free is always the right price!

Free isn't a four-letter word

Free just for trying!

Free midweek admission

Free miles, don't pass it up!

Free next day delivery!

Free popcorn this weekend

Free postage and handling with purchase

Free reasons why you should...

Free roadside help

Free room and board

Free sale all month long!

Free samples: Please take one!

Free shipping and handling

Free today and tomorrow!

Free trade-in appraisals

Free trial offer!

Free with any purchase!

Free! Absolutely free!

Free, if you're registered now!

Free: A vacation in the sun!

Free... Please take a copy!

Free... Welcome back gift!

Freebie of the week!

Get a free upgrade

Get more free with bonus values!

Get one free!

Get Out of Jail Free card

Get your free stuff here!

Get your kicks for free at...

Hassle-free zone

How does a free meal sound?

How does free sound?

Hurry and send for free information!

If it's free... take it!

If we don't beat your best price...
it's free!

If you're not satisfied, it's free of charge!

If your birthday is in October, you
eat free!

Included at no extra cost

Is anything free, worth it?

Is there anything better than free food?

It's a risk-free deal!

It's almost like getting money free

It's always free!

It's automatic! It's extra! It's free!

It's better than free

It's easy and it's free!

It's free and it's fun

It's free for the asking!

It's free, baby!

It's free, just for trying now!

It's free. That's right, free!!!

It's fun, informative and free

It's headache-free

It's like getting the stamps free!

It's nice to offer a free service

It's on us!

It's simple, quick, and best of all
it's free!

It's yours to keep absolutely free!

Join us and get a free...

Just buy a ham, and you'll get a
turkey free!

Kids are free!

Free

Last call for free tickets!

Loads of free stuff for the whole family

Look inside for a free...

Lots of free things to do, see and enjoy

Make sure it's really free

Mention this ad and receive a free gift!

No cost for you!

No strings attached

No wonder it's popular... it's free!

Nothing can compete with free

Nothing is free... what's the catch?

Now we're throwing in the free stuff!

One free year!

Our free gift to you!

Park free for the holidays!

Pay for one... get two free!

Play for free!

Please send me free samples

Plus, get this extra item free

Receive a free gift card with every purchase

Register today for free admission!

Risk-free offer

Send for your free idea kit today!

Send in for this free offer!

Simple! Fast! Free!

So, how do you know when free really means free?

Some of the best things in life are free

Starter kit included free!

Take a look... it's free!

Take advantage of the freebies!

Take our free one-month trial offer

The fast, free, easy way to...

The hassle-free way

The price is right... it's free!

There's a free hamburger hiding in today's newspaper

They're all free!

This advice ain't free

This event is free!

This is a free offer with no obligation

This is your last free one!

Try it for 15 days, free!

Try it for yourself... risk-free!

Try me... I'm free!

Want to free up some time?

We have a simple creed... nothing is free!

We offer it to you free of charge

We put the emphasis on free

We'll do it for free!

We'll give it to you free... if you can find a better value at the same price or lower price!

We're fraud-free!

We've got a lot of freebies!

What's better than free?

What's even better is that it's free!

What's new? What's not? What's free?

When free isn't cheap!

Whenever we see "free", we immediately wonder: What's the catch?

Who can't resist a free dinner?

Who doesn't like getting something for free?

You get a free ride

You next trip is free!

You'll agree or get one free!

You'll love it or it's free!

You'll stay free and you'll eat free!

Your next one is free!

Yours free for the asking

Yours free if you respond right now!

Fun

72 hours of shopping fun!

A fun adventure for kids and parents

A fun-size offer you can refuse

A lot of good laughs! A lot of good food! A lot of good music!

A menagerie of fun

A new age of whimsical fun

A wonderful place filled with fun

Action-packed fun

Add up the fun, thrills and chills

All for fun and fun for all

All kinds of fun for all kinds of folks

All the fun at half the price!

All we sell is fun... that's it!

All you have to do is sit back and enjoy the fun

An evening of down-home fun

Barrels of fun... barrels of savings!

Belly-aching good times are in your future

Big savings on big fun!

Capture the fun!

Catch the spirit of electrifying fun!

Come early so you don't miss any of the fun

Come join the fun; you could be a winner!

Come on in for some great fun

Do more! See more! Have more fun!

Don't sit at home... go out and have fun

Experience something really fun

Eye-popping, toe-tapping good time

Fast, furious and fabulous fun

Fill your weekends with fun

Follow the sun to the fun!

From the Department of Fun

Fun for the ho-ho-whole family

Fun included in every box

Fun is our business!

Fun Time Bargain Days!

Fun, thrilling, exciting

Fun-believable deals!

Get a taste of the fun... get a taste of the savings!

Get dressed for fun with these fabulous...

Get in on the fun

Get on the fast track to fun

Get ready for fun because it's coming your way

Get ready for the fun stuff

Go where the fun takes you

Have a handful of fun at...

Have you had your fun today?

Have you tried our fun-o-licious snacks?

Here's what's new, cool and fun

Hip-shakin', foot-stompin' place

If it's fun you're after...

If you like fun, go for it!

Imagine the fun you'll have with these bargains!

It all adds up to fun... fabulous savings!

It's a hoot and more!

It's a sure bet for fun!

It's a ton of fun

It's all fun and games with these deals!

It's for fun-seekers of all ages!

It's fun to make a meal with super savings!

It's irresistible fun

Fun

It's whimsical and enjoyable

Join in on the fun!

Jump on the bandwagon headed toward sheer fun

Just add a dose of fun to create excitement

Just come and join in on the fun

Last chance to join the fun

Let the fun begin

Let us bring out the fun in you!

Let's go out there and have some fun

Make time for fun

More fabulous, free fun!

Never-ending fun and fascination

New, cool and fun

Now the real fun begins

Number one for fun, fun, fun!

Oh, what fun it is to...

Old-fashioned fun

Only an hour drive to fun time!

Open for fun!

Pile on the fun

Plan to be one of the fun people!

Pour on the fun with...

Put a little fun in your kids' lunchboxes with...

Put the fun in motion for...

Rock 'em, sock 'em good time at...

Shake up the party with fun!

She's more fun than a fortune cookie

Sizzling night for...

So easy! So joyful! So fun!

So sit back, relax, and enjoy the fun!

Stop in and grab a handful of fun!

Take a walk on the fun side

Take advantage of all the fun

The best place for fun

The fun starts here

The fun-filled world of fun

The only rule here is to have fun!

The savings are half the fun. Your satisfaction is all the fun!

There's more fun to come

This fun's for you!

This is the place to come and have fun

Time for the real fun to begin

Tremendous fun for the whole family

Twice as much fun

Wacky ways to have fun

Wanted: Wild West fun!

We are selling pleasure and fun

We bring out the kid in adults

We guarantee it'll be a fun time for all!

We serve plenty of fun, morning, noon and night

We sprinkle a little fun on every meal

We take our fun very seriously

We'll put the fun back in your life with these funtastic savings!

We'll show you some "wheel" fun

We're #1 for fun!

We've got all the fun stuff

What are you doing for fun?

When was the last time you had this much fun?

Where the fun never ends!

Where the good times roll

Why should the big guys have all the fun?

Win a fun night out on the town!

You'll have a fun time at the Sale Event of the Year!

You'll have plenty of fun with these savings!

You'll never run out of fun at...

Your quest for fun starts now!

Furniture

4th of July savings on all American classic furniture!

A chair fit for a king

A full line of ornate hand-carved French and Baroque furniture

A great variety of styles and a wide range of affordability

A home without a sofa is an uncomfortable place

A large selection of furniture for every room!

A wide selection of styles and categories

All customized furniture is on sale

American-made, solid pine furniture

An elegant solution for a studio apartment or a guest room

And speaking of exquisitely crafted furniture

Annual Floor Sample Sale!

Be sure the furniture you buy is styled to your needs

Beautifully crafted quality upholstery

Before you buy any furniture, do some research

Buying furniture is not an expensive proposition with us!

Buying used furniture is a great idea if you can't afford new

Comfort is another key factor in selecting furniture

Craftsmanship is the hallmark of our furniture collection

Designed for comfort and to withstand generations of wear

Distinctly different furniture

Entertainment center values

Every piece of furniture has been reduced from our everyday low prices!

Every piece of furniture is on sale!

Exciting home fashions and fantastic values await you at...

Explore our furniture store of possibilities

Express yourself with custom furniture

Famous name home furnishings throughout the store

Fine handcrafted furniture and accessories that endure the test of time

From traditional to modern, country to eclectic

Functional. Elegant. Comfortable.

Furnish your penthouse living room at...

Furniture for today that will definitely stand the test of time

Furniture is very big with us

Furniture that does it all

Furniture to grace your living room for decades

Furniture you can live with at a price you can afford

Gigantic home furnishings clearance sale

Hand-crafted in the USA

Heirloom quality at an incredible price

Home furnishings from around the world

Huge wall-to-wall carpeting sale!

If you don't have a comfortable chair, it's time to get one

Imagine what you can do with furniture like this

Incredibly comfortable!
Incredibly priced!

Invite a piece of American heritage into your home

Is your furniture older than you?

It's possible to fall in love with this couch

Furniture

It's quality, affordable and casual styling

Livable and affordable home furnishings at tremendous savings!

Looking for furniture?

Looks great and is a space-saver, too!

Luxury furniture and accessories to fit your lifestyle

Modern furniture in stock and ready to ship

No other store has furniture or accessories like...

Now during our Ultimate Showroom Sale!

One of the best investments you can make is a good quality sofa

Our Annual Furniture Spectacular Sale Event

Our daybed serves as a sofa by day, as a bed at night

Our furniture can last 500 years!

Our furniture clearance will change your house!

Our furniture comes ready to assemble and finish

Our home furnishings department is filled with great items

Our once-a-year savings on furniture you won't find anywhere!

Our rugs will fly forever! Our sale won't!

Outstanding styles, beautiful details at incredible values

Perfect for today's living!

Prices that are compatible with your taste and budget!

Proof that the artistry of hand craftsmanship can still be had

Put together a grouping that works for you

Quality furniture at competitive prices!

Resist bargains and buy the finest furniture you can afford!

Save during our annual furniture sale!

Shop here for wonderful home furnishings

So why can't you bring yourself to buy custom furniture?

Striking furniture to complement your décor

Take a magic carpet ride to an unbelievable carpet sale!

The best in design and craftsmanship and still able to offer you a tremendous value!

The chair to come home to at day's end

The finest furniture made today!

The right furniture at the best price!

There's a lot to like in leather furniture

There's a certain sense of pride in owning fine wood furniture

These pieces are easily rearranged for flexibility in setting up a room

Today only! All furniture up to 50% off!

Traditional styling and exceptional versatility

Truly livable furniture

Unbelievable selections... Unbelievable savings!

Unique home furnishings and decorative items at very affordable prices

We can grace your living room for decades

We Know Furniture... Sale Event!

We take the bore out of furniture shopping

What this couch needs is a couch potato

When comfort is your first consideration

Where all things come together, room after room

Where your money is well spent!

Why buy refurbished?

You needn't sacrifice style for quality

You'll find unique furnishings that make a room come to life

Gambling

A royal flush is in your future

A safe bet for gamblers

Beat the dealer... Beat the odds... Be a player!

Beginner's luck starts here!

Bet your bottom dollar

Betting the odds is fun!

Break the bank at...

Buy a lottery ticket. Somebody has to win!

C'mon big money!

Cashing in...

Catch the gaming excitement at...

Chances are, you're a winner!

Deal me in!

Deal yourself a winning hand at...

Don't be afraid to bet on a sure thing

Don't gamble... you're already a winner!

Don't pass the dice... Roll 'em and win!

Don't you just love a sure thing?

Establish a line of credit at our casino

Everybody wants a piece of the action

Everybody wins!

Everyone comes out a winner at...

For high rollers only!

Games of chance

Get a hunch... bet a bunch

Get ready to play

Go for broke

Go home a winner

Go with a sure thing

Happy gambling

Have you tried your luck lately?

Here's how to stake your claim

Here's how you can be a player

Here's one winning combination... that really beats the rest

Here's your chance to clean up

Home of the best odds

How to beat blackjack

How to beat the odds

How to clean up on craps

How to score at slots

I beat the odds!

I'll bet you a dollar

If you're feeling lucky, you're at the right table!

It all adds up to one exciting time!

It pays to play!

It sure beats working

It's a free weekend, if you can hold your own

It's a great time to roll the dice!

It's a rock and roll of the dice

It's a sure bet that we have a fun time for you

It's all in the cards!

It's easy to play and win!

Know when to hold 'em, know when to fold 'em

Legalized gambling here!

Let it ride... Baby... I'm hot

Let the sweet times roll

Like to gamble?

Looking to hit the jackpot?

May the dice roll in your favor

May the odds be with you

Name your game

Need a sure bet?

Gambling

OK, hit me... hit me again

Only for high rollers

Place your bets at our casino

Pretty good odds for all seniors

Roll the bones, make it happen

Roll the dice with the odds in your favor

Shoot craps! Win a...

Sky's the limit for gamblers

Take a seat at our blackjack table

Take a spin on the roulette wheel

Talk about making out like a bandit!

The best place to gamble is at...

The best poker deal... anywhere!

The big jackpot is waiting for you!

The next jackpot is just a silver dollar away

The nicest place to throw away your money

The roll of the dice! The spin of the wheel! The ringing of the slots!

The sky's the limit

There is still plenty of cash to win

Three of a kind and they're all aces

Today... is your lucky day!

Walking away a winner

Wanna bet? Wanna play? Wanna win?

We bet you'll come away a winner

We have the loosest slots and the best odds

We put the jack in the winning jackpots

We welcome all big-time players

We'll deal you a winning hand

We'll roll out the dice for your grand entrance

We're here for the gamblers to enjoy

We're ready to deal your ace in the hole

We're serious about playing poker

We've got enough games to keep you going strong

We've got slots that leave you smiling!

What have you got to lose?

When you're hot, you're hot!

Where jackpots really, really flow

Where players get a better deal

Where she'll stop, nobody knows

Where the games never end

Where the roulette wheel spins

Why would anyone go to Las Vegas to gamble?

Win a fruit salad when you come up with a cherry, a lemon and an orange

Win big at your favorite casino

Win what you spend at...

Winners wanted!

With odds like this, you can't lose

Work all day, play at night

You can afford the odds; it's a piece of the action

You can hear the coins drop

You decide if you like the odds

You just hit the jackpot! Congratulations!

You like to gamble?

You may think the odds are against you

You roll the dice and you'll win!

You will be rolling in the dough

You wouldn't think a few hours could be so exciting!

You'll feel like you've hit the jackpot

You'll make out like a bandit at...

You'll win big!!!

You're a sure bet to have an exciting time!

You're a winner at...

You're always dealt a winning hand at...

You're our ace in the hole

You're the luckiest draw in the deck

Games

A challenging game that's been enchanting kids for generations

A fun way to get brain cells moving

A game of wit and gamesmanship

A game to keep kids busy for hours

A quick game of tag

A terrific selection for game freaks and game junkies

A wondrous selection of games that delight the child in us all!

All fast-action games on sale!

All games should be like this... sensational savings!

All your favorite games on sale!

Amazing savings on fun-time games!

An exciting game for all ages!

Are you game for big savings?

Backyard games for the family

Bargains that won't cost you the game!

Big deals in games!

Big savings on popular games for the whole family!

Car bingo can keep children occupied for hours

Children learn, live and grow through games

Crazy over fighting and shooting games

Each time you play it's a brand new game

Everyone loves a dart game

Fast-action games for explosive fun!

For all game junkies

For the biggest selection of kid-friendly games...

From the Fun and Games Department

From top to bottom, this game is a winner

Fun and games the whole family will enjoy

Fun and Games... Savings Event!

Games and accessories you'll love!

Games for all ages... anytime savings!

Games for the 10-and-over crowd

Games from bygone eras

Games fueled by your imagination

Games kids really want

Games that are educational and fun!

Games that help kids develop creativity and hand-eye coordination

Games that offer educational value!

Games that youngsters can't resist

Games to take on the road

Games, games and more games

Gaming fun for everyone

Get the game with exciting savings!

Get the game... today!

Give the gift of gamin'

Great games available for kids of all ages

Great games... great prizes!

Guaranteed to provide hours of amusement

Hard-to-resist savings on all video games!

Hot savings on all sizzling table games!

Hottest video games... on sale!!!

Hours of enjoyable, frustrating fun

Hours of imaginative play

How about a rousing game of...

Is your brain up to the challenge?

It all adds up to one fun game

It's a game within a game

It's a great kids' game!

139

Games

It's harder than you think

It's just one great game

It's not important whether you win or lose, but where you buy the hottest games!

Let us play! Let us play! Let's play!!!

Looking for exciting new games?

Now here's a game you can sink your teeth into

Now how can you not love a game like this?

Our wildest game yet

Play it smart with outstanding savings on all computer games!

Playing the game is so riveting

Playtime fun with cool games

Poor man's games at bargain prices!

Save on every game and toy!

Save on games for the whole family!

Savings by the bundle on gaming excitement!

Super savings on all hot games!

The best board games ever!

The best game you'll ever play, hands down!

The coolest game on the planet

The game that challenges the way you think

The game that really lives up to its name

The game that takes their imagination to the max

The game you always wanted as a kid

The greatest games in the world come from...

The headquarters for all your superheroes

The hottest games are all on sale!

The most challenging game ever invented

The most stimulating thing you've ever seen

The only game you have to play is ours

The perfect game for fun-loving kids

These games ain't over 'til they're over

This is the greatest game in the world

Today is Family Fun Games Night!

Two Can Play the Game... Sales Event!

Two games in one, for double the fun

Unbelievable savings for all game freaks!

Unreal video game savings!

We challenge you to pass up these bargains!

We don't sell games that promote violence!

We have the newest games in town!

We'll baffle you with the savings!

We're not playing games with the savings!

We're slashing prices on all violent computer and video games!

We've got all the hot games

We've got the games Santa forgot!

We've got the games that challenge your skills

We've got the latest games in town!

We've got your game

What a fantastic cool game!

What a great game for kids!

You don't have to play games with our prices!

You don't need to buy a vowel for amazing game values!

You Name The Game... Savings Event!

You wouldn't think a game designed for kids could be so much fun

You'll flip over our huge selection of games

You'll love the savings! You'll love the games!

You'll love this best-selling game!

You've never seen a game like this

Your fun source for all games and toys!

Gifts

A gift for all seasons. A gift for all reasons

A gift of beauty. A gift of choice. A gift of devotion.

A gift that speaks of love

A gift that will leave a lasting impression

A great gift to commemorate that special day

A memorable gift for just about anyone for any occasion

An all-time favorite holiday gift

Attention all gift givers...

Beautiful gifts at great prices!

Business gift-giving is our specialty

Can't decide what to get that special someone on your holiday gift list?

Choosing a gift should be a pleasure

Claim your gift certificate now!

Clueless about choosing a gift?

Complete your gift-giving list at...

Delicious gifts at sweet savings!

Don't forget to put yourself on your gift list

Easy gifts for the most difficult names on your list

E-gifts for the techs

Exceptional gifts make great impressions

Exclusive gifts for exclusive people

Express yourself through the gift you give

Feel-good prices for feel-good gifts!

Finding cool gifts easy

For the man who thought he had everything

For those special occasions or just because

Free gift card for every shopper!

Gift certificates available

Gift savings throughout the store!

Gifts at great savings!

Gifts for everyone you love

Gifts for the ultimate procrastinators

Gifts from every corner of the world

Gifts guaranteed to please!

Gifts mom will treasure

Gifts of good taste! Gifts of gratitude! Gifts of joy!

Gifts that are memory-makers

Gifts that are on your list

Gifts that are sure to delight her

Gifts that gesture more than friendship

Gifts that stimulate the mind and stir the imagination

Gifts that will keep you out of the doghouse

Gifts that will make her go, "Hmmm"

Gifts that will make you a hero

Gifts they will love to unwrap

Gifts with character, gifts with charm, gifts with memories

Gifts with lots of choices at...

Gifts you can afford! Gifts you gotta have! Gifts you'll absolutely love!

Give the gift that makes everyone smile

Giving a gift that makes dreams come true

Great gift givin' doesn't have to cost you a fortune

Great gift ideas ready for wrapping

Great gift-giving ideas

Great gifts galore

Here's a gift that will really jingle your bells

Holiday gift ideas for the family

Gifts

Holiday memories are made with memorable gifts

Hot gifts people want

How to satisfy everyone on your list with the perfect gift

Huge hits! Great prices! Perfect gifts!

If it's on your gift list, we've got it

It's gift-giving time!

It's the thought that counts

It's who it's for, not what it's for

Just add a bow

Last-minute gift ideas

Looking for a gift everybody will love

Memorable gift with notable savings!

No one will ever say, "Gee... another gift!"

Not all Christmas gifts arrive by reindeer

One gift short for the holidays?

One-of-a-kind holiday gifts

Outstanding gifts make an ordinary occasion a memorable event

Please give a gift to a kid who doesn't have much

Put a gift certificate under the tree

Relaxing gift ideas... priced right!

Simply pick your favorite gifts from our...

Small gifts that make big impressions

Smart family gifts

So many tempting gifts to choose from

Some gifts are best when they have a surprise inside

Sound holiday gift ideas

Special memories start with exciting gifts

Stop searching for the perfect gift

Straight from Santa's workshop... Great holiday gift giving

Stumped on what to give?

Sweet treats for the angels on your gift list

Take a look at our pout-proof gifts!

The gift that only you can give

The gift to let that someone know you care

The gift you'll want to give

The ideal gift for everyone on your list

The perfect gift at just the right price!

The perfect gift without all the fuss

The ultimate housewarming gift

These are absolutely-positively-have-to-have gifts

Think of it as the ultimate gag bag gift

Thinking about a special gift?

This gift will deserve a thank you!

This holiday season... Give the gift of health

This is one gift that won't be returned

We have the finest gift all wrapped up for you

We have the gifts that are on every wish list

We invite you to experience the excitement of gift-giving

We're your gift destination

We're your gift store

We've made gift-giving easy

What in the world do you give someone who has everything?

When in doubt, buy gift certificates

When the occasion calls for a special gift

When you want to send a truly extravagant gift...

Where the best gifts come from

Whether for yourself or for someone on your holiday list

Worth giving... Worth getting

You'll be proud to give these gifts

Your holiday gift guide

Golf

2 for 1 green fee!

4 days! 4 golfers! 4 signature courses!

A Ball, a Tee, a Driver Sale!

A golf sale that isn't over until it's over

A Once-In-A-Lifetime
Hole-In-One Sale Event!

A sale for the golfer who can't get
enough of the game

A sale that will challenge your game

A sale that will make you a better golfer

A sale that's par for the course

Add this to your foursome

Add Zing to Your Swing Sale Event!

Attention: Golf addicts!

Beat the Pro Sale Event!

Call early for preferred tee times

Can one million duffers be wrong?

Can't Get Enough of Golf Sale Event!

Closest to the pin wins a...

Die-Hard Duffer Sale Event!

Do you complement your set of golf clubs?

Don't leave home without your golf clubs

Don't Tee Me Off Sale Event!

Drive your golf buddies crazy with
these savings

Essential ingredients for a daily dose
of golf

Everybody wants to save a few strokes
and a few bucks

Everyone's crazy about our golf sale!

Exceptional golf courses! Exceptional
hospitality! Exceptional value!

Featuring lush greens entwined
by carefully preserved desert terrain

For All Link Nuts Only Sale Event!

For people who like to golf but don't
take it too seriously

For the golfer who can never get enough
of the game

For your convenience we have included
golf carts in our fees

Fore... Get It Sale Event!

Foursome specials

Get a grip on these exciting savings

Get a hole-in-one deal at...

Get set to tee off on a great sale event!

Give golf a try

Golf comes to life with below par savings

Golf fans, don't despair, this sale is
for you!

Golf is still a great bargain

Golf packages with the following courses:

Golf widows, it's time to unite at...

Golf, golf and more golf deals

Grab your clubs and come out to
swing at...

Grip It and Rip It Sale Event!

Happy-Go-Lucky Golfer Sale!

Have clubs, will travel

Hey duffers, we've got a great sale
for you!

Hey... Golf Fans!

Hit a perfect drive every time with...

Hit the fairways in flying colors

Hit the sweet spot with sweet savings

Hole-In-One Sweepstakes

How to enjoy the game you love

How to knock 10 strokes off your game
without really trying

How to shoot under par at the...

Golf

I'd Rather Be Golfing Sale Event!

Improve your image on the green with our golf apparel clearance sale!

It's a gimme deal!

It's easy to plan a golf getaway

It's more than a golf sale!

It's never too early to begin thinking about golf season

It's prairie-style golfing at its best

It's time to dust off those putters

It's time to tee 'em up

It's worth the greens fee

Just a chip shot away from big savings

Just Smack the Ball Sale Event!

Keep this sale under your golf hat

Lost golf balls not included

Maybe it's time for a lesson, huh?

Mulligan sale! Buy one, get one free!

No mulligans... during our closeout sale!

One lucky golfer will win 9 rounds of golf

Our golf sale is bigger than your golf sale!

Pick a Bag, Pick a Club Sale Event!

Play golf at any of these exceptional value area courses

Play where champions play

Ready to tee it up?

Save some green before you get to the green

Savings for the golfer who doesn't take himself too seriously

Shave strokes off your game

Some golf rules to live by...

Spend a little on a retriever and save a lot on golf balls

Stop in for a round after 18 holes

Summer Golf Clearance Sale!

Take a cold one with you!

Take a swing at golf

Take your best shot at the savings

Tee it up with the pros

Tee off early to get the best prices

Tee-Time Early Bird Sale!

The best golf value

The course that tests both your skill and imagination

The Grand Slam Golf Sale!

The grass isn't greener, but the golf is great

The total golf experience

The ultimate course!
The ultimate challenge!

There are no penalty strokes with these savings

This is golf at its purest, surrounded by nature at its finest

Tips from an old pro

Turn the Green Into Gold Sale!

We Have Your Golf Game in the Bag Savings Event!

We'd like to tee off our best customers

Weekend Hacker Super Spectacular Sale!

Welcome to the pro shop

When every stroke counts and when every dollar you save counts

Where excellence is par for the course

Why settle for par?

Wide open fairways and undulating greens

Win free golf!

Win over 36 rounds of golf

Win the Longest Drive Contest and you'll be playing golf the rest of the season... free!

You have the ultimate combination for a spectacular golf vacation

You'll even shave a few strokes off your game with these savings

Graduation

A bright future lies ahead for you

A great day for the graduates

A piece of paper that took 16 years
to acquire

A sale celebration for this year's graduate!

A world is awaiting

Advice for grads

After graduation, you can start saving

And, to all our graduates, we wish you
every success in your future endeavors

Are you ready to go out and conquer
the world?

Are you ready? It's cap-and-gown
gift-giving time!

Awesome gift savings for this
year's graduates!

Bursting your buttons

Capture the memory with a...

Cause for applause

Celebrating our students'
accomplishments

Clueless about choosing a graduation
gift for your favorite grad?

Congrats on your accomplishments

Congratulations and best wishes for a
bright future

Congratulations on all your
academic achievements

Congratulations to the graduate

Congratulations, little grad

Congratulations, you have made us all
very proud of you!

Congratulations, you've joined the
millions who've already graduated

Congratulations... This is a very
special day!

Cool gifts to give to cool graduates

Excellent graduation gifts at
exceptional prices

Exceptional gifts for the most important
moment of their life

Extraordinary gift-giving ideas for
your graduate!

For every graduate, there is a future

From diapers to degrees

Get a little something extra for
the graduate

Get ready to celebrate the completion of
an education...

Gifts for a day to remember

Gifts that are sure to delight
any graduate!

Gifts to cap off that memorable day!

Give him or her a graduation gift
with memories

Give your grad a gift with plenty
of gusto

Give your graduate the gift they
really want!

Giving the perfect graduation gift
ain't easy

Go on, Grads... Strike it Rich!

Good luck to our graduates

Graduation day! It's that special moment!

Graduation gifts at savings that will
make them proud!

Graduation gifts that make a
big impression

Graduation gifts worth giving... worth
getting... on sale now!

Graduation gifts you can afford.
Graduation gifts they'll absolutely love!

Graduation is a time to look forward
and a time to look back

Graduation memories are made with
memorable gifts

Graduation

Graduation Party Headquarters

Graduation time is memorable
gift-giving time

Graduations call for special,
memorable gifts

Hats off to our college grads

Here's to the start of something wonderful

Hey, Pop! Look at me now!

Honor your graduate...

Hooray graduate

I'm going to celebrate my graduation
with my degree

I'm very proud of my son

"I've Made It" Graduation Day
Sales Event!

It feels pretty good knowing you did it

It's a new day!

It's cap-and-gown time

It's graduation gift-giving time!

It's time to reap the rewards

It's worth hooting about

It's your time to shine with a gift of time

Just what a high-school kid wants for
his graduation

Let us do the honors at your celebration

Let us point you in the right direction

Looking ahead to a bright future

Making the grade for new graduates

Memorable gifts for just about
any graduate!

Memories of a lifetime

Not sure what to get the grad?

Notable savings on all memorable
graduation gifts

On sale now! The best gifts that wish
them the best

One of the most important moments of
your life

Onward and upward

Our little girl is a graduate

Outstanding gifts to commemorate that
special day

Pomp and circumstance...
proud and happy

Send a proud graduate packing

Smart graduation gift ideas

Solve your graduate gift-giving
problems here!

Stumped on what to give your graduate?

Tack this to the graduate's door

The best four years of your life are
not over

The best years are yet to come

The big day... Graduation Day!

The commencement of real life

The dream is now realized

The grad is on the move...
watch out world!

The graduation festivities

The joys of graduation day

The perfect graduation gift at just the
right price

The pomp and circumstance
of graduation

The Tassel is Worth the Hassle
Sales Event!

They wore their caps and gowns proudly

They've earned it!

This is a proud day

Tradition, excellence and pride
never graduate

We commend the parents and families of
all graduates

We're your graduation
party headquarters

We've made graduation gift-giving easy!

Ya done splendid!

You'll be proud to give a graduation
gift from...

Grand Opening

A grand opening celebration that's really grand

A grand opening fit for a king

A grand opening is happening in your neighborhood

A grand opening that is truly grand

A grand opening that will knock you off your feet

A grand opening that's right down to the last detail

A grand opening to get fired-up about

A grand opening too great to wait for

A grand opening... and a grand opportunity for...

A grand opening... and grand values!

A grand, grand, grand opening

A special grand opening

A Super Duper Grand Opening!

A truly unforgettable grand opening

A whale of a grand opening

Announcing the grand opening of our new...

Are you a sucker for grand openings?

As we open our doors for our grand opening...

Be our guest to our special Grand Opening Sale!

Big, fun-filled grand opening party

Bring your family and join us at an awesome Grand Opening Party

Celebrate our grand opening at our new location

Celebrate our grand opening in style

Celebrate the opening of our new store

Check out our grand opening

Click here! Grand Opening!

Closed for the grand opening

Come and be a part of the largest event of the year. Our Super Grand Opening!

Come celebrate our sensational grand opening

Come celebrate the grand opening of...

Don't just sit there... come on over to a unique grand opening

Don't just take our word for it... it's a Real Grand Opening

Don't miss the official grand opening

Everybody is welcome to the Grand Pre-Opening Sale

Everything is on sale for our grand opening

Exclusive grand opening for you

Eye-opening savings! Grand Opening Excitement!!!

Fabulous grand opening that touches your heart

Follow the crowd to our explosive grand opening

Get a great deal during our outrageous grand opening

Get to know our friendly staff during our grand opening

Giant Grand Opening Sale!

Grand assortments, grand values, all at our grand opening

Grand opening bonus coupons

Grand Opening Celebration Contest!

Grand opening event on now!

Grand Opening Extravaganza

Grand opening for special customers

Grand opening is happening today!

Grand Opening Jamboree!

Grand opening of homes for the way you want to live

Grand Opening Sale-bration!

Grand Opening

Grand opening special pricing!

Grand Opening Super Sale!

Grand Opening Sweepstakes!

Grand Re-Opening Celebration!

Have you heard? We're having a grand opening!

Help us cut the ribbon... today!

Help us get our grand opening on the road

Here's a grand opening that can save you big bucks

Here's your chance to be part of our grand opening

Here's your personal invitation to our Grand Opening Celebration!

Hold on for a fantastic grand opening

In case you missed our first opening, we're having another one and you're invited this time

Join our open house celebration

Join us for our outstanding grand opening

Look inside for over $50 in grand opening savings!

Make a grand entrance at our grand opening

Markdowns at grand opening prices!

No Purchase Necessary Grand Opening

Open For Business Grand Opening!

Opening Day Celebration Sale!

Our grand opening is not over 'till we say it is

Our grand opening isn't just big! It's monstrous!

Our grand opening will blow your mind

Our Opening Night Grand Opening!

Pre-Grand Opening Specials!

Smile when you say... it's a grand opening!

Spectacular Grand Opening Sale!

Take me out to the grand opening

Thank you for stopping by our grand opening

The biggest and the best grand opening ever

The celebration starts this weekend

The gala opening is set for...

The Grand Opening Bash of the Year!

The Grand Opening of Grand Openings

The grand opening that stands out from all others

The Grand, Grand, Grand Opening Sales Event!

The Great Grand Opening Event is going on now!

The greatest grand opening spectacle in history

They don't have grand openings like this anymore

This grand opening is pure gold

This is the grand opening you've been waiting for

Time to celebrate our grand opening with you

Visit our grand opening

We are proud to announce our awesome grand opening!

We're celebrating the grand opening of our...

We're having an unbelievable open house and you're welcome!

We're throwing a grand opening celebration

We're turning on the charm at our grand opening

Welcome to a colossal grand opening event!

You are invited to a personal Pre-Grand Opening Night

You just might find more than you bargained for... grand opening

You'll love our opening act!

You're cordially invited to attend our grand opening

A cordial invitation is extended to all

A very special invitation just for you!

All I do is greet people

By special invitation only

Come celebrate with us

From our family to your family...

Greetings from party central

Greetings from the top

Greetings straight from the heart

I sincerely hope you can join us to make the event a great success

If you're reading this, you're invited

It gives me great pleasure, on behalf of...

It is an invitation we certainly hope you will accept

It is with deep gratitude that we...

It is with great pride and excitement that...

It would be an honor and a thrill to be...

It's by invitation only, and the food's great!

It's nice to be appreciated

Looking forward to meeting you personally

May God bless you and be good to you

May we have the pleasure of your company?

May your gifts be love, joy and good health

Now accepting all invitations

Now here is a man who needs no introduction

Our warmest wishes for a wonderful...

Please be our guest

Please bring this invitation with you

Please bring your sense of wonder

Please join us... refreshments will be served

Please mark your calendar

Please, let us re-introduce ourselves

Regrets only

Thank you in advance for your kindness

The favor of a reply is requested

The most polite and appreciative greeting you'll get all day

The time is long overdue, so let's get together

This invitation just says party

Treat yourself like a guest

We are extremely excited to inform you of...

We are pleased to announce...

We are very fortunate and honored to...

We bid you good cheer

We hope you'll be able to join us, and we look forward to your participation

We hope you'll take advantage of this opportunity soon

We truly appreciate the pleasure of your company

We want you to be our guest

We'll be thrilled to host your...

We're looking forward to meeting you

We're so pleased that you're coming to visit us

Won't you join us?

Y'all ready to be our guest at...

You are cordially invited

You are invited to a unique, wild, fun-filled evening

You're cordially invited

Your attendance is requested

100% guarantee will always be our commitment to you

100% satisfaction guarantee with full refund privileges

90-day no-risk guarantee

A guarantee that it will be good forever

A guarantee that we may be worthy of your high esteem

A guarantee you can count on

A lifetime guarantee

A refund of full purchase price of the merchandise. Guaranteed!

A warranty that lasts to the finish

All backed by a lifetime warranty

America's best guarantee

An ironclad money-back guarantee

Any reason, any time... you may return it for a prompt refund or exchange

Better than a money-back guarantee

Certificate of authenticity and one-year money-back guarantee

Complete satisfaction or your money back

Comprehensive, lifetime guarantee

Don't forget... our guarantee is unconditional

Double-your-money-back guarantee

Every item is guaranteed unconditionally for its normal life under standard use

Every item, everyday, is 100% guaranteed... no questions asked!

Everything we sell is guaranteed

Everything you buy comes with a money-back guarantee

For over 150 years, we have offered the strongest guarantee in the business

Full money-back guarantee, not a pro-rated portion

Guarantee of a lifetime

Guaranteed 100%! No questions! No exceptions!

Guaranteed by us without reservation

Guaranteed for as long as you think it should be

Guaranteed to last as long as you think it should

I personally guarantee your 100% satisfaction

If for any reason you are not completely satisfied, simply return it for a refund

If it's not right for you, we will gladly exchange it or issue a refund

If you are not completely satisfied, we'll assist you with a prompt exchange, refund, or credit

If you're not happy, we're not happy... that's our guarantee

It's a guarantee... and you can bank on it

It's as simple and ironclad a guarantee as you'll find

It's guaranteed, no matter what

It's simple: If you're not satisfied we will refund your money. No exceptions

Money-back satisfaction guarantee

No cost! No obligation! Guaranteed!!!

No excuses. No fine print. If you are ever disappointed in any item, please return it

No questions, no hassles. That's our guarantee

No risk, double-money-back guarantee

Nobody can beat our guarantee

Nobody has ever used our lifetime guarantee

No-fault lifetime warrantee

Not completely satisfied? Return it for a refund or exchange!

Our exclusive guarantee means what it says

Our guarantee helps you buy with ease of mind

Our guarantee is backed by 30 years of dependable personal service

Our guarantee is forever

Our guarantee is our creed

Our guarantee is straightforward and the very best in the industry

Our name is our guarantee and promise

Our no-nonsense guarantee

Our non-risk guarantee protects you for a full year

Our pledge to you: We guarantee your satisfaction

Our products are guaranteed to give 100% satisfaction in every way

Our rest-easy guarantee

Our service is guaranteed for a lifetime

Simple no-nonsense guarantee

So good it's guaranteed for a lifetime

Take advantage of our exceptional guarantee

That's a guarantee you can't get from anybody else

The guarantee to blow your mind

There is no 'small print' in our guarantee

There is no way you can lose a penny with our guarantee

There's no time limit to our guarantee, so you take absolutely no risk

Trust our guarantee

Unconditional guarantee of total satisfaction

We absolutely, unequivocally, positively guarantee our...

We accept unused items for a full refund, credit or exchange

We guarantee it!

We guarantee our quality unconditionally

We honor all other guarantees

We never guarantee anything

We offer a simple guarantee. You'll be 100 percent satisfied with your...

We offer an incredible guarantee

We offer an unconditional guarantee on every item we sell

We offer the best warranty... whether you need it or not

We promise 100% guaranteed

We strive to live up to our guarantee everyday

We take great pride in our reputation for quality and excellent value

We want you to be completely satisfied, so remember... it's guaranteed

We will cheerfully exchange or substitute the item, or refund your money

We will promptly exchange it or issue a refund, whichever you prefer

We won't even raise an eyebrow

We'll assist you with a prompt exchange, refund or credit. No sale is final!

We'll even guarantee the weather

We'll gladly make an exchange or refund at anytime for any reason

We'll send you a full refund for the entire amount you paid

We're proud of the products we sell, and we back them unconditionally

You must be satisfied with your purchase or return it for a full refund. No questions asked!

Your complete satisfaction is always guaranteed. No questions asked!

Your no-risk 100% money back guarantee

Your satisfaction isn't an option... it's guaranteed!

Your total satisfaction is always guaranteed

10% off anything black or orange through Halloween!

3-Days Of Madness Sale Event!

A frightfully good deal!

A Halloween sale worth screaming about!

A Halloween spooktacular!

A haunting sale... Haunting savings! Haunting values!

A juicy, terror-filled Halloween... Guaranteed!

A monster-mash bash

A night of diabolical terror

A scream of ghoulish delights

A spine-tingling deal

A treat so cool it's scary

A-haunting we will go

All jacked up for Halloween

And to all a good bite

Are you a ghost hunter or a ghost watcher?

As the final doorbell has been rung on another Halloween...

Batty-low prices!

Be my pumpkin?

Be prepared to be scared

Be safe... Be seen on Halloween

Beware of low-ball pricing

Beware; you're in for a Halloween scare

Bewitching bargains! Bewitching buys! Bewitching savings!

Bone-chillers! Spine-tinglers! Goosebumps!

Boo bucks, just like cash

Boo-dacious bargains!!! Boo-tiful buys!!!

Calling all old ghosts and young goblins

Cash prizes for the best costumes!

Catch the evil spirit of Halloween at...

Check out these hair-raising haunts for a safe Halloween

Check out these Halloween-Octoberfest happenings

Come in, if you dare, to the Most Frightful Sale Event!

Come scare yourself up a great deal!

Come to our store and carve out some savings!

Count Stanley says... Our prices won't take a bite out of your pocketbook

Devilish deals!

Don't be scared! Get a handle on Halloween with very scary prices

Don't be tricked... Treat yourself to the...

Don't forget the candy or it could come back to haunt you

Don't miss the free Halloween offer inside

Don't miss the scare of your life at...

Don't run out of candy on Halloween

Dressed to thrill

Enjoy a day at our annual Scarecrowfest

Enter At Your Own Risk... Sale Event!

Experience the height of freight

Eye-popping tricks and treats

Fill your bag with...

Fill your Halloween with treats and surprises at...

For a hauntingly delicious Halloween dessert

For a truly frightening experience...

For goblins of all ages

For Halloween enthusiasts

For your haunting pleasure

Free pumpkin giveaway!

Frightening fun all week long

Frightening savings for your Halloween party!

Fright-night fashions

Full moon, witches and magical Halloween savings!

Get into the spooky spirit of...

Get ready for Halloween early!

Get ready to party at our Halloween festival... A real treat!

Get your picture taken with the ghost of Halloween

Ghostly galas for grown-ups

Ghostly sweet deals!

Ghosts are included in the purchase price!

Ghosts aren't the only creatures stirring things up this time of year

Ghoulish fun and games

Give your little monsters some wholesome Halloween fun

Go a little crazy this Halloween

Go ahead and scream... we do!

Goblin alert, stock up!

Goblin' up the savings!

Grab all the horror you want... it's free!

Hair-raising values!

Halloween can be a real nightmare if you don't look the part

Halloween expires frightfully soon

Halloween fun starts here

Halloween Hollow Festival of Savings!

Halloween madness, no tricks but plenty of savings!

Halloween spectacular here, prices so low... they even scare us!

Halloween Spooktacular Sale Event!

Halloween starts at our front door

Halloween treats for candy-happy kids and saving-wise grownups

Halloween trick-or-treat savings!

Halloween... a treat for the kids

Halloweenies do your thing

Happy Halloween specials!

Haunted house sale!

Haunting for a good time?

Have a cautious and happy Halloween!

Have a ghostly evening with us!

Have a great spooky Halloween

Have a monstrous, tricky, wicked, frightening, spellbinding Halloween!

Have you decided what to be for Halloween?

Hayride of horror

Here's an invitation you can't resist... the most wicked Halloween costume party... ever!!!

Here's wishing all kids a safe and successful Halloween

Hey, be scareful out there!

Horrors... A hoedown all weekend

How many bats, vampires, witches and ghosts can you find?

How you can become a vampire

Howling great deals!

Imagine... your worst nightmare, then come...

In the mood for a quick scare?

Is the thought of facing trick-or-treaters terrifying you?

It will send you away screaming for more!

It's a foot-stompin' Halloween party!

It's A Happy Haunts Halloween Festival

It's a monster of a sale!

It's a treat to shop at...

It's B-A-A-A-A-CK! The ultimate Halloween experience!!!

It's beginning to look a lot like Halloween

It's fun... It's free... It's scare-iffic!!!

It's Halloween and we're here to scare you!

It's no trick... we're treating you!

153

Halloween

It's pumpkin giveaway time!

It's sale-o-ween at the mall-o-ween!

It's scary how much fun stuff we have for Halloween!

It's scary how much you save

It's time to get those customers in order

Join the Goblin Jamboree this Halloween!

Join us for a ghoulishly good time

Join us for an eerie tale or two of terror

Looking for a little after-midnight delight on Halloween?

Looking to do a little ghost hunting of your own?

Make your reservation for a frightfully delicious Halloween dinner

Monster Mash Sales Bash!

Monstrous savings on Halloween treats!

Mummies love our prices!

No tricks, just savings!

No tricks… Treat yourself to savings!

Octoberfest specials!

Our prices are so low, it's scary!

Our prices won't scare you!

Our sale will haunt you!

Sales are a real howl!

Save on Halloween's best treats!

Savings are un-boo-lieveable!

Savings to scream about!

Scare up some real bargains at…

Spellbinding savings during our Halloween fright nights!

Spellbinding savings on a haunting selection of Halloween customs, decorations and treats!

Spine-tingling… Scare-raising… Outrageously frightening!

Spooktacular family fun!

Spooktacular specials… Ghoulish buys!

Spooky Halloween favorites at the sale of a lifetime!

Spooky savings… Haunting values!

The Halloween Fantasy Extravaganza!

The most bone-chilling sale you've seen in a decade!

The place to be on Halloween night!

The savings are our treat!

The store for the best trick and treats in town

The treat is in the price

There's no trick to saving money at…

This Halloween, the treat is on us

Time to go buy a pumpkin

Treat yourself to some Halloween bargains!

Trick-or-treat savings from…

Un-boo-lievable Halloween savings!

We have thrillingly spooktacular deals on costumes!

We won't bury you with high prices like the other stores!

We'll make you a deal so scary, it's scary!

We'll treat you to extra savings!

We're having a Halloween weekend non-stop party!

We're selling goose bumps by the pound!

We're your Halloween headquarters

We've created monster savings!

We've scared up some savings!

Who knows what lurks on the shelves of our store?

Witch store gives you the best deal?

You won't be spooked by these tricky prices!

You wouldn't want to be caught dead in our costumes

You'll be shocked to see all the low Halloween prices!

You'll get spine-tingling savings to scream about!

Happy

A cheerful heart is good medicine

A happy ending to a happy year

A happy person is a productive person

A place where people are happy

A Smiling, Happy-Go-Lucky Sale Event!

A whirlwind of happy deals!

Am I in heaven, or what?

And they all lived happily ever after

Are you a happy camper?

Are you happy or satisfied?

Be happy now!

Be Happy... Sale Event!

Being happy is the best thing you can do for your health

Boy, you just can't make some people happy

C'mon, Get Happy... Sale Event!

Cheered! Hooted! Hollered!

Cherish the happy bargain days!

Color us happy... color me happy!

Come, let us talk about happy things

Confident! Satisfied! Happy!

Do what makes you happy

Everybody is deliriously happy

Fat, dumb and happy deals!

Find work that makes you happy

Footloose and Fancy-Free Sale Event!

For a happy life

For those who can't get enough of a good thing

Get happy! Be happy! Stay happy!

Happiness is conducive to good living

Happy couples, included

Happy Hunting Bargain Days!

Happy kids make happy parents

Happy people create happiness

Happy Times Are Here Again Sale Event!

Happy trails to you!

Have I told you how happy this sale makes me?

Have the happiest of happy

Help us be happier

Here's a slaphappy type of deal!

Here's something worth cheering about

Hey, I'm happy with the deal!

Hey, look at me, I'm happy

Hey, you gotta keep the people happy

Hip, hip, hooray! Sale event!

Hot savings for the happy barbecuer!

How do you spell happy?

How happy do you want to be?

I feel good! I feel happy! I feel really fortunate!

I'm completely happy! I'm definitely happy! I'm feeling very happy!

I'm on top of the world right now

I'm the happiest cat in the world

I'm very happy with my deal!

If that's what makes you happy

If you are happy, I am happy

If you can do what makes you happy, why not?

If you really want to make me happy...

If you're happy and she's happy, then I'm happy

If your feet aren't happy, you're not happy

Is everybody happy?

It's a happy way to start a new year

It's all about happy

155

Happy

It's National "Admit You're Happy" Day!

It's okay to be happy

It's pure happiness

It's time to let loose

It's-your-happy-day deals!

Just be happy that you're happy

Keep it happy!

Keep your customers happy and you'll keep them coming back

Laugh and the world laughs with you

Let us cheer you up!

Let's just say I couldn't be happier to be here

Let's whoop it up

Lucky people are happy people

Make someone happy... make yourself happy

Not just happy but happy, happy

Now that's something to scream about

Our job? To make you happy!

Prepared to be delighted and bedazzled

Relax and be happy

Savings to howl about!

Searching for true and lasting happiness?

Show your merriment

Sunny, happy times are coming

Take the shortcut to happiness

That makes me really happy

The happiest people on earth shop here!

The pursuit of happiness starts here

There is more than one way to spread a little sunshine

There's a happy ending

There's no better place to find happiness than at our Grand Opening!

This is a happy sale event!

This is the happiest day of my life

This weekend, get happy

Time for happy hour!

Time to spread a little cheer

Trying to cheer you up... After the Holiday Sale!

Vibrant! Happy! Excited!

We are serving a side dish of cheer to everybody!

We don't put happiness on hold

We just want to make everybody happy

We make kids happy

We make so many people happy with...

We'll be happy to tell you all about it

We'll put you on cloud nine with...

We're full of happiness to give and get

We're happy that you're happy

We're happy to follow up on our...

We're happy to have you back as a customer

We're tickled to death about the deal!

What we do... ultimately making people happy

What will make you truly happy?

Whatever makes you happy

Who says only fat people are happy?

Whoop-de-do!

Why limit happy to an hour?

Wishing you buckets of cheer

Yeah! Goody! Hallelujah!

You bet your booty I'm happy

You look absolutely ridiculous, but you look happy

You make me deliriously happy

You will know if I'm unhappy

You'll be whistling a happy tune with your deal

You're Happy, We're Happy Sale Event!

Your customers are happy. Hey, even you are happy!

Health

A bad back is bad news

A different look at women's health

A healthier body starts with a healthier you

A healthy body leads to a healthy mind

A joyful heart is a healthy heart

A large belly is a big fat risk

A positive approach to good health

A Public Health Announcement

A simple truth about your health... ignore it and it will go away

A toast... to your health!

Adopt an active lifestyle today... and you will have many healthy tomorrows

An all or nothing approach to a healthy lifestyle

Any excuse is a good excuse for a man not to take care of his health

Are you sick and tired of being sick and tired?

Are you taking your health for granted?

Attitude is 90 percent of good health

Be a fat buster!

Be healthy, wealthy and wise

Blood pressure on target?

Body, mind, soul, spirit

Bone up on your calcium needs

But first check with your doctor

Cars aren't the only things that run better with regular maintenance

Color yourself healthy

Designed to promote good health

Discover a new lifestyle of health

Do you have a cholesterol count that won't quit?

Do you suffer from poor health?

Do you take care of yourself?

Does heartburn take your breath away?

Don't be blasé about your health

Don't gamble with your heart

Don't let chronic pain manage your life

Don't let your health take a vacation

Don't trust your health to just anyone

Drink more water for a health purpose

Ears going, eyes going, brain... forget it!

Eat right. Look right. Live right.

Eating healthfully will only make you feel better

Enjoy life, stay healthy

Exercise and nutrition are the basis of good health

Exercise for the heart, chocolate for the soul

Fat people can be healthy, too

Feel whatever your body is feeling

Foot pain comes in all shapes

For once in your life think of your own health first

For your heart's sake

Fungus among us

Get a 50,000-mile check-up

Get healthy... stay healthy

Get more living out of your life

Get on track for a longer and healthier life

Get the information you need to stay healthy

Give yourself a little tune-up with...

Good common sense is still the best approach

Good food is the No. 1 secret to being healthy

157

Good genes or luck?

Good health increases the quality of life

Good health is a great gift to leave to the kids

Good health isn't just physical, it's mental too!

Has your get up and go... got up and went?

Have a health problem?

Have you seen a doctor?

Heal thyself... make your friends jealous

Healing from within is in

Health comes before work

Health is power

Health is your most prized possession

Health problems don't automatically mean exercise

Health to wealth to happiness

Health! Happiness! Vitality!

Healthier than what?

Healthy doesn't just happen

Healthy habits have a positive effect

Healthy, emotionally satisfying and happy

Here's to your health and peace of mind

Hey... don't take chances with your body

How can you learn when your body is not healthy?

How healthy are you?

How to build resistance and remain healthy

How to keep your health picture-perfect

How to lead a healthy lifestyle

How to live longer, better, wiser

How we help granddads be granddads longer

I don't want to live to 100, I just want to feel good

I feel healthy! I feel happy! I feel terrific!

If one arm feels numb, here's what to do with the other arm

If you don't have your health, you've got nothing

If you have your health, you have everything

If you take care of your body, it will take care of you

If you think you're a big shot... tell it to your heart

If your weight is uncomfortable, it's probably unhealthy

Improve your health through behavior change

In for a check-up? Why not check this out!

Indulge in a healthy lifestyle

Is chronic pain ruling your life?

Is your body cheating you?

It can do wonders for your health

It costs less to stay healthy than to get healthy

It could cost you a fortune to ignore your health

It feels good to feel good

It's an important investment in your health

It's never too late to get healthier

It's not healthy for you to sit around and do nothing

It's time you got serious about your health

It's your health... it's your life

Jump on these healthy values!

Just for the health of it

Keeping kids healthy

Learn more about your health and how to stay healthy

Live the bright, healthy life you deserve

Looking good is as important as feeling good

Make a commitment to a healthy way of life

Make a wise investment in your good health

Make good health your goal

Make health a top priority

New answers to old health questions

No matter how young you are, you have to take care of your health

Nothing is more precious to you than your health

Obesity is a health epidemic

Once you lose your health, it's hard to get it back

Pay attention to what's going on with your body

People must learn to take responsibility for their own health

Poor nutritional habits of children

Raising healthy kids

Recipe for a long, healthy life

Rocketing down the road to good health

Rx for women's health

Sick of being told that everything is bad for you?

Sleep tight for better health

So, you say you want to be healthy?

Sometimes, it helps to take off a little pressure

Start a health plan today

Start living a little healthier

Stop smoking and start exercising

Super health, super stamina, super strength

Take a healthy bite out of good health

Take care of yourself; you're all you've got

Take charge of your health, today!

Take control over your own good health

Take responsibility of your overall health

Thank God every day for the health you do have

The benefits of healthy living

The best advice for staying healthy

The body is made to be healthy

The center for all your health needs

The gift of health

The human touch in health care

The measure of good health care

The new approach to healing

The only way to come out ahead is to put your health first

There's never a good time to be sick

Things to worry about if someone in your family has poor health

Time for a checkup?

Tips on staying healthy

Wanna do something healthy?

We help you... stay healthy

We support health and well-being

We'll give you an owner's manual for your health

What can you do to stay healthy?

What you need to know about good health

When you care about feeling good...

Why think about potential health problems when you're feeling good?

Why wait until you're ill to start thinking about health?

Win the blood pressure battle

You may never be sick another day in your life

You owe it to yourself

Your body is telling you something

Your energy. Your attitude. Your health.

Your guide to good health

Your health is your business

Your heart needs a Valentine wish, too!

Your lungs need spring training, too!

Your passport to health

Your prescription for healthy living

159

Hockey

A booming shot of a sale!

A hockey thrill that will last a lifetime

A power play of savings!

A sale for hockey fans of all ages!

A sale for hockey kids only!

A shot and a save sale!

A sure shot of savings!

A truly exciting game

Aggressive, hard-hitting savings!

An ice feeling

An on-ice extravaganza!

Are you going to be ready when the puck drops?

Are you ready for an all-star hockey sale?

Be a big savings forward in our league of values!

Between the posts

Bold on ice

Call it a hat trick of a sale!

Cool as Ice Sale Event!

Don't be caught off-sides

Don't get caught in the penalty box... buy it today!

Drive to the net with these savings!

Drop the puck and let's go after the savings!

Explosive hockey action during our year-end sale!

Fast-paced, hard-hitting sale!

Feel it on the ice

Feel the blade savings!

Fight for the puck

Fire on ice

For hockey fans of all ages

For puck enthusiasts everywhere

For the Ultimate Hockey Fan Sale Event!

From the face-off circle

Get in front of the speeding puck at...

Get ready to face off at the sale event of the season

Get the puck in the net for big savings!

Get the Puck Sale!

Get the puck, get the savings!

Get your tickets for the next ice age

Give hockey a shot

Guts of steel

Hard-hitting hockey action

He shoots... He scores!!!

Hockey and more hockey savings!

Hockey doesn't get any better than this

Hockey fans aren't the only ones who love a good fight

Hockey fans of all ages

Hockey is heating up

Hockey mania savings!

Hockey moms... have we got a sale for you!

Hockey players stick together

Hockey... speed, action and savings!

Home ice can make the difference

Hot steel on ice!

Improve your slapshot without slapping at...

In the attack zone for great deals

Inside hockey

It takes guts of steel to have a sale like this

It's a great hockey sale!

It's face-off time!

It's not required that you be a hockey player

It's the real deal on ice!

Join the hockey club

Join the top-scoring team with top-scoring values at...

Just drop the puck

Just put the puck in the net

Learn real hockey from real hockey players

Let the puck fly!

Let's play hockey

Let's talk puck

Make the winning goal

Men of steel

No puck intended... this is our final sale of the season!

Off the boards! Offsides! 50% off on all sale items!

On the other side of the glass

Once the puck drops, all sales will be final!

Our game is straight up and down the boards

Our sale talks better than we skate!

Our slap shot of values makes you the winner !

Pucker power... savings power!

Pucks and sticks and things are on sale... now!

Put a little sauce on the puck

Put the game on ice

Put the puck in the net

Savings from the face-off circle!

Selling the game is on the ice

Slapshot values!

Slashing prices! Dazzling savings! Crunching deals on all hockey equipment!

Slashing sticks! Dazzling speed! Crunching deals!

Start firing the puck

Steel against steel

Stick-it-to-'em deals!

Super fast sure-shot savings!

Support your local youth hockey association

Sure-shot savings!

That's the mark of a great hockey sale!

That's where goal-scorers shoot the puck

The best game on ice

The fastest team on ice

The magic is on the ice

The puck drops at this sale!

The puck drops here

The puck is always in play at...

The road map to the net

The shots! The skates! The savings!

The stick! The skates! The puck! All on sale!

There's nothing like playoff hockey

This is hockey excellence

This is our old-fashioned hockey sale event!

This is what we call fast-moving hockey

Time to sharpen those skates

Tough on the ice... sale!

We fight for the puck

We ice the competition

We're dropping the gloves on all sale items!

When the puck drops, you know who'll be in there

Where the puck doesn't freeze

Who gets the puck in the net, gets the win!

Who's minding your net?

You get more than exciting hockey

You shoot... you score with big savings!

You won't get shut out with these game-winning savings!

You'll get plenty of ice time here

You'll see some unbelievable hockey

You're going to see hockey like you've never seen it before

A door that's tough to knock

A fresh paint job can do wonders for your house

A good furnace is built to last

A roof to top all others

Add a warm, country look to your kitchen

Are you putting off a home improvement project?

Are you too busy doing home repairs?

Are your heating and cooling costs out of control?

Are your heating bills going through the roof?

At the heart of every home is a beautiful kitchen

Beautify your surroundings... Remodel your home!

Behind every great home is a great deck

Best quality at affordable prices!

Big or small... we do it all!

Call for a no-cost estimate

Can your air conditioner keep you cool through another long, hot summer?

Cold winds blowing through the windows?

Contemplating a major home improvement?

Cook up a new kitchen in minutes

Deal Direct with Owners Home Improvement Sale!

Do home improvement projects have you running in circles?

Does your bathroom need more than just fresh towels?

Does your kitchen suit your needs?

Don't let a remodeling project wreck your life

Don't let home improvement drive you crazy

Don't let your hard-earned cash go up in smoke... Be energy-efficient!

Don't move, improve!

Enjoy your next vacation at home

Everything for your windows but the curtains

Expand your outdoor living

Fall Home Fix-Up Sales Event!

Fall Home Improvement Value Days!

Fed up with the post-war kitchen?

Free estimates. Design services. Financing. On-time completion.

Free roof analysis

Full service home improvement specialists

Get it done right, get it done for less!

Get your bathroom ready for the holidays

Get your house in shape before winter winds blow

Getting the most out of your home improvement dollars

Give us a call for a free consultation!

Give your house a facelift

Giving your home a fresh new look

Got the home improvement bug?

Greatest remodeling value ever!

Guaranteed work. Lowest price possible. Immediate service.

Holding off on home repairs?

Home improvement is a wise move

Home improvement needn't mean sawdust and bills

Home improvement will pay off in the long run

Home improvements worth making

How to avoid home improvement headaches

How to avoid remodeling fraud

How to improve the value of your home

How to make your remodeling job easier

If something needs to be done, do it now!

If you don't know roofs...
Know your roofer

If your house isn't energy efficient, you're losing more than just heat

Imagine what an addition could do for your home

In a remodeling mood?

Increase the value of your home and never paint your house again

Inviting ideas for your home

Is your deck ready for summer?

Is your handyman a couch potato? Then call a professional

It's never too late to insulate

It's time to focus on home improvement

It's time to invest in fixing up your home

Keeping up with home repairs is essential

Landscaping is a home-improvement project

Let our professionals help you with your...

Let this be your year for a kitchen or home addition

Make your home improvement dream come true

Make your home more secure, more attractive

More furnaces burn more than just gas

Need home improvements and repairs?

No job is too small... Call for a free estimate

Nobody takes care of your old house like we do!

Now is the perfect time to plan your remodeling ventures

Now... you can afford to fix up your home!

Old windows need replacing?

Old world craftsmanship

Our reputation is home improvement!

Our siding will never rot, crack or need painting

Perhaps the home improvement you make this year should be to your garage

Planning to rehab your kitchen?

Preserve the value of your property

Problem-solvers for fast and easy fix-ups

Protect and beautify your home

Quality bath remodeling

Quality work and reputable professional contractors

Read what satisfied customers have to say about...

Remodeling clearance event going on now!

Remodeling your home doesn't have to be painful

Repairs. Maintenance. Remodeling.

Room additions, built to blend

See it, plan it, do it!

See your kitchen come to life

Sit back, enjoy the results

So it's time to fix it up

Some advice when picking a contractor

Stop getting soaked by your old water heater

Summer without air conditioning can be tough

Take the plunge on remodeling

Take your time to develop plans before you start a home project

The ABCs of home improvement

The best deals for fall fix-up

The best place in your home to invest money... the kitchen!

The best way to eliminate home repair costs, is not to have any

The biggest remodeling sale ever!

Home Improvement

The home improvement pro

The last word in home remodeling... yes!

The most cost-effective way to protect, beautify and increase the value of your home

The need for more living space

The payback value of home remodeling projects in unknown

The time to save on home remodeling is now!

Think of our home improvement loan as opportunity knocking

Think spring fix-up specials

Thinking about painting your house?

Thinking of adding a new bedroom?

Time to remodel?

Tired of your kitchen?

To request an estimate online, visit our Web page

Transform your kitchen into a five-star restaurant

Warm up to window savings!

We are the ones who can fix your leaky pipe

We can enhance the value of your home

We complete the job, follow through and stand behind our work

We do everything in your kitchen but the dishes

We do timely repairs

We like to let our tools do the talking

We make home improvement painless

We make your home remodeling dreams come true

We stand behind our work

We think additions belong on your home, not on your loan

We'll give your garage door a lift

We'll help you stretch your remodeling dollars

We'll make your deck look as good as new

We'll nail down those home improvement projects

We're in the home improvement business

We've built our reputation one home improvement project at a time

We've got 'em all, when it comes to windows

We've got all the answers to all your home improvement questions

We've got great ideas for fixing up your house

What good is a roof that lasts 20 years if the company that put it on only lasts 5?

When it's got to get done... get it done right!

Whether it's a small fix-it project or a major renovation...

Why remodel your mobile home? Just move it!

Why replace your furnace when the winter is over?

Will remodel to suit

Winter is fast approaching... will your roof be safe from the cold?

You can afford to fix up your home

You have a 30-year mortgage, shouldn't you have a 30-year faucet?

You're going to have to do it sooner or later

You've got to look at it as a home improvement value!

Your air conditioner could be cooling you out of house and home

Your cure for home improvement headaches

Your front door is the opening statement for your home

Your old house will never be the same

Horse Racing

A battle down to the wire

A big day of racing

A day at the races

A horse lover's dream come true

A new breed of horse racing fans

A race for the big money!

A sale for horse racing enthusiasts!

A Triple Crown champion

A triple-threat on any racetrack

Aaaaaaaaand they're off

After the mint juleps...

Always play the favorite

America's most celebrated race

And the winner by a nose is...

And they're off to big savings!

Attention horse lovers

Bet on the best thoroughbred racing has to offer

Bring 'em home with a win!

By a nose

Call it good old-fashioned horse sense

Calling all horses

Come to the track for some horseplay!

Coming strong in the stretch

Daily double to double your savings!

Deals right from the horse's mouth!

Derby Dollars Days!

Do you read the Racing Form before going to the race?

Don't be left at the gate

Early entries make you a winner

Everyone wants to ride with a winner

Flying down the backstretch

Food, fun, and horse racing

For horse lovers

For the best live racing...

For the non-horse fan

For those of us that love horses

Free horse and buggy rides!

Get ready to ride

Get the green sheet

Got a Derby favorite yet?

Harness racing is a great sport

Have you ever camped out at the racetrack?

He found the winner's circle

Here they come, terrific savings down the stretch!

Hoof it and win

Horse lovers will be ecstatic with these bargains!

How to pick 'em!

How to spot a winner

I feel like I just won the Kentucky Derby

I just did a little horse tradin'

I ride to win!

I wouldn't trade my horse with anybody

If a horse keeps losing, sooner or later you have to get different oats

It's a horse race now!

It's a trifecta sale, buy 3 and get 1 free

It's Derby Day everyday at...

It's Derby time!

It's the granddaddy sale event of 'em all!

It's time to buy a new horse!

Jockeying for position at the biggest sale of the year!

Keyed up... ready to go!

Horse Racing

Let your stallions go out there and win!

Let's go to the races!

Let's ride!

Looking for a good horse to ride?

Make your move to super savings!

Maybe it's time to change horses?

Now in the home stretch

Off to the races

Off-track betting puts you there

On the road to Louisville

Once the gates open the horses are running for the...

Our barn door's open for bargains, values and deals!

Our racing heritage

Picking a winner is not going to be easy

Post time is our sale time!

Put the right spin on horse racing

Racing action

Racing's Biggest Day!

Raising, training and selling some of the finest horses around

Recreational horses for your riding pleasure

Roaring out of the gate

Run free with these magnificent horses

Saddle up with these tremendous deals!

Should I buy a horse?

Start every race from the right position

Step into the winner's circle

Stop by our starting gate

Take your pick, but make it quick

The biggest horse race of the year

The classic horse derby

The excitement of horse racing

The finest racetrack in the world

The greatest horse there ever was

The greatest show on turf

The horse show of the western world

The jockey of today...

The race of the year

The Run for the Roses Sale Event!

The thrill of a horse race

The wonderful wacky world of harness racing

The world's richest horse race

They shoot horses, don't they?

They're off and running

This horse is for rent!

This horse is going to the winner's circle

This is horse country

Thundering around the turn towards exciting savings!

Until the starting gate opens...

Use a little horse sense and take advantage of the deal!

Watch the final stretch

We can put you in the winner's circle

We pick 'em... but don't put your money on it

What a race!!! What a horse!!! What a sale!!!

What's a day at the racetrack without a little...

Where you're always at the right track

Which horse do you want to ride?

Why not get started with your own horse?

Wild about horses

Win, place and charge it!

Winning horses can't keep you away

Would you like to buy a piece of the horse?

You could find yourself nose to nose

You don't have to be a jockey to fall in love with a horse

You'll be the winner by a head at...

Hospital

A compassionate, friendly hospital staff

A good hospital can make the difference between life and death

A great community hospital

A hospital that handles the needs of the family

A hospital with a community spirit that knows no limits

A hospital's commitment to education

A top-rated hospital for heart surgery

A warm and cheerful place to get well

Are you the patient who was killed?

Ask about nurse-to-patient staffing ratio

Avoid costly medical disasters

Be an informed patient

Be Medicare smart

Best physicians. Best nurses. Best quality care.

Committed to delivering the very best patient care

Compassionate care that meets the needs of every patient

Continuing to serve your health care needs

Crisis knows no schedule

Day-to-day functions of a hospital

Do you have white-coat hypertensives?

Do you trust your hospital?

Doing what we can to make patient care better

Don't mess with your life! Have a mammogram!

Don't wish upon a star, when it comes to your heart

Fantastic nurses. Exceptional care.

For what's most important to you... patient outcome

Getting the best care

Getting to the right hospital may be more important than getting to a hospital quickly

Giving blood is one of the best ways to give a precious gift

Have you ever gone to the wrong hospital?

Health care is too important to be a privilege

Heart care, recognized among the best anywhere

Helping people to get well

High-quality health care services

How are your doctor's bedside manners?

How many doctors does it take to get you healthy?

I owe them my life

Improving the community's wellness and health

In keeping with our commitment to you...

In the patient's best interest

It's all part of putting the patient first

It's time to expect more from your hospital

It's nice to have someone who really cares about you

Life threatening, urgent but not life threatening, and less urgent patient care

Making health care a basic human right

Meeting the needs of today's patients

New techniques and treatments for improving patient care

No one will be turned away

No price tag should be put on patient care

Nurses are the heart of our hospital

Nurses make it happen

Hospital

On your hospital stay...

One of the lowest mortality rates in the healthcare industry

One of the nation's top pediatric hospitals

Organ donors needed

Our cardiac team doesn't miss a beat

Our doctor-patient ratio is astronomical

Our doctors speak multiple languages

Our first concern is the well-being of every patient

Our mission is to provide exceptional care for patients

Our physicians are as diverse as our patients

Our physicians are board-certified

Our professionalism and dedication to patient care is the key to our success

Our state-of-the-art hospital

Our surgeons are among the nation's best

Patient care is a responsibility we never take lightly

Patients are enthusiastic about our bedside services

Patients value being treated as people

People facing serious medical conditions count on us

Place your care in our hands

Quality care can have a dramatic effect on whether a patient lives or dies

Real people taking care of real people

Recognized for quality care

Share the gift of life... be an organ donor

State-of-the-art health care services

Striving to be the best hospital ever ends

Surgery in the morning, home in the evening

The attitude of our staff is very obvious...

The best hospital is right here in your neighborhood

The best time to visit our hospital is before you have to

The high quality of care we provide our patients

The hospital with the human touch

The most advanced pediatric care available

The world's most advanced hospital

There's no emergency we can't handle

We are a stand-alone specialty hospital

We are one of the nation's best trauma hospitals

We are proud to service our customers day and night

We are the most preferred hospital in the country

We are trained to understand your health condition

We believe an emergency room is more than an emergency room

We care for patients, whole heartedly

We hope we never see you in our emergency room

We maintain the highest quality of care for each patient

We make your hospital stay a little more hospitable

We represent virtually every medical specialty

We take pain seriously

We're here for you, all of your life

What a difference a good hospital can make

What's your doctor's bedside manner?

Where the patient always comes first

Whether you're 7 or 77... it's all about you

You're not just a gown, but a patient at our hospital

Hot-Cool

30 red-hot doorbusters!

A cool deal before cool was cliché

A flat-out cool deal!

A hot new offer!

A Hot Time in the Old Store Sales Event!

A hot, hot, hot winter sale!

A hotbed of savings activity!

A real hot sale event!

A sale as hot as the summer sun!

A super-hot savings extravaganza!

An unbelievable selection of all your hot favorites!

Be as cool as you want to be

Blazin' hot deals!

But what's really hot are the...

Caution! Hot savings inside!

Caution: Hot prices ahead!

Caution: Hot, hot, hot stuff inside!

Check out the hot picks!

Cool bargains... hot deals!

Cool down on a hot deal!

Cool down with a refreshing...

Cool for sure savings!

Cool looks priced right!

Cool prices... hot savings!

Cool stuff that makes you tick

Cool stuff you just gotta check out

Cool ways to stay warm

Darn, that's a hot deal!

Don't miss these hot deals!

Enjoy it while it's hot!

Extremely hot deals!

Find out what's hot before it's not

For girls who know the cool stuff!

For Hotheads Only Sales Event!

For the guys who just like looking cool

Get 'em while they're hot!

Go with the hot hand

Here's a hot tip just for you!

Here's what's hot; right here, right now!

Hot buys you can't pass up!

Hot damn... what a deal!

Hot dang! What a sale!

Hot deals throughout the store!

Hot deals... hot buys!

Hot features... cool prices!

Hot grub... Cool pub

Hot hand of a deal!

Hot item of the week!

Hot new products for today's new markets

Hot news about cold sores

Hot nights... cool deals!

Hot off the truck... Truckload Sale!

Hot on the heels of explosive bargains!

Hot prices on the stuff you want!

Hot prices! Hotter values! What a great pair!

Hot savings... right now!

Hot Stuff Sales Event!

Hot tickets for a hot time!

Hot times... cool deals!

Hot tips for smart shoppers

Hot values at cool prices!

Hot? We're on fire!

Hot-Button Issue Sales Event!

Hotfoot it down to...

Hot-Cool

Hotter Now Than Ever Sales Event!

Hotter than a summer sales event!

It's a hot seller

It's as white-hot as any deal can get

It's back and it's red hot

It's cool to like it hot!

It's getting hotter and it's hotter than ever savings!

It's hot and it's an exclusive deal!

It's hot and it's an incredible bargain!

It's hot and we've got it!

It's one of the hottest things around

It's the hottest rage

It's what's hot today!

Just for you... cool stuff inside!

Know what's cool

Last of the red-hot deals!

Look inside for cool freebies!

New is what's cool!

Nothing is cooler than steaming savings on a hot day!

Now that's really a cool deal!

Off to a hot start

One hot price! One hot sale!

Our hot prices just got hotter

Our hottest sale of the year!

Our sale is red-hot!

Our savings are sizzling hot!

Plug into what's hot... now!

Prices so hot, no one can touch 'em

Pssssst! Want a hot tip?

Push the hot button for sizzling savings!

Red hot and cool deals!

Red-hot rates just in time for your summer vacation

Red-hot savings!

Red-hot values for winter shoppers!

Show off your cool

Some like it hot!

Strike while the iron is hot

Summer deals so hot you better bring your sunscreen!

Super hot buys!

The dish on what's hot for...

The hot buzzword is...

The hot event of the year!

The hot new look!

The hottest thing going is going fast

The latest! The hottest! The most current!

The only things hotter than the coffee are the savings!

The season's hottest looks

They're going like hotcakes!

Time for a hot deal!

Today's hot picks

Totally new! Totally hot!

Vales at hot prices!

We put the cool into savings!

We're always all over the hot new things!

We're back with red-hot deals!

We're hot as fire

We're Not Just Blowin' Hot Air Deals!

We've got what's hot!

What's hot for the holidays?

What's hot? What's new? What's next?

What's new! What's good! What's hot!

What's the hot look?

When we say hot, we mean hot!

When you're hot, you're hot!

Where The Uncool Is Cool Sales Event!

Where to get the hot stuff

Why settle for a lot of hot air?

You're Going To Be Hot Stuff Sales Event!

A free hotel night is reserved for you

A good choice for the night

A good night's sleep is our promise to keep

A hotel known for impeccable service

A little down-home hospitality

A natural place for people to hunker down

A new definition of luxury

A place where niceness and acquiescence rule

A resort for meetings of the mind

A resort isn't a business, it's a way of life

A safe guest is a happy guest

A small hotel with a big, warm heart

A whole herd can bed down here

Absolutely the best place to stay

Accommodations are sumptuous

All you need to do is check in

Allow us to make your stay a truly memorable one

An experience unlike any other

An incredibly luxurious resort

And remember, it's the little things that count

Award-winning service

Be our guest and experience an extraordinary getaway

Be our guest... Be our quest

Catering to your every whim

Check into luxury!

Comfort is key in our hospitality program

Comfortable accommodations. Excellent facilities. Great service.

Convenience... comfort... impeccable service

Deluxe and affordable accommodations

Don't just sleep anywhere

Enjoy our award-winning service

Enjoy our hometown hospitality and our welcoming open-arms attitude

Everyone expects southern hospitality, and we certainly provide it

Everything you expect in a four-star resort

Everything you've ever imagined a resort to be

Exceptional service that will create a lasting impression

Executive class suites designed for business travelers

Experience a luxurious night's sleep

Experts in hospitality

Fantastic guest rooms and family suites

Far from anything you've ever experienced

First class just got easier to take

Gracious accommodations in old world tradition

Great service at a great price!

Have a great stay with us

Have it your way at our hotel

Hospitality has your name on it

Hotel rooms with rates to suit every budget!

If you don't like your room and would like to go elsewhere, then be our guest

If you haven't been to our hotel lately, you haven't been here at all

Impeccable service and attention to detail

It is a pleasure having you with us!

It is our policy to respect the privacy of our guests

It will change the way you look at hotels

It's a place like no other

It's called proactive hospitality

It's just like your own room, only we treat you better

It's our unspoken goal to exceed your expectations

Just call room service. No charge!

Just right for a romantic weekend

Leisure time takes on a whole new dimension at...

Let our people make your stay an experience

Let us do the digging to find a place for your...

Let us put your butt in our bed

Let us shower you with luxury

Life's luxuries for a lot less

Looking for a place to spend a quiet evening?

Luxury accommodations, affordable price!

Luxury isn't an option

Luxury, elegance and personalized service

Meeting the highest standards of excellence

Nothing like old-fashioned hospitality

Nothing sets the mood like a classy room

Odds are you'll love staying here

One of the nation's premier resorts

Optimal comfort throughout your stay

Our bellmen are always standing by

Our guests are our highest priority

Our hospitality is more than just a tradition

Our job is making sure your stay is arranged exactly the way you like it

Our job is to meet your needs

Our secret? Years of five-star service!

Our staff takes great pride in taking care of our customers

Our standards will meet your highest expectations

Peace of mind is a piece of cake at...

Personalized service. World-class amenities!

Pets are welcome here!

Privacy is, indeed, the ultimate luxury

Providing our guests with friendly personal service

Sleep for less at the best

Sleep tight or it's a free night!

Some hotels may call you demanding. We satisfy your demands!

Southern hospitality at a very comfortable price

Staying at a four-star resort is not the same as our four-star resort

The benchmark by which enjoyable stays are measured

The best part of our job is to make you happy

The Good Choice Hotel

The hotel of budget luxury

The hotel that is a home away from home

The intimacy and highly personalized service one would expect

The kind of hospitality that makes you feel at home

The most complete resort complex in America

The most hospitable hotel in the hospitality industry

The most technologically advanced hotel in the industry

The pleasure of your company

The quality of our service is the reason for our success

The ultimate hotel, with service to match

The ultimate luxury of a world-class resort

The VIP treatment that you deserve

There is no better place to relax than here

There is no getting up on the wrong side of the bed at our hotels

There's no place that shows you hospitality like we do!

There's room at the inn... always!

This hotel is full of attitude

Treat yourself to our hospitality

We are committed to hospitality

We are delighted that you have selected our resort

We are totally in tune with everything you need

We do not charge for extra service

We exceed your expectations

We go out of our way to make our guests feel welcomed and right at home

We go the extra mile to accommodate you

We handle everything so you don't have to!

We have high-tech room service

We invite you to return, so please buckle up and drive carefully

We learn from complaints... that's how we get better

We live up to our reputation

We make sure you have exactly what you need

We make your experience with us enjoyable

We make your stay a lot more rewarding

We may be exaggerating a little, but our service is fantastic

We only answer to you!

We provide nighttime pampering that goes beyond chocolates on a pillow

We provide you with the best of everything

We strive to make your stay a delight

We take the lug out of luggage

We treat our guests as if they were staying at a four-star hotel

We treat you with kid gloves

We welcome the opportunity to be of service to you

We will make your head spin with our service

We will make your stay truly memorable

We'll even put you to sleep!

We'll treat you like a celebrity

We'll treat you like you own the place

We're changing a lot more than the sheets

We're committed to ensuring that you receive the service you expect

We're not your typical resort

We're your home away from home

We've thought of everything, so you don't have to

Western hospitality with natural splendor

When comfort counts

When nothing else will do but your own virtually private resort

When you stay with us, prepare to be pampered

Where first class never ends!

Where individual privacy is respected

Where you get the treatment you deserve

Will coddle you with creature comforts

With all the first-class amenities guests have come to expect

You won't feel like a room number

You'll know just how special a night's rest can be

You'll like the affordable rates!

You'll really enjoy being here!

You're only a few miles away from a good night's sleep

You've just discovered what separates the good hotel from the great ones

Your room is always ready!

50% more cleaning power

A great bacteria fighter with a knockout punch

A place for everything, and everything in its place

A simple and effective way to treat dirt and stains

A solution for germs

A stopped-up sink drain can really be a pain

After all, when you're cleaning your house, you can always use an extra vacuum cleaner

All household essentials... now on sale!

April showers bring spring-cleaning

Are you ready to fight clutter?

Be a neat freak... special purchase of mops, brooms and brushes!

Better ways to have a healthier home

Call the exterminator!

Chalk one up for clean living

Clean and sanitize the easy way!

Clean it till it sparkles and shines with...

Clean Sweep Sale Event! For all your household cleaning needs!

Clean up and clean out

Clean up at our big household sale event!

Clean up the mess when you clean up with these super savings!

Clean up with our best household savings!

Clean your whole house with...

Cleaning day is an adventure

Cleaning made easy!

Cleaning, without a doubt, is the least-expensive home improvement

Cleanliness is Next to Godliness Sales Event!

Clear the decks with these super cleaning savings!

Disinfects while you clean

Do germs call your house their home?

Do you have a smelly problem to solve?

Do you have to wear a gas mask when you open the refrigerator door?

Does your home look, feel and smell fresh?

Don't be a victim of spring-cleaning

Don't forget to clean behind the sofa

Don't just push germs around. Get rid of them with...

Double your cleaning power with...

Drawbacks of clean living

Drive the drudgery out of housework with...

Experience the fresher feeling of...

Fantastic for small spills to hard-charging cleaning!

Feel the clean

Ferocious spring-cleaning savings on all household products!

Flush out toilet problems with...

For a fresh, clean spring look...

For the quickest clean in every room, use...

Fresh. Clean. Shining.

Get a fresh start on house cleaning with...

Get out the brooms!

Get rid of household dust, pollen and mold spores before they get you!

Get tough cleaning action with...

Get tough on germs

Good, clean advice:

Great for small spills to hard-charging cleaning

Has clutter overrun your life?

Has your room passed its health inspection?

Here's the dirt on cleanliness

Hire your high-tech spring-cleaning pro!

House cleaning's a snap with...

How many microbes are crawling around in your bathroom?

How to avoid germs

How to keep the dirt out of your home

If your bathroom is dirty, what condition is your kitchen in?

If your kitchen is clean, all is right with the world

Is spring-cleaning bugging you?

It cuts through dirt like a missile

It treats dirt like scum!

It's a dirty shame

It's a great time to clean up at our Power Vacuum Sale Event!

It's neat to be clean

Join the war against germs!

Killing bacteria without killing you

Latex gloves... the solution not only for health care workers

Let's team up to clean up!

Life's necessities all on sale!

Make housework fun

Make your cleaning efforts more efficient with...

Make your home sparkle with...

No more messy rooms with...

No scrub! No wipe! No work!

Nothing's tougher on grease than...

Now's the time to tackle spring cleaning!

Now... the bucket brigade can hang up its mops, brooms and brushes

OK, we've come clean... 25% to 50% off on all housecleaning products!

Protect your family from harmful germs

Put an end to clutter in no time at all

Reduce the work in housework with...

Refresh your home during our marvelous Housecleaning Sales Event!

Refreshingly cleans away dirt, stains and bacteria

Remove the stains... kill the germs

Sanitary fresh

Save on household cleaners... big time!

Simple, superior clean

Spring Cleaning Sales Event for tidy and sloppy people!

Stamp out germs with...

Stock up on cleaning supplies

Stop dirt in its tracks

Super household savings that sparkle and shine!

Take home fantastic household values!

Take spring-cleaning one shelf at a time

The best cleaner/polisher ever invented is elbow grease

There's no better time to clean up... Sale Event!

There's nothing like coming home to a clean, wonderful-smelling house

Tips to make spring-cleaning a breeze

Wage germ warfare in your kitchen

We clean it all!

We clean to your satisfaction!

We have what you need to keep it clean

We offer high-tech spring-cleaning

We took the work out of housework

We treat dirt like dirt

We will make your home shine

We're tidying up with fabulous household savings!

We've got all the kitchen and bathroom cleaning solutions you'll ever need!

When tough stains can't be removed, get...

Your kitchen hosts more germs than your bathroom

Hunting

A great area for hunting

A hunter's paradise

A perfect time to go hunting

A single shot deal!

A successful deer hunt... guaranteed!

A-hunting we will go

America's hunting tradition of values!

An abundance and variety of birds for
your hunting excitement!

Archery deer season begins...

Are you ready for this year's
hunting season?

Avid outdoorsmen yearn for the wild of...

Begin the day empty-handed, go home
with hands full of savings!

Big game hunter specials!

Big Game Hunters Sale Event!

Bow hunters get their arrows here

Buck the odds with super savings!

Careful! This gun's loaded with
great deals!

Catch the annual deer fever outbreak

Catering to the needs of hunters

Caution: Deer crossing

Come up and enjoy the hunting season

Deer Season! It's that time again

Done a little bit of hunting?

Double-barreled sales excitement!

Duck season opens today!
Are you ready?

Early-season archery hunters

Everything you need for the hunt

Finest hunting companion ever

Follow the deer tracks to
incredible savings!

For hunting enthusiasts

For the serious deer hunter

From one sharpshooter to another

From the duck blind

Get camouflaged from head to toe at...

Get the jump on the rabbit

Get your sights on some easy bucks

Getting on the right track

Go bow hunting with a champion

Going deer hunting with Dad

Good hunting to you

Goose hunting at its best

Grab a bow and go for the hunt

Happy hunting out there,
you sharpshooters

Happy hunting to all!

Head for the woods

Holiday Hunting Special!

How to be a champion duck caller

Hunt where the geese are

Hunter safety classes... sign up today!

Hunters pay the bill for
wildlife restoration

Hunting for bargains?

Hunting for something?

Hunting is more than guns and killing

Hunting licenses available here

Hunting Opener Sale!

Hunting the way it used to be

Hunting wild sheep is the ultimate

If you are hunting for the best deals,
you'll find them here!

If you're a big-game hunter...

Is it duck season or is it deer hunting?

Is your hunting license expired?

It's a "good deal" hunting

It's a fine day for hunting down good old-fashioned prices!

It's Take Your Boy Hunting Day

It's the season to gun for the wild gobblers

It's the Thrill of the Hunt Sale Event!

It's the time of the years when hunters get antsy for hunting bargains!

Last-minute hunting sale!

Lock, stock and barrel savings!

Locked and loaded explosive savings!

Looking ahead to deer season

Make the most of this hunting season

More hunters needed

Nail your trophy white-tailed...

Nature needs hunters

No hunting beyond this point

No payments till hunting season

No shooting experience is necessary

Now it's time to improve your aim with great deals on all hunting equipment!

One-stop hunter's supply headquarters

Opening Day Annual Sale Event!

Outfit yourself with state-of-the-art hunting intelligence

Prepare now for hunting season

Pull the trigger on these great buys!

Reload for another shot at these bargains!

Renewing your hunting license

Sharp Shooters Sale Event!

Superb hunting is our main attraction

Take dead aim at these savings!

The age of big-game hunting lives

The annual deer hunt starts here!

The annual kickoff to hunting season

The bucks stop here

The ducks are coming, the ducks are coming

The End of Another Hunting Season Sale!

The geese are still up north, but the savings are down south!

The hunt is on

The hunting season ahead

The key to hunting success

The thrill of the hunt is exciting savings!

The total experience of hunting...

There's nothing like the thrill of the hunt

They went for the bucks, we went for the savings!

'Tis the season for hunting

Tomorrow is Opening Day... Today is Savings Day on all hunting needs!

Track down a great deal at...

We can improve your hunt

We have everything that makes hunting so special

We have the largest populations of geese and ducks... anywhere!

We make hunting a big game

We offer unparalleled pheasant hunting

We put the hunt back in hunting

We take deer hunting seriously

We've Done the Hunting For You Sale Event!

Where the pros go for bird hunting and clay target shooting

Who are the hunters and who are the bargain hunters?

Why hunting in the wilderness is more fun!

You have to take a shot at these deals!

You'll get a better shot on ducks and geese with us!

You'll get a double-barreled advantage with these super deals!

You'll get your deer for sure

You're in true, rugged wilderness when hunting here

Zero in on savings!

Hygiene

A clean body is a basic human right

A solid, well-groomed, impeccably-dressed, flawlessly polite man

An incredible sale for embarrassing problems!

Appearance is a quality you deserve!

Are you a clean freak?

Body odor is no laughing matter

Chase germs away with...

Clean never felt this good

Clean up with terrific savings on all personal care products!

Could your body pass the stink and smell test?

Do you have to look like a slob before you buy our personal care products?

Don't take it personally... 30% off all personal care products!

Extraordinary personal hygiene products... on sale!

Fabulous savings... all in the name of health and beauty!

Fill your shower caddy with savings at...

For a cleaner feeling all day long

For men who don't wear deodorant

For that unkempt hairstyle, try...

Get that fresh, clean feeling with...

Good personal habits start with savings on...

Great fragrances for all your bathrooms

Has your deodorant called it a day?

Head for the showers with...

Head on over for savings on all hair care products!

Here's what you need to smell fresh as a country breeze!

Hey man, it's time to get a haircut!

How come you smell so good?

How do you smell success?

How to keep that unkempt look...

How to tell your friend he has bad breath

Hygiene is a personal issue

Hygiene rules for underwear... change everyday!

I'm off to scrub up

If I had body odor, would you tell me?

If you can't look good, you better smell great

If you can't stand the smell, get out of the bathroom

If you're worried about hygiene...

Image is everything

Is a hairbrush a foreign object to you?

Is your toothbrush covered with bacteria?

It deodorizes you from the inside

It feels fresh and cool and bracing

It pays to look good!

It won't stop perspiration... just the smell

It's easy to keep feet smelling good when you use...

It's nice to look good

It's really good hygiene

It's the smell of clean

It's the soap that makes life smell sweet

Keep looking your best, all the time

Keep up your hygiene habits

Keep your skin looking healthy

Make sure you wash up before chowing down

Make your bathing experience a delight

My deodorant doesn't always work

Neatness counts

Neatness is most important, and that applies to attire, hair, shoes, etc.

No man should be without a barber

No one likes to shave every morning... so face up to it!

Nobody knows if they have a severe personal hygiene problem. But we do!

Now that's refreshing!

Outrageous savings on all personal hygiene products!

Overall good hygiene is a definite turn-on

Personal-grooming guidelines

Polish yourself up with these unique hygiene savings!

Practice good hygiene... every day!

Savings reminder! Don't forget to brush your teeth!

Shaves, facials, mudpacks... full service

Showered, shaved, ready to go!

Smell better... feel better with exceptional savings on...

Smell like a winner!

Super savings for all clean freaks and real slobs!

Sweating is not an option

Take 50% off all personal care products. Now that's refreshing!

Take a shower... it's great for the soul

Take time off for grooming

Talk about a dirty dozen!

Teaching kids good hygiene habits

That so-fresh feeling

The fight between bad breath and mouthwash

The freshest way to feel clean

The hands you wash could save lives

The importance of keeping clean

The new word... clean!

The next stop: The shower

The perfect odor killer for bathrooms

The perfect partner for body odor

The right attitude on neatness

There are no rules when it comes to personal hygiene

There's something therapeutic about good hygiene

This is strictly a hygiene hypothesis

Tired of smelly socks and shoes?

Turn bath time into fun time

Unreal bargains for bad breath, body odor and greasy hair!

Upgrade your image with these personal care savings!

Use only for smells at crisis level

We're more than just a dry cleaner

What are your personal hygiene habits?

What has your underwear done for you lately?

What's your idea of a clean body?

When it comes to maintaining proper body odor...

When you don't take showers for weeks, deodorant is a must

When you stink, you stink!

Who's the biggest slob of them all?

Why don't barbershops have a sale?

Why gamble with your appearance?

With a sweet scent and fresh breath

You can smell better than a magnificent perfume

You don't have to brush hard to brush well

You feel different when you look different

You know you're supposed to floss everyday!

You'll feel clean and fresh with...

You'll have a healthy head of hair in days!

You'll not only smell good, but the savings will make you smell even better!

You've got to start somewhere! Let us do your dry cleaning!

A deductible is a deductible with us

Affordable life and health insurance for the entire family

An insurance plan that offers cash benefits

Are you doing enough to protect your family?

Are you getting more health care for your money?

Are you paying too much for life insurance?

Are you properly insured? Or are you underinsured?

As a homeowner you do need life insurance coverage

Be overprotective without overpaying

Beating the high cost of health insurance

Benefits we all can use

Buying insurance can be a torturous experience

Can you afford to go without insurance?

Choose the plan that's best for you

Choosing the right health care plan can be confusing

Coming to terms with life insurance

Cut your current insurance premium in half

Did you ever have a sick feeling your health plan doesn't cover...

Disability insurance will provide you with monthly checks

Do you get the health insurance blues?

Do you know where your insurance agent is?

Does insurance make you a bit squeamish?

Don't buy life insurance until you call us!

Don't you owe it to yourself, and your loved ones?

For quality insurance and superior service... call

For yourself. For your family. For your security.

Free! Prescription discounts

From one of the world's most respected insurance names

Get auto insurance at the best rate!

Getting the best value for your insurance dollar

Have you reevaluated your life insurance needs lately?

Having problems finding enough life insurance?

Having proper insurance coverage can make the loss easier

High-benefits, low-costs and excellent service

How about long-term care insurance?

How much protection is enough?

If you don't need insurance, don't buy it!

If you're not insured, you're playing with fire

Insurance designed to help cover it all

Insurance is a small price to pay

Insurance is something you have to have but don't want

Insurance... it's a fact of life!

Is your present coverage inadequate or too expensive? Check us out!

Isn't it time you consider buying insurance?

It's time to give your health insurance a checkup

Let's start by asking how much insurance is enough

Life insurance is important, but so is disability insurance

Low-cost, high-coverage health insurance

Lower your premiums and get the same or better coverage

Make sure your life insurance policy is up to date

No medical exam required

Now's the time to buy that asteroid insurance!

Our team will be on the site of a disaster within 24 hours

Paying too much for health insurance?

Peace of mind is accompanied by insurance

Premiums that meet the most frugal budget for health insurance

Protected by a solid, secure company

Sit down with an expert before you buy insurance

The advantage of this valuable coverage is its low cost

The cure for health insurance

The health plan that gives you more

The lowest cost insurance plan available anywhere

The most protection you can get for your money

The most respected name in the insurance industry

The premium is high, but the benefits are great

The price for not having the best protection just isn't worth it

The right way to protect your loved ones

Think all health insurance plans are alike? Think again!

Thinking about switching insurance?

Tragedies do not have to mean financial devastation

We can never emphasize enough to have the right insurance

We make life insurance easy

We only offer top-quality insurance programs!

We pay full benefits for as long as you're hospitalized

We take a load off your mind

We understand your insurance needs

We'll get you over, under, around or through it

We're driving down the cost of auto insurance

We've got you covered!

What exactly is your insurance doing?

What is your insurance worth?

When a disaster strikes, we strike back quickly!

When should you start thinking about long-term care?

When you're up against it, you don't have to be

Where there's smoke, there's insurance

Why pay more than you have to for the coverage you need?

Without disability insurance you're tempting financial fate

You can avoid a catastrophic event by buying insurance

You can count on our comprehensive coverage and affordable rates

You can have complete confidence in the company behind you

You can't be turned down for this insurance

You can't imagine living without insurance

You owe it to yourself and your family

You want the best care for those you care about!

You won't miss a single day of protection!

You'll get more for your insurance dollar with...

You'll like the coverage and the savings!

You've heard the words... peace of mind

Your coverage will never be canceled!

A click away from being a winner!

A web of opportunities awaits you

A whole new world of sale, deal and value possibilities

An educational gateway to the future

And don't even ask about a website. Of course!

And for all you Net surfers...

And what are your sales doing on the Internet?

And with just a double click, you can come along

Anything your phone system can do, the Internet can do cheaper and better

Are you a dot-com or a dot-bomb?

Are you addicted to the Internet?

Are you cashing in on the Web?

Are you concerned about privacy and safety?

Are you crying out for information?

Are you in Internet time?

Are you rethinking the Internet?

As the online world grows...

Blaze a trail to your site

Can you trust companies on the Internet?

Click here and be there

Click me now!

Click, click. Who's there?

Coming to a website near you

Competing for those clicks

Discover the real power of the Internet

Do you speak Internet?

Don't get caught in the Net...

Everything you need to surf the Internet

Exclusive Internet offer!

Explore a world of information without leaving home

Find something! Do something! Buy something!

For Internet users everywhere

From novelty to must haves

Get online and join us today!

Get the dot-com out of here!

Get to where you want to go, even faster

Get your feet on the Net

Getting customers in a very competitive www world

Getting surfers on board

Giving people their window to the world

Has the Internet changed the way you work?

Have we got a Website... for you?

Here's how to protect yourself against the Net threat

Here's looking at your site!

Hop onto the World Wide Web and save...

How can you make your website more profitable?

How sweet the Web is for phenomenal deals!

How to surf the Net and not get soaked

I found a great bargain in one click

I miss my Internet bargains!

If you don't know where you're going, the Web will get you there

In the Net we trust

Information on the go

Internet people are able, ready and willing to spend money

Is it your ultimate source for information?

Is your email about to burst?

Is your website getting enough traffic?

It takes a lot more than a glitzy website to create sales!

It's a candy land of personal consumer information

It's a dot-com delight

Just get plugged in, and whammo!

Learning how to web is easy with...

Make sure they can find you!

Making the Internet whatever you want it to be

Making the Net work for you!

Never fear, the Internet is here

Not all Internet sites are created equally

Oh what a tangled Web we weave

On this side of the Internet

Only on the Web

Put your site on primetime

Reach anyone, any time, anywhere

Reach out and Web someone

Remember when "it absolutely has to be there overnight" was good enough?

Rules for Net success

Save on stuff you need for networking

See us on the Net

Smile! You're online

So where do you surf?

So, log on right now!

Staying plugged in with us!

Stuck in a Web jam?

Talk to your local Internet guru

The click you've been waiting to hear

The dot starts here!

The Internet can be an amazingly powerful tool for...

The Internet is coming to an office near you

The Internet is the place to find us!

The Internet means business

The Internet works free for us!

The magic word is... Internet

The most revolutionary sales tool ever invented!

The new frontier! The new pioneers! The new gold rush!

The wheel. The printing press. The Internet.

The world at the click of a mouse

There is no night on the Internet

Things to buy for online shopaholics

This is no spam...

Understanding the Web customer

Visit us on the Web

We are the dot in the dots of the Internet business

We connect you with the world!

Web business can open your life like a can of beans

Welcome to our website

What has your website done for you lately?

When you need it now, download it

Where are you spending all your time on the Net?

Where can the Internet take you today?

Where the www do you want to go today?

Wow! 250,000 Hours Free!

Yes, you can get a free lunch off the Internet

You are now in dot-com land

You can find a goldmine on the Internet

You just need to log on and see what you can buy!

You're a click away from being a winner!

Your home's most vital connection to the world

Your reputation is your website

Your website is your ultimate Yellow Pages ad!

You're only as good as your Web page!

A free, 30-minute consultation

A good decorator can give you what you want

A good interior designer doesn't have to cost a fortune

A house doesn't become a home until you decorate with what you love

A modernist twist... and within your budget!

A new viewpoint on decorating your home

A professional designer to help you put it all together

A true reflection of your individual taste

A very stylish home doesn't have to cost a lot of money

A world of decorating ideas!

Affordable elegance

An ensemble that looks like you spent a fortune

An extraordinary decorating sale!

An eye for beauty and a craving for comfort

An inviting feeling

Be your own decorator

Beautify your home... one room at a time

Before you begin decorating, call...

Call for free swatches!

Can you imagine your room looking like that?

Comfort is of No. 1 importance in decorating a home

Create a showcase home of your own

Create your personal lifestyle with us

Custom Decorating Sale!

Decorate your home with us

Decorating on the cheap

Designing a room that's just right for you

Designing for your lifestyle

Do-it-yourself decorating service!

Dress up your walls! Save 25%!

Enhance your home's beauty

Entertaining ideas of redecorating?

Express your personal desires and passion through decorating

Fill your home with warmth and comfort

For those who don't have their own interior designers

Free in-home measuring!

Getting a room facelift has never been easier

Great decorating is essential to beautiful living

Here's how to redo a room in minutes

Home decorating savings!

Home furnishing you can afford

How cool can you make your kid's room?

How do you know what looks best in your home?

How to create a room that says "Wow!"

How to work with an interior designer

Hung up on decorating?

Ideas for your home without taking a second mortgage

If your budget allows, consult an interior decorator

Interior decorating... today's alternative

Interior design on a budget!

Is it time to change the look of your living room?

It's not about cost; it's about style!

It's time to wake up the home with a little life

Jazz Up Your Room Sales Event!

Leave the decorating to us!

Let our professional decorators create a look that's right for you

Let us create the room of your dreams

Let's talk decorating

Luxury is only expensive when it's overpriced

Make a statement about yourself

Make all your decorating decisions with professional help and confidence

Make your decorating dreams come true

Nobody brings it all together like we do

Our design pros have the perfect answers

Our remarkable attention to detail is our trademark

Relaxing and casual, yet decidedly tasteful

Revitalize your home with color

Simple solution to decorating your windows

Smart living

The decorating expert

The finishing touch for any room

The right interior fashions for the right rooms

The room of your dreams

The thought of redecorating your home can be a gut-wrenching experience

They won't believe you did it yourself

Thinking about decorating your home

Together we will decorate your dream home

Total home concept

Turn ordinary into... extraordinary

Turn your bedroom into a boudoir

Visit our custom home fashion department

We bring rooms to life!

We bring the perfect designs right to your home

We bring warmth and comfort to your home

We can help you put it all together

We create just the look you're after

We do the decorating your way

We do windows beautifully!

We give free decorating advice

We love making your home special

We make house calls!

We make it easy for you to fulfill your decorating dreams

We make rooms unique

We pay attention to your taste

We personalize your home to your taste

We take great care in creating a beautiful home

We will brighten any room in your house

We will create a home that is uniquely yours

We work with what the customer wants

We work within the means and taste of our clients

We'll cook up a new interior for you

We'll make your home cozy and warm

We'll make your room a showplace!

We'll spruce up your interior decoration

We're proud to reinvent your living room

What can you expect from an interior designer?

Window treatments... all on sale!

You can spruce things up without spending a fortune!

Your complete window decorating source

Your home is a statement you make to the world

Your interior designer can find someone who can do the job for you!

Investments

A good way to grow your money

A great return on your investment

A safe place to put your money

A smart investment gives you more for your money

A sound investment? A wise investment? A lucrative investment?

A unique investment for your future

A word of advice to investors:

An investment plan won't work if you don't start one... Now!

An unique opportunity for you to invest in the future

Are there too few eggs in your basket?

Are you financially set for life?

Are you getting the right financial advice?

Are you living on easy street?

Are you sitting on your assets?

Be investment smart

Build your financial future today!

Building your portfolio

Children should learn to save... It's an investment for all their parents

Concerned about investment risk?

Consider our past in planning your future retirement

Contact your investment professional, call...

Continue to earn. Continue to save. Continue to invest.

Could your money do better elsewhere?

Do it now, and avoid financial disaster

Do you know what a good investment looks like?

Do you know what to do with your money?

Does your investment need a shot in the arm?

Do-it-yourself investing

Don't blow it... invest!

Don't leave your estate in the hands of the government

Don't let anyone clown around with your money

Don't let your money get dusty

Enhance your financial future

Every penny really does count

Exciting opportunities for investment

Feather your nest with us

Feel like you need a crystal ball to figure out your investments?

Financial fitness takes precedence over physical fitness

Financial protection for the family

Get a handle on what your worth is today!

Get a nice return on your investment

Get the jump start on your financial future

Getting a grip on your finances

Got a few thousand to invest?

Haphazard about savings and spending?

Have cash, will invest!

Helping people make the most of their investments

Helping people manage their finances

Here's how to get the most out of your retirement assets

Hit a home run with your investments

How do you feel about your financial future?

How does your investment garden grow?

How independent do you want to be?

How much money will you need to retire?

How not to manage your money

How safe are the havens in your investment portfolio?

How to get control of your financial life

How to invest more safely

If you want to retire rich, your best bet is to invest like crazy!

If you're in need of investment intelligence...

In financing, like life, timing is everything

Invest in your child's future

Invest wisely, your family depends on it

Invest your money on proven performance

Invest your money where you'll get the greatest return

Investigate, before you invest

Investing is about making money

Investing that makes financial sense

Investment ideas that can create an interest in investing

Investments pay dividends

Investments today can lead to big returns tomorrow

Investments work for you instead of you working for them

Isn't it time to put your money where you can enjoy it?

It all comes down to return on investment

It pays to consult an expert

It takes a smart person to recognize a smart investment

It's about your money!

It's an excellent way to save for your future

It's like you're making money the old-fashioned way

It's never too early to start learning money management

It's never too soon to start investing

It's time to start investing!

It's time to stop and smell the dividends

Keep your cash hard at work!

Know your broker better than your wife

Let us be your personal finance trainer!

Let us help you make all your money work together

Let us show you the way to grow your money

Let your money start working for you!

Live like a millionaire on your retirement investment

Looking for a place to park some cash?

Looking for a return on your dollar?

Looking for a smart place to put your money?

Looking for financial advice?

Looking for financial independence?

Make a wise investment for your well being

Make plans now... for retirement comfort

Make your money last a lifetime!

Managing your money isn't just how to spend it, but how you can save for a rainy day

Money has the power to grow

Never fall in love with your assets

Not taking risks may be the biggest risk of all

Now is the time to invest!

One-stop shopping for financial products

Only you are responsible for your financial security

Our mission is to help you make money

Plan for income today and tomorrow!

Plan now for a comfortable future!

Plan now to have more later!

Planning today might save your tomorrow

Put a little something aside for the future

Put your money to work for you!

Puzzled about your financial future

Investments

Recommendations that can make you a fortune!

See how far we can take your money

Small investments, big results!

Smart investors work with smart brokers

So, what's going on with your finances?

Start investing now!

Steer your money in the right direction

Take a breather from financial stress

Take control of your financial future

Taking the first step towards financial security

That penny can be the start of your financial success

That's why it's called estate planning

The key is investing the money you have wisely

The key is return on investments

The key to a lifetime of security!

The power of compounding returns can work wonders

The right investment may not always be obvious

The smart money says...

The way to a sound future

There is still plenty of time to grow rich

There's a better way to spend your money, invest

Think about your financial fitness

Think first, then invest!

Think of your retirement as a major purchase

This is the new age of financial planning

'Tis the season for stock tips

To invest or not to invest?

Turn liquid assets into solid gold, today!

We can take your IRA to more places

We let you know where you stand!

We pledge allegiance to your investments

We save your investment from commissions

We think about retiring... more than you!

We'll help you feather your nest!

We'll put you on Easy Street!

We're going to recommend exactly nothing

We're here to make our investors money

We're your financial life preserver

Welcome to Financing 101

What are your financial targets?

What is your money doing today?

What to do in financial crisis?

What's the best way to save for college?

When it comes to managing your money, don't be a turkey

When money works hard for you, you don't have to work so hard for your money

When you need advice... go to the professionals

Who do you call with questions about your finances?

Who says you have to wait until sixty to retire?

Why bury your money with an expensive funeral?

Will taxes eat up your kids' inheritance?

Will your money retire before you do?

Worried about your family's finances?

You don't have to be an analyst to invest with us!

You need to start investing today!

You should invest with someone you trust!

You're rarely too young or too old to invest

You've got to start somewhere, sometime!

Jewelry

24-karat savings!

3 carats of dazzle

50% off all fashion jewelry!

50% to 70% off fine and precious jewelry!

A 3-carat princess cut diamond is a bargain beyond belief!

A bevy of diamond beauties

A carat or more, one in a million

A cut above the rest

A dash of fine artistry

A dazzling diamond celebration

A diamond makes a girl happy

A diamond says everything

A diamond-in-the-rough deal!

A gem too good to pass up

A girl never has enough jewelry

A jewel at a great price

A jewel more precious than gold

A maze of 14kt gold

A once-in-a-lifetime purchase!

A pouch of sparkling baubles

A rainbow of gemstones

A real diamond in the rough

A spectacular conversation piece!

A stone of exceptional quality and brilliance

A symbol of infinity: Rings

A thousand glittering treasures

A true gem for the money!

A truly romantic keepsake

An exquisite strand of silver beads

An extraordinary necklace of amber beads

Beautiful jewelry at fantastic prices!

Buying a diamond can be a significant purchase!

Buying a diamond can be intimidating

Choose a jeweler as you would choose a wife

Classic design jewelry never goes out of style

Clueless when it comes to jewelry?

Customer design services and jewelry appraisals

Dazzling diamond sales event!

Diamond savings extravaganza!

Diamonds are a girl's newest best friend

Diamonds are forever

Diamonds beyond all expectations

Diamonds say it all

Diamonds to cherish forever

Diamonds... the gift of a lifetime!

Each piece of jewelry is one of a kind

Earrings for that special occasion

Every lady ought to have pearls

Exciting, beautiful, quality-crafted jewelry

Extraordinary values on fine jewelry!

Fabulous finds in fine jewelry

Fabulous jewelry on sale!

Fine jewelry clearance event!

Fine, fashion jewelry

For all gem lovers

For that pinkie finger

Frank advice about diamonds

Free jewelry cleaning!

Gems that glow like stars

Gems to make you look like the sun

Gemstone and diamond extravaganza!

Jewelry

Gemstone blowout sale!

Gleaming objects of wanderlust

Gold, sterling, platinum, emeralds, diamonds and much more

Hand-crafted sterling silver jewelry

Here's a good reason to love diamonds!

How do you know if your jeweler is reputable?

If you can't decide between the diamonds or the fur... buy them both!

If you don't know your jeweler, you'd better know jewelry

Incredible savings off fine jewelry store prices!

It gleams with a priceless sparkle

It'll make a deep impression... period!

It's hard to beat a diamond

It's jewelry you don't have to think about

It's the accessories that make the woman

Jewelry that flirts with the eye

Jewelry that is customized and personalized

Jewelry that is unique as you

Just looking at jewelry can make you feel good

Keepsake jewelry all on sale!

Let your jewelry speak for itself

Like people, no two diamonds are alike

Mad About Diamonds Sale Event!

Magnificent jewels

Memorable moments with diamonds

Million-dollar jewelry sale!

Nothing lingers like a ring's glow

One of our most precious jewels

On-staff certified gemologist

Opulence! Splendor! Brilliance!

Priceless is just a word

Recycled jewels on sale!

Ring her finger with sapphires and diamonds

Select fine and precious jewelry all on sale!

Shopping for gems!

Simply dazzling

So precious to the touch

Sparkling diamonds. Opulent gemstones. Precious gold.

Sparkling savings!

Stunning in every detail

Tell him a little ice is all it takes to melt your heart

Tennis bracelets are not only for tennis players

The cure for a diamond craving

The diamond symbolizes the expression of love and commitment

The gem of the day!

The true value of jewelry

The ultimate gift is jewelry!

The world's finest gold jewelry

These pearls are brought to you by...

This is one diamond that's a cut above

Wanted, your old jewelry!

We have the expertise to ensure your purchase is brilliantly flawless

Welcome to the gem show of shows

What to look for in a quality diamond

When flowers just won't do... diamonds will!

When it comes to beauty, these are true gems

Where your diamond dreams come true

Wrap a wrist in gold

You can never go wrong with diamonds

You can't go wrong spending money on jewelry

You can't go wrong with anything that sparkles

July 4th

4th of July Celebration of Savings!

4th of July hot buys!

4th of July Marathon Sale!

4th of July Savings Explosion!

4th of July specials to shout about

A cool blast for a hot Fourth

A flag-waving sale!

A great patriotic serving dish

A salute to savers

Add a little July 4th spirit to...

All-American sale that's out of the blue

All-American Savings!

An explosion of savings!

And we're even open July 4th

As American as the Fourth of July

As sizzling as Fourth of July fireworks!

Awesome star-spangled savings on July 4th party starters!

Bang-up specials!

Bargains born in the USA!

Blush Red! Offbeat white! Tastefully blue!

Bright lights... big celebration!

Cap off the Fourth of July festivities with a bang!

Capture all the excitement of the Fourth of July

Celebrate America's birthday on the 4th

Celebrate the 4th of July with your independence

Celebrate this Fourth of July in a truly patriotic way

Color your 4th of July picnic with...

Cook up a colorful celebration

Declaration of savings!

Did you ever have red, white and blue hot dogs?

Don't forget the Fourth of July Parade

Don't let the parade pass you by

Dynamite offers for the 4th

Exercise your freedom for the best price with flag-waving savings!

Explosive Fourth of July savings!

Explosive star-spangled savings for patriotic picnics

Festival of freedom

Fired up for the Fourth of July

Fireworks on the 4th of July are as American as apple pie

Fireworks Sale Extravaganza!

Flag waving savings!

Flag-wavin' values to get your attention

Food! Fun! Fireworks!

For a revolutionary July fourth celebration!

For your bang-up Fourth

Fourth festival frenzy

Fourth of July explosion of savings!

Fourth of July firecracker of a sale!

Fourth of July Sale Blowout!

Fourth of July Weekend Savings Extravaganza!

Freedom, opportunity and the Fourth of July

Friends, fun and fireworks add up to a fabulous 4th

Get ready for the biggest barbecue day of the year!

Go 4th and celebrate!

God Bless you, America

Happy birthday America, hats off to you! **191**

July 4th

Happy Fourth of July specials!

Have a blast on the Fourth of July

Have an all-American 4th of July

Have breakfast with Uncle Sam

Here's a new way to celebrate the 4th

Hot 4th of July sale!

Hot fireworks and explosive savings!

How's this for a red, white and blue celebration?

It's a star-spangled celebration!

It's a Yankee Doodle Dandy of a deal!

It's our star-spangled salute

It's the way to say happy birthday to America

Join us for a celebration of the birth of our nation

July 4th blowout, you gotta go see it!

Just an old-fashioned Fourth of July celebration with good old-fashioned prices!

Kick off your holiday with a bang at...

Let us light your fuse

Let's make July fourth safe

Life, liberty and the pursuit of a cookout

Looking for a big bang this 4th?

Make a day of the Fourth of July and bring a picnic

Old Glory in all its glory

One Yankee Doodle celebration!

Parade of values, it's the talk of the town!

Red, white and blue savings!

Savings that sparkle!

Savings worth saluting!

Savings-American style!

Spectacular 4th of July savings!

Star-spangled after July savings sale!

Star-spangled Fourth of July excitement!

Star-Spangled Sale Event!

Star-Spangled Savings Blast!

Stock up for the 4th of July weekend

The fireworks display is free!

The Independence Day bargain blast

The stars and stripes celebration kicks off with a bang

There will be plenty of fireworks at...

They'll all want seconds on the Fourth

This Fourth of July is on us

This holiday weekend catch the big fireworks

This July 4th, enjoy the rewards of freedom

Three cheers for the red, white and blue

Today is our country's birthday

Toot your horn on July 4th

Wave the flag... it's time to celebrate!

We have a lot to be thankful for this 4th of July

We're blasting high prices with explosive deals!

We're bursting with savings!

We've got the fireworks for your 4th of July

Wear a bit of history, tell it like it is

What are you doing to celebrate the birth of our nation?

What better time to one-up Uncle Sam than the Fourth of July?

What better way to enjoy the Fourth of July than...

What's on tap for July fourth?

Why not hold an old-fashioned 4th of July picnic?

Wow... What a Fourth of July!!!

You'll be saying oooooh, ahhhhh, wow, ohhhhh at our 4th of July Fireworks Sale Celebration!

You'll salute the savings this 4th of July!

You're invited to our nation's birthday party

Kids / Teens

4th of July savings for every red-blooded American teen!

8 out of 10 teens shop here!

A fresh approach to quality kid care

A sale that clicks with teens!

A special sale just for kids!

All about teens

Attention all kids!

Bargains for teens who act like complete idiots!

Bargains just for teens!

Be a champion for kids

Be a kid again at...

Be the first kid on the block to have one!

Big kids... little kids... just for kids!

Big savings on all the latest stuff!

Big-time kid stuff!

Bring on the teens... bring on the savings!

Buy Anything You Want... Sales Event!

Calling all kids

Can you spare a kid?

Child care: What parents want

Cool stuff... cool teen savings!

Everybody's Doing It... Savings Event!

Exciting kid's stuff savings!

Fashions for fresh-thinking teens

For big kids only!

For kids with special needs

For little kids! For big kids!
For grownup kids!

Fun for kids... funky for adults

Fun kids love

Fun things for kids to do

Get a glimpse of the glam at...

Give kids a chance

Go from ho-hum to yum-yum with...

Going where the teens are

Helping kids do the smart thing

How to make a kid "special"

How to raise great kids

If they're very, very, very good, they can go to the mall!

Investing in children is worth the price

It brings out the little kid in everybody!

It's dazzling! It's hot! It's irresistible!

It's sure to delight the kids

It's the cool thing to do

It's what kids want

Just ask your kids

Just what teens expect and more!

Keep it kid-friendly

Kid bits! Kid power! Kid stuff!

Kids are where it's at

Kids come in all sizes and shapes

Kids eat 'em up

Kids go free!

Kids just wanna have fun

Kids know where the cookies are

Kids love 'em

Kids need you now!

Kids: Don't try this at home

Kids' days! Free admission!

Kids' fun guaranteed

Kids' summer specials!

Kid-tested

Look alike! Dress alike! Act alike!

Making teens smart customers

Kids / Teens

Off-the-wall savings for all teen shoppers!

On track with teens

Our kids need your help

Our No. 1 priority is our children

Outrageous savings for sportos and freaks!

Pay attention to kid-power

Peer pressure is not allowed in this store!

Reaching out to kids

Satisfy your kid's curiosity

Savings fit for a kid!

Savings time to be a teen!

Send kids to college, send yourself to the bank

Small kids! Big kids! All kids!

Smart buys... for smart teens!

Smashing savings for all teeny-boppers!

So, okay, we messed up... everything is on sale!

Soon-To-Be-A-Teenager Sales Event!

Special savings for special kids!

Stepping up for teens

Stuff for your hip-hop lifestyle!

Surf's up... prices down, dudes!!!

Teen fashions for that all-around sloppy look!

Teen time

Teenager for hire

Teenagers are customers too!

Teenagers are teenagers wherever you go

Teenagers Rule Sales Event!

Teens are everybody's best customers!

Teens gravitate toward the latest stuff

Teens love us!

Teens speaking out

Teens take action

Teens Will Be Teens... Sales Event!

Teens' time is now!

The American kids have spoken

The fun-filled snack is just too cool for any kid to resist!

The Kids Corner

The kids will just flock in

The savings are awesome for every teen and kid!

The store for teens' needs and wants!

The teen audience is a marketer's dream

The ultimate teen dream

The wide world of kids

The "Wow" store for teens!

Thinking of getting your belly button pierced?

Totally unteen... totally uncool

Ways to raise great kids

We appreciate our teen customers!

We care about kids

We cater to all kids

We focus on kids and teens

We give kids the world

We make kids happy

We sell baggy pants and logo-driven t-shirts

We sell the things that teens want and love!

We'll make you feel like a kid again!

We're kid-friendly

We're telling it like it is... Hot Stuff... Cool Savings, Weekend Sale!

We've got the hottest teen look!

We've got what every teen needs!

What teens want, we've got!

What's new for kids!

You could be the teenager of the year!

You're not just a number in our store!

You've got it, kid...

Labor Day

A day for all hard-workin' folks

A day for special recognition of our work force

A Labor Day cookout is fuel for the day

A Labor Day salute

A Labor Day workout to start the day with a smile

A special thanks to all those who labor

A time to celebrate your livelihood

A time to honor the industrial spirit

Ah, Labor Day. Nothing to do but...

All Americans are honored on Labor Day

All work clothes on sale... Labor Day only!

America works. Today America plays!

An incredible sale for all hard-working Americans!

As the Labor Day weekend gets under way...

As the nation pauses to celebrate Labor Day...

As you enjoy this Labor Day weekend...

Be happy in your labors, be happy today with terrific savings!

Big Labor Day weekend storewide sale!

Bonus buys for Labor Day celebrations!

Celebrate Labor Day with honest-to-good prices!

Celebrate Labor Day... you deserve it

Celebrating Labor Day with working pride

Celebrating the fruits of your labor

Celebrating the hard work and diligence of American workers

Chalk up another Labor Day weekend

Check out these hard-working values

Don't belabor the Labor Day fun

Don't do Labor Day without one

Easy entertaining for Labor Day

Enjoy a well-earned holiday this Labor Day

Enjoy Labor Day and let the good times roll

Enjoy the fruits of your labor

For all those who worked through the holiday, thanks!

Free labor today!

Get ready for your Labor Day guests with...

Get the goods on Labor Day!

Give thanks for a day off

Hats off to America's work force

Have a Labor Day bash with us!

Have a labor-saver weekend

Have a picnic this Labor Day

Hooray for Labor Day!

It's a Blue Collar, White Collar Sale Event!

It's a day off for all you workaholics, too!

It's a day to honor the American work force

It's just pure and simple... a Labor Day Sale!

It's not just a sale... it's a Labor Day sale!

It's our big Labor Day sale!

It's the Unofficial End of Summer Labor Day Savings Celebration!

Join your Labor Day parade!

Labor Day bargains never sounded so good!

Labor Day bonanza, just for today!

Labor Day buys to wake you up today!

Labor Day Closeout Extravaganza!

Labor Day

Labor Day inventory sell-off

Labor Day is a labor of love

Labor Day is a time to relax and dine with us

Labor Day picnics that'll make your day

Labor Day price blast!

Labor Day projects for your kind of day

Labor Day Save-a-Thon!

Labor Day Savings Event going on now!

Labor Day special treats!

Labor Day Stock-Up Bonanza!

Labor Day Summer Clearance on all...

Labor Day values worth celebrating

Labor Day Weekend Sale!

Labor Day... a time for new beginnings

Labor-saving Labor Day buys!

Let the hard-working folks enjoy Labor Day

Looking for something to do over the long Labor Day weekend?

Magnificent savings in honor of our country's workforce!

Make a Labor Day meal an event!

Make your last cookout the best of all

Next day service, even on Labor Day

Now through Labor Day

On the go for Labor Day

Open Labor Day for our Sale of Savings!

Open Labor Day... Thank you for today!

Our biggest sale ends Labor Day!

Our Labor Day savings work for you!

Party on Labor Day

Pre-Labor Day specials!

Pre-Labor Day spectacular savings!

Saluting hard working Americans

Savings Days... Friday through Labor Day Monday!

Send off summer with a Labor Day blowout!

Sharing the fruits of your labor with exceptional savings!

Smart money won't miss this Labor Day sale!

Start your Labor Day weekend now!

Summer's last holiday cookout! Make it special with...

Super Labor Day deals all day long!

Super spectacular savings for all hard-workin' folks!

Taste the fruits of your labors at our cookout

This is why they call it Labor Day

Today... all your labors are rewarded

Today... enjoy the results of your labors!

Try this for a Labor Day treat

We salute the American laborer

We salute the working mother

We're celebrating Labor Day and giving our employees the day off to spend with their families

We're having our Labor Day Spectacular... again!

We're open Labor Day!

We've got our work cut out for us today! It's our Annual Labor Day Sale of Sales!

We've taken the labor out of Labor Day picnics

What do you say we have a Labor Day picnic?

You won't work up a sweat with these prices!

You work hard, so we work hard to save you...

You'll enjoy the results of your labors with these bargains!

You're invited to a Labor Day jamboree

Your favorite Labor Day thirst quencher

Your hard-earned money won't miss a great Labor Day sale!

Lawn/Garden

A Big Green Thumbs Up Sensational Sale!

A garden of values

A gardener's guide to summer chores

A gift to inspire green thumbs

A harvest of values!

A lavish garden for a little green

A must-have for your garden

A planting project you can share

A spring trip to a garden center can be...

Add a token of your personality to your garden with...

Add life to your garden with unbelievable spring savings!

All I want for Christmas is a yard full of black dirt

All the gardening tips you need to know

Are you a plantaholic?

Are you an organic gardener?

Armchair gardening in January is smart!

Ask the garden guy!

Bargains for money-wise gardens!

Before you start planting, make sure you have the right tools

Breaking new ground on lawn and garden prices!

Bring joy to your garden with...

Bursting with bargains!

Buy 'em and watch 'em grow!

Catch the gardening fever!

Celebrate a garden of savings!

Check out our greenhouse values!

Creating your own garden is easier then you think

Discover the excitement of gardening!

Do you have anything you need planted?

Do you have the tools to garden?

Do you use pesticides?

Don't leave the garden without it

Early Bird Sale Event!

Eliminate that sneezing and wheezing from gardening with...

Everything under the sun... Annual Garden Sale!

Fall garden spectacular savings!

Fertilizer Face-Off Fabulous Sale!

For folks with green thumbs

For gardeners who appreciate art as much as plants

Fun begins the day you start your garden

Garden bargains for people who want to get down and dirty!

Garden time-savers!

Garden-inspired gifts

Get a grip on gardening

Get a lush, green lawn for very little green!

Get more fun out of gardening with...

Give someone the gift of gardening

Give your garden a whole new fresh look with...

Good gardening requires well-maintained tools

Good gardens start from the ground up

Good time to plant, great time to save!

Grace your garden with...

Great ideas for your own garden

Great savings for early bird gardening!

Grow a Garden Sale Event!

Grow a garden... It can be therapeutic

Happy planting!

Lawn/Garden

Have you taken a walk in your garden this spring?

Here are 10 good things to plant and one great one!

If you plant it, they will grow!

If your garden is beset by squirrels, deer and rodents, don't despair

Is your garden wilting in the heat?

It is time to order your seeds and enjoy the beauty of the garden

It's not too early to think about the spring garden season

It's time to head out to the garden center!

Jump-start your garden this spring with us!

Keep the garden free from weeds, diseases and destructive insects with...

Keep your grass up to par

Last call for lawn and garden savings!

Let it Grow, Let it Grow, Let it Grow Sales Event!

Let us show you the magic gardening touch

Make Your Garden a Work of Art Sales Event!

Next year's garden starts now!

No garden is complete without an...

One-step gardener's shop

Our garden tools sale is growing!

Our savings watering bucket runneth over!

Plant a row for the hungry!

Plant-tastic plant sale!

Remember, great gardens began in the fall

Save some green at the garden center

Savings are in full bloom at...

Savings for weekend garden diggers!

Scent-sational Garden of Savings!

Show Off Your Garden Sale Event!

Start your garden off right with...

Terrific savings for gardening enthusiasts!

The best gardeners shop for...

The best gardening bargains anywhere

The countdown to planting time has begun

The End of the Gardening Season Sales Event!

The Growin' o' the Green Sales Event!

The only thing we can't plant is our quality

This offer is nothing to sneeze at!

This week's garden report

Time for gardeners to start planning for spring

Tips to protect your green thumb

Today is the time to plant mid-summer bulbs

Turn your garden into a spring wonderland

Wake up your garden with...

Wanted: Green thumbs!

Watch your savings grow!

Ways to grow! Ways to save!

We make it fun in garden planning

We make your garden grow!

We're the hapless gardener's best friend

We've got everything you need for a lush summer garden

We've got everything you need to get growin'

What More Could A Gardener Ask For Sales Event!

When you don't have a green thumb... see us!

Why not grow your own?

Winterize Your Garden Sales Event!

Yards of savings sale!

Your garden pharmacy

Your garden starts with us!

Magic

A Little Black Magic Sales Event!

A magic world of...

A magical wonderland of utterly unbelievable savings!

A touch of magic makes things happen

A Whiz of a Wizard Sales Event!

Add a magic touch to...

All it takes is a few magic words to do the deal!

Come feel the magic

Could it be magic? You bet it is!

Do you believe in magic?

Don't miss this act. It's magic!

Every moment is magical

Every trick comes with a how-to demonstration

Experience the magic behind the magic

Fly with us on the Magic Carpet Sales Event!

Get Ready To Be Amazed... Sale Event!

Holiday magic is in the wrappings

It all adds up to a magical show of unreal savings!

It works like magic

It's going to be a magical evening!

It's incredible... you must see it to believe it!

It's a moment of magic for the young and old

It's like magic to be here

It's magic at its very best

It's your magic number!

Magical gifts for every generation

Maybe you need a new crystal ball?

Money-makin' magic

Remember the magic word... Save!

Rub the lamp and say... Wow, what a sale!

Savings are in the cards

Savings that are absolutely magical!

Show 'em your magic wand

Simply magical!

Spread the magic throughout the holiday season

Step into the magical world of fantastic savings!

The fashions of today are sheer magic

The magic number is 50% off!

The magic of Christmas

There is nothing magical about it... everyday low prices!

There's something magical about going to a toy store

These deals work like magic!

This sale puts a touch of magic in your pocket!

Want to add a little magic to your life?

We are going to amaze you!

We have nothing up our sleeves... just magical deals!

We want to hear you shout these magic words... I love the savings!

We'll put the magic back into your life

We'll show you the magic with unbelievable savings!

We're going to have to pull a rabbit out of a hat to...

Welcome to a magical world of excitement!

You'll freak out with these deals!

You'll have the magic touch with these bargains!

Your wish is our command

A note to the germ-conscious people

A second opinion never hurts

A sure cure for the common cold

Ah, the miracles of modern medicine!

All your drugstore needs for less!

Allergy-free zone

Always take your medications seriously

An apple a day keeps the doctor away

Are you at risk for heart disease?

Are your feet a pain in the neck?

Ask your doctor

Be your own doctor

Beyond the stethoscope

Cancer doesn't discriminate

Celebrating Cancer Survivors' Day

Change your life and you'll improve your health

Choose a doctor you can trust and feel comfortable with

Discover relief that can last and last and last

Disease of the week

Disease recognizes no frontiers

Do what the doctor says!

Do you have an ax to grind with medicine?

Do you have high blood pressure?

Do you want to lower your high cholesterol?

Don't forget to take your medicine

Don't go to a doctor on April Fool's Day

Don't let chronic pain manage your life

Don't let your allergies slow you down

Don't wait until it's too late

February is heart month

Fill your medicine cabinet with healthy values at...

Fill your prescription while you shop

Finally, a medical breakthrough

Find a doctor... Before your body needs one

Finding a good doctor isn't easy

For chronic pain suffers

Get smart: Get the right medication

Get the medical test you need... today!

Give your spine the right backing

Great buys on pain relief!

Has the health care crisis affected you?

Have you ever had an ulcer?

Here are the flu facts

Hey, you can get diabetes too!

How strong are your bones?

How you can save on medical costs

I don't listen to doctors because they give me heartburn

If cosmetic surgery is for you, here are some options:

If your back is out of whack, go see a chiropractor

In an age of miracle medicines

In the hunt for new medicines

Insist on seeing an audiologist for your hearing health care needs

Is it an allergy? Is it in my head? Is there a cure? What do I do?

Is there a doctor online?

It could turn into pneumonia if you don't catch it in time

It's a fact of life. Kids get sick!

It's deadly if not treated

It's evidence-based medicine

It's our professional opinion

It's time to roll up those sleeves and face the needle

Join the fight against AIDS

Just listen to what another doctor has to say

Kiss your cold sore goodbye!

Look and feel your best for less!

Looking for a family doctor?

Medical poll reveals 8 out of 10 doctors take a vacation for good health

Medical research makes a difference

Must-have for your medicine cabinet

Need a chiropractor?

Need a great physician?

Nighttime pain relief...

Nine out of 10 doctors recommend...

No more back pain

No prescription can make you feel this good

Obesity is a major disease! What are you doing about it?

Pain is a very personal experience

Pain-ending alternatives

Play two rounds and call me in the morning

Prevention is the best medicine

Protect your medical records

Putting the right medicine into your body

Quality-of-life pharmacology

Questions about your medication?

Racing toward a cure

Raising healthy kids

Rent-a-doc

Rx for change

Seeing a doctor can be a real pain

She is the poster child for early detection

Shopping for a doctor?

Smart medicine that will cure your aching body

So, how long should you put up with pain?

Sports medicine has come a long way

Stay healthy this winter... Get a flu shot

Take your medicine

Taking the ouch out of a shot in the arm

Talk to your doctor about your symptoms

Talk to your doctor before you take any drugs

Thanks to medical progress, people are living longer

The best time to choose a doctor is before you need one

The doctor will see you now!

The first step is always call a doctor

The latest state-of-the-art digital hearing aid is sold at...

The medicines you trust today!

The most widely used general medical book in the world

The product doctors recommend most

The right care from the right doctor

The war on disease

The yearly check-up

Tips from an old doc

Warning signs are not to be ignored

Watch out for the flu bug

We can give you the key to a fat-free future

We've got the cure

What are you doing to help protect your heart?

What is the future of medicine?

What lurks in your medicine cabinet?

What would life be like without medicine?

Why risk a heart attack?

You don't need more medicine, you need the right medicine

Your doctor is always there for you!

20% off and no sales tax this weekend!

A 21-Gun Salute Sale Event!

A Memorial Day salute

A parade of values

A really big Memorial Day sale event!

A Salute to a Memorable Day Weekend

A time to pay tribute to...

A time to remember

After honoring the nation's war dead on Monday, begin a holiday from road rage

All fired up for Memorial Day

America bows its head in thanks to our father heroes

America is taking Monday off to observe the holiday

And gladly they served

And remember... In your own way

Are we worthy of their sacrifice?

Armed for Memorial Day

As we honor those who paid the ultimate price for freedom

Be a Memorial Day parade hero

Big weekend, little prices

But remember we must, remember we will

Buy a poppy and wear it proudly on Memorial Day!

Catch the Memorial Day sale wave!

Celebrate an All-American Memorial Weekend with us!

Crowd pleasers for Memorial Day

Day of remembrance

Drive safely over the holiday weekend

Flag a winner this Memorial Day and save!

Flag-wavin' savings!

Free flags for remembrance

Got any plans for the Memorial Day weekend?

Grilling season officially starts this weekend

Have a great American picnic!

Have a great Memorial Day weekend

Heading into the Memorial Day frenzy

Here's memorable savings!

Hey you... Pre-Memorial Day sales you'll remember

History will not forget them

Hold a special place in your heart for the celebration of Memorial Day

Honoring America's armed forces, past and present

Honoring the fallen

How soon we forget

How will you spend the Memorial Day holiday?

If you know a veteran who served our country, be sure to say "thanks!"

In memory of those who made the supreme sacrifice

It happens every Memorial Day

It's a memory to all the soldiers who were left behind

It's Memorial Day, and the country is kicking back

It's your patriotic duty

Join the Memorial Day parade on Main Street, USA

Join us for a moment of silence

Just in time for Memorial Day

Lest we forget

Let us teach our children the meaning of this tradition

Let's celebrate Memorial Day with honor, respect and gratitude

Make Memorial Day feasts memorable

Make your Memorial Day meaningful this year

Memorable savings!

Memorial Day essentials: Family, friends and fun

Memorial Day extravaganza!

Memorial Day is a time to celebrate America

Memorial Day memories

Memorial Day Parade of Values!

Memorial Day picnic & barbecue specials!

Memorial Day Sales Invasion!

Memorial Day savings are in the bag!

Memorial Day savings events!

Memorial Day savings really sizzle!

Memorial Day savings the American way!

Memorial Day Sell-a-Bration!

Memorial Day weekend blasts off!

Memorial Day Weekend Extravaganza!

Memorial Day Weekend Sales Event!

Memorial Day... Great savings to remember!

Memorial Weekend Sell-Off!

Memories make Memorial Day memorable

Not forgotten

Observe Memorial Day, go to church!

On this Memorial Day, let's not forget them

Our day to honor the memory of fallen heroes of all wars

Pay tribute to the memory of...

Re-examine the true idea of Memorial Day

Remember Memorial Day

Remember those who served

Remembering the brave

Remembrance is key to Memorial Day

Rev-up your Memorial Day party with...

Revving up for the long Memorial Day weekend

Salute the men and women of the armed forces this Memorial Day

Salute these savings in a blaze of glory!

Salute to America... there's no place like home

So we gather today to honor them

Take time to remember all those silent heroes

Thanks to Monday's Memorial Day holiday

The race is on for exciting Memorial Day savings!

The true meaning of Memorial Day

They deserve our thanks and our reverence

They gave their lives for American freedom

They made the supreme sacrifice so we can enjoy all that we have today

They shed their blood for our flag

Things to do over Memorial Day weekend

This is not just a day to celebrate, but a day to remember

Time again to stop and remember

Timeless reminders that valor is rare

To remember the gallantry

Ways to salute Memorial Day

We gather on Memorial Day to commemorate the fallen

We proudly honor the men and women of our armed forces, of all wars

We've cooked up a big batch of savings for the Memorial Day weekend!

What could be better than a Memorial Day cookout?

What's your Memorial Day menu?

You're invited to our Memorial Day Indy Party

Money

A cash bonanza!

A dollar saved is a dollar earned

A few coins a day

A million dollars buys a lot of pizzas

A stash of cash

Adding up to the penny

After all, it's only money

All it takes is time and money

Always keep an eye on your money

As they say, go where the money is

Be a penny saver!

Before you know it, you could be rolling in the green

Before you plunk down megabucks for...

Best way to stretch a dollar

Bet your bottom dollar you'll...

Beyond the dollar signs

Bring home the bacon

But dollars and cents aren't the only factor

Cash and carry

Cash in a flash

Cash in on the money craze

Cash on the barrel

Cash... when you need it

Dial 'M' for money

Did someone say money?

Do not fear. Your fortune awaits you!

Do you know how to euro?

Do your wallet a favor and shop at...

Does money grow on trees?

Does the buck stop in your pocketbook?

Doesn't cost you a red cent

Dollar for dollar, pound for pound

Don't pay one penny till...

Don't waste your money on gimmicks or hype

Easy On Your Pocket Sale Event!

Everything runs smoothly when you pay with cash

E-Z money

Fast holiday cash

Fatten your piggy bank with...

For those with more cents than money

Gawrsh, that'll buy a lot of cheese!

Get out your checkbook

Get the most bang for your buck at...

Get those co-op dollars working for you

Get your money's worth, or your money back. That's our promise!

Go ahead, it's your money

Great money-saving tips!

Hard up for cash?

Hey, look what a buck buys!

Ho, Ho, Ho, who's got the dough?

How can you be sure you're getting your money's worth?

How I became a spendthrift

How to be a zillionaire!

How to gamble away your money

How to spend other people's money

How to stretch your dollar with...

Hurry, there's "Big Money" to be made

If you've got the money, go do it!

Improving your net worth

Is there a cash machine somewhere?

Is your pocketbook getting thinner than you'd wish?

It boils down to two bucks a month

It comes down to dollars and cents

It takes money, Honey!

It's a guaranteed moneymaker!

It's expensive, but it's only money

It's how to make extra cash

It's just another way to stretch
your dollars

It's like money in the bank

It's money in your pocket

It's only a dollar a day!

It's worth every single penny

It's your money... take it with you!

Just say... Mo' money! Mo' money!
Mo' money!

Just think of all the money you'll save!

Let's hear it for the dollar

Looking to make a little money on
the side?

Make money the new-fashioned way

Money isn't the only perk we offer

Money truly well spent

Money-saving efficiency

More For Your Money Sale Event!

More ways to make a little scratch

More zip and zap for the money

Need some extra cash for the
holiday season?

Need money, now!

No money down

Not one red cent more!

Now you're talking real money

Now... you'll stop saying "If I only had
the money"!

Other ways to spend your money

Our mission is to help you make money

Pay as you go!

Put your money where your mouth is

Raking in the cash

Save money fast!

Save some green for...

So, don't waste another dollar or
another moment

Splurge on yourself...

Still only 10 cents

Take the money and run

Tapping the piggy bank again?

The buck is welcome at my desk

There's big money in fortune cookies

Two bucks a pop

Want to make tons of money?

We are willing to take your money

We take anything... Cash! Checks!
Credit cards!

We watch every dime that comes in
the door

We'll give you your money's worth

We'll put you on a spending spree with
the savings!

We'll take it in cash!

What do you mean you don't take
real money?

What do you think, I look like an
ATM machine?

What would you do with a million dollars?

Whatever happened to a penny saved...?

When money talks most
people understand

When you've got money, who needs luck?

Where the buck stops, no one knows

Whose hand is that in your pocket?

Why throw money out the window?

Worth the extra bucks

You can save money at the same time!

You don't have to spend a lot of clams
for that!

You don't have to spend a wad of dough
to do it

You don't need to pay a penny extra!

You've hit pay dirt!

More

A great deal and a great deal more

A store with more

A taste for more...

All of the above and a whole lot more

All that you expect and more

Always room for one more

And much, much, much, much, much more

And now there's even more to save!

And the more the better

And there's more where that came from

And you'll come back for more

And, oh so much more

Big is better, so is more

Bigger, better and more

But wait, there's more

But we can do much more than that

Buy more... save more!

Buying yourself more time

Can't ask for much more than that

Click here for more

Committed to giving you more

Curious? Want to know more?

Do more, charge less and get it done faster

Do more. Achieve more. Gain more. Earn more.

Do we need to say more?

Don't spend more; spend less and get more

Driven to do more and more

Everybody shops around for somebody offering more

Everyone knows that less is never more

Everything you expect and more

Expect more, pay less

Find out more today!

For more good ideas...

Get more than one opinion

Get ready for more

Gives you more, costs you less

Go ahead and expect more from us

How to make more and more money?

If you are paying more, you are going to get more

If you want us to do more, you've got to pay more

In short, is more really better?

Is it wrong to want more out of life?

It's all that and more

It's more than just new

It's more than that... much, much more

It's nothing more noble than that

It's the first of a lot more to come

Just another way to get more for less

Just what you'd expect and more

Keep 'em coming back for more

Learn more. Make more. Do more.

Less is sometimes more

Like to know more

Live a longer life and do more things

Looking for something more?

Make room for more

Make the time to give yourself more time

More bargains than you bargained for

More big savings

More business... more profit

More cash. More savings. More power.

More choices than ever before

More choices... more opportunities

More coming

More dizzying than dazzling

More effective. More efficient.
More satisfied.

More for the road

More for your money

More fuller. More exciting.
More difficult.

More money means more money

More of the good stuff is on sale!

More questions and answers

More reasons? Take your pick!

More room in front

More than ever before

More than more

More than one way to get it done

More than you ever imagined

More than you expected

More to come

More values than meet the eye

More! Better! Faster!

No one cares more than we do

No one deserves it more than you do

No one gives you more

Now with more chances to win

Ready for more?

Save more... get more

Search no more

Show me more

So why not enjoy it more?

Sometimes more is just more

Sometimes you get more than what you
paid for

Spend less, get more

Take a minute! Tell us more!

That's believable. But there's more

The more the merrier

The more we hear from you, the more
we can do for you

The more you give, the more you get

The more you look, the more you see

The more you put into something, the
more you get out of it

There's always bigger, there's always
better and there's always more

There's more where that came from

There's still room for more

They always come back for more

To get more, you have to pay more

Wait, there's more

Want more ways to go?

We are more than ready to deal!

We do more than say "look at me"

We do more than you think

We give you more time to do more

We want more bang for our bucks!

We're going to continue to do more

What more can we do?

What more could you ask for?

When less is more... when more is less

Where do you go to get more?

Who doesn't need more savings?

Whoever pays more gets more

Why pay more?

Working together to achieve more

Would you like to know more?

Wouldn't we all like a little more space?

You can expect more... and you'll get
more at...

You can spend more, a lot more

You get all this and more

You'll do more than survive...
you'll thrive

You'll get more, more and more

You'll want more than one

A gift of love will match the sparkle in Mom's eyes

All mothers are eligible to...

Are you looking for something different on Mother's Day?

Be good to your mother-in-law... today!

Bring her a hug, a kiss and a delightful surprise

Bring you mom to brunch

Cater to Mom... today!

Celebrate Mother's Day with us!

Champagne and roses for Mother... compliments of...

Dazzling gifts for Mother, as enduring as your love

Did Mother's Day land you in the doghouse last year?

Don't forget that special lady in your life

Enter our Mother's Day brunch contest

Even if you're a mother, go ahead and take your mother out to dinner on Sunday

Exceptional gifts as special as Mom!

Fabulous gifts that say she's the very best!

Families make great Mother's Day gifts!

Fantastic gifts for her! Fantastic savings for you!

Fit for a queen... queen for a day!

Five ways to say Happy Mother's Day

For all she does, remember Mom on her day

For Mom, may we suggest...

For the world's best mom

Free Mother's Day wrap

Free rose for Mom!

Get Mom a gift that will last year round

Get Mom fit for life, give her the royal treatment

Gifts for Mother's Day with love

Gifts she'll really use and really enjoy

Give her something from the heart

Give Mom something truly special

Give Mom what she really wants

Give Mother something that will really charm her

Go ahead, make Mom's Day!

Great gifts for Mom at great prices for you!

Guaranteed Mother's Day delivery!

Guess what Mom wants most

Have we got a sweet deal for Mom!

Have you made your reservation for Mother's Day?

Honor Mom on Mother's Day by getting her out of the kitchen

Honor Mom's memory on Mother's Day

Honor thy Mother

How can you top a bouquet of flowers as a Mother's Day present?

If mothers had their druthers, they'd ask for...

If you really want to pop for Mom...

It's a nice way to honor your mother

It's never too early to think of Mother's Day

It's something that says Happy Mother's Day

It's that time again to honor the most important women in your life

It's your gift that'll bring a smile to her face

Just a Mother's Day sale!

Just in time for Mother's Day

Just shopping for plain old Mom

Last minute gifts for Mom

Leave the cooking... cleaning...
and coddling to us

Let us cater to Mom... today!

Let us cook for Mom

Let us do the pampering

Let us help you reward that
special woman

Looking for a Mother's Day gift?

Luxuries for Mom. Savings for you!

Magnificent gift ideas for Mother's Day!

Make Mom's Day shine with...

Make Mother's Day unforgettable

Make this a Mother's Day she'll
never forget

Mom deserves the best

Mom's Big Day Sale of Values!

Mom's Day sale!

Moms enjoy 20% off dinner with this ad

Moms get in free at...

Mother loves gifts from us

Mother's Day gifts for non-moms

Mother's Day gifts from the heart

Mother's Day planting spectacular!

Mother's Day Sale! Starts today!

Mother's Day, make it sparkle

Mother's Day... need look no further

Mothers come in all sizes

Order Mom's gift today!

Pamper Mom on Mother's Day

Positively everything for Mother's Day

Pre-Mother's Day sale!

Pulling your hair out over what to get
for Mother's Day?

Put a sparkle in Mom's eye. And on her
ears, wrist or neck

Remember Mom on Mother's Day

Roses for Mudder's Day

Savings specials with moms in mind!

She deserves something special

She spoiled you... now spoil her!

Shock your mom... today!

Show Mom you inherited her good taste

Six wonderful ways to say she's beautiful

So many tender ways to tell Mother you
love her

Something just for Mom

Special Mother's Day offer!

Spoil your mom this Mother's Day

Spring into summer with great deals
for Mom

Super gifts for super moms

Surprise Mom with a loving gift of...

The best gift to give a mother is the gift
of time

The Mother's Day gift that's heaven sent

The perfect gift for a special mom

The perfect gift for Mother's Day!

The ultimate Mother's Day special

This Mother's Day give Mom our
special gift!

This Mother's Day say thank you with a...

This Mother's Day, it's impossible to
pick the wrong gift

This Mother's Day, we have a special
gift for you!

This year for Mother's Day honor a
woman you love

Thoughtful gifts show Mom how much
you care

Unique gifts for every kind of mom!

We have one word for Mother's Day...
flowers!

We have the gift she prefers!

What do you give the most special
person in the world?

Where the gifts are for Mom

With prices like these, there'll be enough
left over to take Mom out!

Move

A wise move

Are you looking to move?

Be smart and move with the best

Call the truck, boys, it's moving day

Call us before you move

Choosing a moving company

Don't you think it's time to move on?

Find out where everybody is moving and don't move there

Follow the moving van

For families on the move

Hassle-free moving from...

Have you decided to move yet?

Here's a moving experience to enjoy

Hey! We're moving!

It certainly beats doing the move yourself

It's a great time to make a move

It's a smart move worth shouting about

It's your move and it's easy to make

It's your move... make it now!

Keep that in mind when you consider moving to...

Keep the moving vans busy

Let's get moo-vin'

Make a calculated move that really adds up

Make us a part of your moving routine

Make your move, now!

Moooooving day is today!

Move up to quality

Move your stuff in today

Move your things in today

Moving made simple

Moving sale! Everything must go!!!

Moving the loot

Moving tips to get you where you're going!

Moving to serve you better

Moving up. Moving on. Or just plain moving.

Need more reasons to move?

Nervous about moving?

Nothing to do but move in

Now is the time to make your move

On your mark. Get ready. Move in.

Overwhelmed by moving?

Pondering your next move?

Service that will move you

So what's your next move?

The best move is the right one

The low-cost move is on

The time has come to make your move

There's no time like the present to start preparing for your move

Thinking about moving yourself

To move or not to move, that is the dilemma

We can make your move a little easier

We dig holes and move it

We do all the heavy lifting

We hustle to haul

We make movin' easy

We're moving... so we'll be closed until...

Well, it's moving time... again!

When you move, we move with you

When you're ready to move, so are we!

You made the right move

You won't have to cut corners to move

Your best move is now!

Music

A concert as great as all outdoors

A dazzling night of music!

A gift of music is a token of love

A musical sales blitz!

A new age of beautiful music

A passion for the sounds of music

A sale for music lovers!

A sale that will make music history!

A world of music

All Gospel music on sale this Sunday only!!!

All the latest hits available now!

All the music... all the memories... all on sale!

Are you a music lover?

Bargains for true music lovers!

Believe in the miracle of music

Big savings on jazz and rock just make people feel good!

Big, big, big band era savings!

Country music's sale of America!

Crank up the volume... with huge volume discounts!

Cutting prices on all heavy metal music!

Dear music lover:

Easy listening

Ever been to a rock concert?

Everybody buys their music at...

From pop to classical savings!

Give the gift of music!

Give yourself a music tune-up

Good music is good medicine

Good songs and a great sale make a winning combination!

Great savings for making music, too!

Great savings on songs of the season!

Groovin' in the grove

Hear the music come alive

Hot hits on sale now!

Hot, musical fun in the summertime

How to listen to great music

How to make your get-together sing

Hungry for good music?

If you can feel the beat, you will feel the savings!

If you love music, you'll love our sale!

In the great musical tradition of...

It all starts with a song

It's funk! It's rock! It's folk! It's blues!

It's music for you!

It's "singing in the aisles" time

Jammin' with jazz!

Join us for the musical escapades of...

Just a great music sale!

Just sit back and enjoy the music

Let there be music

Life in the rap lane

Listening pleasure

Live in concert

Live music every Thursday

More Music For Your Money... Sale Event!

Music fans from all over the world, shop here!

Music Fest Sales Event!

Music for now people

Music for the headphone set!

Music is the language throughout the world

Music

Music of the great one

Music of the season at unheard-of savings!

Music on the move

Music that comes straight from the heart

Music the family appreciates

Music to set the mood

Music to thrill the heart and lift the soul

Music to Your Ears... Sale Event!

Music you've never heard before

Name That Tune Sales Contest!

New age music at yesterday's prices!

Now that's music to anyone's ears

Now that's something worth singing about

Old tunes... new tunes... your tunes!

On the pop music concert front

Our live music is an event!

Our music sale speaks for itself!

Our sale is back at the top of the charts!

Play it again, Sam... It's our annual sale again!!!

Real cool music... really cool savings!

Round-the-clock music marathon

Savings filled with musical delights

Say it with a song

Soothing New Age music

Stop the music! Drastically slashed prices on all...

Strike Up The Band Sale Event!

Take a musical trip back in time

Take your favorite tunes with you!

Teen pop music on sale!

The beat stops here

The coolest music this side of...

The finest music-making America has ever heard

The hauntingly beautiful sound of...

The home for great music

The most exciting way to hear music

The most thrilling, heart-pounding music of all time

The music never stops... the sale starts this weekend!

The music that brings back memories

The music you grew up listening to

The musical event of the year!

The only place to buy exceptional music!

The sheer joy of making music

There's only two kinds of music: good and bad

This music sale is an event!!!

Thrills your heart and touches your soul

Top it off on a musical note

Unheard-Of Music Sale!

Unreal savings on all Country and Western tunes! Guitar not included!

We call it feeling music

We do more with music

We give you savings to sing about

We're playing your song... When the Savings Come Marching In!

We're your one-stop shop for all music

We've got hot music at cool prices!

We've got it all here! Classics, pop, country, jazz and rap

We've got what you want to keep the music playing

Whatever your musical pleasure...

When it comes to great music...

You can't listen to music on an empty stomach

You'll be rockin' and rollin' again with these old-fashioned prices!

You'll dig the savings!

New

A glimpse into a new you

A great new idea

A look at the new... and a review of the past

A new body in weeks!

A new line of makeup from...

A new look for a new vision

A new look!

A new take on an old tradition

A new way to bring up the future

A new way to live

A new world of home entertainment

A new year begins today!

A new you!

A nose for what's new

A special new offer from us... exclusively for you!

A truly new shopping experience

A whole new way of looking at anything

A world of new ideas

Accent the new

Ain't new grand?

All new merchandise drastically reduced!

All that glitters isn't new

Allure of the new!

Amazing new prices... awesome new stuff

An exceptional new offer from...

An idea so old it's new

An old-world past, a new-world beginning

And now for something completely new

Another new twist

Anything new?

Appreciate the new...

Are you prepared for the new?

As good as new

As new as tomorrow's technology

Better than new

Bigger. Better. Newer.

Blending the old with the new

Brand spankin' new

Build your future on a new...

But what else is new?

Come and see what's new

Create an entirely new look

Discover the new

Do the new

Do you have anything new?

Don't be afraid to try new things

Don't you ever buy anything new?

Everything is so new and up-to-date

Everything old is suddenly new again

Everything that's new is on sale!

Everything's new

Explore a new dimension in living

Finding what's new?

Fishing for something new?

For those who demand the new...

From enduring old ways to exciting new ways

Get with the new spirit

Go ahead, ask me what's new

Great new stuff

Has something new caught your eye lately?

Here's a new approach to life

Here's fantastic new news

Here's something completely new!

Here's to a new you!

Here's what's new

How do you know it's new?

Hungry for something new?

I can't wait to see what's new

If it's new... it's here

Isn't it about time for a new...

It all begins with the word "new"

It's a brand new look

It's a new and exclusive sale event!

It's a new kind of cool

It's a new phenomenon

It's a new twist

It's an entire new venue

It's better than new

It's brand new!

It's different because it's new!

It's fresh! It's new!

It's new and exciting

It's new and inexpensive

It's new and nifty

It's new but looks old

It's new to all of us

It's new! It's affordable! And it's on sale!

It's new! It's dazzling! It's...

It's new! It's hot! It's irresistible!

It's new, it's fun, it's different

It's not new... just weird

It's so new it's newer than new

It's the eyes that see something new

It's the new thing

It's the newest...

It's the next best thing to new

It's the start of something new

It's time for something new

It's time to try something new

It's totally new!

It's weird. It's different. It's new.

Just like new!

Just out!

Like new... like now!

Look for this new display

Look what's new

Looking for new meal ideas?

Looking for something new?

Looking for the hottest new look

Make everybody happy with something new

Make way for the new

Maybe it's time to try something new

Never before

New and exclusively yours

New and improved

New and nifty

New and noteworthy

New attitudes. New ideas. New solutions.

New deals... new prices!

New features included

New from...

New is exciting whether it's a...

New look. New attitude. New you.

New low price

New on the scene

New possibilities. New challenges. New frontiers.

New Prices Sale Event!

New roads to success

New rules! New tools! New thinking!

New stuff to buy

New this year

New ways to save for your investment

New ways to save more money

New ways to say "I love you" every day

New year... new you!

New! Better than ever!

New! First ever!

New! See it now!

New, and we have it!

New, cool and fun

New-fangled! New-fashioned!
New and improved!

No kidding: it's new and improved

No one else can offer you our new...

Not everybody believes "new and improved" is better

Not new, but improved

Now... try something utterly new

Open now... sensational new stuff inside

Our new is fresh and novel

Out with the new

Outrageous new deals!

Presenting the new...

Put a new spin on...

Put in the new and throw out the old

Red, white and new

Refreshingly new!

See for yourself the bright big new...

See the latest! See the hottest!
See what's new!

So dare to compare the new...

So is it old... or is it new?

So smart... so new!

So what's really new?

Something new and exciting

Something new can become an old favorite!

Something new down every aisle

Stay with the new

Stop in, see what's new

Swing by and see what's new

Thank you for trying our new...

The all-new...

New

The beginning of something new

The best of what's new

The fun is in the new stuff

The hunt for something new

The new is back

The next best thing to new

The road to new profits

The same old, but with a new name

There is nothing wrong with trying something new

There's always something new going on at...

There's always something new to see

This is your new world

Try it today! It's all new!

Try something new!

Unique and daring and new

Wake up to something new

Want to see yourself in a whole new way?

We take old ideas to new places

We're sportin' a new look

Welcome to a new beginning

Welcome to the new age

What else is new?

What's new becomes old... what's old becomes new again

What's new in your world?

What's new! What's cool! What's for you!

What's new? What's hot? What's not?

What's new? What's now? What's next?

When only the new will do!

Why not try something new?

Wowing the world with something new

You never ask, "What's new?"

You'll be taken back by our new offer

New Year

A great reason for saying "Happy new year"... awesome savings!

A great way to jump-start the beginning of the year

A Heck of a Year Sales Event!

A new look for a new year

A new start! A new challenge! A new opportunity!

A new tradition begins at...

A new year special!

A New Year's Eve gala!

A new year's resolution... shop with us and you'll save big bucks!

A New Year's savings celebration

A once-a-year sale!

A party this special only comes along once a year

A smart start for a big year

A whale of a New Year's Eve celebration

All champagnes and sparkling wines are on sale!

An awesome New Year's Eve celebration

An Eve-ning to remember

Beat the Clock Sale Event!

Beginnings of the year are a wonderful time to...

Blast into the new year with explosive savings!!!

Break out the bubbly

Bring in the new year in impeccable style

Celebrate in style this year

Celebrate the new year with great savings!

Check the savings out next year!

Come celebrate our New Year's Eve Sales Celebration!

Continue a holiday tradition. Or start one!

Dance in the new year with us!

Do we have a resolution for you

End of the Year Sales Spectacular!

Get a bang out of New Year's savings!

Get a New Start Sale Event!

Get more savings before this year's done!

Get ready today for another year of the best...

Get the new year started with...

Great year-end savings!

Happy New Year Sale!

Have a ball this New Year's Eve at...

Have a rocking New Year's Eve

Have New Year's Eve dinner with us

Here we go again... New year... New opportunities!

Here's help to get the new year started right!

Here's the safest and cheapest way to party on New Year's Eve

Here's to our New Year Sale Celebration!

Hey, whatcha doin' New Year's, New Year's Eve?

Holiday hangover sale!

Hurry in for our new year's buys!

Hurry! Because it all ends January 1st

It Only Happens Once a Year Sales Event!

It's a brand new year with good old-fashioned prices!

It's New Year's Eve... know where your bubbles are?

It's sure to be one of our best Sales of the Year ever!

It's your last chance to splurge before the end of the year

Kick off the new year with...

Let us be among the last to wish you a happy new year

Let us bring in the new year with you

Let us make your New Year's celebration the best ever

Made your New Year's date today?

Make this New Year's Eve one that you'll remember forever

Make us part of your new year's resolution

Make your New Year's Eve party a success with...

Make your reservations and resolutions now!

Need a New Year's Eve date?

New Year's Clearance ends today!

New Year's Eve savings excitement!

New Year's sale-a-bration!

No plans! No reservation! No fun!

Noisemakers and hats are included in the deal!

Now here's a great way to start the new year

Now through New Year's Day

Old prices, new year!

Our New Year Sale starts today!!!

Reservations are required on New Year's Eve

Ring in the new year with savings from...

Ring in the new year with unbelievable deals

Ring Out the Old and Ring In the New Bed and Bath Sale Celebration!

Savings for those who want to ring in the new year

Say farewell to last year with last-minute savings!

Say farewell to last year with unbelievable buys!

Shopping in the new year at old year prices

Solutions to your new year's resolutions

Start the new year with a "Big Bang" of a deal!

Start the new year with a new...

Start this year off with fantastic savings!

Tear into these New Year's values

Ten ways to celebrate the year's end

That's the No. 1 resolution people make and break

The ball-dropping extravaganzas

The big bash is back for another year

The biggest New Year Eve's party ever

The celebration is about ringing in wildly incredible deals!

The last big party of the year

The obligatory year-end celebration

The place to be on New Year's Eve

The place to be when the clock strikes midnight

The year to forget... a sale to remember!

Toast the new year from our huge selection of couches!

We look forward to serving your needs in the new year

We're taking stock of the new year... drastically slashed prices!

What a great way to start the year

What's new for the new year?

Will start your new year with a smile

Wrap up the new year with a...

Year's up! Prices are down!

Year-End Countdown Sell-a-Thon!

Year-end deals are underway!

Year-End Savings Days!

Year-End Savings Spectacular with no payments 'til the new year!

Year-end sell-off!

You're invited to our Pre-New Year Sale Celebration!

Your place to shop for the new year!

Now

Absolutely! Positively! Now!

Act now and ignite your life like never before

Act now! Later may be too late!

All the more reason to buy now!

And I need it now!

And if you think it's big now, just wait

Available now!

Be there now!

Buy it now... use it now!

Buy it. Buy it now!

Buy now, pay much later

Call now for reservations

Clearance specials now at...

Come back into the now

Come on everyone, all together now!

Do I really need it now?

Do it now!

Do yourself a favor... get started now!

Enjoy the here and now

For the way you live now

Get 'em now!

Get a fresh start now!

Get in the spirit of now!

Get one... now!

Get what you need now!

Go for it now!

Going on now!

Great selection! Super values! Save now!

Have it all now!

Hey! That was then, this is now!

Hey, look at me now!

I can hear you now

I have to have it now!

I want it now!

If you start now...

In great demand now!

It happens now!

It isn't happening "someday"... it's happening now!

It's all gravy now!

It's going on now!

It's got to happen now!

It's here... it's now!

It's no longer the future... it's now!

It's now or never

It's time to buy now!

It's very now saving!

Just what you need, right now!

Living in the now

Look at us now!

Need savings now?

Next year begins now

No better time for action than now

Nothing can stop us now!

Now about now!

Now all on sale!

Now even better

Now get to it

Now hear this

Now in your neighborhood

Now is a great time to...

Now is the perfect time

Now is the time to buy! Don't wait!

Now is the time to save!

Now isn't that special!

Now it can be told

Now it's your turn

Now more than ever

Now on sale!

Now open for a limited time

Now open! For your convenience!

Now or Never Sale!

Now save on everything you need for...

Now that's a bargain... pure and simple

Now that's convenience

Now that's nuts

Now that's tradition

Now there's a carrot

Now this is inexpensive

Now we've got your interest

Now will actually mean now!

Now with a great new look!

Now you can have it both ways

Now you know

Now you see 'em

Now you're cookin'

Now you're talkin'

Now, at an amazing price

Now, everything is possible

Now, how can we help you?

Now, it's official

Now, more than ever

Now, you don't have to look your age

Now's the best time

Now's the time for new innovation

Now's the time for you

Now's the time to try...

Now... it's all in one place

Now... means now!

Now... prepare to be astounded

Now... when you need it, we've got it

OK, what are you doing now?

On sale now!

Pay me now or pay me later

Right here, right now!

Save right now!

Save the best for now!

See it now!

So now you know... the real story

So what's cool now?

So why not do it... now!

Start now!

Start putting more money in your pocket now!

The answer is now!

The fun starts right now!

The look that's now

The power of now

The right place! The right price! Right now!

The sale to grab now!

The time to be happy is now!

The time to buy is now!

The time to take action is now!

The wait is over... the time to buy is now!

There has never been a better time to buy than now!

Things you need to know about now

We put the emphasis on "right now"

We'll show you how to get it... now!

Well guess what, now you can

What now?

Why act now?

Why not just start now?

Why not now?

Why wait? Right now!

You hear it every day... "I need it now!"

You live for now

Your benefits start now... today!

Your time is now!

OK

All is not OK

An OK look, an OK feel, but it's not OK to touch

But it's OK, as long as you stayed reasonably within budget

But let's just say OK!

But that's OK. Everyone's entitled to an opinion

Cut some slack, OK?

Don't change a thing, OK?

Go ahead, it's OK to smile

Having a great OK time

Here are two ways to say okay

Hey everybody, it's "OK" deal time!

I'm like, okaaay... what's the big deal?

I'm OK, you're OK

I'm waaaaaiiiiiting, okay?

If it looks good, it is OK

If you've got the money, we'll okay the deal

In other words, everything will be OK

It's a wonderful life, OK?

It's an OK thing!

It's just an OK deal

It's OK to be one step ahead of everybody else

It's OK to say no

It's OK with us

It's OK, we can deal with it

Just follow the directions, OK?

Just hop on, it's OK

Just say OK

Low prices, OK values

Not just the first time, OK, but every time

Oh... But... If... OK!

OK to photocopy

OK, first the good news

OK, here's your turn

OK, I won!

OK, it's quiz time

OK, let's set the record straight

OK, let's work together

OK, OK! I get the idea

OK, so show us the money

OK, so what's next?

OK, we sell experience

OK, what do we do now?

OK, what is it?

OK, you get the savings!

OK... I'll bite... what's the gimmick?

Okay, I'll give it a try

Okay, now forget it

Okay, show me what you've got

Ooooooookay!!!

Outlandish. Outspoken. Outrageous. Okay.

The odds are you'll be OK

The performance is OK! The productivity is OK! The profitability is OK!

The world is an OK place to grow up in

This is your OK day!

We want action, okay?

We'll OK it!

We're giving it away! Is it OK with you?

When it's OK, start the ball rolling with...

Whoa, wait a second, OK?

You decide if it's okay

You write the check, OK?

Olympics

A dynamic go for the gold sale!

A Feat of Gold Sale Event!

A golden showcase for you

A gold-medal favorite

A good shot at taking home the gold

A medal-winning performance

A new gold standard has been set

A Pitch for the Gold Sale Event!

A quest for the gold

A Race for the Gold Sale Event!

A small price to pay for Olympic savings!

A solid gold performance of savings!

A solid-gold sale!

A touch of gold savings during the Olympic Games!

A tribute to our Olympic Sale!

A true Olympic deal!

An awe-inspiring Olympic sale!

An Olympic moment

An Olympic spirit of community

Are you ready to be a medal winner?

Are you tough enough to go for it?

As a kid you dreamed about it

Be a guardian of the flame

Be an Olympic champion!

Big... Bold... Gold

Bringing the great times to the great games

Bronze, Silver, Gold, Three-for-Three Sale Event!

Buff up that tarnished Olympic gold

Can't get enough of the Olympics?

Carry on the spirit of the Olympic games

Catch a dose of the Olympic spirit at...

Catch the Olympic Spirit Sale Event!

Chasing the Olympic gold

Congratulations on winning an Olympic gold deal!

Dreams of gold

Enjoy these savings during the Olympic Games!

Everyone has a dream of being part of the Olympics

Everyone is a winner during the Olympic Games

Everything is on sale during this Olympic year!

For a true Olympic experience...

For the glory and the gold

For the spirit of the medal

Fulfill their dreams of winning the gold

Get a hold on the gold with record savings!

Get in on the gold medal game

Get Into the Games Sale Event!

Get into the spirit of the games

Get on the fast track to pocket the gold

Get the taste of the Olympic experience

Get your five rings of big savings here!

Get your shot at the gold

Go for all-out savings!

Go for the bold!

Go for the glory! Go for the bold! Go for the savings!

Go USA!

Gold medal savings that add up!

Gold medal sparkling savings!

Gold medal values!

Grab a gold medal deal!

Olympics

Great games! Great excitement! Great savings!

Great savings throughout the Olympics!

Having the best sale is our goal

Here's a golden opportunity...

Here's your shot at the gold

How 'bout them gold medal savings!

Ignite the Torch Sale Event!

In the Hunt for the Gold Sale Event!

In the True Spirit of the Olympics Sale!

Isn't it time you went for the gold?

It's a Gold Medal Day Sale Event!

It's absolutely a gold medal deal!

It's not an Olympic feat to bring home the savings!

It's our Olympic Sales Event!

Join the Gold Medal Club and save!

Last stop before the Olympic Games

Let the deals begin!

Make an Olympic clean sweep on savings!

Medal-winning savings on all your favorites!

No matter who wins the gold, you can still share the glory

Olympic champion deals!

Olympic festival of savings!

Olympic fever is at full pitch during our...

On the fast track to win the gold

Our deals are like winning a gold medal!

Own a piece of Olympic history

Quest for the gold prices!

Savings that make you feel as good as gold!

Show the world your competitive spirit

Show Your Olympic Spirit Sale Event!

Take a swing at the gold

Take home the Olympic spirit

Take the Olympic savings challenge!

That's what the Olympians eat

The five interlocked rings: Sale! Save! Sale! Save! Sale!

The flame burns on!

The greatest games ever

The greatest Olympic sale ever!

The Olympic gold or the pot of savings

The Olympic year. The sale of the year!

The Opening Ceremonies Sales Event!

The pain! The drive! The glory! The sale!

The sale is here, judge for yourself

The thrill of victory! The thrill of big savings!

The torch is lit with magnificent savings!

There is nothing like an Olympic Games Sale Event!

This is an Olympic year

This sale is pure gold

We cover the games

We got a gold medal deal for you!

We salute the US Olympic team

We're bringing home big savings!

We're going after the gold with savings!

We've got an Olympic Gold Medal Sale to live up to!

Where the action is and loving it

Winning the gold begins at...

World records come and go, but this sale is world-class

You deserve a gold medal

You don't have to be a world-class athlete to go for the gold

You don't just wear it. You earn the savings at...

You'll go home with a gold medal at...

Your headquarters for Olympic savings!

Your Moment of Glory Sale Event!

Party

A little pre-party planning never hurt anyone

A party that will make you say, "Wow!"

Add some punch to your party

All in favor of a great party... say "I"

Are you ready to rrrrrumbllle???

Attention all partygoers:

Bring a bottle of wine and a friend

Call now and meet thousands of party animals just like you!

Can you say "party"?

Catch the fun at party central!

Come as a guest, act like one, and you'll be treated like one

Come for the wildlife, not the nightlife!

Come party with us!

Did someone say "I need a party planner"?

Don't let another fun evening float away

Don't miss the real thing

Don't wreck your house, have a party at...

Every day's a party at...

Everything is up for grabs

For an ooh-la-luscious good time

For parties, you supply the guests... we will do the rest

For the wildest wild time ever...

Get keyed up for a great time

Go ahead, have a ball

Go hog wild

Good times to be had by all

Great parties start with smart planning

Have tux, will party!

Have we got a party for you!

Here's a winning lineup for a super footbowl party

Hey, Bud, let's party!

Hey, don't ask questions... just party!

How stressful party planning can be

How to make a scene at a party

How to throw a fabulous party

How to top off a great party

If all the festivities, celebrities and hoopla didn't get your attention, how about this?

If you want to enjoy your party, hire me!

If you're up for it, so am I

It never hurts to plan ahead for a big party

It's a party that happens to have dinner

It's going to be a party bigger than a carnival

It's how the world parties

It's like the Boston Tea Party

It's not so hard to throw a dinner party

It's party time all the time at...

It's the biggest party in the world

It's time to be the life of the party

It's time to party!

It's time to stop talking and start partying

It's time to throw a real soiree

It's time to whoop it up

It's your night to fly

Join the fun!

Keep the party buzzin' with...

Keep the party going with a...

Leave it to the party planners

Leave the partying to us

Party

Let the festivities begin!

Let the good times roll

Let the howling begin!

Let us host your next party or special event

Make your holiday party the best ever!

Make your next shindig a rockin' time

Maybe you should have hired a party planner

More party for your birthday

Now that's a party!

One party you don't want to miss

Overflows with good cheer

Party down with a big bang

Party hearty

Party of the season

Party on

Party on down with the fun party

Plan your holiday party at...

Plan your party with us!

Put on a party face

Shirt and tie optional

So, you want to throw a swanky party

Some people just know how to throw a great party

Start the countdown for the big party now!

Start the party with a bang with us!

Stir up the party spirit

Tell the sun to get up so we can start partying

The big dance starts here

The gang's all here

The party starts here!

The place for progressive people

The place to be on Saturday night!

The preferred place to party...

The quest for a good time

There's no rain on this party

There's somethin' happenin' here

This is your kind of party

This place has got the "go" going

Throw yourself a party

Throwing a bash?

Throwing a party can be a piece of cake

To get a free party planning kit, call...

Tonight we're gonna party

We can add life to any party

We decided to use a caterer

We make parties easy so you can celebrate

We'll get you in the party mood with a...

We'll have you swinging from the rafters!

We'll help you make a great impression

We'll make you the biggest cheese at your party!

We're running out of potato chips

We've got everything for your party

What did you bring to the party?

What if you threw a party and nobody came?

What you need for a great party

Where adults can come to party

Where the good times keep getting better

Why isn't everyone partying?

Wildest party of the year

Wise men party here!

You are the biggest excuse for having a party

You don't need an invitation to have a party

You'd never forgive yourself if you missed it

You're going to have a hell of a good time. Rock on!

You're invited to be the life of the party!

Party Themes

A "Whooooooo's That?" Halloween Party

A Down-Home Jamboree

A Hint of Spring Fashion Show

A Razzle Dazzle Bash

A Touch of Broadway Cast Party

Adopt-A-Family Ball

An Evening With The Stars

And The Beat Goes On Party

Apples and Acorns Fall Celebration

Autumn Nights Black Tie Affair

Ball of Laughs Birthday Party

Barbecue Bash Party

Beach Bash Wing-Ding

Beat the Winter Blahs Get-Together

Behind the Masks Ball

Blast from the Past Party

Bring Your Teddy Bear Party

Buckle up your boogie shoes and
let's party!

Bucks and Does Hoedown Night

Cap and Gown Beer Blast

Carrying On the Tradition Get-Together

Catch a Falling Star Singles Party

Chill out at the "Big Chill Out"

Chip-and-Dip Pool Party

Circle of Friends Spring
Salad Luncheon

Coosome Twosome Valentine's Party

Die-Hard Duffers Ball

Dinner Party in the Park

Election Night Get-Together

Evening in Black and White

Eye-Popping Fashion Show

Fall Dinner and Fashion Show
"Pretty Women"

For Couples Only Square Dance Hoedown

For The Time Of Your Life Under The
Stars Party

Frank-en-stein Festivity

Fresh As A Spring Breeze Cocktail Party

Gallery Hop Party

Give Your Heart to Us Party

Glitz of Tinsel-Town Party

Good Times are Poppin' Party

Harbor Light Ball

Harvest Moon Festival

Hip-Hop Party Jam

It Sure Beats Working Labor Day Party

It's a Pajama Party

It's a Party Animal Party...
Bring your pets!

Jump and Jive on the River

June Jam-Up Party

Keep the Good Times Rolling Party

Lemonade on the Green

Let Freedom Ring Fashion Show

Let the Corks Fly New Year's Fling!

Let's Go to the Hop 50's Shindig

Let's Live It Up Soiree

Let's Rip the Roof Off Party

Light Up the Jack-O-Lanterns Party

Live at Five Party

Lobstermania Get-Together

Made in the Shade Retirement Party

Mardi Gras Mania

Masquerade Ball

Medieval Times Party

225

Party Themes

Midsummer Night's Dream Party

Monster Mash Party

Moonlight Barbequefest

Moonlight Masquerade Ball

Moonlight on the Verandah Party

Nautical and Nice Fashion Show

Old-time Yule Log Christmas Party

On-Side Kickoff Party

Pain In The Butt Party

Palette of Fall Colors Fashion-Show

Party Down With A Big Blast Party

Party On The Pier

Party Pooper Round Up

Pretty Nifty 50 Birthday Bash

Pumpkin Patch Bazaar

Put a Yellow Feather in Your Hat Fashion Show

Put on your bobby socks and lace up those saddle shoes... it's a Fifties Party!

Put on Your Green Derby Shindig

Puttin' On the Airs Party

Quest for the Gold Affair

Return to Elegance Ball

Reunite For A Night Party

Rockin' Sock Hop Party

Sailor's Delight Dinner Dance

Savor the Taste of Summer Dinner Party

See You On The First Tee Social

Singin' in the Rain Party

Sizzlin' Summer Patio Party

Skinny Monday Before Fat Tuesday Party

Slam-Bam-Birthday Blast

Slumber Party Fun

Social Butterflies Gala

Stampin' Stampede Wingding

Star-Spangled-Birthday Blowout

Take a Break from Holiday Shopping Party

The Abominable Snowman Sleigh Ride Social

The Annual Daddy-Daughter Party

The Annual Summer Sunrise Get Together

The Belle of the Ball

The Caterpillar Ball

The Crystal Chandelier Ball

The Dullest Party

The Eve of the Eve New Year's Party

The Gobble Wobble Run and Walk Party

The Great Pumpkin Party

The Last Hurrah Party

The Musicians Ball

The Shamrock Shuffle Beer Blast

The Spirit of Fall Get-Together

The Starry Night Ball

Those Lazy, Crazy Days of Summer Get-Together

Trick and Treat A-Thon Party

Tropical Bash Party

Un-boo-lievable Halloween Party

Wacky Sock Contest Party

We're Going To Rock Party

We're having a Dinosaur Party

Wet-N-Wild Pool Party

White-Tie Extravaganza Ball

Winter Wonderland Soirée

Wood Chopper Ball

Ya Gotta Have Heart Valentine's Party

You're invited to a Musical Jungle Jam Session

You're invited to a Spooky Sleepover

You're the Only One for Me Valentine's Party

Zany, Jazzy, Crazy Party

Patriotism

A time for American pie instead of apple pie

A timely opportunity to show your patriotism

A tribute to America's patriotic spirit

Ain't a flag big enough for our pride

All for one and one for all

All-American patriotism

All-American style that's red, white and you!

America in every way

America; a symbol of hope and freedom

American pride

And that's what makes America great

As a concerned American citizen...

Be patriotic... be an American

Be respectful to the times we're living in

Buy American

Call me patriotic or whatever, this is where I want to be

Capture your American pride

Catch the spirit of patriotism

Display the flag in a show of patriotism

Do it loud and proud

Every day, be proud to be an American

Everything I stand for as an American

Evil people can't destroy our spirit and our freedom

Fly it high, fly it proud

Give. Care. Help. Live.

God bless America

God, I love this country

Hang-together patriotism

Be the first one who's going to stand up for our country

Home of the brave

How Americans are pulling together

How very American

I am proud of our United States of America

I believe in my country... I believe in myself

I feel proud

I would give my life for America

I'm a red, white and blue American

I'm awfully proud to be an American

I'm one voice, but I want to do my part

I'm proud of the fact that I'm an American

I'm so proud to be an American

I've never been prouder

If my country needs me, I'll be there

If you can't respect your country, then get out

If you're not proud to be an American today, you never will be

In times of great tragedy, people shine as they unify in a common purpose

It evokes a sense of pride in being an American

It is a grand old flag

It's my duty

It's not their America, it's all of ours

It's the American way

It's the pride that comes with waving our flag

Jump-start the patriotism

Just because you wave a flag, it doesn't make you a patriot

Let's take care of our country first

Long live the United States

227

Patriotism

Lucky to be Americans

More united than ever

My country, right or wrong

My stars, my stripes, my flag

Now is the time to be tougher than nails

Now is the time to fight even harder

On to spreading the American way of life

Our actions come from the fierce love of country

Our flag of freedom always rises to the top

Our love of the flag and the country

Our nation is forever grateful

Our sweet land of liberty

Outpouring of patriotism

Patriotism in time of war

Patriotism is a badge of honor

Patriotism is not blind love of your country, but knowing your country for what it is

Patriotism is the right thing to do

Patriotism is year-round

Patriotism-driven

Praise our flag... protect our flag

Protect the land you love

Pure patriotism

Rally 'round the flag

Reaffirming the American spirit

Red, white and you

Rekindling the American spirit

Respect for the flag

Show your patriotism

Show your true colors

Stand proud, America

Stand united as a nation

Standing up for what you believe

Stars and stripes forever

Support the red, white and blue

Terrorists make me proud to be an American

That's patriotism! That's freedom! That's America!

That's what real patriotism is about

That's what this country is all about

The American flag... a symbol of honor, strength and freedom

The courage to be an American

The resilience of America begins with each of us

There's just something real about America

They have answered the call to duty

They will do America proud

Think of it: American flags made in America

This country belongs to you

This is America, my friend

Tolerance and patriotism

United we stand – divided we fall

Wave it with pride

We are with you. God be with you

We believe in unity. Peace and love are up to you

We can be afraid, or we can be ready

We do things the American way

We make us great

We salute bravery, compassion and patriotism

We will prevail

We're flying the flag proudly

What can I do?

What's your commitment to your country?

When it comes to patriotism, we rise to the occasion

When you have a choice, buy American

Who says "Made in the USA" doesn't cut it anymore?

Your love of flag and country

Pets

A Dog's Best Friend Sales Event!

A dog-and-pony show of savings!

A good meal for your most finicky friend

A higher-quality alternative to kennels

A pet's medical bills can add up

A shaggy dog savings story!

A world of pet fashion

Adopt a pet

Affordable and loving care for your pet or pets

Are people who buy insurance for pets crazy?

Are you a cat or a dog person?

Are you killing your pet with kindness?

Are you wondering why your dog is looking at you funny?

Ask your veterinarian

Be a friend to man's best friend

Be kind to your pet

Because pets are people too! We're there when you can't be!

Bow-wow!!! Meow!!! Wow saving on all pet supplies!!!

Bring this ad and save 10% off puppies!

Calling all cat lovers

Calling all pet enthusiasts

Can a goldfish be a friend?

Check the chew toys you give your dog

Could this be your dog?

Crazy for cats

Does your dog pull you down the street?

Does your kitten need extra nutritional care?

Does your pet suffer from anxiety?

Doesn't every dog deserve a bone?

Dog Days Sale Event!

Dog or cat boarding or grooming

Doggy dinners served here!

Dogs aren't just pets... they're family

Dogs like to dine in style, too

Don't forget your furry or feathered friends

Don't pussyfoot around with this pussycat

Don't take chances with your pet's health

Energy for active dogs

Everything your cat desires

For conscientious cat owners

For dog lovers

For dogs who run in the fast lane

For the pet in your life

For those people who are allergic to dogs and cats

Free dog wash with every...

Free dog-training consultation and evaluation

Free to a good home

Furry friends welcome

Getting a bath is not a dog's favorite pastime

Give fleas that one-two punch

Give your dog a reason to wag his tail

Give your pet a bed that's every bit as comfortable as your own

Give your pet the best

Has your dog been vaccinated against diseases?

Have we got a puppy for you!

Help a homeless puppy

Help prevent homeless pets

Hire a professional dog walker

229

Pets

Hot diggity dog... Pet Sale Event!

Hot savings for fat cats... cool mutts!

How much is that doggy in the window?

If your dog's toys aren't being chewed, what's wrong with them?

Is your pet home alone?

It's the Cat's Meow Sale of the Summer!

Keep your pet healthy with...

Look who's the top dog

Love and attention. Pet-sitting. Dog walking. Pet feeding.

Love your dog, but not that doggie smell?

Make your new pet one of the healthiest companions available

Make your pet part of our family while you travel

Making life better for your pet

May is National Pet Month

Now your pets can travel with you

Obedience training is good for your dog

Oh, to live the life of a dog

Pamper your pet with...

Pet Adoption Week

Pet identification is important

Pet of the month

Pet safety

Pets are dogs, cats, hamsters, fish, turtles, hermit crabs and monkeys

Pets need medical care, too!

Pets on parade

Professional pet-sitting and compassionate dog training in your home

Protect your pet

Protect your pet from fleas, ticks and heartworms with...

Remember, spring is the time for heartworm testing

Savings for feisty felines and furry friends!

See your vet before you get your pet

Solutions to the top 10 dog problems

Stuffed animals do not require feeding

Super savings on all self-cleaning litter boxes!

Terrific savings for your furriest of friends

The best values for man's best friend

The way to a dog's heart

There's always pet insurance

These little critters need a home

They don't call them "Man's best friend" for nothing

Training your dog?

Treat your pet to good health

We scoop the poop so you don't have to

We teach you to teach your dog

We're not your typical pet store

We've got everything for your pooch

What a great way to tell your dogs how much you love 'em

What a way to keep your dog looking his best

What do you do if your pet is overweight?

What to expect at the vet

What's better than having a cat?

Whether he likes it or not, your best friend needs a bath

Which pet is right for your family?

Why cats make great pets

Why do you love your dog?

You and your dog both need training

You can help homeless dogs

You'll never have to clean a cat box again

Your dog will lap this up

Your pet deserves the best

Your pet is also invited to the party

Your pet never had it so good

50% more anytime minutes

A lot more talk time for the money

Act now... talk forever

All cell phone users have the right to remain silent

All phones advertised are EnergyStar compliant

All top-brand cordless on sale!

All you do is pick up the receiver and talk

America's love-hate affair with cellular phones

And stick this in your phone jack

Be the 10th caller and win...

Big selection of cordless phones!!! Super low prices!!!

Bought a new phone lately?

Buy a wireless phone and get 50% off

Call anytime, even Sundays

Cell phones are annoying! Cell phones are prohibited! Cell phones are ubiquitous!

Cell phones make you incredibly accessible

Change your mood – change your phone color

Choosing the right wireless phone has never been easier

Dial up while you fill 'er up!

Do you have a cellular phone glued to your ear?

Do you have a phone card?

Do you understand your phone bill?

Don't be a victim of telemarketers

Don't tell your mother you have a cell phone

Driving while under the influence of a cell phone

Dropped signals. Bad reception. Dead zones.

Ever feel like throwing away your phone?

Every call is like a local call

Everything you need to talk while you drive

Final notice prior to disconnection

For people who are addicted to the phone

Free corded Caller ID phone

Free up your phone

Get 2 phones for the price of one

Get more phones without more jack

Get on the phone and bend someone's ear

Get the latest wireless phone

Give me the good old telephone days

Give the gift of chit-chat

Great phone... great prices!

Have you ever tried to shake hands over the phone?

Hot deals on wireless phones

How to keep your call center profitable

How to stop telephone solicitors from invading your privacy

I can't hear you! I think we're breaking up here

I have a call! Where's my phone?

I just called to say nothing!

I'm thankful for cellular telephones

If only you had a cell phone

If you've ever waited on hold, you know that a minute can feel like an eternity

In the old days, if you needed a phone, you called the phone company

Installation services include phone jacks, lines, satellite systems and more

Phones

Is that your beeper or my beeper?

Is your child ready for a cell phone?

It's as simple as making one phone call

It's like trying to provide your own phone service

It's phone-a-thon time

It's simple. Just pick up your telephone

It's worth a phone call...

Just kick back and give us a call

Long distance made easy

Make the switch, keep your number and save $50-$200 instantly

More ways to stay in touch

My cell phone 'eeps 'reaking up!

My fees are eating my phone bills

Need a phone hookup? We've got it!

One phone call, and you're on your way

Our phones are the talk of the town

Pay-as-you-go cellular phone cards

Phones that can... snap it! Style it! Share it!

Phones, service, special offers may not be available in all areas

Pick up the phone and start savings

Please stay on line. Your business is very important to us

Please turn off all cell-phones

Post these numbers by your phone

Press 3 to speak with a service representative

Put our phone number on your speed dial

Questions? Don't hesitate to call us at...

Save time... phone ahead

Smart phone applications go on sale today!

So what's everybody talking about on their cell phones?

Super phone savings!

Take your call center to a new dimension

Talk anywhere, talk longer

Talk hands-free and keep both hands on the wheel

Technology that lets you do more with your phone

Ten free minutes of phone time

The most common and popular way to communicate

The way to keep your call center up to pace

The wireless phone is a wonder invention

There are still people who want a phone to look like one

Think before you beep

This call may be monitored for quality assurance

This is a phone-free zone

Tired of losing your cell phone?

To learn more about everything, call...

Today, phones are indispensable

Unlimited night and weekend minutes

We have a phone and service ready for every budget and need

We have traditional cell phones in stock!

We have your phone number

We make other wireless phones obsolete

We treat all calls confidentially

We're as close as your phone

We're only a phone call away

We're waiting for your call

Well Worth The Dial... Sale Event!

What ever happened to the busy signal?

What would Superman have been without a phone booth?

When a business tells you on the phone that "your call is important to us," is the company lying?

When is the best time to call you? When I'm eating dinner!

You get instant answers over the phone

Presidents' Day

2-day Presidents' Weekend Sale!

A Presidents' Day sale you've never seen!

A sale event of presidential proportions!

A sale four years in the making!

A sales event bigger than the Washington Monument and Lincoln Memorial!

All Democrats and Republicans are welcomed to our Convention of Values!

All donkey and elephant coupons honored here!

All items are priced for George!

America the beautiful begins with our Presidents' Day Sale!

Are you ready for Presidents' Day?

As the nation pauses for Presidents' Day...

Be honest, George!!! You always wanted a Birthday Sale Celebration!

Big Presidents' Day Sale!

By George... It's a holiday sale!

Celebrate Presidents' Day with a 21 sales salute!

Celebrate the birth of two great Americans with two days of savings!

Come to our President's Day celebration!

Complimentary cherry pie and coffee while you shop!

Don't get caught in a lie this Presidents' Day

Don't miss our month-long Presidents' Day Celebration!

Drastically-slashed prices in honor of two great men!

Enjoy cherry pie, coffee and some of our biggest savings!

For my money... It's a great presidents' sale!

Free cherry pies all day long!

George and Abe are not running our big value of savings!

Get into the spirit of Presidents' Day!

Give yourself a Presidential pardon from high prices!

Good old-fashioned prices in honor of our first president!

Great Pre-Presidents' Day bargains!

Hail to Presidents fantastic money-savings sale!

Hail to the chief... What a relief... It's sale time!

Happy birthday to the father of our country

Hey! At least I was honest... today!

Home of the great Presidents' Day savings!

Honest Abe deals!

Honest Abe says, "You can't beat these prices!"

Honest values George and Abe would be proud of!

Honestly, our sale starts today!

Honor our Commander in Chief with deep price cuts!

Hooray for Presidents' Day!

How are you planning to celebrate Presidents' Day?

How many candles will these presidents be blowing out during our blowout sale?

Hurry! Presidential savings going on now!

I cannot tell a lie... It's all on sale!

If your name is George Washington, it's free!

In honor of Presidents' Day...

It's a Presidents' Day tradition

It's Abe Day, today!

It's Abe Lincoln Day, after all

233

Presidents' Day

It's Washington's Birthday, so we are serving everything cherry-flavored

Just in time for Presidents' Day

Lincoln Day breakfast special

Monumental sale of the year!

Once-a-Year Presidents' White House Sale!

One of these presidents is going to be up for sale at...

Penny off everything... all day!

Presidents' celebration... free delivery!

Presidents' Day bargains, values, deals!

Presidents' Day Bonus Days!

Presidents' Day Clearance Sale!

Presidents' Day Price Chopper Ritual

Presidents' Day Red, White, Blue Bargain Blast!

Presidents' Day sale-bration... Hats off to you!

Presidents' Day savings bigger than Mt. Rushmore!

Presidents' Day savings extravaganza for every citizen!

Presidents' Day Sell-Off!

Presidents' Day Storewide Sale!

Presidents' special item of the day!

Presidents' week sell-a-thon!

Ready, willing and Abe-l sale!

Remarkable George Washington's birthday savings!

Remarkable Presidents' Day values!

Salute our Presidents by exercising your rights to save more here!

Save lots of Lincolns and plenty of Washingtons during our great Presidents' Day sale!

Special President's weekend savings!

Super Presidents' sale!

The biggest Presidents' Day bash from here to Pennsylvania Avenue!

The Once-a-Year Presidents' Day Sale!

The people's choice...

The Presidents' Day sale that gives you something to celebrate!

The White House white elephant sale of the year!

This Presidents' Day sale is up for grabs

This Presidents' Day, elect to...

This sale is revolutionary... By George

To honor a president you got to have a sale

Today is Lincoln's B-day

Today, come turn your Washingtons into Lincolns at...

Unprecedented Presidents' Day Sale Event!

Vice Presidents' Day sale... Come in and deal with the boss!

Washington's first birthday sale!

We cannot tell a lie! Best prices guaranteed during our Presidents' Day Weekend of Savings!

We cannot tell a lie... You'll save a bundle!

We don't lie about our quality, value and prices!

We'll give you a Lincoln if you...

We'll make you the deal that gets the seal of approval

We'll treat you to a Presidents' Day birthday gift

We're open Presidents' Day, all day!

What awesome Presidents' Weekend savings!

Whatever you say, Abe!

You might not believe it, but it's our Presidents' Bargain Day Celebration!

You'd be crazy to miss our Presidents' Day party sales celebration!

You'll remember this Presidents' Day Sale Event!

Puns

A 21 buck salute

A real glass act

A sale of two cities

All quite on the wardrobe front

All the bright stuff

As time flows by

Back by unpopular demand

Back-to-shoe sale

Bags to riches

Bait and twitch

Be on the cookout

Beauty and the feast

Best of the worst

Bills are ringing

Can't judge a chair by its cover

Car wars

Claws for celebration

Clothes call

Diamonds in the tough

Dinner of champions

Do the bright thing

Don't leave earth without it

Don't pay through the hose

Duty and the beast

Eat your art out

Everything she touches turns to sold

Feeling label pains

Field of screams

Food for naught

For the man who has lost everything

For whom the cash rolls

Franks for the memories

Free reasons to buy...

From soap to nuts

Funds and games

Get the debt out of here

Glove me tender

Go with the glow

Good fences make good decor

Good to the last crumb

Grape expectations

Grin and wear it

Have an ice day

Have friend will travel

Have your bike and ride it too

Hell on heels

Here's the beef

Hey, my pork is missing

I did it my weight

I'm not my brother's sweeper

If books could kill

In cash we trust

It was glove at first sight

It was love at first taste

It won't "quack" your budget

It's a lawn story

It's a mall world after all

It's art, for feet's sake

It's like money in the tank

It's survival of the biggest

It's the wheel thing

Knife and easy

Lawn and order

Leaf of the party

Let there be night

Let your fingers do the talking

Puns

License to grill

Life's a pitch

Like a fish out of money

Love it or heave it

Man's best snack

May the phone be with you

Mind over mattress

New world odor

Now ear this

Off the beaten aisle

One hail of a sale

One of the greatest shows above earth

Our berry best

Our runners runneth over

Pay as you grow

Planting the town green

Pluck of the Irish

Pop goes the wallet

Put a woof over your head

Put your best face forward

Reach out and bug somebody

Read between the vines

Ready, willing, and unable

Say it ain't snow

Shop 'til you pop

Shop ahoy

Show and sell

Show us the honey

Skyway robbery

Smooth selling

Soaring at the speed of data

Sod, but true

Some enchanted reading

Some like it cool

Someday my profit will come

Stand by your van

Stars and gripes forever

Stock it to me

Stop and smell the money

Stop spreading the news

Strike while the shopper is hot

Study as she goes

Take a load off your couch

Take a walk on the sale side of the street

Take me out to the mall game

Taming of the screw

Teach fire with fire

Tell the tooth

Thank goodness for mall favors

The families that live together move together

The byte at the end of the tunnel

The frill of it all

The grass is always browner on the other side of the fence

The greatest savings on earth

The lawn ranger

The proof is in the pasta

The sweet smile of success

There is something new under the sun

Think of us as see-mail

Ties wait for no man

To hill and back

Truck or treat

Try this on for sighs

Wake up and smell yourself

We aim to freeze

We don't fuel around

We're up-sizing

What a difference a stay makes

Who gives a shirt?

Yule be sorry

Quality / Craftsmanship

A commitment to quality and the pride of accomplishment

A fierce sense of pride, and respect for craftsmanship

A level of quality that defines everything we do

A passion for excellence

A quality that's legendary

A renewed commitment to quality and excellence

A standard that is tough to beat

A thirst for excellence

American quality, in every detail

An old-fashioned sense of craftsmanship and pride

As timeless as the tradition of quality

Building a reputation for quality, excellence and service

Built by hand, through innovation

Built to last a lifetime

But don't take our word for it

Buying quality with confidence

Carefully hand-crafted

Commitment to the highest standards of quality

Committed to quality first

Compare the quality! Compare the prices!

Crafted in the spirit of American craftsmanship

Craftsmanship should be a key factor in your decision

Damn right... we're quality!

Discover a big difference in our quality

Don't settle for anything less

Excellence is our only standard

Expect and appreciate the quality

First in quality

For more than fifty years, we have been committed to quality

For over one-hundred years, our quality and craftsmanship has known no equal!

For people who expect the best in quality

Guaranteed quality at...

High quality, low price, we know it

High-end quality without the high-end prices

If it's not pure quality, don't settle for less

If we don't give you quality, then we have failed

Imitations exist but none measure up to our quality

Impeccable quality

In pursuit of excellence

Inherent quality craftsmanship

Introducing a whole new measure of quality

It is our testimony of the quality

It stands for a commitment to quality

It whispers quality

It's a level of quality and pride that makes our product the very best

It's all in the quality

It's not a claim we make lightly

It's not the money... it's the quality that counts

Its quality is unparalleled

Just about the only thing we didn't change was our standard of quality

Let's talk quality

National brand quality... guaranteed!

No one can match our quality

Nobody knows quality like we do

237

Nothing assures quality like pride

Nothing handmade is ever ordinary

Now that's quality you can really trust

Often imitated... never duplicated

Old-fashioned quality and conscientious service

Our commitment to quality is reflected in our performance

Our commitment to you, quality first

Our company value is quality

Our craftsmanship takes quality one step further

Our customers drive our quality

Our name says quality

Our pledge of quality goes into everything we make

Our quality can and will stand the test of time

Our quality is 100 years in the making

Our quality is a symbol of excellence

Our quality is built-in

Our quality never has an expiration date

Our quality shows and tells

Our reputation stands behind our quality

Our standard of excellence

Our standards of quality will be measured by you

Our success stems from our quality

Outstanding quality at fantastic prices

Painstakingly made by hand

Perfection is always made from scratch

Proven quality, proven performance

Quality always saves more than it costs

Quality and dependability run in our company

Quality and service because we care

Quality and service to meet existing customer needs

Quality and value must go hand in hand

Quality and value you just can't beat

Quality becomes your reputation

Quality counts and counts and counts

Quality craftsmanship and ingenuity

Quality first, service second, price third

Quality has become our hallmark

Quality has lasting value

Quality is a proven formula

Quality is always a good value

Quality is expected... excellence will be accepted

Quality is first and foremost

Quality is most important to you... and to us

Quality is not just a commitment

Quality is one of our key ingredients

Quality is our cornerstone

Quality made the old-fashioned way

Quality management, quality process, quality standards

Quality people. Quality products. Quality company.

Quality that comes with a guarantee

Quality that exceeds your every expectation

Quality that lasts forever

Quality that people demand today

Quality that's uncompromised

Quality through innovation is our philosophy

Quality to measure up to

Quality with a capital Q

Quality without a compromise

Quality you can see and count on

Quality, craftsmanship and excellence sets us apart

Quality, when reality exceeds expectations

Quality. Value. Commitment.

Reach for the top quality

Same quality... better prices

See the difference quality makes

Setting the pace for excellence

Shopping for quality, value and service can pay off

So much quality, so much value

That's what sets us apart... quality

The benchmark of quality

The craftsmanship behind the quality

The name you know for quality

The only thing that will outlast the service is the quality

The perfect blend of quality and craftsmanship

The pride in craftsmanship and attention to detail

The proof is in the quality

The quality is outstanding and the value is superb

The quality is priceless

The quality makes us different

The quality you can always count on

The quality you value

The tradition of real craftsmanship still lives on

The true meaning of the word quality

The word says it all... quality

There is no substitute for quality

There's more to our quality than just words

Think quality... it makes a difference

Timeless quality. Timely values

To create quality like this does not come easily

Top quality at an affordable price

Total quality commitment

Uncompromised quality, performance, reliability and service

Unsurpassable quality

Variety, service and quality you can count on

We are often imitated, but never duplicated

We care about quality

We didn't invent quality. We just defined it

We make quality a priority

We make them like they used to

We offer the quality and integrity you expect in a leader

We pay great attention to detail and quality

We stake our name on our quality

We stand behind the quality of our products

We take great pride in our reputation for quality and excellent value

We take quality to a whole new level

We're committed to delivering quality

We're very proud of our quality

We've built our reputation on quality

We've got a passion for perfection

Welcome to the company of quality

What's behind our quality? Our people!

When it comes to quality, good enough is not good enough

When only quality will do

When quality counts!

When we say value, we mean quality

Where quality and value meet

You can afford quality

You can't have one without the other. Quality and craftsmanship!

You don't build quality like ours overnight

You have only one choice, when quality counts

You should never have to compromise on quality

You'll appreciate the craftsmanship

Zero tolerance is what creates quality

A doozy of a fixer-upper

A fantastic penthouse with a view of the bay

A great home to raise a family

A great location deserves a beautiful home

A great place to put down your roots

A great value at an affordable price

A home as unique as your family

A home for every lifestyle

A honey for the money

A hot property that's a cool place to call home

A house like this isn't built overnight

A little house that can grow

A move-up house at a starter home price

A new home is waiting for your family

A nice fit for both family and budget

A perfect home for the perfect family

A real difference in condominium living

A small house with big ideas

A true handyman special

A unique house needs a unique buyer

Absolutely fantastic, absolutely gorgeous

Achieve the dream of owning your own home

Affordable living at its best

All I want for Christmas is a new home

All our happy homeowners can't be wrong

All the comforts of country living

All this house needs is you!

An impeccable house, in pristine condition

Anyone can show you a place to live, but we'll show you the house to buy

Are you looking to buy your first home, but don't know what to do?

Are you struggling to save for the down payment?

At a price that's easy to swallow

Away from city congestion... back to nature

Buy a home, build equity, save on taxes

Buying a house? We'll make you feel right at home

Buying your dream home doesn't have to be a nightmare

Buying! Building! Remodeling!

Call us today for a property preview

Can't afford a new house? Not a problem!

Country living is closer than you think

Cramped? Crowded? Squeezed? Jammed?

Don't put your dreams on hold

Easy living is country living

Easy to own... easy to qualify

Elegant! Exciting! Extraordinary! Exquisite!

Enjoy the comfort of a suburban lifestyle

Escape the bustle of city life

Estate sale... don't miss this!

Every day that your home is on the market, you're losing money

Every house is a gem... every home is a jewel

Exceptional buy... quick possession

Fantastic location... low association fee

Find your dream home on the net

Fit for a king, fit for a queen, fit for a family!

For families buying their first home, we'll open the door

Free market analysis!

Get moving before the house is sold

Give your landlord the notice

Go house hunting with the best

Gracious one-owner home

Great value... quiet neighborhood

Has your dream house gone sour?

Have we got a house for you!

Have you thought about owning your own sand castle?

Here's a nifty little fixer-upper

Here's the front door to your new home!

Homes that are as individual as your family

Hoping to buy a home before the kids return to school?

House hunters welcome!

House to sell? No problem!

How much house could you afford to buy?

How to buy, sell and borrow

How to sell your home for all it's worth

I'm sold on buying a house

If you don't want to do renovation, this house is for you

If you have questions about buying a home! We have the answers!

If you need more space, now's the time to take action

If you're hunting for a home, set your sights on us

If you're looking for a new home, you're in the right neighborhood

In move-in condition

It really is maintenance-free

It's a place you can call home

It's not just the money you save, it's the house you buy!

It's the biggest investment you'll ever make

It's the home of your dreams

Kick the rent habit

Let me show you what your new home will look like

Let us be your guide to a beautiful home

Let us help you find a house to make your home

Live very inexpensively and enjoy other things in life

Look both way before buying a house

Looking for a good small house that doesn't cost a ton of money

Low-maintenance and affordable

Maintenance-free living at its best

Must be seen to be believed... a dollhouse

Need a bigger house?

Need more information on home buying and selling?

Nothing to do but move in

Now's the time to make that move

Our amenities will make you feel right at home

Our reputation is built on recommendations

Owner itching to sell

Perfect in-law arrangement

Planning a long-distance move?

Puzzled about where to buy your home?

Quality, location and commitment to value are why you should plant your roots at...

Read this before you even think about buying a new house

Rent, don't buy!

Shop for money before shopping for a home

Should we rent or should we buy?

Simply put, it's the price that makes this house

So you want to be a landlord?

Someday you'll be able to afford a new home. Is Thursday too soon?

Real Estate

Specializing in first-time home buyers

Stop throwing rent money out the window

Take home a house... today!

The beauty of this house is that it needs work, but it's also very livable

The best things in life aren't free, but we make them affordable

The home that works for you

The impossible is now affordable

The kind of place where you would like to live

The little extras you want can be easy to afford

The perfect place for families of all ages

The right location! The right price! The right home!

The sooner you can sell, the sooner you can buy

They may not be home this Sunday, but we are

Think of your house as a purchase, not an investment

Think of yourself as an owner, not a buyer

This castle can be your home

This could be your home for the holidays

This house requires a special buyer

This one is a steal

Time to trade up!

Tired of house hunting?

Tired of shelling out rent every month?

To move? To sell? To stay?

Treat yourself to easy living

Value-priced homes

Want a prime location?

Watch your kids walk to school

We are the real estate experts

We are your realtors for life

We bring experience to every home we sell

We create the magic when selling your home

We give an honest approach to your real estate options

We have a house that fits your lifestyle

We make house calls

We make the home buying process easier and less confusing

We open doors to some of the finest places

We'd be glad to go house hunting with you

We'll show you more home for your money

We're selling homes with a human touch

We're the best way to get into a new home

We're the key to your new home

We've got a home for you!

What does a dream home look like?

What's the right house for you?

When it comes to real estate, no one has the key like we do!

When you're ready to move, so are we

Where you live does make a difference

Who says you can't buy happiness?

Why rent when you can own?

Why settle for an ordinary home?

Why shouldn't you be picky about your next home? We are!

Wish you could buy a house?

World's best place to raise your family

Would you like to sell your home even faster?

You may be able to afford more home than you think

You'll feel so at home, you'll forget you aren't

You're going to love living here

You've worked for your house, now let us work for you

Your boat will love this house

Your next home could be just a couple of ads away

Religion

A heavenly value today!

A little soul with soul savings

Always wear your Sunday best for church

Are you a beeeeeliever?

Are you a lion or a Christian?

Are you a religious right person or a religious left person?

Are you right with God?

Ask not what God can do for you...

Calling all sinners

Catch the new spirituality in America

Change is good for the soul. But it's murder on the body

Come worship with us without leaving your car

Commit your life to God... today!

Do only nice people go to church on Sunday?

Do you have a tremendous hunger for spirituality?

Do you think you'll make it to heaven?

Does breaking bread create too many crumbs?

Don't leave your loved ones home alone, bring them to our home

Every person has a right to religious freedom

Excite your soul and amaze your mind

Find a church and say a prayer

Fish is good for the stomach but not for the soul

Forgiveness can be your spiritual spring-cleaning

Freedom of religion must be respected by all

From the pulpit to the pew

Get a little piece of heaven right here on earth

Get in tune with God

Get more out of life with Christ

Give us three minutes, we'll make a believer out of you

Going to church is a privilege and a joy

Going to heaven? Come in and plan the route

Have the 10 Commandments become multiple choice?

Have you tried going to church?

Heaven isn't in your neighborhood, but it could be

Here's a new way of looking at God

How can you best serve the church of the future?

How can you worship a homeless man on Sunday and ignore one on Monday?

How is your faith?

How to give more to charity and receive more in return

I was born again and again and again

If God wants to forgive you, fine... we can't

If spirituality were a drug, we couldn't make it fast enough

If the church won't defend the poor, who will?

If you ain't afraid to praise God, then make some noise

If you are looking for God, you came to the wrong place

If you don't have faith, get some

Is religion going to church and pious talk?

Is your faith not worth the investment?

It's a joy to share your faith

It's got to be good for the soul

243

Religion

It's significant to give back from what has been given to you

It's time to count your blessings

Join the flock

Keeping the faith pays off!

Let's get ready to be humble

Like love, faith is only kept by giving it away

Listen to God for guidance

Looking at the Bible from a different point of view

Made fresh every Sunday

Make your church your health club

Missing God?

One prays to God in the manner he believes suits him the best

One way to avoid trouble is to avoid temptation

Only God can make a tree

Open your mind to the divine powers within and around you

Our country needs all the help it can get... including God

Pass through the doors and visit God

Pay attention to your soul

Plug into a powerful source

Pray for what you want, work for what you need

Pray today for world peace

Prayer is cool, but sometimes you need a little steam

Prayer is valuable. So is common sense

Reach out and turn on the light

Ready for Sunday services

Reaffirm your faith... today!

Rediscover the art of prayer

Regardless of what god you might believe in...

Remember your religious heritage

Say yes to God

See you Sunday!

Sin six days during the week and get salvation on Sunday

Skip rope, not church

So, how do you spread the Word?

Stop complaining and count your blessings

Sunday worship is nourishment for the soul

Take a retreat from materialism

Take the path to spirituality and moral high ground

They have been misunderstood by every culture since the beginning of time... the 10 Commandments

This house of God welcomes everyone

Those who go to church regularly are physically healthier

To be born again is to experience a tremendous change

Today is a National Day of Prayer

We can't promise life everlasting, but we can promise life right now

We feed your soul every Sunday

We welcome you regardless of race, creed, color or the number of times you've been born

We'll give you a start you'll never forget

We'll make you a believer, too

Welcome to the Lord's table

What does God do for you?

What should a Christian be in today's society?

Why go to the gym when you can go to church?

Would you rather your kids learn about love from a big purple dinosaur, or the Bible?

You can accomplish anything if you just trust God

You've come to the right place

Restaurant

A culinary delight you'll never ever forget

A deliciously diverse dining experience

A dining experience of historic proportions

A fabulous feast for the frugal

A feast for the eyes, heart and stomach

A free steak-and-eggs breakfast

A fun family restaurant

A glorious dining experience awaits you at...

A good assortment of friendly, moderately-priced food

A good place for a quick, late dinner

A gourmet dining experience

A great meal at a great price!

A homey, old-fashioned breakfast served every morning

A lot of love goes in our food

A neighborhood restaurant that just happens to serve some of the best Italian food anywhere

A real eating experience at a real bargain price!

A restaurant that's out of this world

A romantic menu, featuring foods meant to be shared

A second helping is offered to anyone with an empty plate

A truly extraordinary dining experience

All seconds will taste as good as the first

All you can eat breakfast buffet... every Sunday!

All you can eat for $368.00

Aloha and good eating!

An exquisite Epicurean affair

An exquisite menu to please all tastes

Are you an adventurous diner?

Are you looking for a "diet" kind of meal?

Belly up to a chicken-fried steak platter

Breakfast on sale!

Building relationships is our bread and butter

Casual dining for casual people

Change your routine and dine out

Clearly the best cup of coffee ever served

Close your kitchen and come out to ours

Come home to a homestyle breakfast

Country-style casual dining

Delectable dining

Dine on traditional southern delicacies

Dine out with the best

Dine where the locals dine

Dining is always a pleasure at...

Dinner and parking for a song

Do you have a taste for a juicy hamburger?

Down-home southern food

Eager to eat the Senior Special dinner at 4:30

Eat at your own risk

Eat the best for less!

Eating heart-healthy meals has never been easier to order

Eating in our restaurant won't blow your budget!

Eating out is one of the pleasures of life

Enjoy an evening of heart-healthy gourmet dining

Enjoy the outdoor dining and experience the great view of the lake

Enjoy your holiday meal at a restaurant

245

Every Friday, we're serving up Fish, Fun and Fellowship

Everyday food with a sensible price!

Everything from caviar to spoiled milk

Everything is prepared from scratch

Everything we serve tastes good

Exceptional food in a casual, comfortable setting

Exotic tropical drinks and Polynesian cuisine

Experience island dining at its finest

Extra value meal

Favorite all-you-can-eat restaurant

Feast on delicious entrées at our fabulous dining establishment

Feast on our gastronomic delights

Featuring home-style cooking for breakfast, lunch and dinner

Featuring sandwiches of every kind

Feel like Italian tonight?

Fine dining in a rich French tradition

For a fantastic dining experience

For a leisurely lunch or dinner

For a meal that's fast, fresh and delicious

For a one-of-a-kind gourmet meal

For an intimate and sophisticated evening of fine food

For anyone who loves great eating

For discriminating palates

For good food that bites back

For lunching and munching

For people who love good food

For serious eaters only

For the discriminating palates

For the hearts, minds and taste buds of American diners

For wickedly hot food, this is the place

Free breakfast bar!

From finger food, to a full barbecue, to a sit-down dinner

From hearty home cooking to sophisticated French cuisine

Give the gift of great dining!

Give your stomach a treat

Good country eatin'

Good food and service... if you have that, price doesn't matter

Good fun. Good music. Good food to satisfy every appetite.

Good values and great grub

Great meals at affordable prices!

Have we got a table for you!

Healthy, tasty and interesting food at budget prices!

Home of the best chicken-fried steak

Homemade goodness without the fuss

How can you beat these eats for just a few bucks?

If cooking isn't your cup of tea, then have a cup of tea on us!

If we don't smile, your meal is free!

If you could make good food at home, who would want to eat out?

If you like more in your food... try our new menu

If you like onion rings, this is the place to order them

If you want to make it a special night out, look no further

If you're a "fishy" person, we are the restaurant for you

Indulge! Enjoy! Eat on!

It's a greasy spoon, but really good

It's never too late to eat an early breakfast

It's not just another restaurant... It's the only one

It's our pleasure to serve you a meal

It's time to enjoy a true five-star dining experience

Join us for dazzling ocean views and fresh island cuisine

Juicy and delicious from the first bite to the last

Just bring your appetite

Just sit back and enjoy honest-to-goodness cooking

Kids eat for 99 cents!

Leave your diets at home

Let the banquet begin!

Let us be your steady diet

Let us do the cooking for you

Looking for a great place to dine on a budget?

Looking for somewhere different to eat out?

Make your dining-out experience something more than just a refueling

More sizzle! Great steaks! Less money!

Mouth-watering food prepared before your very eyes

No one comes to our restaurant without falling in love with our food

Not fancy food, but food that makes you feel good

Oceanfront dining has never been so good

Old-fashioned home cooking

Omelets and waffles made while you watch

One of the world's most electric dining adventures

Open all night!

Our appetizers start your meal off on the right foot

Our chicken never had it so good

Our fish come with everything but the hook

Our food is for the gut

Our food is safer than White House food

Our food looks great, but tastes even better

Our kids' menu makes mealtime fun!

Our meals are always an adventure

Our policy is first come, first serve

Restaurant

Our restaurant is an extension of everyone's home

Our restaurant is farmhouse friendly

Our ribs are the next best thing to heaven

People come to our restaurant for our food

Point. Click. Your table is ready!

Put a little South in your mouth

Remember the last time you tried something different?

Satisfy your appetite with us!

Savor the meal at a leisurely pace

Seems like every cop in town eats here

Serving the recreation of the Titanic's last dinner

Sink your teeth into our menu

So by all means, treat yourself to a feast

Soul-food style dinners

Special four-star dinner for families and friends

Start your day with our breakfast!

Steak and seafood at a reasonable price!

Stop for a quick bite or stay for a relaxed meal

Stuff your face with our food

Sugar-free, meat-free, and smoke-free eatery

Swamp cuisine and live Bayou boogie

Take-out: For at-home dining pleasure

Tease your taste buds... here!

The $3 late-night steak dinner!

The beauty of real Japanese cuisine and sushi

The best food this side of your grandmother's kitchen

The best place to grab a quick sandwich!

The best restaurant you never heard of

Restaurant

The best steak in town from the best restaurant in town

The best sushi in town

The best-kept gastronomical secret

The casual place to go for delicious food

The catch of the day is up to you

The coziest restaurant... anywhere

The food is always good; it's always hot!

The food is delicious and reasonable

The freshest seafood in the world

The full flavor of old-time, real barbecue

The healthiest gourmet food in America

The meals are incredible

The most diverse menu for a value-packed, American-style meal

The most incredible meal you will ever eat

The only restaurant for your holidays

The perfect setting for seafood lovers

The place to pig-out

The right choice for dining, any day of the week

The southern-style seafood is fabulous

The ultimate restaurant award... our customers!

The world's finest restaurant!

There's nothing quite like our steaks

This is a restaurant where food is taken very seriously

This is very much an experience; it's not just a sandwich

Thrill your palate... choke your arteries

Traditional American cuisine

Treat yourself to a relaxing breakfast

Try our mouth-watering, world-famous chicken and ribs

We are a stick-to-the-ribs kind of place

We are just a very good steakhouse

We are the nuts and bolts of everyday eating

We don't just set tables. We set standards

We have the most brilliant cook alive

We invite you to a dining atmosphere all its own

We invite you to dine with us

We make an everyday meal into a special occasion

We proudly serve the freshest and most creative dinners... anywhere!

We put your money where your mouth is

We serve "diet-friendly" meals, too!

We serve duck with everything but the quack

We serve ethnic delights

We serve picky eaters

We serve the best new taste in the west

We'll kick your taste buds into high gear

We're big on burritos

We're known for our Mexican food

We're the "off the beaten path" family restaurant

What are you gonna do for dinner?

Where do you get your most value for your dining dollar?

Where good people meet and eat

Where people eat just for the halibut

You can dine in... but takeout is an excellent option

You can eat here without blowing a bundle

You can sink your teeth into it... big time!

You don't need teeth to eat the sweet-sauced ribs

You don't need to be a big shot to get a reservation

You won't be able to wait to sink your teeth into our steaks

You'll always ask for a doggy bag at our restaurant

You'll be licking your chops at...

10K or Marathon Deals! It's your choice!

5K race... register here!

50% off all carbohydrate meals before the big race!!!

A good pair of shoes can win the race for you

A run a day keeps the doctor away

A sale that inspires runners of all ages!

A sale to take your breath away, not your money!

Are you ready for the run of your life?

Are you up for a quick twenty-mile jog?

Awesome savings for the long run!

Be a sponsor of this year's triathlon

Be the pace-setter

Biggest sneaker sales event ever!

Can you go the distance?

Deals that are faster than fast!

Endurance is the big thing

Every participant receives a T-shirt

Every runner owns a pair of our shoes

Everything is on sale during our marathon savings event!

Experienced runners know a great sale!

Explosive deals for weekend joggers

For fun on the run... get everything you need here!

Get a jump on this year's running season

Get a running start on these values!

Get on the fast track

Get on the running shoes

Get the spirit for running

Get your second wind during our first sale extravaganza of the year!

Go the distance with super values!

Going fast, faster, fastest bargains on all...

Going the distance with amazing savings!

Going the Extra Mile Sale Event!

Great savings for all joggers!

Have you run a marathon before?

Have your pre-race pasta dinner at...

Hit the savings running!

I'd rather be running

In the race to win

It's a runner's world

It's not a sprint, it's a marathon

It's not where you start but where you finish

Just how prepared are you for the big race?

Just in time for revving up your spring running

Just jump into your running shoes and...

Let Your Spirits Run Wild Sale Event!

Make a run for it

Make tracks to the best sale possible!

Makin' tracks

Making running a part of your life

Meet me at the finish line

Monday through Thursday... phenomenal savings for weekend joggers!

Normally running shoes aren't something we can get too excited about, but these are different

Off the Beaten Track Sale Event!

Off to a flying start

On your mark for the sale event of a lifetime!

On your mark... Get set... Bang!!!

Running

Passing mile markers becomes easier when you're running with our shoes!

Prices that get you running

Pushing yourself to the limits

Put your shoes on and ruuuuuuun!

Race to the Finish Savings Event!

Racing for your favorite cause

Reaching the finish line

Ready to go the distance

Ready... set... finish!

Run for the record

Run for your life

Run strong. Run smooth. Run fast.

Run with the best

Run with the power

Runners don't let the grass grow under their feet

Running a marathon is an extraordinary achievement

Running for a cause

Running is a great way to keep in shape

Running is one of the best ways to lose weight and keep it off

Running is the spice of life

Running is the ultimate time machine

Running like a pro

Running Shoes for the Season Sales Event!

Running with gusto...

Savings like this will give you a runner's high!

Savings set the pace!

See you on race day!

Setting the pace

Sign up for the race of a lifetime

Sprint like a champion

Start the outdoor running season with great bargains on...

Stretch those muscles before the race

Taking it to the limit

Terrific deals for the long run!

The finish line... you did it!

The fuel that powers your running

The joys of running

The mother of all marathons

The race is on with explosive deals at...

The race to fast-pace savings!

The win-win sales event of the year!

There's nothing like winning a race

Think you can pass up a sale this outstanding?

This is no run-of-the-mill running shoe

This is the place to race

This sale will give you a runner's high!

Time Is Running Out Sale!

To inspire runners of all ages

Training for the marathon? We have all the equipment you'll need and it's on sale!

Treat your muscles with a little respect

Up and running savings!

Wake Up and Smell the Shoes Savings Event!

We'll help you reach the finish line

We'll keep you in the running with these sensational savings!

We're setting the pace with unbelievable savings

Wearing the right gear is a smart choice

When you take a hike, take it for a good cause

You can run... you can WIN!

You Get What You Sweat For Savings Event!

You won't get lost in the crowd with these bargains!

You're off and running with incredible savings!

A burglar-friendly environment

A child's safety never can be guaranteed

A clean fireplace is a safe fireplace

A little vigilance can save lives

A new kind of security blanket

A security camera is the best way to protect your property

A sense of security about safety

A small price to pay for safety

A trained dog can provide safe and effective protection

According to the National Safety Council

Add an ounce of prevention to keep your family safe

Adding more security to your home is always a good deal

After all, everybody wants good security

Are we on an orange alert or a red alert?

Are you a target for a break-in?

Are you concerned about your safety?

Are you throwing caution to the wind?

Are your kids safe? Are your valuables safe?

Around-the-clock protection

Awareness can save your life

Be alert. Be aware. Be careful.

Be alert... don't be fooled

Be aware of hazards at home

Be protective of your own turf

Be safe... instead of sorry

Be smart... be safe... but don't worry

Being cautious about being cautious

Burglar alarms... fire alarms... for your protection

But having a man around is no guarantee of safety

But wouldn't you rather be safe than sorry?

By the time you realize you've been robbed, it's too late!

Check hazardous points around the house on a yearly basis

Check the batteries of each smoke detector at least once a month

Child safety is our main concern

Concern about privacy or concern about security

Cut your chances of being burglarized

Do something now before it's too late

Do you need extra security?

Don't be alarmed!

Don't be caught off guard! Be ready!

Don't be complacent... a little bit of paranoia is good

Don't be the next victim

Don't let a thief come between you and your valuables

Don't let this happen to you!

Don't make a burglar's job easier

Don't play it safe; just play it smart

Don't wait till it's too late

Ducks sleep with one eye open for safety

Enjoy life with a high degree of safety

Ever get the feeling you're being watched?

Everybody could use a little safety checkup

Everybody needs security

Expand your security system with video protection

Finding potential household hazards before they find you

For the safety of your children

Free security analysis

Get a guard dog

Get serious about security

Here's how to protect yourself

Hide it! Lock it! Or lose it!

Home safety is an often-overlooked factor

Home safety is priority number one

Home-alone safety

How can you tell when you're suffering from carbon monoxide poisoning?

How kid-safe is your home?

How much security do you need?

How to avoid becoming a victim

How to prevent home break-ins and fatalities

How to protect the ones you love most

I don't want to tell you I told you so, but I told you so

If home is where your heart is, your security system should also be there

If security is the question, we've got the answers

If you don't have the best security, you don't have any security

If you're worried about safety...

Ignore safety at your own peril

In the interest of safety... let's get tough

Increasing caution makes good sense

Install a complete home security system for only...

Investing in safe habits

Is there danger lurking in your medicine cabinet?

It's a small price to pay for safety

It's about safety and security

It's as safe as a bank vault

It's for our safety as well as yours

It's wise to stay alert

Keep chemicals locked away from children

Learn the ABC's of safety

Learn to save a life

Made with your safety in mind

Make a commitment to safety

Make break-in tough for burglars

Make plans for home safety

Make safety part of your lifestyle

Make your home safe and secure

Making your home that's safe even safer

Never compromise safety

Never let down your guard

No one knows how many ill-minded adults are lurking in the shadows

Nobody leaves the house in the morning thinking they will be on the 6 o'clock news

Nothing is going to be 100 percent, but we'd rather be on the side of caution

Nothing is more important than security

On the outside. On the inside. On the safe side.

Pay heed to security

Peace of mind protection

Prevention is the best defense against burglary

Prevention is the key to safety

Protect your privacy! Protect your property! Protect your family!

Putting safety first makes a great deal of sense

Quit beefing about it and do something about it!

Raise your consciousness about safety

Residential fire and security systems installed by professionals

Safe schools are safety-smart

Safeguard your home from thieves

Safety begins with you

Safety could become a problem if you don't take care of it

Safety first! Security second! Convenience last!

Safety is everybody's business

Safety is first and foremost

Safety is no accident

Safety measures help ensure the family safety

Safety should not be sacrificed for convenience

Safety starts with you!

Safety: Do you take it for granted?

Security and safety is our highest priority

Security is not a joking matter. All comments are taken very seriously

Security isn't a product; it's a process

Shouldn't you feel the same way about security?

State-of-the-art security system... now on sale!

Steps to achieve good security

Take responsibility for your own safety

Taking simple steps to make your home safer

The benefits of security and safety are peace of mind

The highest in safety standards

The Home Security Break-In Sale Event!

The more precautions you take, the safer you'll be

The only thing foolproof is responsibility

The risk of disregarding security

The state-of-the-art security system

There is no substitute for your own vigilance

There is no such thing as being too safe

Think of safety as you do your underwear... not meant for the public to see

Think of us as your safety net

Think safety! Think security!

Think seriously about a home security system

This home is protected by...

Total home protection

Trust us to protect you

Turning the spotlight on safety

Warning doesn't solve the problem... being alert does

Ways to avoid potentially dangerous situations

We are concerned about your safety

We burglar-proof homes

We don't take safety for granted

We emphasize safety

We give you a sense of security

We have an obligation to provide for your safety

We have the security you can count on

We provide the security you need

We really do care about your safety

We stop smart thieves

We've built our reputation on keeping you safe!

What are you going to do about it?

What's the price of security?

Where should you turn for safety?

Why leave your valuables unprotected?

Why put yourself at risk

You can be certain that we'll keep a vigilant watch over you

You can't live your life in fear

You can't move away from crime; you have to deal with it

You don't have to be paranoid to be worried about your privacy

You think you're protected and you're not

You want security? Go buy a blanket!

Sailing

A classic yachting adventure for only...

A full service marina

A good time for all downriggers

A well-maintained boat is a thing of beauty

A world-class yachting marina

A yacht's eye view of...

Ahoy, adventure seekers

Always sail with the best deals!

Anchor and come get the savings!

As another sailing season comes to an end

Batten down the hatches for extreme buys on all...

Boating tips for a safe summer

Buy the captain's choice at...

Catch the fresh wind in our sale event!

Chart your course for success

Check the rigging and stock the galley

Climb aboard and leave your worries behind

Come aboard for a sale adventure!

Come sail away with us!

Deals nothing short of piracy!

Dedicated to boating safety and fun

Discover what a little wind in your sales can do

Don't abandon ship just yet... the sales are coming!

Don't miss the boat on these discounted items!

Don't set sail without one

Drop your anchor and join the excitement at our Yacht Club Day!

Enjoy the pure joy of sailing at...

Everyone should try sailing

Follow the trade winds to drastically slashed prices!

For a breezy day on the water...

For people who are serious about sailing

For the best in the world of sailing, call...

Fresh as a sea breeze

From on-deck to decked out

From Sea to Shining Sea Sale Event!

From stem to stern, bargains, values, deals!

Get equipped to weather the storm with...

Get in shipshape for the race at...

Get on board with...

Get ready to sail into...

Great deals for you and your crew

Great savings for boat buffs!

Great values for getting the yacht shipshape

How about a weekend sea adventure?

I'd rather be sailing

I'm heading out to take a sailing lesson

If you can sail here, you can sail anywhere

If you sail in any direction, you're bound to find awesome savings at...

Is your boat Coast Guard-approved?

It puts you on deck to save big!

It's a clear-sailing sale event!

It's a fun boat to sail

It's a spectacular sail of values!

It's a sport for all ages

It's not mutiny... it's our final sale of the season!

It's your dream boat

Know the ropes before you set sail

Let us help chart your course

Let your imagination sail with us

Look What Washed Ashore...
Sale Event!

Looking at buying a used boat?

Looking for a qualified coxswain

Mark your calendar and chart your course for fantastic bargains throughout the store!

On dock or deck, we go overboard to deliver...

Our boats are as reliable as the tide

Put the wind back into your sales at...

Ready to set sail for another season

Really, now who wouldn't want a boat?

Row, row, row your boat to a seaworthy sale event!

Sail ahead of the rest to the best buys!

Sail in for sensational savings!

Sail into summer with...

Sail the sea... on us!

Sail through the sailing season with...

Sail where the savings take you!

Sail with your own captain and crew

Sailing on Sale!

Sailing season underway

Sailing through the season will be a breeze with big savings!

Sale away!

Sea Maine at its best

Seaworthy savings for every Jolly Roger!

Set a course for adventure

Set sail for rest, relaxation and fun

Set sail for warm-weather savings at...

Set your course full speed ahead and cruise by...

Set your sails for a delightful day

So climb aboard, you'll enjoy the ride

Special purchase goods for the sailing crew

Steady as she goes

Stem to stern everyday deals!

Take me where I can buy a boat

The joy of boat ownership

There is no nicer place for sailing than...

This will float your boat... guaranteed!

Tie up at your favorite year-round yachting playground!

We are strictly sailing

We are the authority on sailing

We can keep you afloat for any emergencies!

We sail when others can't

We'll put you back on course with...

We're clearing the decks... now is the time to save!

We're flying the flag on old-fashioned prices!

We've raised our sails for a gala of a sale!

Weather or knot: Big savings!

Welcome aboard for an...

Welcome aboard to our annual Nautical Sales Event!

Welcome to the world of sailing

When the ocean calls...

Why not climb aboard?

Would you like to spend the day sailing with me?

Yo ho ho, a pirate sale event for all swashbucklers!

You can bet your dinghy you will save big money on...

You can't afford to miss a boatload of savings

You couldn't find anything like it in any marina

You'll make out like a pirate with these savings!

Your ship has come in with drastically slashed prices on all...

13-Hour Sale! Every 13 hours!

50% off the whole time we are open!

72-hour shockers!

A blanket sale you'll warm up to!

A cheap but good sale!

A Customer Satisfaction Sale!

A fabulous sale for saveaholics!

A garage sale isn't a bad idea

A magnificent sale! A monstrous sale! A monumental sale!

A nifty thrifty kind of sale!

A no-brainer sale! Everything must go!

A Once in a Lifetime Sale!

A One-Two Punch Sale!

A Penny Saved Is A Penny Earned Sale!

A roaring sales blowout!

A sale just too good to pass up!

A sale like this can't last forever!

A sale so big it only happens once a year!

A sale that will leave change in your pocket!

A sale that will make your hair stand up!

A sale with a great WOW to it!

A sale worth dying for

A super, super, super sale!

A very special sale that's... Top secret

A 'May'zing Sale!

Absolutely everything on sale... now!

Absolutely! Last day, today!

Act fast... When they're gone they're gone!

All For One Sale!

All the Bells and Whistles Sale!

All the best, all for less, all on sale!

All This for Just a Dollar Sale!

All your favorites, now on sale!

Amazing sale on stuff you need!

Amazing Savings Sale!

An Everyday Sale!

An Extra Special Sale!

An incredible 3-day sale!

An OK sale is 25% off, but a good sale is 40% off

Are you ready for a sale like this?

As you always wished it would be on sale

Ask about our easy payment plan!

At 15% off, our hot prices just got hotter!

At a good, old-fashioned price

At these prices, you'll really clean up!

At this price, you can only hope your friends didn't see it first

Back-In-Time Sale!

Best Buy in America Sale!

Big weekend... huge sale!

Biggest and best sale of the year!

Billion Dollar Sale!

Blowout Sale of Excitement!

But-Do-You-Need-It Sale!

Can't Resist Sale!

Cash Back Sale!

Catalog Sale Only!

Catch the sale at great savings!

Clearance! Closeouts! Floor samples! And more!

Code-red clearance sale!

Customer Only Sale!

Do not miss this incredible sale!

Dollar Days Sale!

Don't Let the Price Fool You... Sale!

Don't miss this sale!

Don't wait! This sale ends soon!

Due to overwhelming demand, the sale is still on!

Dynamite day sale!

Early Bird Smart Money Sales!

Early weekend sale!

Easy as 1-2-3 Sale!

End-Of-Season Sale!

Entire stock sale for her and for the kids!

Even our rummage is on sale!

Ever walk away from a sale feeling this good?

Every day is a great sale day!

Everybody is raving about the sales!

Everything a sale should be!

Everything is on sale! Absolutely no exceptions!

Everything that isn't nailed down is on sale!

Everything's on sale... nothing held back!

Factory Direct Sale!

Final sale of the season!

First time on sale!

For a great sale! And a great deal of savings!

For a limited time only!

For one night only!

Funny Money Sale!

Garage sale! Sidewalk sale! Yard sale! Rummage sale! Take your pick!

Get more bang for your buck at this sale!

Get out your sunglasses 'cause you're going to be dazzled

Get what you want on sale!

Go ahead and knock yourself out at our Annual Knockout Sale!

Going for the sale!

Going Into Business Sale!

Good, Better, Best Sale!

Gotta Get It Sale!

Greatest sales time of all times!

Guaranteed to bring big sales smiles!

Guess what's half off?

Hail Damage Disaster Sale!

Half Price Sale!

Hang onto your money. It's on sale!

Held over due to popular demand!

Help us make this sale a success!

Here's a sale that's just ducky!

Here's a sale you can't walk away from

Hot Sizzling Super Sale!

Hot, hot, hot! Truckload sale!

Hottest sale of them all!

How about a sale that's a real family value?

How to avoid getting hung-up by our unbelievable sale!

How to profit from every sale!

Huge spectacular sale!

Hurry in! Sale ends tomorrow!

Hurry!!! This week only sale!

Hurry, before this sale is history!

I bought it at an estate sale!

I want it! I need it! I have to have it sale!

If it ain't one sale... it's another!

If it isn't 50% off, it ain't a sale!

If our savings grabbed your attention, so should this sale!

If they don't see an "on sale" sign, they don't buy

If you see it... it's on sale!

If you're asking if everything's for sale, yes!

If you've been looking for that big sale, don't miss this one!

Instant Rebate Sale!

In-Store Sidewalk Sale!

It only happens once a year!
Don't miss it!

It takes a smart shopper to save at a sale

It's a hoot of a sale!

It's a humdinger of a sale!

It's a sale you can sink your teeth into

It's a Sell-A-Thon!

It's a sensational sale!

It's a Star-Studded Sale!

It's a steal of a sale!

It's a walk-away sale!

It's all on sale!

It's an amazing sale! It's an irresistible sale! It's better than a sale!

It's Closeout Time Sale!

It's definitely not your average sale

It's never on sale for less

It's not a sale! It's great prices every day!

It's not easy to pass up this sale!

It's only once a year that we put our best on sale!

It's our anniversary sale!

It's our Annual Giant Warehouse Sale!

It's our Jumpin' January Sale!

It's our only sale of the year!

Join the sale for one day

Kick Off the Season Sale!

Last Blast Sale!

Last Chance to Save Sale!

Last-Minute Sale!

Look what's on sale!

Looks Like A Million Bucks Sale!

Lots of neat stuff on sale!

Lowest Prices Ever Sale!

Luggage Trade-In Sale!

Made in the USA Sale!

Make tracks to the terrific sale of the year!

Make your own sale with our low prices!

Markdown Madness Sale!

Midnight Special Sale!

Million-Dollar Sale!

More sales for you!

Moving sale!

Name Brand Sale!

Name Your Own Price Sale!

Never underestimate the power of a great sale!

No Bull Sell-a-thon!

No Hassle Sale! No Runaround Sale! No Baloney Sale!

No Sales Tax Sale! We'll pay your sales tax!

Not your ordinary closeout sale!

Now all on sale!

Now or Never Sale!

Off the Ceiling Sale!

On sale at incredible sale prices!

On sale now!

Once-In-A-Lifetime Sale!

One fabulous big sale!

One heck of a sale!

One Price Sale!

One-Stop Sale!

One-Week Super Sale!

OOPS! We Must Have Goofed Sale!

Operation Must Sell!

Our Annual Famous Sale is going on right now!

Our best customers are invited to a one-day sale!

Our best sale of the year!

Our biggest sale of the year is online, too!

Our Cheesiest Sale Ever!

Our Magic Markdown Sale!

Our sale is worth waiting for

Our sale prices beat their sale prices!

Our sale vs. on sale

Out-of-this-world savings

Outrageous sale... today only!

Overstocked sale!

Parking lot sale!

Phenomenally exciting sale!

Pick Your Price sale!

Power buying is the key to this sale!

Pre-moving sale!

Prepare to be dazzled by this
amazing sale!

Price Smasher Sale!

Really big sale... The biggest event of
the season!

Red-hot 3-day sale!

Remember when a sale was really
a sale?

Rockin' and Shoppin' Sale!

Run In Before You Run Out Sale!

Sale in progress

Sale of sales!

Sale price... today only!

Sale prices you'll really love

Sale specials of the week!

Sale? You bet!

Sale... today only!

Seize the sale!

Senior citizen sale day!

Shop For Yourself Sale!

Sizzlin' with sales!

Something for Everyone Sale!

Special limited time... layaway sale!

Starving Artist Sale!

Stock-up Sale!

Storewide Clearance Sale!

Straight Talk Sale!

Such a Deal Sale!

Sunday Silent Sale... Shhh

Sale

Super Duper Sunday Sale!

Super sale, super service, super
selection, super savings

Super Savings Weekend Sale!

Take a look at some of the most exciting
stuff on sale!

Take me out to the garage sale!

Terrific Tuesday Sale!

That's a humdinger of a sale!

That's right... everything is on sale!

The Bare Minimum Price Sale!

The Best for Less Sale!

The best little warehouse sale ever!

The best-kept sale is out!

The Big Super Sale!

The biggest sale of them all!

The Brand Name Sale!

The champion of all sales

The competition can't touch our
lower prices

The early bird catches the sale!

The frenzy sale of the month

The Gigantic Warehouse Sale of
the Year!

The good buy sale of the year!

The Great Sales Jam!

The Great Stuff Sale!

The greatest sale imaginable

The Last Great Sale of the Year!

The last real sale!

The Million-Dollar Sale!

The Money-Saving,
Pantry-Stocking sale!

The right time, the right date, the right
price, the right sale!

The sale blitz is on!

The Sale of all Sales!

Sale

The sale of sales at fantastic savings!

The sale of the hour!

The sale you'll fall in love with!

The sale you've been waiting for!

The sale, the whole sale, and nothing but the sale!

The sales event everyone has been waiting for

The sales war has started

The Smart Money Saver Sale!

The stuff you need at prices you'll love!

The stupendous one-day sale!

The sun is shinin', the bees are buzzin', and we're having a sale!

The wait is over! Sale starts...

The world's greatest sale ever!

There should always be sale

There won't be another sale like this for years

There's a method to our sale-of-madness

Think you can pass up a sale this great?

This is a no-hype, no-gimmicks... Year-end sale!

This is not just another sale

This is one big cushy sale

This is our final, final, final sale!!!

This sale is guaranteed to lift your spirits!

This sale only happens once a year!

This sale packs a punch!

This sale will shock you!

Time flies when you're getting 50% off

Time is running out sale!

Unbelievable savings at an unbelievable sale!

Up For Grabs Sale!

We have more stuff on sale than you can shake a stick at!

We honor all competitors' sale prices!

We meet you more than halfway... 55% off

We'll beat the pants off anyone else's sale!

We'll stack 'em up against any other sale!

We're dropping everything... including prices!

We're having a lunch sale!

We're having an "Old Times" sale!

We're stirring up a sensational sale on...

We're throwing in the free stuff with this sale!

We're Under Construction Sale!

We've got the stuff for any sale imaginable

Welcome to our Annual Thank You Sale!

What a discount... What a sale!

What a great sale is supposed to be!

What a great time for a sale!

What's yer hurry? Sale!

Whatever you put on, we'll take 20% off

When does it go on sale?

When we get a price break, you get a sale!

When we say sale... we mean it!

Where everything is for sale!

Where the sales never end!

Whoomp, Here It Is Again Sale!

Worth Every Cent Sale!

Y'all must be having a sale, right?

You can't afford to miss this sale!

You Don't Need To Pay Top Dollar Sale!

You'll be taken back by our sale!

You'll flip for our sale!

You'll Love It Sale!

You're invited to a private sale!

You're too smart to pass up the sale

You've gotta sale!

Sale Events

$1,000,000 Closeout Sale Savings Event!

2-Day Blast Sales Event!

A Five-Star Sales Event!

A great sales event with fabulous buys!

A Lot For A Little... Sale Event!

A sales event that will make your day!

A sales event to call your own!

A truly exceptional sale event experience!

All The Bells And Whistles Sales Event!

Annual Colossal Warehouse
Sales Event!

Annual Inventory Clearance Sale Event!

At The Right Time, At The Right Price
Sales Event!

Baby Boomers Sales Event!

Back By Popular Demand Sales Event!

Back In Time Sales Event!

Bang for the Buck Sale Event!

Bare Minimum Price Sales Event!

Be the life of the sales event!!!

Best Buys In The USA Sales Event!

Best Customer Only Sales Event!

Best For Less Sales Event!

Best Prices Sales Event of the Year!

Billion-Dollar Sales Event!

Bring Home The Bacon Sales Event!

Business Savings Event!

Call Us Crazy Sale Event!

Closeout Time Sales Event!

Closing Our Doors Sales Event!

Construction Sales Event! Going on in
spite of the mess!

Cure For Cabin Fever Sales Event!

Customer Satisfaction Sales Event!

Deep Discount Event of the Year!

Dirt-Cheap Sales Event!

Dollar Mania Sales Event!

Don't Let The Price Fool You Sales Event!

Don't miss the biggest shopping sales
event of the year!

Don't you just love it? Sales events!!!

Dynamite Days Sales Event!

End-Of-Season Sales Event!

End-Of-Year Sales Event!

Everything On Sale Event!

Exceptional sales event for
savvy shoppers!

Exceptional, Sensational Sales Event!

Expect More For Your Money
Savings Event!

Extra Special Sales Event!

Extra, Extra Sales Event!

Factory Direct Sales Event!

Final Markdowns Sales Event!

Foot-Stomping, Heart-Pounding
Sales Event!

Get Carried Away Sales Event!

Get on board at the sales event of
the season!

Get What You're Looking For...
Sale Event!

Go ahead, knock yourself out! Annual
Knockout Sales Event!

Good, Better, Best Sales Event!

Grab A Shoppin' Cart Sale Event!

Great American Sale Event!

Great Door-Buster Sales Event!

Great Stuff Sales Event!

Greatest Sales Event Of All Time!

Greatest Sales Event Of The Year!

Greatest Savings Event Of All Time!

Half-Price Sales Event!

Hassle-Free Sales Event!

Healthy Living Sale Event!

High-Five Sale Event Of The Season!

Home Sweet Home Furniture Sale Event

Hoot of a sales event!

Hot Hit Sales Event!

Hottest Sales Event Of The Season!

Indoor Sidewalk Sales Event!

Instant Gratification Sales Event!

Introducing... the Five Million Dollar Sales Event!!!

Inventory Blowout Sales Event!

Is It Worth It? Sales Event!!!

Isn't that what a sales event is all about? Savings!!!

It's A Beautiful Thing Sales Event!

It's A Helluva Sales Event!

It's A Wonderful Life Sale Event!

It's All About You... Sale Event!

It's Irresistible Sales Event!

It's our Extraordinary Sale Event Of The Year!

It's our Last Hurrah Of The Year Sales Event!

It's our Thank You Sales Event!

It's the best time of the year for a Savings Event!

It's The Price That Counts... Sale Event!

It's your time to shine at our fabulous sales event!

Jump into our sales event with both feet!

Let The Good Times Roll Sale Event of the Year!

Let's Cut All The Bull... Sale Event!

Lowest Prices Ever Sales Event!

Lucky Seven Sales Event!

Made In The USA Sales Event!

Madness and Mayhem Sales Event!

Men's Half-Yearly Sale Event!

Midnight Madness Sales Event!

Mid-Week Madness Sale Event!

Million Gallon Paint Sale Event!

Moonlight Madness Sales Event!

Mooooovin' The Merchandise Sale Event!

Move Fast Sales Event!

Name Brand Sales Event!

Now Hear This Sales Event!

Off-The-Wall Sale Event!

Old Times Sales Event!

Once In A Lifetime Sales Event!

One Big Happy Family Sales Event!

One-Day Savings Event!

One-Two Punch Sales Event!

Operation Must Sell Sales Event!

Our Magical Markdown Sales Event!

Out With The Old And In With The New Sales Event!

Parking Lot Sales Event!

Pay-As-You-Go Sale Event!

Pick Your Price Sales Event!

Pinch yourself... this sales event isn't a dream!

Price-Blaster Sales Event!

Prices You Can Afford... Sale Event!

Price-Smasher Sales Event!

Procrastinator's Sale Event of the Week!

Put It On Spin Sale Event!

Put On A Happy Face Sale Event!

Red Tag Sales Event!

Rib-Ticklin' Sale Event!

Rockin' And Shoppin' Sales Event!

Saved By The Bell Sales Event!

Savings For A Rainy Day Sales Event!

Secret Savings Night Sales Event!

Seize the Moment... Sale Event!

Shop 'Til You Drop Sales Event!

Smart Money Saver Sales Event!

Snap It Up... Sale Event!

Something For Everyone Sales Event!

Star-Studded Sales Event!

Strike Up The Band Sales Event!

Sunday Silent Savings... Shhh!
Sales Event!

Super Saturday Preview Sale Event!

Super Spectacular Sales Event!

Super store! Super savings! Super
Sales Event!

Sweet Dreams Sales Event!

Talk Of The Town Sale Event!

Terrific Tuesday Sales Event!

The Big Super Sales Event!

The Biggest One Day Only Sales Event!
of the year!

The Gang's All Here Savings Event!

The Great Sales Jam... Savings Event!

The Last Great Savings... Sales Event!

The making of an unbelievable
sales event!

The most unexpected sales event ever!

The sales event for smart shoppers!

The Super Sell Sale Of Savings Event!

The unlimited savings event!

There's No Better Time To Clean Up
Sale Event!

Think Big Sales Event!

This is a sales event in all its glory!

This is one sales event you don't want
to miss!

This is what you've been waiting for...
Tremendous Sales Event!

This Is Your Last Chance To Dance...
Sale Event!

This sales event is a 7-day celebration!

This sales event is for you!

Time to enjoy the buzz! Join the Sales
Event Celebration!

Treat yourself to a terrific savings event!

Truckload Sales Event!

Up For Grabs Sales Event!

Warehouse Overstock Savings Event!

We Saved The Best For Last Sale Event!

We'll Make It Worth The Trip
Sales Event!

We're Clearing The Shelves Sale Event
Of The Season!

We're On Your Side Savings Event!

We're Out Of Our Minds Sales Event!

We're the proud sponsor of our
sales event!

We've pulled out all the stops... Savings
Event of the year!

What more can we say? It's the Sales
Event of the year!

What More Could You Ask For
Sales Event!

When Every Dollar Counts Saving Event!

Where The Action Is Sales Event!

Whoozits and Whatzits Sale Event!

Won't Believe It Sales Event!

World's Greatest Sales Event!

Worth Every Cent Sales Event!

Year-End Sale Event!

You asked for it! You got it! Sales Event!

You can profit from the sales event of
the season!

You Don't Need To Pay Top Dollar
Sales Event!

You Have The Edge Sale Event!

You Won't Believe It Sales Event!

You'll Love It... Sales Event!

Your Lucky Day Sale Event!

Zero Down Sales Event!

Savings

10% to 30% off any one of our hundreds of thousands of items!

2 weeks of great savings!

20% off already-discounted prices!

24 hours of non-stop savings!

25% off all previously marked items!

30% to 50% off on everyday low prices!

7-Day Savings Stampede!

A big event! Bigger savings!

A Spectacular Sale! Unbeatable Savings!

Absolutely, positively unbeatable savings!

Act fast. The time to save is now!

Action-packed savings!

Ain't the savings terrific?

All merchandise drastically reduced!

All prices cut to the bone!

All the savings at one place!

Always 10% to 30% senior discounts... everyday!

Always save more on...

Amazing savings, all at the right price!

An especially sweet offer at half the regular price

An invitation to excellent savings!

Any way you look at it... you save!

Around-the-house savings, at sensational savings!

At prices moms love!

Be part of the tremendous savings!

Better move fast... savings this great won't last!

Big discounts! Huge savings! Big time savings!

Big excitement!!! Big savings!!!

Big savings on an exceptional selection of...

Big savings... limited time!

Big time savings... you bet!

Bring home Big Savings!

Celebrate the savings year-round

Cheap at half the price

Cheers for dirt-cheap prices!

Clean up with fantastic savings on...

Colossal savings... limited time

Come and check out fantastic savings!

Come in early for big savings!

Compare for yourself and save!

Compare our prices to what you've been paying and save more!

Count on savings on your favorite...

Delivering real savings

Discover the savings you've always wanted

Do it the discount way and save

Dollar day savings!

Don't wait! These savings won't last!

Doorbuster discounts!

Double Discount Days!

Down to the bone, rock-bottom prices!

Dynamite deals! Dynamite values! Dynamite savings!

Earn 10% back on just about everything

Enjoy the unbeatable savings!

Everyday savings, every dollar counts!

Everyone falls in love with lower prices

Exciting savings? You better believe it!

Experience the savings excitement!

Eye-popping savings!

Fantastic savings! Super-low prices!

Feast your eyes on these savings!

Fill up your piggy bank with big savings!

Final price reductions...
additional savings!

Five ways to relax and save

For the low, low price of one cent!

From morning 'till night, we're saving
you money!

Fun-time savings!

Get 4-star savings now!

Get a jolt of savings during...

Get in the circle of savings

Get ready for bigger and better savings!

Get the price and performance you're
looking for

Get the things you need at prices
you want!

Get your money's worth!

Go for all out savings!

Go to the green arrow and save big time!

Great savings and great values!

Great savings in every aisle, every day!

Great savings... low warehouse prices!

Groundbreaking savings!

Half-price savings!

Hello, cash back!

High-voltage savings!

Home is where the savings are

How 'bout them savings?

How low can our prices go? Come in
and see!!!

How to keep the green in your wallet

Huge savings in every department!

Hurry in for exceptional savings!

Hustle in for great savings!

I'm hungry for savings. Please put me
on your mailing list!

In savings we trust!

Incredible prices on everything in
the store!

Incredible selections! Amazing savings!

It can be yours at incredible savings

It goes without saying... great savings!

It's a special day of savings for
senior citizens

It's an all-out Savings Blitz!

It's our biggest savings event of
the season!

It's ridiculous... how much you can save!

It's savings insanity time!

It's the perfect time to stock up and save

Jumbo-size savings!

Just when you thought our prices
couldn't get any lower

Just-in-time savings!

Kiss your savings hellooooo!

Last call for our end of the season savings!

Last minute savings markdowns!

Let us fill your wallet with savings!

Log on and save

Look for our lowest prices ever on...

Look for the yellow dots in store
and save!

Look inside for weekend savings!

Lots of savings... lots of selections

Low prices that make a difference!

Low prices... great choices!

Lowest prices every day, guaranteed!

Magnificent savings!

Make a beeline for the savings!

Make a clean sweep on savings!

Make the switch and save

Marathon of savings!

Massive savings on all...

May we interest you in some
serious savings?

Mega-savings on all your favorites

Money-Saving Deals!

Monstrous savings will floor you

More for your quarter

More ways to save on everyday essentials

Nail down those savings with...

New lower prices every day!

New price reductions that will make
you happy

New services and great prices make a
great combination

New, easier way to save!

No gimmicks! No games! Just savings!

No gimmicks! You pay 1/3 the price!

No sales pitch, only savings!

No waiting for savings

Nobody beats our everyday low prices!

Non-stop savings!

Nothing to sneeze at these
super savings!

Now at prices you can't pass up

Now... save up to 50% every day!

Oh, baby! What savings!

Old-fashioned savings

One million miles of savings!

Only today you can double your savings!

Our best prices of the year!

Our prices speak for themselves!

Out-of-this-world savings!

Plenty to smile about savings

Plug into savings

Posted prices that everybody knows
nobody pays!

Power savings!

Quality products at prices you can afford

Quality, selection and savings...
every day!

Quantities are limited, but savings
are not!

Red-hot savings!

Reduced ticket clearance prices

Round up some real savings on...

Run in for Spectacular Savings!

Satisfy your appetite for savings!

Save $100 instantly!

Save $15 on your first purchase

Save a buck, buck, buck

Save a fistful of cash!

Save a little, save a bundle, savings for
the family!

Save a potful of savings!

Save a wad this weekend

Save an extra 10% on all clearance items!

Save big $$$ now!!!

Save more money, save right now!

Save on everything you need

Save on everything you're looking for!

Save on what you really wanted!

Save the Sale!

Save up to 70%... everything must go!

Save-a-bundle

Saving money has never been easier

Saving you money... makes us happy!

Savings are only important when you
are really getting the savings!

Savings are packed and ready to go!

Savings around the clock!

Savings for every pocketbook!

Savings for her, for him and for
the children

Savings like this come only once a year!

Savings on gadgets you don't need!

Savings on products you use every day!

Savings so big it'll make you smile!

Savings that call for a celebration!

Savings that sizzle

Savings that we pass on to you

Savings that'll knock your stockings off!

Savings to make your life easier!

Savings you can't pass up

Say hello to sensational savings!

Scare up a whole nest of savings!

Sensational savings on your favorite brands

Shovel up the savings

Show me the savings!

Slam... Jam... Savings!

Slamming the door on high prices!

Smart savings for the savvy shopper

Smart savings from A to Z

Smart ways to save

Smile! It's all 50% off!

So, hurry in today and save, save, save

Special savings for seniors!

Special savings just for you!

Spectacular save-a-thon!

Spectacular savings every department!

Spectacular savings on leading brands!

Spend less and save more!

Splurge and save!

Start counting all the money you will save

Steep markdowns

Stock-up savings start here!

Stop here for great savings!

Stop inventing excuses! Come on in and grab the savings!

Sumptuous savings!

Super closeout savings!

Super sale... super savings!

Super saver savings

Super savings blowout!

Super special savings!

Sweetest savings ever

Take advantage of our "hassle-free" savings!

Savings

Take advantage of our lowest prices of the season

Take advantage of these never before savings!

Take an extra 25% off on regular low prices!

Take the savings challenge!

Take-off to savings!

Tap into big savings!

Tax-time savings!

The best prices in town

The best savings ever

The best savings in life are right here

The best savings... ever

The bigger the sale, the nicer the savings!

The difference is in the savings

The early bird gets the savings!

The fun way to save

The king rules when it comes to savings

The lowest prices in America... every day!

The money-saving way to a...

The more you spend... the more you save!

The place for savings!

The price tag is steep, but the savings are 50% off!

The right time to save!

The savings are absolutely incredible!

The savings are all yours

The savings are really piling up

The savings are unbelievable!

The savings make the difference!

The savings never stop!

The savings will make you smile

The search for savings ends right here

The time to save is now!

Savings

There has never been anything like these savings!

There's no limit on how much you can save!

These savings will bowl you over!

They've Got To Be Kiddin' Savings!

Things to do with the money you'll save

Think big savings!

Think of the money you'll save

Thirsty for savings

This is the weekend to save big!

This way for great savings!

Today's lesson... math made easy with big savings

Top pickings, top savings!

Total savings... in every aisle!

Unbelievable savings on everything you need!

Up to $500 cool cash factory rebate

Want your dollars to go further?

Warehouse club prices without membership fees

We cut out the middleman so you can save

We have no problem saving you money

We have what you want at the right price!

We put the money back into your wallet

We save you money, morning till night

We sell more for less!

We won't say we'll save you up to five hundred bucks. We'll prove it!

We'll make you happy with super savings!

We'll save you a ton of dough

We'll show you how your dollar gets more at...

We're cleaning house. You clean up!

We're unloading the biggest savings ever

We're your bull's eye for savings

We've got the prescription for savings

Weekend jam-packed with outrageous savings!

What a difference a savings makes!

When it comes to the best price, the buck stops here!

When it comes to the price you pay... You make the call

Where the savings keep coming!

Where you always save more money... or we'll give you the difference back in cash!

Workin' to bring you the best savings

Wouldn't you like to pay wholesale like the big guys?

Year-end sell-off

You can count on great savings, every day!

You can't afford to miss these incredible savings!

You get more for your bucks!

You have only 10 days to enjoy these fantastic savings!

You won't believe the savings!

You'll appreciate the savings

You'll flip over the savings!

You'll get our savings rockin'

You'll have to clip a lot of coupons to get savings like this!

You'll love our low prices!

You'll save a fistful of dollars

You'll save a pot of gold at...

You'll save a pretty penny

You'll save more than ever before

You're going to love the savings!

You're looking at big savings!

You've got 24 hours of savings!

Your dollars go further during our Dollar Day Savings!

Your favorites are now 30% off

Your to-do list savings!

Zip away with big savings

Service

24-hour service, 7 days a week

A century of service

A no-nonsense approach to great service

A professional staff with efficient service that delivers fast

A service company that cares

A world-class service organization

All it takes is a phone call to get the ball rolling

All the service you want when you want it

Announcing something new in service: Service!

Anyway you look at it, no one serves you better

Anywhere, anytime, everywhere, all the time!

Are you getting the service you are paying for?

Big on service, not on price

Call any time, even on Sunday

Call the experts today at...

Championship-caliber customer service

Chill out with our AC service

Committed to the quality of customer service our customer expect

Customer service with a human touch

Do we measure up to your expectations?

Don't gamble with customer service

Dy-na-mite service!

Earth-shaking and crisis-averting service

Everybody promises. We deliver!

Excellence in delivering customer-driven quality service

Excellent service is our priority

Exceptional service at a sensible price

Extra service, no charge!

For service you can count on!

For us, success is defined by providing quality service

Get to know us before you need us

Give us a call and we'll roll up our sleeves

Good old-fashioned service never goes out of style

Here are twenty-seven thousand two hundred and fifty-one reasons to use our service!

Here's one number you can count on!

How much is free service costing you?

How to avoid being a service statistic

If anyone can fix it, we can!

If business is war, then our service is the ultimate weapon

If not now, when? If not us, who?

If you're not entirely satisfied, we'll take care of it

If you're not happy, we're not happy

It's a headache you shouldn't have to deal with

It's all about service and customers' needs

It's as simple as making one phone call!

It's everything you've heard and much, much more

It's not your problem... it's ours!

It's one of the ways we deliver great service

It's our service that will bring you back

It's our spirit of service

It's your support and our service that makes us shine

Just let us know what you need when you need it

Let us be of service to you!

Let us dazzle you with our service

Loyal, dependable, trustworthy

Make one call and relax

Make us your first call... not your last resort

Making extraordinary service ordinary

No matter how small your job... call us!

No one offers a better way to provide great customer service

Nobody does it faster, better, cheaper

Now let us service you!

One call gets the things you want done... done!

Our business is to provide service

Our people make the difference

Our service is made up of three words... reliability, reliability, reliability!

Our service is not only great, it's fantastic

Our service is priceless

Our service is so good; you don't even notice it

Our service is your solution

Our service makes your life a lot easier

Our service now comes in person

Our service says a lot about ourselves

People who know you, people you can rely on, today and tomorrow

Professional personalized service

Professional service results at a great value

Providing the highest quality of service in the industry

Put our superior service to the test

Quality people, excellent service

Quick service with a smile!

Ready to serve you!

Service faster than you ever thought possible

Service is as important as the product

Service is everybody's business. Service is our only business!

Service is the first word in our dictionary

Service is the key to our success

Service isn't service if it's only a promise

Service like ours is nothing to sneeze at

Service that meets your specific needs

Service that's above and beyond

Service with a smile now has a new meaning

Service with pride and integrity

Service you can trust

Service you expect, demand and deserve

Service you've come to expect

Service, the way it used to be

Service... anytime, day or night

Someone you can count on!

That is our commitment! That is our promise!

The best way to judge a company is by its service

The cheapest prices and fastest service

The company that goes the extra mile to solve its customers' problems

The difference in our service is dedication

The emphasis is on unparalleled customer service

The last time you had this kind of service you were probably eating at a fine restaurant

The problem is gone or we do it over

The proof is in the service

The service business is our business

The service is incredible... absolutely priceless

The service that makes a difference

This is the kind of service you need

Today's new technology, yesterday's old fashioned service

Under the influence of great service

Under-promise, over-deliver

Unparalleled personal service

Urgency knows no bounds

We always deliver on our promise

We are in business to deliver the best service

We are the ones who get it right

We do not walk away from our commitments

We exceed your expectations

We get it right the first time

We give a whole new meaning to the word service

We give service, not a sales pitch

We give the service you demand

We go the extra mile to make sure you're satisfied

We hate to brag about our service

We never promise what we can't deliver

We never rest on the 7th day

We not only meet, but exceed your expectations

We pride ourselves on friendly customer service

We provide a good service at a good cost

We serve you better

We service one thing no one else does. Everything!

We stay awake so you can sleep

We take great pride in our level of professional service

We take service calls seriously, so you can relax

We treat you with exceptional service

We want using our service to be an enjoyable experience

We won't be satisfied until you are satisfied

We'll be there to serve you!

We'll knock ourselves out for you

We'll put ourselves in your shoes

We're a small company, but you'd never know it by the service you get

We're as reliable as a community landmark

We're available morning, noon and night

We're going to spoil you with our service

We're here to service

We're not kidding... we're service

We're ready to jump through hoops for you

We're serious about our service

We're the service pros

We're the someone you can count on

We're there when you need us most

We've never lost our sense of service

When it comes to service. When it comes to satisfaction. Come here!

When we say we're going to be there, we're there

When we service, we mean service

When you say jump, we fly

When you want service, faster than ever before, who do you call?

Wherever you need us, whenever you need us

Will get the job done day or night

Worry-free service

Wow! Now that is service!

Yes, we do make house calls

You demand... we deliver

You get it all... savings plus service

You need it tomorrow, we have it today!

You probably don't even remember our kind of service

You've got a million things to think about. One of them is not service

You've got our beeper number

Your business is your business. Service, however, is ours

Your emergency is our priority

Shopping

7 reasons to shop smart

A new way to shop and save!

A once-in-a-lifetime shopping binge!

A sale for compulsive shoppers!

A shoplifter's sale event!

A shopper's dream come true

A shopping environment you'll really like

A shopping spectacle!

A Thrifty Shopper Sale Event!

A truly unique shopping experience

Add this to your shopping list

Added value to the shopping experience

Are you a shopaholic?

Are you a smart shopper?

Are you getting your money's worth when you go shopping?

At prices the average shopper can afford!

Attention all shopaholics

Attention shoppers! No waiting at checkout counter seven!

Be a superachiever shopper with superachiever savings!

Be a wise shopper

Be smart... shop at...

Born to shop

Come shop with us!

Comparison-shopping is welcome

Don't forget to put it on your shopping list

Enjoy great shopping

Finish your holiday shopping here!

For a delightful shopping experience

For a late-night shopping fix

For compulsive shoppers only!

For men who hate to shop

For shoppers addicted to discounts

Get what you need while the getting's good

Go forth and spend

Good guys shop at...

Good news for procrastinating shoppers

Got the urge to splurge?

Handy shopper's guide

Happy shopping!

Hurry up, home shoppers! You only have five minutes to order!

I'll do just about anything to avoid shopping

I'll get it for you, wholesale!

I'm off to the mall to do my part for the economy

I'm your designated shopper!

If he had to pay for his stuff, he'd shop here too

If you should find a lower advertised price, we'll match it

If you're going to shop, shop at the best!

Is shopping entertainment?

It makes shopping an ultimate excursion

It pays to shop strategically

It's a lovely day to shop

It's always time to shop

It's shoppertainment!

It's the reason to shop

It's wise to be a cautious consumer

It's yours, if you want to pay the price

Kick off your shoes and shop

Last minute shopping

Learn the value of buying on sale

Let us make your shopping easy
and enjoyable

Let's go shopping today!

Like we've said for 50 years, shop for it
anywhere, you'll buy it at...

Look but don't touch!

Marry rich... and go shopping the rest of
your life

More than ever it's easy to shop
the Internet

Nobody makes shopping easier... nobody!

On a never-ending shopping spree!

On your mark! Get set! Shop!

Other great ways to shop

Our goal is to make your shopping
experience as satisfying as possible

Perfect for early holiday shopping

Prepare to shop till you drop

Priced to please you

Read this before you shop

Say yes to shopping!

Shop around the clock

Shop comfortably indoors

Shop early and get more of what you want

Shop early and shop often

Shop online and save even more!

Shop us first!

Shop! Compare! Choose!

Shopper satisfaction

Shopper stoppers savers!

Shoppers be aware of pickpockets

Shopping in cyberspace is a way of life

Shopping on your mind?

Shopping the way it should be... simple!

Shopping with us is quick and easy

So go ahead. Get carried away

So you think you're a savvy shopper?

Squeezing every last penny out of your
shopping dollar

Stretch your shopping dollars at...

Take in great shopping at...

Take your money shopping

Thank you for shopping with us!

The lazy man's shopping guide

The one stop for shoppers

The perfect place to find just what you
are looking for

The shopping experience every woman
craves for

There's no place like the mall

We make shopping a breeze!

We make your shopping easy
and enjoyable

We never charge you for roaming

We want to make your shopping
experience the very best

What are your shopping habits?

What you want! What you need!

When in doubt, go shopping

When price matters... shop here!

Where men love to shop

Where shopping is really fun

Why shop anywhere else?

Win a $500 shopping spree!

Win a 10-minute shopping spree!

With us, you'll know exactly what your
cost is

World-class shopping... here!

You don't have to dress up to
go e-shopping

You have boldly gone where no shopper
has gone before

You look! You purchase! You pay!

You won't go home empty-handed

You'd better get shopping!

You'll like our way of shopping

You're always welcome to come
and browse

You're in for a shopping expedition!

Signs

Always close gently, no matter what

Always open! No waiting!

Authorized personnel only

Avoid dropping air conditioner out of window

Back in 10 minutes

Be a watt watcher: Turn off lights when not in use

Break It... If It Ain't Broke

Caution: Highway construction next 100 years

Caution: Hot surface. Do not touch!

Caution: Invisible wall ahead

Caution: This vehicle makes wide turns

Check your ego here!

Closed by order of the health inspector

Closed due to inclement weather

Counselor in training

Crime Scene – Do Not Enter

Danger: Watch for falling rocks

Designated Smoking Area

Do not enter due to hazardous conditions

Do Not Feed the Moat Monsters

Do Not Stop On Tracks

Do not turn upside down

Don't buy here, non-union

Don't even think of parking here

Employees must wash hands before going back to work

Flamethrowers for rent

For emergency use only

For the general public only

For those who do not work here, please do not enter at all

Fragile: Handle with care

Fresh paint, but it's also wet paint

Give 'em a brake

Handicapped Parking Only

Handle with care

Hard hats only beyond this point

If negligent driving is observed, please call:

If you can read this, you're too close

If you value your privacy, keep out

In case of emergency, break glass

It is unlawful and dangerous to dispense gasoline into unapproved containers

Keep for reference, not revenge

Knock hard! Doorbell out of order

Lazy Help Wanted

Look for this sign in store

Lost and Found

Need a penny? Take one!

Never mind the dog. Beware of the owner

No admittance without valid ID

No cash on board

No chewing in the chat room

No dogs allowed

No loitering prohibited

No parking – parade today

No person may enter the pool area alone or swim alone

No personal checks accepted

No shoes! No shirt! No sympathy!

No solicitors or peddlers

No tie or jacket required

No turns either way

No wrestling in the restroom

Nobody parks here

Not open to the public

Now under construction

Office space available

Official use only

Open to the public

Out to lunch

Passengers only beyond this point

Pick up order here

Please don't talk to the operator, they are already confused

Post no bills

Precious cargo on board

Private property, keep out

Proceed at your own risk

Proper attire required

Put your sales message here

Reading classes begin here today for those who can't read

Reserved for the elite

Restroom only for customers who spend more than $10

School's open, drive carefully

Sensitivity training here

Serious inquires only

Shoplifters will be prosecuted

Short guys can stand tall here

Sign up for tomorrow, today!

Slippery when wet

Sorry: We're closed

Speed zone ahead

Spitting on Walls and Tables is Prohibited

Standing or loitering is not permitted

Standing room only

State prison: Do not pick up hitchhikers

STOP: No visitors beyond this point

Take a number, please

Temporarily out of service

Thank you for not smoking

The law of gravity is strictly enforced

This bus stops at all railroad crossings

This door to remain locked at all times

This space could be yours

This space for rent... cheap

Toilet out of order

Try Me

Unauthorized vehicles will be towed away at owner's expense

Under penalty of law, this tag not to be removed except by the consumer

Unemployment Dept.: new claims only

Unlawful to remove alcoholic drinks from premises

Use caution when opening

Used car salesmen need not apply

Walk this way

Want to save a lot of green? Look for the red sign

Warning! Do not walk in front of bus

Warning! Going wrong way

Warning: It is forbidden for any person to go beyond this point

Warning: No Loaded Guns

Watch out for falling expectations

Water on road when raining

We accept these size packages only

We apologize for any inconvenience this may cause

We are unable to make change for bills larger than one dollar

We break for coffee

We hire safe drivers

We report suspicious activities

We're raising children, not grass

Yield to pedestrian in crosswalk

You are here "X"

You pay for what you break

275

A bad day of skiing still beats a great day at the office

A skier's paradise

A snowboard made for grown-ups

After all, this sale is all downhill!

After every thrilling run...

All ski trips now on sale! And all the paraphernalia!

Anyone who is a true skier only has to put a board on the snow and enjoy it

Back on the slopes

Be aware... ski with care!

Before you hit the mountains, hit our ski sale!

Boards and boots for guys with big feet!

Boots off, party's on

Buy one ski, get the second one free!

Cross-country ski sale!

Cushy slopes and posh creature comforts

Don't blow off pre-season sales!

Don't forget your ski gloves

Don't leave for the slopes without your helmet

Equipment rentals are free with lift tickets!

Family fun on the slopes

Feeling that itch to ski?

For a real snowboarding experience without buying a board!

For boots, bindings, apparel and all the rest!

For less than the price of a lift ticket!

For the traditional ski enthusiast

For those who take their skiing too seriously

Free day of skiing!

Free skiing lessons!

From the ski slopes to the streets

Gearing up to go snowboarding

Get a grip on your ski poles

Get an early start on the ski season

Get in gear before you go

Get to a ski school

Getting in shape for the slopes

Good news for the beginner

Great deals for advanced skiers or just beginners!

Great ski deals for families!

Great skiing! Great savings on all...

Great times! Great fun! Great skiing!

Guaranteed skiing means one thing. You'll love it!

Head for the great white outdoors

Heads up on the slopes

Hey skiers!!! Have we got the snow for you!!!

Hit the mountain with...

Hit the slopes with great savings!

Home of great ski value!

How to be a ski bum

How to look good on the slopes!

I love skiing; it's my favorite sport!

If you've never skied before, take some lessons!

It's a breeze for young and old

It's a Rocky Mountain fantasy

It's a skier's paradise

It's all downhill from here

It's powder paradise

It's ski time

It's the pinnacle of snowboarding

It's time to start thinking to dust off your skis

Join a ski club!

Last one down buys the beers!

Learn to ski this winter

Let's go in the snow

Let's go skiing

Lift ticket not required

Looking for a ski bargain?

Looking to buy, sell or trade your old ski equipment?

Make our store your lift ticket to top values!

Making lifelong skiers out of kids

Max out your ski-time savings!

Maybe you should learn snowboarding?

Mountains of fun for everyone!

Night skiing under the stars

On the beginners' slope

On the cutting edges of your skis

On the go on the snow!

Once you get there, it's all downhill from there

People ski here because they can bring their kids and not break their wallets

Ready for the chair lift or the wheelchair?

Sick of crowds and lines?

Ski all day... play all night!

Ski deals for ski bums!

Ski early, ski often, and you'll be a skier for life

Ski expo sale!

Ski for less here!

Ski free!

Ski slopes that would terrify most people

Ski the excitement

Ski vacation package to...

Ski your hearts out

Skiers say... "bring on the snow!"

Skiing is an invigorating, active vacation

Skiing is for winter-sports enthusiasts

Skiing the Rockies with your family

Snow makers, snow sale!

Snowboarding is what we do!

Snowboards are fun!

Taking a ski trip out west?

Taking skiing to new heights

Talk about great conditions for winter savings!

The best little ski shop in Utah

The best ski resort in America

The better the fit, the better you ski

The boots have it all

The growing activity is snowshoeing

The right place to ski, eat and play

The ski resort of your dreams

The ultimate ski sale!

They come. They ski. They conquer.

Think snow... think skiing

Thinking of a ski vacation?

To ski or not to ski? That's not even a question

Warning: Do Not Ski Into Tree

We have a lift ticket for you!

What to do after an exhausting day of skiing!!!

Whatever your ability, we have the board to take to your performance level

When was the last time you went skiing?

When you live to ski

Where people are born on skis

Where the skiing's powder-perfect

Why not just ski for fun?

Winter belongs to skiers

You'll be skiing in a blizzard of savings!

Your lift ticket to high living

Ain't it funky?

Ain't that a trip?

Are you into glamming it up?

Are you jerking me around?

As the kids say, it rocks

Aw quit your bellyaching

Aw, chin up, dude

Blow a gasket

Boogie on down

Buzz off

Can you dig it?

Catch my drift?

Chill out

Chomping at the bit

Clam up

Cool as a cucumber

Cool it

Cool your jets

Cruisin' for a bruisin'

Cup of Joe

Cut me some slack

Cut the baloney

Dawg, that's smooth

Deep six

Dig this

Doesn't mean squat

Don't dump on us

Don't flip your lid

Dropped a dime on him

Eat crow

Enough already

Far out, man

Feed your face

Freaked out

Friggin' cool

From the get-go

Get outta my face

Get ready to rock

Get real

Getting some face time

Gimme five

Give me some skin, my friend

Go ballistic

Go bananas

Groovy, baby

Ham it up

Hang loose

Hang ten

Hardy-har-har

He's a loose screw

He's a sleazeball

He's brain dead

He's yanking your chain

Heavy, man. Heavy

Hey, stuff happens

Hold the phone

Howzit goin?

I kid you not

I'm like, "Who cares?"

I'm outta here

I'm pumped big time

If you don't got it, then get it

In your face

It drives me bananas

It's a beaut

It's a doozy

It's a great gizmo

It's a hoot and a holler

It's a humdinger

It's a lot of moolah

It's a total blast

It's all peachy-keen

It's been a slice

It's been a trip

It's just ducky

It's like, who cares?

It's so uncool, it's cool

Keep your shirt on

Know what I mean?

Let's cut through all the bull

Let's go to my crib and chill for a while

Make tracks

No way, Jose!

Not so fast

Now, that's a howl

Nutty as a fruitcake

Oh, get real

Oh, spare me

OK! Let 'er rip

Okey dokey

On the cheap

On the flip side

On the fritz again

On the front burner

Out of the groove

Packed with pizzazz

Put the kibosh on it

Rollin' with the homies

Same ol' same ol'

Say what?

'Scuse me?

Show me some heat, baby

Snap out of it

So buzz off

So's your old man

Stick it in your ear

Strut your stuff

The big squeeze

The jig is up

The nitty-gritty of it

This place is nowhere

Totally wired

Up the wazoo

Wait a sec

We got our derrieres kicked

Whaddya want? We got it!

Whasssup!!!

What a marshmallow

What a rip-off

What a schmuck

What's the buzz

What's the diff?

What's your beef?

Whatever floats your boat

Whatever pops your cork

Whatever turns you on

Who'd have thunk it?

Who's really da man here?

Who's your daddy?

Works for me

Ya know... well, ya know

Yadda, yadda, yadda

Yeah, whatever, man

You big wuss

You can hack it

You can hang with me

You da ma-a-a-n!

You know what I mean, man?

You're dead on

You're pulling my leg

279

Sleep

A Cozy Night's Sleep Sales Event!

A good mattress is a good cure for insomnia

A good night's sleep is important to good health

A good night's sleep is what we're selling

A good sleep on a good mattress is a good morning

A mattress pad will help you protect your investment

A summer snooze of a sale!

Advice for selecting the best mattress

All you need for a good night's sleep is...

An expensive mattress will last you a long time

And to All a Good Night Sales Event!

Are you getting enough sleep?

Are you getting up on the right side of the bed?

Are you sleeping well at night?

Bedding bargains to cure insomnia!

Better yet, don't sleep on it... buy it today!

Breakthrough sleep technology

Bright-eyed and bushy-tailed values!

Catch up on your beauty sleep with a...

Common causes of sleeplessness

Do you wake up during the night and can't fall back to sleep?

Do you wake up tired, achy and sore?

Don't ask us what it's like to sleep on a...

Don't deprive yourself of sleep... buy a...

Don't neglect your sleep! Buy the right mattress!

Down pillows, any size, one low price!

Every mattress comes with a good night's sleep

Fantastic closeout savings on brand-name mattresses!

For a great night's sleep, try...

Free 30-day comfort guarantee!

Free pickup of your old bedding!

Free set-up and removal!

Free! Next-day delivery guaranteed or your mattress purchase is free!

Get a good night's savings of 50%

Get a good night's sleep every night with...

Get an expensive pillow for a good night's sleep

Getting a good night's sleep is very important

Getting enough shut-eye?

Give your body the deep and restful sleep it deserves

Here's a sale you don't need to sleep on!

Hit the hay, hit the sack, hit the greatest bedding sale ever!

How to sleep safely!

I want to wake up in a bed that never sleeps

Ideal for a pillow fight!

Is looking for a new mattress tiring you out?

It lulls you to sleep

It may not help you sleep, but at least it will...

It's a bedding savings bonanza!

It's a Sleepover Party Sales Event!

It's like sleeping on air

It's like sleeping under the stars

It's our annual Good Night's Sleep Sales Event!

It's Something to Sleep On Deal!

It's time to wake up to monstrous savings during...

Live boldly. Sleep blissfully!

Manufacturer-discounted mattress sets and closeouts on sale today!

Maybe a new mattress would help you sleep?

Never Disturb a Sleeping Man Sales Event!

Now you won't be experiencing sleepless nights

Rise and Shine Bedding Sales Event of the Season!

Savings for die-hard night owls!

Savings that give you a few minutes of extra sleep!

Savings that will put to sleep walking zombies!

Say goodbye to insomnia!

Should your pillow have been laid to rest years ago?

Sleep good tonight on a...

Sleep Like a Baby Sales Event!

Sleep On It Sales Event!

Sleeper sofa savings!

Sleepless nights, tired days... gone forever!

Sleepwalkers Special Savings!

Snuggle up for a good night's sleep on a...

So comfortable, you'll never count sheep again

Spring bedding sale!

Spring Into Savings Mattress Sales Event!

Stop counting sheep. Get a new mattress!

Surround yourself with a comfortable pillow

That was the best night's sleep I've ever had

The Best Price Mattress Sale!

The first words out of your mouth will be "Good morning!"

The king-size mattress for you!

The mattress that makes you rejuvenated, restored and revitalized

The mattress that will conform to the shape of your body and support it

The National Sleep Foundation never sleeps

The quality of sleep is in the quality of the mattress

The savings will wipe the sleep out of your eyes!

The ultimate bedding sale!

Times are hard, but that doesn't mean your bed has to be

Wake up and take a look at these fantastic deals!

Wake Up Fresh As A Daisy Sales Event!

Wake up to the value of sleep!

Walking the floors all night?

We guarantee you'll wake up with a smile!

We sell sleep!

We'll give you great reasons to sleep on a...

We'll have you jumping out of bed with great deals!

We've got the greatest sleep system in the world

You can be sleeping on a new bed... tonight!

You deserve the very best night's sleep

You must sleep on it to believe it

You will sleep well at night. You made the right decision.

You won't be counting sheep! You'll be counting the savings!

You'll always wake up with a smile when you sleep on a...

You'll get more than a good night's sleep

You'll sleep tight tonight, guaranteed!

281

A gorgeous smile is a girl's best accessory

A huge smile lights up the savings!

A smile is the best gift of all

A warm smile is always in style at...

An incredible sale can really make you smile!

At a price that will make you smile!

Bargains that will make you smile!

Betcha we can make you smile

Big smiles for our customers

Can't Stop Smiling Sales Event!

Cash in on your smile

Celebrating 50 years of smiles!

Deals that'll put a smile on anyone's face

Double smiles... today only!

Fortune smiles on you with these deals!

Get the official smiles contest T-shirt

Give a holiday basket of smiles!

Guaranteed deals to make you smile!

Guaranteed Smile-Maker Sales Event!

How could you not smile with these low, low prices?

It always makes you smile with savings like this!

It's just one more reason to smile

It's the place with saving smiles

Just put a big smile on every customer

Lots of smiles! Lots of bargains!

Miles and miles of smiles

More reasons to smile

Our job is to keep the smile on the customer's face

Savings from ear to ear!

Savings that will definitely put a smile on your face!

Savings... sure to make you smile!

Service with a smile!

Show us your smile... we'll show you the savings!

Smile when you say "It's on sale!"

Smile-maker deals!

Super deals guaranteed to put a smile on your savings!

Super values that'll make you smile!

Thank you for making our salespeople smile

That smile on your face tells everyone you got a deal!

The benefits of greeting customers with a smile

The Million-Dollar Smile Savings Event!

This is the place with smiles!

Values that'll put a smile on any face!

We definitely will put a smile on your face with these savings!

We give you a lot more to smile about

We love your smile... you'll love our prices!

We make our customers smile

We'll have you smiling from ear to ear with these deals!

We'll make you smile with...

We'll put a smile on your savings!

We're looking for America's best smile

Where customers are met with smiles

Where smiles and good spirits never fade

Where the smiles are real and the deal's sincere!

Who wouldn't smile at these savings?

You earned it... the smile!

You have the smiles we need

250% delicious!

A delicious snack that keeps people smiling

A delightfully chocolate experience

A great super snack to feed the whole family

A little pick-me-up treat

A melt-in-your-mouth treat

A smile in every bite

A snack that is as healthful as it is delectable

A snack you simply must try

A special treat for the sweet

A super-sweet, super-treat

A treat for kids of all ages

A treat with just a little guilt

A zesty snack sensation

Absolutely yummy

America's favorite snack

An all-time treat

Bet you can't eat just one

Buttery smooth

Candy the whole gang will love

Candy time is fun time

Contents will taste delicious

Delectable edibles

Delicious and good for you!

Delicious! Scrumptious! Delicious! Satisfying!

Delightfully delicious! Downright delicious!

Doggone good

Dollar Day savings on great-tasting treats!

Everybody loves sweets, especially ours

Everyday indulgences

Everyone's favorite snack

Explore the tangy delights of...

Fantastic prices on candy favorites!

For a real taste-tempting treat

For those who are on a mission to munch

For your next snack attack

Give your stomach a treat

Good to the last bite for those on the run!

Goody goody goody snacks

Grab-and-go snacks

Great-tasting gourmet candies

Have a snacking good time

Healthful snack facts

Here's a great snacktacular treat for everyone

I'll be the designated chocoholic driver

Incredible savings to satisfy your sweet tooth

Indulge your sweet tooth

Irresistible treats! Irresistible urge! Irresistibly good!

It'll hit your sweet spot

It's a hysterically unexpected treat

It's a whole candy store in a box

It's delicious as you can get

It's just pure indulgence

It's munchin' crunchin' snackin' time!

It's the perfect snack for...

Kids just eat them up

Let the munching begin

Let us satisfy your sweet tooth

Lip-smacking treats

Lunch box treats

Luscious! Irresistible! Amazing!

Snacks / Sweets

Make snack time easier and fun

Melt-in-your-mouth sweets

Mmm... Yummmy!

Mouth-watering treats

Munch! Crackle! Crunch!

Munching at its best

Nothing is more deliciously decadent than...

Oh, that's sweet! Oh, those sweets! Oh, how sweet!

One crunchy snack you can't resist

One-bite delights

Ready to bring a chocolaty smile to your face

Relax with a delicious snack

Satisfy the sweet cravings with...

Satisfy your sweet tooth with these treats

Savings that are mmmmmmm good

Savor the delicious delights of...

Scrumptious sweets!

Smooth, creamy, rich and decadent

Snacks that are decidedly different

Snacks you'll love to eat

Snacktacular savings!

Stuff yourself with our candy

Sugar-free... and fabulous

Sure to satisfy your sweet tooth!

Sweet deals on candy and treats!

Sweet favorites for the whole family

Sweet temptations

Sweet treats and good things to eat

Sweet! Yummy! Delicious!

Sweets for the most demanding sweet tooth

Tastier because they're tastier

Tasty snacks to satisfy your hunger

The biggest treat on earth

The delicious, sweet crunch of...

The dreamiest sweets from heaven

The most incredible and delicious treats

The most incredible candy you will ever eat

The perfect snack for any kid

The sweetest snack in the world

The treat you're looking for

They'll gobble them up

They're flavorful from the first bite to the last bite

They're scrumptious!

Totally irresistible! Simply delicious! Better than ever!

Treat yourself and treat your family

Treat yourself to our special values!

Treats only dentists love

Treats to overindulge your sweet tooth

Turns your snacks into instant energy

Twice the snacks, twice the fun

Unbelievably sweet!

We satisfy your craving for...

What a pick-me-up

When you crave that sugar fix...

When you crave the very best

When you just feel the urge to snack

Wholesome snacks

Wildly delicious!

You are in for a real treat

You'll fall in love with our candy treats!

You'll get more sweet taste because they're sweetened with love

You'll go nuts over our healthy snacks

You'll love the homemade taste in every bite

You'll really dig 'em! You'll simply love 'em!

You've never tasted anything so deliciously...

Soccer

A kick-start to a great soccer season

A playmaker in every game

A soccer sale for the ages!

As the soccer season kicks off...

Bitten by the soccer bug?

Checking out women's soccer

Finally, a soccer game worth watching

For all those hard-core soccer fans out there

For people who love soccer

Free soccer clinic for kids

Get a free soccer ball with...

Get the Ball in the Net Sale Event!

Get your kicks over the kick

Give it your best shot

Hit the field running

I believe in the sport of soccer

If you call sell anything... why not soccer?

It's crunch time for soccer!

It's fun to be surrounded by soccer

It's soccer madness

It's soccer season!!!

Just for kicks

Just kick it into awesome savings

Kick off the soccer season with us!

Kick with power

Kicking's the name of the game

Live and breathe soccer

Loyal soccer people

Make soccer a major priority

Much more than soccer

Nobody knows why they like soccer. It just happens

Now that's what we call soccer mania!

Now! Catch soccer fever!!!

Once the ball rolls, anything can happen

Our sport is worldwide

Polishing your soccer skills... sign up here!

Scoring goals is what soccer is all about

Set the ball on fire!

Smart soccer people

So much for taking soccer seriously

Soccer is a fine sport for kids

Soccer is a kick

Soccer is a safer, less expensive sport

Soccer is just not America's game... yet!

Soccer is my game

Soccer is the fastest-growing sport in America

Soccer Shocker Savings Event!

Soccer springing into action

Soccer... you'll get a kick out of the savings!

Soccermania monstrous savings!

Swept away by soccer

Take it from a soccer dad

That's what's so great about soccer

The start of the soccer season... are you ready?

The ultimate soccer challenge

This is the ultimate in soccer

We take our soccer seriously

Whack the ball into the net of values!

Where soccer kicks

World Cup Fever Bargain Days!

You'll get a kick out of these deals

Sounds

Aagggh	Fwink	Pssssst	Whoa
Ah-chooo	Fwong	Rarrooom	Whonk
Ah-oooh	Fwooosh	Riiippp!!!	Whooooooo
Arrooooooo	Gadzooks	Schlurp	Whooopeee
Arrrghhh	Gasp	Screeech	Whooops
Ba-bum, ba-bum	Geez	Shmack	Whoooosh
Biff! Pow! Crash!	Glug	Shooonk	Whoop-dee-doo
Blammmo	Glunk	Shuddap	Whoopee!!!
Blatt	Gonk	Skazeech	Whoowee
Blecccch	Gotcha	Skooosh	Whump
Blppb	Gronk	Skritch	Wooooooosh
Boink	Hi-yaaaaa	Slurrrp	Woweee
Bonk!!!	Ho Heee	Smak	Wump!
Brappp	Honk!	Smoooooooooch	Ya hooo
Burritt	Hrrrumph	Sooo-eey	Yaaaaahh
Buuurraap	Jeeeeeeez	Splappp	Yap
Buzzzzzzz	Kaaa-boom	Splat	Yawww
Bwik	Ka-boosh	Sploit	Yeahhhhhhh
Charboom	Ka-ching	Splooosh	Yeccch
Chooo	Ka-jillion	Sploot	Yee haw
Clickity-clack	Karash	Splut	Yeeeooow
Clonk	Ker-sploosh	Spritz	Yeeesss
Clumpf	Klang Krash	Sssshhhhhhh	Yee-ikes
Doink	Klik	Swat	Yeow
Doof	Klunk	Swish!	Yipes
Eeeeeeeee	Krash	Swoosh	Yoo-hoo
Eeep	Ooh, eee!!!	Ta-Daaah	Yuck
Ee-haw	Oooch	Thonk!!!	Yummmy
Eeooow	Ooops	Thump	Yup
Flifflaff	Oowaww!	Tweeeee	Zazz
Flump	Plop	Ugggh	Zing
Flussshh	Plunk	Vrooom	Zooom
Foom	Poing!	Whammo!	Zzzappp

Spring

#1 choice for spring

A downpour of values!

A fresh new look for spring

A hint of spring. Spring preview!

A sneak peek at spring sale!

A Spring Break extravaganza!

A spring energy boost of savings!

A spring renaissance celebration

A spring sale so hot, you'll think it's summer!

A springtime shower of savings!

Add a festive touch of spring to...

After this winter, you deserve to make the most of our Spring of Value Sale!

Ah, spring! The time of year when everything comes alive

Ahhh, the smell of a spring sale!

All merchandise is reduced for our Giant Storewide Spring Sale!

Amazing spring savings!

An absolute must for spring

Anytime, we're ready for spring

April showers bring you big savings at...

April showers save you dollars!

Are you ready for spring?

Arrival of spring marks the start of home repairs

As spring-cleaning time nears...

Bargains are sprouting up all over!

Be a part of our spring tradition

Be prepared for April showers

Be ready for spring

Beat the Spring Rush Sale Event!

Blast into spring with...

Blooming with buys!

Blossoming deals!

Breaking new ground... on lawn and garden prices!

Budding values!

Cabin fever! Spring fever! Shopping bug!

Cash in on your planting purchasing power

Catch the fever!

Celebrate the beginning of spring with us

Clean up on spring sale!

Did you forget to turn your clock forward?

Don't let April showers ruin your spring

Don't miss your last chance till next spring

Drive into spring and save!

Early bird sale!

Early spring values!

Emerging from Hibernation Wake Up Sale Event!

Every day is spring at...

Everybody Deserves A Spring Break Sale Event!

Everyday spring values for outside and inside!

Everything feels fresh and new again

Everything's coming up bargains!

Experience the feeling of spring at...

Fall in love with our spring fling!

Fantastic spring savings!

Fast-forward into spring

First sign of spring sale!

Fresh new ideas for spring

Fresh with the green of spring

Freshen up your home for spring

Full speed into spring savings at...

Gear up for spring

Get a great selection! Get great savings! Get ready for spring!

Get a head start on spring with...

Get a jump on spring fever

Get a lush, green lawn for very little green

Get a running start on springtime sales!

Get a spring break on prices!

Get Everything in Shipshape for Spring Sale!

Get hoppin' into spring

Get ready for spring with a shower of values!

Get ready for spring! Get a great selection! Get great savings!

Get set for summer with a spring shopping spree!

Get swept away this spring at...

Getting the lawn in order

Great blooming buys!

Grow-a-garden sale!

Happy spring to all our customers

Have a great spring shopping spree, on us!

Have you anticipated the arrival of spring?

Hooray for spring! Hooray for savings! Hooray for the sale!

How does your garden grow?

How to face your spring-cleaning

Invite spring to your home

It might as well be a spring sale!

It promises to be a dazzling spring season

It will always be springtime when you shop at...

It's a thunderstorm of incredible savings!

It's about spring! It's about savings! It's about time!

It's April Fools Day... Remember that when you shop our competitors' ads

It's everything you need for spring

It's finally here... Spring Cleanup Sale!

It's green thumbs up for savings!

It's high time for spring spruce-up savings!

It's not too late to take a family spring break

It's perfect for anyone who's just coming out of hibernation

It's raining savings!

It's the spring fever sales event challenge!

It's the ultimate in spring beauty

It's Think Spring Week Sale!

It's think spring... sale!

It's time to roll out the lawn mower

It's time to watch the grass grow

Jumping the gun on spring

Just in time for spring gift giving

Kick off spring with our super sale!

Let the spring clean-up sales begin!

Let us help you welcome spring

Let's all scream for spring savings at...

Like spring temperatures, sales are on the rise!

Making spring happen... for you!

Must-haves for spring

No foolin'... spring really is here

No payment 'til spring

Nothing to sneeze at these magnificent savings!

Now's the time to get the jump on spring savings!

Oh, the joys of a spring sale!

One-day spring coat blowout!

Our best and brightest collection for spring

Our newly-arrived spring merchandise

Our spring sale can chase away the winter blues!

Our spring sale is in full bloom!

Outdoor living sale!

Overstacked, overstocked... Spring sale!

Planning a spring move?

Plant your dream garden with our Spring Fever Sale!

Plantastic plant sale!

Pre-spring inventory blowout!

Pre-spring inventory wacky, wild, wow sale!

Prices are melting during our Spring Thaw Sale!

Revvvvvvv up for our spring sale!

Rise and shine, it's clean-up time!

Sail into spring's huge savings on...

Sales catching, springtime specials!

Savings are sprouting up at...

Savings in bloom!

Savings with the green of spring!

Sensational spring savings... for every spring day!

Shower of savings!

Singing in the Rain Sale Event!

So long winter, hello spring savings!

Soak up the savings!

Spring ahead with savings!

Spring awaits you at...

Spring blossoms at...

Spring break specials!

Spring Celebration Days!

Spring Cleaning Inventory Sale!

Spring cleanup with fresh savings!

Spring clearance starts tomorrow!

Spring Decorator Sale!

Spring Festival of Values!

Spring fever clearance!

Spring Fever Daze Sale!

Spring Fever Sales Event!

Spring fever? Value days are the cure!

Spring fever... Cash in!

Spring

Spring Fix-Up Sale!

Spring Fling Sales Event!

Spring Freeever Clearance!

Spring has really sprung... get ready for the big sale!

Spring ideas your garden will love

Spring in and save!

Spring into blooming savings!

Spring into low prices!

Spring into our Early Summer Sale!

Spring into Spectacular Savings!

Spring is a wonderful time to renew the look of your home

Spring is the perfect time of the year to...

Spring paint sale!

Spring Parade of Savings!

Spring price break going on now!

Spring price thaw!

Spring project savings!

Spring rebate spectacular!

Spring remodeling clearance!

Spring repair specials!

Spring sale... Hop to it!

Spring sales are bustin' out all over!

Spring sales splash!

Spring Saving Extravagance!

Spring saving time's checkbook!

Spring savings blowout!

Spring savings specials!

Spring savings time!

Spring sell off!

Spring sell-a-break!

Spring Sell-a-thon!

Spring service savings from...

Spring showcase spectacular!

Spring

Spring showers bring plenty of savings!

Spring specials are under your umbrella!

Spring spruce-up specials!

Spring starts here!

Spring Super Savings Event!

Spring tent sale!

Spring Training Annual Sale Event!

Spring values from...

Spring with us. You deserve the best!

Spring zing sale!

Spring's A-Poppin' Up All Over Sale!

Spring's best offerings at...

Spring's Finally Here Sale!

Spring's grand entrance gets a warm welcome during our...

Spring's on sale at...

Springtacular Sale!

Springtime savings!

Springtime specials!

Springtime values!

Springtime-to-Save-Time Sale!

Spruce-Up Sale!

Step into spring with prices to turn you head over heels!

Stop and smell a springtime sale!

Storewide spring sales!

Super Spring Sale!

Swing in for spring savings!

Take big savings at our spring sale!

The best of spring buys!

The First 24 Hours of Spring Sale!

The freshest springtime savings!

The Great Spring Sale!

The right selection, the right sale prices, the right new choices for spring!

The savings are springing up!

The spring season begins with...

The total spring sale for him and her!

The ultimate cure for spring fever... Great values! Great savings!

There's No Fool Like an April Fool Sale!

Think green... spring is here

Think spring fix-up specials!

Thinking about hanging up the snow shovel?

This only happens once a year

This sale is nothing to sneeze at!

This spring put a touch of magic in your lawn

Time to take the lawnmower out of hibernation

Unbeatable spring values!

Warm up fast with our hot spring bargains!

Warm up to a cool spring day with...

We bring spring to your door

We can help you with your springtime to-do list!

We have the cure for spring fever... Lots of savings!

We make all your payments until spring

We put a little spring into your spring at...

We'll shower you with savings on all...

We're jumping the gun on spring with our annual sale!

We're Making Spring Happen for You Sale Event!

Welcome spring with these garden specials!

Welcome to the season of new beginnings!

What more could you want in a spring break offer?

With warmer weather arriving, it's time to think maintenance

Yard sale time!

Younger than springtime savings!

Zing into spring with...

St. Patrick's Day

A day of legend and leprechauns

A gala St. Patrick's Day festival

A hearty toast to St. Patrick's Day!

A salute to the Irish

A special delight for your Irish friends

A St. Patrick's Day bonanza!

A St. Patrick's Day feast!

A St. Patrick's Day tradition

A toast to St. Patrick's Day!

A warm Irish welcome to all

A wee bit o' the green

Add a touch of green to your party

Add a touch of leprechaun magic

Ah, it's the day after the wearin' of the green

Ain't nothing green but the money

All things are green... today!

All we want for St. Patrick's Day is...

An Irish wish from the heart

And the luck o' the Irish to ye

Are you a lad or lassie?

Are you ready to celebrate St. Patrick's Day?

As the great St. Patrick's Day festival approaches...

Authentic Irish corned beef and cabbage served daily!

Back by popular demand, St. Patrick's Day celebration

Be a leprechaun and save lots of green!

Be aware of the buys of March!

Behave yourself... You're Irish today!

Catch the Irish spirit!

Celebrate St. Patrick's at O'Sullivan's

Celebrate St. Patrick's Day with these great savings!

Celebrate the day of the Irish

Celebrate with us for the real green

Color the world green

Cook up an Irish feast

Countdown to St. Patrick's Day!

Decked out for St. Patrick's Day!

Display your Irish blessings

Eat, drink and be Irish

Even if you aren't Irish, join in at...

Everybody's Irish today!

Fetes for St. Paddy

For a festive St. Patrick's Day...

For a rollicking Irish good time

For St. Patrick's Day revelers

For the luck of the Irish and then some

For the perfect touch of St. Patrick's Day green

For the savin' of the green!

For your favorite Irishman

Four leaf clover not required

Four leaf savings!

Free corned beef sandwich, today!

Get a feel for what it means to be Irish

Get ready for the wearin' of the green

Get your Irish blessing here!

Get your Irish up

Get your Irish wit out today!

Get your shamrock rolling early

Go for the green!

Good luck on St. Patrick's Day

Green beer for the men... Irish coffee for the ladies

St. Patrick's Day

Green beer will be a-flowin'

Green is the official color for today!

Hail to the green

Have a wild Irish Day!

Have you ever dreamed of playing the bagpipes?

Help us start a new St. Patrick's Day tradition

Here's a fun way to start your lucky day!

Here's how to make your friends green with envy!

Hey! Let's all wear green all day!

I'm Irish for today!

If you're lucky enough to be Irish... you're lucky enough

Irish expedition sales adventure!

Irish eyes are definitely smiling today!

It doesn't get much more Irish than that

It's a great day for the Irish

It's on us! A green beer with a green bagel

Join the best annual Irish celebration of the day!

Join the celebration of green

Join us after the St. Pat's parade

Kiss a green leprechaun for luck

Let us help you celebrate St. Patrick's Day!

March in for a shamrock of a deal!

Of course, you don't have to be Irish to celebrate St. Paddy's Day

Party on Patty's

Pick a shamrock today!

Plenty of green savings!

Priority one for today: getting green

Put a little green into your life

Put on your green derby, paper shamrock and smiling eyes

Save a lot of green this St. Pat's Day!

Savin' o' the green

See us for all your St. Patrick's Day needs

Shamrocks for sale...

Show everybody you're proud to be Irish

St. Paddy's Preview Sale!

St. Patrick's Day values!

St. Patrick's weekend sale!

Start planning now for St. Patrick's Day!

Start today with a taste of Irish tradition

Stock up for St. Patrick's Day!

The best Irish bash in town

The luck of the Irish might just rub off on you at...

The place to be on St. Patrick's Day!

The world's greatest leprechaun lives here

There's magic in the air on St. Patrick's Day!

There's nothing like a leprechaun to help celebrate St. Patty's Day!

There's plenty of green beer a-waiting

Time for the wearin' of the green

Time to green up

Today we're serving a garden of Irish delights

Unleash the hidden Gael in you

We are ready for St. Patrick's Day!

We have a warm Irish welcome for you

Wear it with Irish pride

Welcome Your Irish Day!

What a great time to be Irish!

When Irish Eyes are Smiling Sale Event!

When St. Patrick comes marching in

You can bet your last shillelagh that...

You'll be savin' the green at our St. Patrick's Day sale!

You're in Guinness country... today!

You're invited to the Shamrock Ball

Store

A great place to shop 'til you drop!

A little store with a big reputation

A neighborhood store that neighborhoods love

A store for all seasons

A store that is fun to shop

A store with a trend setting and distinct identity

A store within a store

A super store! Super selections! Super savings!

All stores now open. Extended holiday hours!

Always a bargain... this store was built on it!

An old-fashioned five-and-dime feel to the store

And, if we don't have it, we'll get it!

Browse and enjoy your store

Buzz in early and often

Can't find it? We'll get it!

Come in and meet our friendly live sales associates

Come see what all the talk is about

Do more with our store

Easy to get to, hard to leave

Enter today at a store near you!

Everything from A to ZZZZZ

Everything you need under one roof

Factory-direct, dealer-direct, right to you, direct

Friendly service that you won't find in any other store

From your door to our store

From your neighborhood store

Get it all... here!

Here are ten reasons to shop at...

How to lure customers into your store

How to manage your store more effectively

Hurry in for the best selections

I'm not buying, but do you mind if I look around?

If it's out there, it's in here

If we don't have it, you don't need it

If you can't find it, we generally don't sell it

If you're giving away the store, you'll go out of business

In terms of service and selection, nobody can beat our store!

It's a fabulous store for...

It's a good store to get in and out

It's always better to shop here!

It's just a great store!

It's where to shop!

Like no other store in the world like it

Make tracks to...

More than a store; it's a shopping experience

No traffic, no crowds, no waiting

Nobody offers a better selection

Now available at a store near you!

One store is all you need

Open around the clock!

Our name says it all!

Our sales associates are top-shelf

Our store has no walls

Our store is never closed!

See 'em, feel 'em, buy 'em, show 'em, save 'em, sell 'em

293

Store

Selections so good, you'll flip your lid

Service. Price. Product quality. Selection. Availability.

Specials throughout the store!

Stop in and see our in-store displays

Store closing... lost our lease!

Storewide savings happening now!

Tell them you bought it at...

That's what makes our store special

The friendliest store in the city

The funkiest store in town

The personal touch is alive at...

The right price, the right value, the right service!

The road stops at these locations

The shelves are alive with the sound of music!

The store is on sale!

The store that knows the outdoors

The World Wide Web is our favorite store

There's more help per shopper at this store

There's something fresh and new every day!

This is your store!

Visit our store at www...

We always take cash!

We are bigger than we look

We built our store by listening to our customers

We conduct sales in person

We got what's hot!

We had to expand to meet the demand

We have a little bit of a lot

We have it all!

We offer something not available at other stores: personal service!

We put the super in supermarket!

We sell only what the customer wants

We want your business and we'll prove it

We're a very kid-friendly store!

We're committed to your satisfaction

We're giving away the store!!!

We're improving the look and feel of our store

We're open during construction

We're selling satisfaction!

We're the small store with big deals!

We've got the things you didn't know you need

We've got what you need right under your nose

Where people come to buy... not shop!

Where shopping's a pleasure, too

Whether you're across town or across the country, you're just across from us

Whisk in for storewide savings!

Why bounce from store to store when we're on the ball?

Why shop anywhere else?

You always get exactly what you want from our store!

You can't go wrong with anything you buy here!

You know what you want... we've got what you want!

You know you can find what you're looking for

You never know what's in our store

You want it, we got it!

You'll love our prices as much as our merchandise!

You're the store's best customer

Your dollar will go a lot further... here!

Your kind of store!

Your neighbor, your store

Zoom in and save big!

Stress

A great stress reliever

A healthy way to cope with stress

Achieving maximum piece of mind with minimum effort

All tied up in knots?

Are you a slave to the clock?

Are you caught in a torture chamber?

Are you having trouble keeping all the balls in the air?

Dealing with stress head-on

Do something new: relax!

Do you feel like a piece of taffy, being pulled on all sides?

Do you think you're stressed out?

Everybody needs a way to relieve stress

Feel wrung out, tired, soggy, very lazy?

For instant stress relief

Fun! Sunshine! Relaxing!
Repeat as needed!

Gently massage away the anxieties and cares of the day with us!

Has the hustle of the job reduced your nerves to a fine dust?

Have another cup of coffee and relax

Here's how to de-stress

How could you feel stressed in a place like this?

How do you spell peace of mind?

How well can you handle stress?

I'm no longer exhausted at the end of the day

Is stress draining your energy?

Is your body aching for a way to unwind?

Is your stress-o-meter on overload?

It's exactly what you need to do... relax!

It's stress management

It's the biggest stress reliever there is...

It's the perfect way to relieve stress and tension

Keyed up, run ragged, dog-tired, worked up?

Let us ease your mind

Living stress-free!

Make stress your ally

Makes your ulcers bleed, doesn't it?

Manage stress, you don't have to eliminate it

Need some laughs to help the spirit? Relax!

Not sure if you're really stressed-out?

One of the greatest stress relievers known to man

Pour a cup of instant relaxation

Rent a guru

Say goodbye to stress

Screw it. Forget it. Relax.

Share some peace and quiet with...

Steps you can take to cope with stress

Stress? Who needs it?

Survival in a world full of stress

Take control of stress

Take the stress out of life

Taking charge of the stress in your life

Tips for handling holiday stress

Understanding the causes of stress

Unwind from the pressures of life

What better way to chase away the stresses of the day and relax?

What do you know about stress?

What, me worry? You bet!

You can't put a price on peace of mind

Summer

24-can salute to summer

A basket full of picnic bargains!

A great escape from summer doldrums

A great summer madness sale!

A hint for summer pleasures...
summer treats

A perfect way to escape on a summer day

A real summer treat

A short sale for a long summer!

A summer blast of a sale!

A summer favorite, and for good reason

A summer sale so big, you'll save in
places where it isn't even summer!

A super spectacular summer getaway!

A super summer sell-a-thon!

A super summer Sunday sale!

A taste of summer all year long

A touch of summer is all it takes

Add a shot of sunshine

Add sizzle to your summer with a
backyard barbecue bash

Ah, summertime, and the livin' is easy

Ah, that blissful season of
outdoor entertaining

Ahhh, summertime!

All at fantastic summer savings!

Amazing summer deals so hot you better
bring your sunscreen!

Amazing summer's end sale!

An endless summer of savings!

An old-fashioned, summertime
one-cent sale!

Annual summer scorcher sale!

Are you ready for summer?

Barbecue season is underway...
everything is on sale!

Bask in the blazing summer glory of...

Be cool! Stay cool this summer with...

Be the first to hit the beach

Beat the heat summer sale!

Big day at the beach. Big night at the...

Big summer values!

Blazin' summer savin'!

Blow the lid off with summer savings!

Breeze through the summer with...

Brighten up your warm summer
nights at...

But watch out for our hot June sale!

Can your air conditioner keep you cool
through another long, hot summer?

Cap things off for summer with...

Capture the essence of summer at...

Celebrate summer with a fun, new
experience for the whole family

Celebrate this summer's main
event with...

Change your summer from fun to
fantastic savings!

Chill out this summer at...

Christmas in July Sale!

Classic summer specials!

Cool deals for hot days!

Cool looks... Hot savings!

Cool off and enjoy the summer at...

Cool off this summer with a...

Cool savings... biggest air conditioner
sale event of the summer!

Cool summer buys!

Cool your heels without burning
your budget!

Cut out for summer fun

Don't let summer pass you by

Don't let the summer sun put a strain on your wallet

Don't sweat out another summer

Ease into summer with our summer values!

End of summer clearance!

Enjoy a healthy summer with...

Enjoy the cooler hours of hot days at...

Enjoying your moment in the sun... now!

Escape the boredom of hot summer days

Everything is on sale for a picnic except the ants!

Everything under the sun is under $20!

Everything you need for fun in the sun!

Everything you need for summer entertaining

Everything you need for your picnic guests. Invited or otherwise

Everything you'll need to help summer grow on you

Exceptional summer values for the beach and beyond!

Exciting savings before we kiss summer goodbye!

Explosive savings for active summer lifestyles!

Extended summer hours

Final summer clearance!

Final summer markdowns!

Finish your summer with our closeout sale!

For a good start on summer

For a slice of summertime fun

For cooling off a hot summer day

For easy days under the sun

For our new summer hours, we're letting our prices slide!

For summer living

For the livelier side of summer

From sunscreen to ice cream... sale days!

Fun in the sun with...

Get a big gulp of sun with a huge gulp of savings at...

Get a head start on summer at...

Get a jump on the sun season

Get into the swing of summer fun

Get ready for an action-packed summer savings at...

Get summer off to a rousing start at...

Good old summertime sale!

Great for cooling off a hot summer day

Great summer buys at...

Great summer roundup of savings!

Guaranteed savings on everything under the sun!

Have you made big plans for the warm months ahead?

Here comes the sun... And savings!

Here's a cool idea for summer... Hot buys!

Here's cool advice on how to beat the heat... below zero financing on all air conditioners!

Here's your summer survival kit

Here's your ticket to a summer of fun

Hot deals... cool prices!

Hot summer savings guaranteed!

Hot summer-daze deals end Sunday!

Hot! Hot! Hot! Sizzling summer savings!

Hottest sale of the summer!

How hot are our prices?

Hurry in for summer sales and great values!

I found my place in the sun at...

Ice down your summer with...

If the sun doesn't shine... we'll give you a 10% discount on all merchandise!!!

Ignite your summer fun at...

Is your lawn mower up to the summer?

It happens every year... as summer fades into fall deals!

It's our biggest sale of the summer

It's our Summer Solstice Sale!

It's outdoor living time!

It's Take Your Pale to the Beach Day

It's the best and most fun way to cool off

It's the coolest way to beat the heat

It's the unofficial kickoff sale to summer!

It's time for those summer getaways

It's your lucky summer sale!

Join our Summer Safari Sale!

Join us for some old-fashioned summertime fun

June Is Breaking Out All Over Sale Event!

Just add the sunshine to all your summer drinks

Just breezin' along savings at...

Just pucker up for a sip of summer's delight

Kaboom! Summer Blast-Off Sale!

Keep your cool without blowing your budget

Kiss the Summer Goodbye Year-End Sale!

Last call for summer fun

Last Sale of Summer!

Last week of summer sale!

Last-minute summer sale!

Let us help you beat the heat

Live it up... it's our Unreal Summertime Sale Event!

Live it up... it's summertime!

Look hot for a shade less

Looking for ways to beat the heat?

Made in the Shade Sale Event!

Make the most of your summer at...

More great finds for hot summer nights

Nothing says summer like our hot sale!

Nothing starts the summer like buying a new swimsuit!

Now's the perfect time to get ready for summer

OK, let's hit the beach!

One hot summer sale!

One hundred ways to beat the heat

Open your home to summer

Our most popular event of the summer

Our savings are a picnic

Plan now for summer

Put a little fun in your backyard with...

Red-hot summer sale!

Rediscover the joys of summer at...

Sales explodes with excitement this summer!

Savings that put excitement into summer fun!

Say hello to summer's good buys!

Sensational summer sale!

Serious summer sidewalk sale!

Sizzling savings on summertime essentials!

Sizzling values on the hottest summer swimsuits!

Soak up the sun... soak up the fun... soak up the savings!

Some cool advice on how to beat the heat

Spectacular summer savings!

Spend an easy day at the beach with us!

Summer Blastoff Sale!

Summer camp... You gotta go do it!

Summer can be a blast at...

Summer cash-back savings are really heating up!

Summer clearance time... So don't waste it!

Summer comfort at its best

Summer fun begins with...

Summer home improvement sale!

Summer is passing very quickly... And so is this special summer offer!

Summer kick-off specials!

Summer lasts forever, but the savings won't!

Summer relief has arrived with great savings!

Summer sale goes out in a blaze of glory!

Summer sale... Hot looks... Cool prices!

Summer savings days are here again!

Summer savings start with these coupons!

Summer sizzzzzzzler savings!

Summer Splash Spectacular!

Summer value daze!

Summer values so hot, they'll melt any resistance!

Summer's R&R starts right here!

Summer's Rolling By Sale!

Summerfest of values!

Summertime is savings time at...

Sun, fun and savings... just for you!

Sun, sand and sensational savings!

Sun-sational sale!

Sunsational... funsational... pricesational savings!

Super saver summer specials!

Super Summer Savers!

Super Sunday Splash Sale!!!

Take advantage of our special summer savings!

Take advantage... summer closeouts!

Tear into summer with sizzling hot savings!

The best buys of summer!

The best sale to happen to summer since sunshine!

The exceptional buys of summer!

The hazy, lazy, crazy days of summer savings!

The hot spot for fabulous summer savings!

The Last Big Weekend of Summer Sale!

Summer

The last fling of summer... deals!

The last of summer on sale!

The savings are hot on summertime values!

The Slice of Summer Price Break!

The sun is shinin', the bees are buzzin' and we're having a sale!

The Super Summer of Savings Sale!

The window of opportunity on summer savings is closing fast!

This is the summer to bag bargains!

This summer will your refrigeration decide to take a vacation, too?

This summer, let us heat things up at your barbecue

Time to crank up the air conditioner

To tan or not to tan?

Totally hot... Totally new... Totally free!

Treat yourself with our smashing summer specials!

Under the big tent... Outdoor Living Time Savings Event!!!

We have it all for backyard leisure

We make summer sparkle

We put sizzle into summer fun

We're celebrating the end of our summer sale!

What a summer sale!

What better place for sipping lemonade?

What makes a great summer sale?

Where to go for great summer weekends

Win a $200 summer shopping spree!

You'll go nuts in the sun with...

You're free to enjoy the summer!

Your backyard will be rockin' with summer savings!!!

Your summer fun kit is available at...

Zoom… into summer fun at…

A simply stupendous savings blitz!!!

A spectacular epic... price-smasher sale!

A surrealistic experience of savings!

Absolutely breathtaking! Absolutely dazzling! Absolutely delightful!

Absolutely utterly delightful savings!

Absolutely... positively... the last sale of the year!

A-maze-ing-ly great savings!

Amazing! Fabulous! Spectacular! Incredible deals!!!

An absolutely spectacular fantastic savings event!

An astronomical sales event!

Aren't the savings fabulous?

Astounding! Amazing! Brilliant!

Astronomical and colossal savings!

Beyond Your Wildest Expectations... Sales Event!

Brilliant spectacle of exceptional savings!

Charming. Exquisite. Marvelous.

Completely, stupefyingly ridiculous bargains!

Dazzling extravaganza buying bonanza!

Dazzling. Stunning. Spectacular.

Delightfully different! Devastatingly beautiful! Distinctively you!

Earthshaking. Stupendous. Perfect.

Elegantly rich and eminently enjoyable

Energetic! Inspirational! Dynamic Sale Event!

Enormously enjoyable bargains

Excellent. Marvelous. Exquisite.

Exhilarating. Emotional. Spectacular.

Exquisite. Enchanting. Enthralling.

Extraordinary... exceptionally great buys!

Faaaaabulous savings!!!

Fantastic! Colossal! Super! Sales event!!!

Fantastic, incredible, or anywhere in-between

Get outrageous during our end-of-the-season savings!

Great expectations... great deals!

Hmmmmmm. Believable?

Impeccable!

Incredibly comfortable deals!

Incredibly, wildly exhilarating values!

Irresistible. Outstanding. Wonderful.

Isn't that a terrific bargain?

It's a phantasmagorical sale!

It's a refreshingly revolutionary sale event!

It's a Superspectacular Truckload Sale!

It's absolutely, positively worth considering

It's almost imaginable

It's awesome, isn't it? Lowest-prices-ever sale!

It's astounding! It's incredible! It's amazing savings on all...

It's colossal! It's gigantic! Our Billion-Dollar Sale Event!

It's colossal... It's stupendous savings!

It's delightful. It's marvelous

It's exciting, it's euphoria

It's extraordinary... it's stupendous

It's flat-out fantastic... out-of-this-world savings!

It's great, simply great buys!

It's great... It's fabulous prices!!!

It's humongous... our big super sale!

It's indescribable... the sale of all sales!

It's just fantastic savings!

It's marvelous! It's dazzling!
It's extraordinary savings!

It's simply amazing. It's simply
incredible deals!

It's toorific... Cash Back Sale!

It's unbelievable, not even imaginable,
good old-fashioned prices!

It's unbelievably real values!

It's unfathomable bargains!

Lavishly sumptuous

Let's get sensational! We did, with these
low, low prices!

Lush, lavish and completely
captivating deals!

Magnificent, absolutely
magnificent bargains!

Magnificent. Outstanding.
Spectacular savings!

Mystique. Heavenly. Elegance.

Oh my goodness gracious...
it's savings time!

Opulent and elegant

Ostentatiously expensive

Outrageously Outstanding Instant
Rebate Sale!

Perpetually magnificent

Phenomenal! Spectacular! Electrifying
storewide savings!

Positively exquisite

Powerful and electrifying deals!

Quietly spectacular

Rapturous! Superb! Daring!

Remarkable. Astounding. Exceptional.

Scrumptious super savings!

Sensational! Spectacular! Stunning
savings that'll knock your socks off!!!

Sensational. Powerful. A gem.

Sheer sophistication savings on
all dresses!

Simply brilliant. Simply eloquent.
Simply fabulous.

Simply spectacular Bargain Hunter Sale!

Sleek. Sassy. Sophisticated.

So fabulously priced

Stunning, genuinely spectacular

Stupendous and spectacular savings!!!

Surprisingly sweet on savings!

Tempting, terrific and tremendous
"wow" prices!!!

Terrific! Sensational! Super
Half-Price Sale!

The fascination is amazing

The feeling is indescribable

They're so outrageously fantastic prices!

This is a one-time absolutely spectacular
sales event!

Thoroughly intoxicating bargains!

Thunderous, magnificent, spectacle of
real savings!

Totally unique and different...
you-won't-believe-it saving event!

Truly magnificent... Truly remarkable...
Truly a phenomenal deal!

Unbelievable... amazing Dynamite
Day Sale!

Undeniably elegant

Unpredictable and glorious

Uplifting! Triumphant! Enlightened!

Utterly amazing. Utterly delightful...
deals!

Utterly overpowering, all-consuming

Voluptuous!

What an unbelievable deal!

Whoopee! It's our annual Sales
Days event!

Wildly exciting warehouse
liquidation sale!

Wonderful! Fabulous! Extraordinary!

You will be ecstatic over our prices!

You'll be absolutely thrilled with the
savings!

Taste

A delicious and delightful taste

A delicious taste your kids will love

A deliciously different taste

A new taste they'll go wild for

A surprisingly delicious taste

A symphony of good taste

A taste of country

A taste so rich, nobody can match

A taste that is perfectly delicious

A taste that truly must be experienced

A taste they all love and a taste you'll love!

A taste to satisfy your appetite!

A tasty breakfast for everyone

A tasty treat

A wholesome taste of...

Acquire a taste for the ultimate...

America's favorite taste

Award-winning taste

Big flavor... great taste

But the difference is in the taste

Can't you just taste it?

Clearly a matter of taste

Come and experience the taste

Create a fantastic taste

Curious about the taste?

Discover that great-tasting, all natural...

Don't just butter it... top it with taste!

Enjoy exquisite taste

Enjoy the irresistible taste of...

Exceptional taste

Fancy your taste

Fantastic taste, lots of variety

Find out how good it tastes

For those with tastes for the bizarre

For women with impeccable taste

Fresh tastes from our oven

Give them the taste they love

Give your family the taste they deserve

Great new tastes to discover

Great taste and variety

Great taste in minutes

Great taste just got better

Great tasting, good-for-you!

Here are all the ingredients for that great taste!

Here's a tasty chew

Hey, this tastes good

Homemade taste you'll enjoy

Homemade taste your family will love

Introducing a new taste to fall in love with

It looks good and tastes as good as it looks

It reflects your taste for the finer things

It tastes like chicken

It's a must-taste

It's time to turn on those taste buds

It's your taste

Just one taste... is all it takes

Keeping pace with changing tastes

Mighty sweet with great taste

Never tasted so good

Nothing tastes like...

Nutrition. Value. Taste.

Once you get a taste of the pie, you'll want more

Once you taste it, you're spoiled forever

One big flaky taste

One taste and you'll know why...

One taste is all it takes

Palate pleaser

Perfect for your family of exquisite taste

Pure authentic American taste

Puts you in the best of taste

Raise your glass to great taste

Savor the natural flavor of...

Serve the taste that's noticeably better

Show off your good taste

Show them you've got great taste, too

Simply the best tasting

So many ways to enjoy exquisite taste

So tasty! How do we describe it?

Staying in shape never tasted so good

Sure, they're fattening, but boy do they taste good

Take home the taste of...

Taste a real delightful sandwich

Taste beyond belief

Taste it, you'll love it!

Taste so great, we guarantee it

Taste that defies your expectations

Taste that keeps flowing

Taste the difference quality makes

Taste the good life

Taste what's fresh this season

Taste what's new

Taste you can't measure

Taste, quality and value

Tastes devilishly delicious

Tastes the way it's supposed to

Tastes they'll really love

Tasty, wholesome and sweet

Tempt your taste buds

That tangy taste sensation

The amazing taste of...

The aroma, the taste

The definition of good taste is you

The great taste of a great meal

The taste people prefer

The taste says it all

The taste sure doesn't get any better

The taste that tops everything

The taste that turns the world upside down

The taste you can't beat

The taste you dream of

The taste your whole family will love

They taste as great as our name

This stuff tastes great

Time is ripe for that old-fashioned taste of...

Treat your taste buds to something different

Trust your senses and indulge in a world of great taste and pleasure

Trust your taste

Try the great taste of...

Unsurpassed taste

Wake up to the great taste and smell of...

We envy anyone taking their first taste

We expand and delight the culinary palette

We welcome you to stop in and experience a taste of...

You gotta taste it

You'll love the taste

You'll never forget the taste

You'll please a lot of palates with...

You've got the taste of summer fruits all year long!

Your taste buds will say...

Your taste is exquisite

Yummy! Scrumptious! Tasty!

Technology

A whole new way to use technology

Acquiring the best-of-the-best technologies

All the way with digital

All things are mobile

And you thought you knew everything about wireless

Applying the new tools of technology... today!

Are you a wireless-starved customer?

Are you out of your wires?

Are you ready for the challenges that new technology brings?

Are you turned on by this digital age?

As the world becomes increasingly digital

At digital speed

At home with technology

At the forefront of wireless technology

At your wireless service

Be the leader with the newest technology

Beat the digital drum

Beyond wireless technology

Blame it on digital-age technology

Brace yourself for the next round of technology

Bringing the digital marketplace to the world

Building the bridge of technology to the new frontier

But what exactly is new about wireless?

Buyers who want tomorrow's technology today!

Call me portable. Call me smart. Call me mobile.

Choosing the right technology

Closed due to technology overload

Competing at digital speed

Cool about digital?

Create with it, apply it and put it to work for you!

Creating with technology, not just using it

Customer care solutions for the digital age

Deploying technology to solve business needs

Developed yesterday. Marketed today. Obsolete tomorrow.

Digital me!

Digital solutions make your life simple

Digital technology brought us a new world

Digital technology is going places

Digital this! Digital that!

Do you have the mobile touch?

Do you have the right digital tools and the knowledge to use them?

Don't be left on the side of the technological road

Facing technology head on

For all your digital, mobile, wireless business solutions

For all your technology needs

From the technology toolbox

Get connected with wireless

Get in step with new, new, new technology

Get the digital edge

Get the technology you need... today!

Getting the most from the wireless world

Go digital and you'll never go back

Go mobile to keep your business running

Go wireless on a budget

Grow your world by mobilizing it

Helping to bridge the digital divide

How can today's technology help you?

How did wireless technology change your life?

How digital is your business?

How the wireless world meets the world

How to get the most out of your wireless world

How to make your business mobile

I don't need technology; I need solutions

If you can't keep up with technology, you might want to close your doors

If you don't understand technology, how will you manage it?

Implementing digital technologies

In a wireless world, everything is possible

In our world of technology, people still make the difference

In the center of the digital landscape

In today's digital economy...

Invest in the new technology, today!

Is digital the best solution?

Is technology driving your company?

Is wireless invading your privacy?

Is your technology completely obsolete?

It pays to be connected!

It's a digital marketplace

It's a fact... digital is better

It's not mental telepathy, just wireless technology

It's revolutionary, not evolutionary

It's the digitalization of the world

It's the optical technology of the future

It's time to go wireless

It's what you expect from a mobile leader

It's wireless communication... today!

Knowing how to use technology

Let us show you how our mobile and wireless solutions can help you!

Look Ma, no wires!

Looking for the real deal in mobile technology?

Make your life mobile

Making technology available for all

Making the right technology decisions

Making the world wireless

Making this a better world through the use of technology

M-business that works for you!

Mobile analysis and problem solving

Mobile is everything you want and everything you need

Mobile products you can count on in the future

Mobile solutions to help you soar above your competition

Mobile success... today and tomorrow!

Mobile. Digital. Network.

Mobilize your business, grow your business

Moving ahead in a technologically-confusing world

Moving into the new wireless world

Moving your business with technology

M-power your people!

Now I'm always in touch, always able to respond to client needs

Now is the time to get wireless

Now it's time to turn to digital living!

Now that is what you call state of the art

Now you can use your phone anywhere in the world

On the digital highway to...

Opening all the digital doors

Our technology will put you at ease

Plug into the wireless revolution!

Put digital services to work for you!

Putting technology in your hands

Putting technology to work for
your business

Reach beyond your wireless dreams

Right now technology!

Space-age technology at your fingertips

Stay one step ahead of the
technology game

Staying ahead in the digital race

Survival in the digital age

Switching to digital?

Take a look on the bright side of mobile

Take a new look at technology

Take advantage of the technology that's
out there

Taking wireless to the next level

Technology can help improve
your performance

Technology in action!

Technology is changing faster than ever
to meet new demands

Technology is the driving force in...

Technology is the tool for growth

Technology like you've never seen before

Technology makes it a possibility

Technology makes life better

Technology now... technology later!

Technology on the move!

Technology tells it like it is

Technology that bridges the wired and
wireless worlds

Technology trends for the coming years

Technology will change the way you
live today!

Technology will never hold you back

Technology with a human touch

Technology you can rely on well into
the future

Technology's new frontier

That's a lot of cool about digital

That's right... it's all digital!

The benefit of using wireless, is wireless

The convenience of digital technology

The digital connection to real information

The digital economy is in your future

The digital frontier! The digital future!
The digital generation!

The digital gold rush! The digital
marketplace! The digital revolution!

The digital home of tomorrow... today!

The digital world has no boundaries

The excitement of wireless!

The good news is that technology works

The industry's best wireless technology

The latest in wireless wizardry

The look of yesterday... the technology
of today!

The low down on top technology today!

The most burning problems are solved
with the hottest technology

The most popular technology on
the planet

The new technologies, which ones
and when

The next generation of wireless service

The next state-of-the-art revolution
starts here

The power advantage of digital

The power of superior technology

The proof is in our technology

The right approach to mobile technology

The right wireless solution

The road to your wireless future

The technology of the future... now!

The technology of tomorrow is today

The way technology is used today!

The wireless future is your future

The wireless wonder does it all

The world is wired for wireless

There are no boundaries in the
digital world

There is a wireless option out there to get the job done!

This is all about technology

This is definitely the way to go

This is not the time for hibernation

This way to new technology

Time to go digital

To succeed, connect with the new technologies

Today's business technology market for tomorrow

Today's most reliable technology

Today's technology with yesterday's service

Tomorrow's technology today!

Trying to keep pace with all the changes in technology?

Turn on to wireless

Understanding mobile technology before you buy

Use technology to do more with what you have

Use the technologies that are right for you

Using the new tools to change technology

Was technology something you took for granted?

We are in the digital economy

We fought in the wireless revolution, and we won!

We have the best minds in technology

We have the technology that is shaping the world

We make wireless work

We solved the chicken-and-egg problem

We tell the truth about this new technology

We'll take you wireless and beyond

We've got the digital touch

We've got the technology to produce your wireless solution

We've opened our eyes and ears to digital reality

Welcome to the wild world of wireless

What a difference wireless makes

What are your digital needs?

What do the new technologies mean for your business?

What does technology mean to you?

What makes digital music so cool?

What technology doesn't make sense?

What's in store for the next generation of mobile products?

What's the value of technology?

What's your digital future?

When it comes to computer technology... just do it!

When people think of technology, they think of...

When was the last time you had a low-tech experience?

Where will technology take us next?

Why we went mobile

Will you survive in the digital economy?

Wireless communication solutions

Wireless knows where you want to go

Wireless takes you a step beyond

Wireless technology, today, tomorrow and into the future!

Wireless? Now we're talking!

World-class technology and reliability

You can't afford to settle for yesterday's technology

You have the technology to change the way you do business

You might say it's mobile

You'll be amazed at what you can do with wireless

You'll get more bang for your technology buck with us!

Your wireless future is now!

Thanksgiving

A feast of ideas for every appetite

A harvest of healthy savings!

A holiday that won't gobble up your savings!

A must for Thanksgiving

A plentiful table begins with...

A Thanksgiving dinner fit for a Pilgrim

A way to give thanks is to share a blessing

After Thanksgiving Sale starts tomorrow!

All who are hungry, let them come and eat

All-time favorites for your Thanksgiving feast

At 40% off storewide, there won't be any Thanksgiving leftovers!

At 50% off, it's time to talk turkey!

Be grateful for the blessings in your life

Before the feast, let's talk turkey

Bountiful food savings!

Bring something festive to the Thanksgiving feast

Celebrate with good reason

Dear fellow pilgrims,

Develop a game plan for Thanksgiving

Don't be a turkey, get a head start on...

Don't let Thanksgiving sneak up on you!

Eat out this Thanksgiving

Eat, drink and be thankful

Enjoy a bountiful Thanksgiving season

Feast on these savings!

Five reasons to give thanks

For that yummy Thanksgiving dinner

Free pumpkin pie with purchase of...

Free turkey giveaway!

From our table to your table... Happy Thanksgiving

Get all the right stuff for Thanksgiving at...

Get stuffed with savings

Give a turkey dinner to a homeless person

Gobble up our Thanksgiving specials!

Gobble up our traditional Thanksgiving dinner

Gobble up these big savings!

Guess what's behind every great Thanksgiving!

Have a happy Thanksgiving... you deserve it

Have you ever thought of celebrating Thanksgiving early?

Here comes the big turkey sale event!

How big of a turkey should I get?

How to keep your Thanksgiving guests out of the kitchen

How to survive Thanksgiving Day

Hurry up and gobble up the savings!

Ideas for your Thanksgiving feast

It's a great bird, no bones about it

It's the time of the year for giving thanks

It's Turkey Savings Time!

It's turkey time

Jazz up those thanksgiving leftovers with...

Join the Thanksgiving Day parade

Join us for our Annual Turkey Day Hunt

Let's talk turkey on...

Let's turkey-in this Thanksgiving

Looking for a way to start off Thanksgiving weekend?

Make this Thanksgiving one to remember

November harvest special

Our After-Thanksgiving Sales begin today!

Our store is stuffed with big savings!

Our turkey dinners deserved five stars

Over 200 years of giving thanks

Pilgrims' helpful hints

Put a free turkey on your table when you shop with us

Put some zip on your table for turkey day

Savings for your Thanksgiving table

Savings you can truly be thankful for

Serve your best at this year's Thanksgiving gathering

Shake up your Thanksgiving dinner with...

Sign up for the turkey shoot... today!

Special Thanksgiving Weekend Super Sale!

Start your Thanksgiving morning off with...

Stuff your turkey with our savings!

Take-out turkey takes the trouble out of Thanksgiving

Tasty Turkey Day treats to top off your celebration

Thanks-For-Giving Sale Event!

Thanksgiving Day food baskets for the poor

Thanksgiving kicks off the holiday season at...

Thanksgiving marathon savings event!

Thanksgiving savings, any way you slice it

Thanksgiving weekend sale extravaganza!

Thanksgiving with all the trimmings

Thanksgiving... a call to give thanks

Thanksgiving... a day for counting blessing, not calories

The finest of Thanksgiving feasts

The hit of your Thanksgiving table

The hotline for turkey trouble

The lowest price on turkeys and everything else

The most anticipated food event of the year... Thanksgiving!

The smart Pilgrims eat here

The start of the Christmas shopping season begins at...

Think Thanksgiving

This deal's a turkey and it's alive and kicking

This Thanksgiving, buy a turkey that isn't a turkey

This turkey has the right bird's eye view of Thanksgiving

Time to gobble, gobble, gobble up these values!

Trimmings for the Thanksgiving table

'Twas the night before Thanksgiving...

Visit us today for Thanksgiving Day deals!

Wanna ruffle some feathers?

We want to make your Thanksgiving something to be thankful for

We're giving everybody something to be thankful for

We're keeping the thanks in Thanksgiving

We're sticking our necks out to save you money

Welcome to our Thanksgiving Day salute!

What could top a Thanksgiving dinner at...

What to look for on a turkey label

What's your Thanksgiving favorite?

Why wait until November to celebrate with a turkey?

You're invited to gobble with us

Your days of hunting for a great deal are over, Pilgrim

Time

5-minute roundup

A race against the clock

An old idea whose time has come

And here's the real clock stopper

Are you an addictive time-waster?

Are you living on borrowed time?

Around the world... around the clock!

At a moment's notice

At the top of the hour

Be smart about your time

Beat the clock before it's too late

But who has the time?

Buy all the time you want

Can you find a few hours to burn?

Caught in a time warp?

Check your local listings for the times

Crunch time

Discover how to save time and money

Don't let time run out on you

Don't say "later" when you can say "now"

Don't wait a minute longer!

Don't waste another minute

Don't worry if time is a problem

Every minute! Every hour! Every day!

Everything still needs to be done yesterday

Experience the suspension of time

For just a minute of your time today

Free up your time with...

Give the gift of time!

Give us two minutes of your time, and we'll give you ours

Going beyond the possibilities of time

Got 15 minutes to kill?

Have you looked at your calendar lately?

Here's how to kill time

Here's what to do with the rest of your time

Here's what to do with those empty hours

Here's your 15 minutes of megabyte fame!

How much is your time worth?

How to make time fly

How to squeeze more time out of time

Hurry, time is running out

If you want to know what time it is, get yourself a clock

Imagine what you can do with 10 extra minutes

Imagine yourself stepping back in time

In this time-is-money era, every minute counts

In topsy-turvy times

It takes time to save time

It's 11 p.m. Do your customers know where you are?

It's commercial time!

It's make-or-break time

It's time to put on the brakes

It's time to put up or shut up

It's time well-spent

It's worth 20 minutes of your time

It's worth every minute

It's your time to shine

Just in time

Just think of all the time and headaches you'll save

Last-second savings

Let us add a new dimension to your leisure time

Long on ideas, but short on time?

Make every minute count

Man of the minute

Next time, save time

No time like now

Now is your time to buy a...

On call, round the clock

On time... every time

One hundred percent of the time

Passing the test of time

Please take a few minutes to...

Practical time-saving tips

Pressed for time?

Put time on your side

Right up to the minute

Saves... big time!

Size the minute

Spend a little time with us and you'll...

Standing the test of time

Start turning back the hands of time

Staying ahead of the times

Take a walk through time with us!

Take as much time as you need

Take time for yourself

Thank you for the time

The clock is ticking... so act now!

The clock will start ticking for...

Time can be your most valuable asset

Time for a commercial

Time for a helping hand

Time Is A-Wastin'... Sale Event!

Time is money. Don't waste it

Time is on your side

Time is running out... don't wait another minute

Time is ticking away

Time marches on

Time saving tips

Time well spent

Timeless elegance

Timely tips

Today's bonus hour

Turn back the hands of time

Until it's late, it's on time

Up-to-the-minute

Watches make a super last-minute gift, and a lasting keepsake

We all know time is precious

We don't want to alarm you... but time's running out!

We interrupt this waste of time

We promise, we'll make it worth your time and effort!

We'll be there in a bird-dog minute

We're available around the clock!

We're cuckoo over clocks

We're on time... are you?

What are you doing with your time?

What time is it? Game time!

What used to take a few minutes now takes a few seconds

What's 20 minutes of your time worth?

When you don't have time to waste...

When you have the time, will you have the money?

Who has time anymore?

Who knows where the time goes?

Working against the clock

You can hear the clock ticking now!

You can save a lot of time...

You don't have a minute to waste

You have no time to lose!

You'll be glad you took the time

You'll save time with...

You're only minutes away from...

Your time is as valuable as your money

311

36 Hours in a Day Sale Event!

A sure way to make your day...
Great deals!

Act today...

And what better time than today!

Apply today!

Bargains every day of the week!

Beating the Monday Blues Sales Event!

Call today... what are you waiting for?

Contact us today!

Daytime! Nighttime! Anytime!

Do you wake up in the morning saying,
"I should have taken the deal"?

Don't let today go by without...

Don't put off until tomorrow what you
can do for less today!

Don't start your day without us!

Every day is special when you...

Everyone needs a sale day like this!

Fast and filling, just like today!

Feel-Good Monday Sale Event!

Feeling lucky today?

For people who need coffee to start
their day!

Fuel your day with...

Get a buzz-alarmed start... today!

Get a jump on today!

Get the great value you've come
to expect!

Get what you need today!

Give us a call today, won't you?

Go Ahead, Make My Day Sale Event!

Go do it today!

Good morning starts here

Great deals don't wait for tomorrow

Here's a great way to start your day!

Here's one reason to look forward to
Monday morning!

Here's the way to start the day with a
good morning

Hit the day at a gallop

How many days before Christmas?

I've been waiting for this day all year

If you didn't buy it today, you can buy
it tomorrow!

Indulge yourself today!

It changes every day

It doesn't make any difference what day
it is... everything is on sale!

It happens every day

It's a delicious way to start the day!

It's a perfect way to ring in the day

It's a wonderful way to start off the day

It's an owe-it-to-yourself day

It's even better the second day

It's sure to brighten your day...
unbelievable savings!

It's up to you to seize the day... and seize
the savings!

It's your kind of day... it's your kind
of sale!

It's your wakeup call to outstanding
bargains and terrific deals that add up
to awesome savings!

Join the sale for one day!

Jump-Start Your Day Sale Event!

Less than a dollar a day

Make a day of it... a shopping spree
sales event!

Make the call today!

Make the commitment today!

Make us part of your morning routine

Make your day special... every day!

Make your day with us

Mark your calendar... today!

Morning, noon, night

No matter where your day takes you, get over to our price-slashing sale event!

Not a bad day's work with prices like these!

Not only will you make your day, you'll make your family's too with outstanding savings!

One day only!

Only 1 day remaining!

Only today you can double your savings!

Our sale starts at the crack of dawn

Pick it up today!

Save the date!

Savings all day... everyday!

Savings as fresh as a morning breeze

Say yes today!

Seize the day... seize the savings!

Shop early... tomorrow may be too late!

Sometimes overnight is too late

Start the day out right with...

Starting today!

Strike up your best deal today!

Sunrise... sunset... one-day sale!

Take one home... today!

That'll be the day when we have a sale event like that!

The buzzword of today is...

The main event of the day

The pulse of today!

The savings start at dawn... end at dusk

The way to survive a day

The word for today is "save"

There's something special every day!

This is an awesome day for phenomenal savings!

This is one lucky day for you

This is something that doesn't happen every day!

This is your "go for it" kind of day!

Tickets on sale today!

Today is a banner day!

Today is a red-tag sale day!

Today is tailor-made for you

Today we filled our store with sensational savings!

Today we interrupt your newspaper with...

Today, tomorrow, next week and right now!

Today's Pick-Me-Up Sales Event!

Today's special is you!

Vote today and we'll tally up the savings for you!

We are all set to have a field day

We need you to join us, today!

We service like there's no today!

We turn every day into a special occasion

We urge you to act today!

We've got the savings to start your day!

Well, it's your lucky day!

What a difference a day makes

What a lovely way to spend a day

What can we do for you today?

What can you do today?

What's on tap for today?

Where do we want to go today?

Why don't you join us today?

Why don't you subscribe today?

Why wait? Get exactly what you want today!

You can count on today!!

Your day! Your way!

Your sale... your day!

A great set of tools for the price!

A new world of tools awaits you at...

A tool ahead of its time

A tool for all seasons and all reasons

A tool that will save the day and every day!

All must-have tools on sale!

All the right tools at just the right price

An Arsenal of Tools Savings Event!

An indispensable tool to better serve you

Anyone can sell you on the tools. It's how you use them that counts!

Are your tools all they're cracked up to be?

Bargain value prices on terrific time-saving tools!

Big savings on all tools!

Build your future with the right tools

But do these tools really save time?

Buy good tools and they could last a lifetime

Buy the toolbox and get 30% off on all tools and stuff you can fit in the toolbox

Buy the woman some new tools!

Can your tool do this?

Cheap tools will fall apart no matter what you do

Choose the right tool for the right job

Choose your tools carefully

Closeout tools for workshopaholics!

Dead or alive trade-ins!

Do you buy power tools?

Do you have the tools to get the job done?

Do you have too many tools for your tool belt?

Easy-to-use tools

Especially designed for you, Tool Sale

Essential tools for essential jobs

Everybody Loves Tools... Sale Event!

Everything you need in one toolbox

Excruciatingly tough

Fill up your toolbox for less!

From Work Boots To Tool Belts... Sales Event!

Get the right tool for your next project

Get the tools and expertise you need at...

Give him the tools for success

Good old-fashioned prices on tools to have and to hold!

Good quality tools are a good investment

Hand tools! Cutting tools! Power tools! All on sale!

Hand-tooled quality

Handy tools to get the little jobs done

Having the right tools makes all the difference

Helping people learn to use the right tools

Here's a tool that looks great in your workshop

Here's the latest gizmo

Hey, here's a handy tool to have in the car

How about a cool tool to do...

How do you know if you're buying the right tools?

I learned my lesson. Buy the best tools!

I'm your task-conquering handyman tool

Incredible tools that you really can use

It never hurts to have a big set of tools

It takes the right tools to do the job right!

It won't do your laundry, but...

It's a cool tool made just for you!

It's a smart tool to use

It's a time-saver tool!

It's a tool that gets used

It's an Incredible Tool... Sale Event!

It's child's play when you have the right tools!

It's not just another tool in the toolbox

It's one tool you should not be without

It's time for new tools

Just for women... all-purpose tools!

Know your tools... know your tool store!

Let him who is without the right tool cast the first complaint

Like they say in the trade, "It's all in the tools"

Man's quest for better tools

More Tools For Your Toolbox Sale!

Never underestimate the power of good tools

New tools, new benefits, new thinking

Once you own this tool, you will never be without it!

Open up our toolbox of savings!

Our tools are tough as nails

Our tools don't take a back seat to anyone!

Our tools speak for themselves

Our tools stand up to any tools from a quality standpoint

Our tools will never let you down

Our tools won't sit in the toolbox and gather dust

Own the tools the pros use!

Power savings on all cordless power tools!

Powershop... sales event!

Primary tools for every DIY!

Real-time tools for real action

Safety glasses are the most important tool you can own!

Savings on dependable tools that get the job done

Say hello to the hottest tool on the market

Sledgehammered pricing on all tools!

Special purchase on all types of hand tools!

Stands up to the punishment

The best quality tools made!

The best tools money can buy!

The choice of the professionals

The drill you want is now on sale!

The job is too important to mess around with second-rate tools

The most powerful tools have the most powerful results

The most versatile tools around

The one tool no one should be without

The one tool that answers all your needs

The only tool that lets you do the work in half the time

The only tool you'll ever need!

The power tool of choice!

The pros say it's a necessity

The right tools at the right time at the right price!

The "Ten Best Tools" for all you do-it-yourselfers!

The tool is now in your court!

The tool that can change the mindset of how you work

The tool that can make an enormous difference

The tool that speaks for itself

The tools that do-it-yourselfers use

The tools that solve problems

The tools you need to do your job quickly and easily

Tools

The ultimate tool for today's price!

The wise workers equip themselves with tools they can use

The world's most powerful tool!

There's a right tool and wrong tool for any job

There's no substitute... the right tool for the job!

These tools are incredibly useful

Thingamajigs and Doohickeys... Sales Event!

This is one tool that you don't realize you need until you get one

Time-saving tools! Time-savvy tools!

Tips. Techniques. Tools... Extravagance!

To be productive... you need the best tools!

To do your best work, you need the right tools

To get the job done right, use the right tools

Today is April Tools Day!

Tool demo day!

Tool of the Week Deal!

Tool Power... Savings Event!

Tool show specials... on sale!

Tool talk

Tool trade-in deals!

Tools every man would love

Tools for fix-up fun

Tools for handy-men and handy-women

Tools for jobs of all sizes

Tools for the creative professional

Tools for the tool junkie... on sale!

Tools for today's craftsmen

Tools for tool-belted women

Tools for tykes

Tools make great gifts!

Tools of the trade... monstrous savings!

Tools that help you work better!

Tools that make it happen

Tools that match your needs can help you overcome the toughest...

Tools that take you from start to finish

Tools that work for you

Tools to Drool Over... Sales Event!

Tools to get it right the first time!

Tools to improve your woodworking skills

Tools to put to work

Tools you don't even know you need

Tough. Rugged. Reliable.

Use the right tool for the job

We carry only the very best tools!

We have the tools you need!

We insist you use the best tools of the trade

We like to let our tools do the talking

We sell tool belts to toolboxes

We've got the tools that work for you!

Welcome to our toolshed

What you do with our tools can make a huge difference

What's in your toolbox?

Whatsits and gizmos for all gadget enthusiasts!

When you have the right tools, there's no limit to what you can do!

You can't rely on just one tool!

You don't build your future with tools of the past

You Get More With Our Tools... Sale Event!

You'll be a fool if you don't buy this tool

You're invited to our Tool Corral Celebration of Savings!

You're nothing without tools!

Toys

50% off toy clearance!

A kid can't have too many toys

A rich man's toy is never on sale!

A super selection of dolls and accessories

A whole new level of excitement and fun

A wonderful toy for all ages

Adorable toys for adorable tots

All action figures on sale!

All cool toys on sale!

All high-tech toys... now on sale!

All the hottest toys and savings too!

Americans Love Toys... Sale Event!

Award-winning toys for kids of all ages

Batteries are always included with our toys

Big savings on must-have toys!

Bring your favorite toy for show and tell

Built kid-tough!

Buy 2, get 1 free toys!

Check out this year's hottest toys!

Christmas In July Toy... Savings Event!

Come play with all the latest toys

Come see all our new toys!

Created by kids for kids

Designed exclusively for children

Did you ever see a dynamic toy like this?

Do you like to play with toys?

Don't you wish you had one when you were a kid?

Donate a toy for a child!

Even you'll fall in love with our toys!

Exciting savings on hot toys and more!

For the toys you want

Fun savings on your favorite toys!

Fun toys for children of all ages

Get it at your local toy store!

Get the toys that are in demand... now!

Give them technological toys

Great toys for great kids!

Happy savings on the best toys!

Happy-go-lucky toy savings!

Here's a toy for all kids of all ages

Holiday toys for every kid's wish list

Hottest toys going fast!

Hours and hours of fun, guaranteed

Imaginative toys for child's play

Interactive toys for active kids!

It's a new toy every day!

It's a Playtime And Toy Time... Sales Event!

It's this year's hottest toy!

Join in on the toy drive

Just for kids who like toys

Learning toys that grow with your kids!

Low-tech prices, high-tech value toys... now on sale!

Must-have toys!

No tools required... assembles in minutes

Now on sale! The toys you want!!!

One magnificent toy sale!

One of the greatest toys for men of all ages

One toy that no child should be without

Play, learn, create and save!

Please... no tears over out-of-stock toys!

Safe, high-quality toddler toys!

Save on cool toys for the kids!

Save on their favorite toys!

317

Toys

See what's new at the toy store!

Share the joy... share the toys... share the savings!

Smart savings on learning toys!

Smart ways for kids to play and for you to save!

Some assembly required

Spectacular Toy Clearance!

Take home your favorite toy... today!

Terrific toys for every kid!

Terrific toys... $10 or less!

Thank heaven for little girls' toys!

The best toys are on sale at...

The Big Toy Box... Sales Event!

The dollhouse of her dreams

The highest quality toys ever built!

The most irresistible toy you've seen in years!

The place to buy classic toys!

The store for the toys you want!

The toy's most difficult feature was the instructions

The Toymania Sale begins today!

The toys they want!

There's joy in Toy Town all year long!

These are your favorite toys... Christmas Sale Event!

This store is filled with toys!

This toy is a must-have

This toy is for someone who doesn't want to grow up

'Tis the toy season!

Totally Toys Sale!

Toy Mania Sale Event!

Toy stories are told here!

Toyriffic values going on right now!

Toy-riffic values!

Toys at wished-for prices!

Toys either for yourself or your child

Toys for all ages

Toys for big boys and little girls

Toys for curious toddlers to discover and play

Toys for dogs and cats of all ages

Toys for Tots... is a great way to share your toys!

Toys that are a joy to play with

Toys that encourage creativity

Toys that get kids excited

Toys that make it easy for kids to learn and play

Toys that no child should be without

Toys that still pull at those old heartstrings

Toys that you didn't have as a kid but always wanted

Toys the way they used to make them

Toys to fill your little girl's wish

Toys to help kids discover a whole new world of fun

Toys to make their imagination soar

Unbelievable savings on the toys they want!

We sell just the right toys!

We're loaded with tons of neat toys!

We're wowing toy shoppers with exciting savings!

We've got the toys Santa forgot!

We've got toys for kids of all ages

Where kids get hooked on toys!

Wind up the toys with these savings!

You're invited to an incredible and beautiful Doll Sale Event!

You've seen them on TV

Your destination for all your favorite toys!

Your kids deserve the best toys!

Your kids won't stop playing with this toy

Your No. 1 Specialty Toy Store!

Training

All you have to do is put your training to work

An entire year's worth of training for less than...

Authorized hands-on training

Be ready! Start your training now!

Did you ever receive security training?

Do you have a hit-or-miss training program?

Don't blame them; train them!

Don't be afraid to invest in training

Even the pros go to training camps every spring!

Find the time for training

Fire up your training!

For initial training, ongoing training or performance coaching

Get busy training!

Get in on the ground floor with training

Get solid quality training without leaving your office

Get the training you need for the tools you use

Getting business training under your belt

Give them the right training, right now!

Got a group to train?

Have you upgraded your training?

High-quality employee training

How much does it cost to train a new employee?

How to leverage your training dollars

If you're not ready to make the commitment, then forget about training

Innovative ways to train employees

Invest in training

Is your training department missing the boat?

It's all about B2B training... back to basics

It's what we do... training!

Just saying you took a training course isn't enough

Just-in-time training

Keep your training fresh and dynamic

Keeping the training process in sync with customer expectations

Learn from a training expert

Life skills training

Live training is still the best way to go

Make it fun, make it effective, make it successful

Making training a necessity, not an option

Missing the mark with training?

Motivated and happy, well-trained and talented

Need help training?

Never underestimate the value, or power, of training

One-to-one training boosts motivation

Our people can make your people better

Our philosophy behind training is...

Our trainers do more than train

Our training makes a difference

Professional training dries up sweaty palms

Put a lot into training, and you'll get the most out of it

Quality of training... not quantity

Ready-to-use training program

Real support! Real solutions! Real training!

Realistic training

Recruit. Train. Promote.

Training

Save time and money with in-house training

Simple to learn, easy to use

State-of-the-art training

Stretch your training dollars with us

Successful people aren't born, they're trained

Tailored to your training requirements

Take advantage of our superior training now!

Take your training to a new dimension

Taught by the top industry professionals

Team training available

The best line of defense is well-trained employees

The best training program in the world

The best value for your training dollars

The essential elements of effective training

The most innovative training in...

The personal touch of classroom training

The right training at the right time for the right people

Think of us as your partner in training

Tips for training

To be the best, train with the best

Train everyone today... for tomorrow!

Train like the pros

Training for challenging times

Training for peak performance

Training is essential to adding value to your company and your customers

Training is our business... it's what we do!

Training needed?

Training salespeople to be salespeople

Training that will work for you!

Training that's guaranteed

Training today for tomorrow's success

Training when you need it, where you need it

Training with the best

Training with the human touch

Training: Now available for whenever you need it

Up-to-the-minute training for your sales staff

View training as a process, not a product

We come to your office with computers and an instructor

We deliver up-to-the-minute customized training

We do the training for you!

We don't stand behind our training; we stand behind you

We invest in people... we believe in training

We know something about training that you don't

We know that you know that training is necessary

We supply the right technologies

We train people how to work together

We train you to train your people

We've got the training you need!

Why do we need training?

Why you shouldn't miss this great training opportunity

With one purpose in mind... training

Work with the professionals

You can never have enough training

You can't afford not to be current on the latest technology

You name it. We are certified!

You provide the people and we provide the training

You'll get more training per dollar with our staff!

Your training includes everything you need now and for the future!

Transportation

A city with a world-class public transit system

A fast, high-quality way for Americans to travel

A hop, skip and jump to your bus depot

A scooter to fit every need

A train is a little slower, but you get to see the country

A world of wheels

Air travel is definitely the way to go

An alternative choice of transportation

Are you a road hazard?

Are you on the right track?

Are you still driving in the slow lane?

Are you taking your lumps at the gas pumps?

Are you tired of the city traffic?

Autos. Trucks. Cycles. Or just wheels.

Buckle up for the next million miles

But carpooling it is

By air. By rail. By truck. By barge.

Choosing your mode of transportation

Coming to a railroad near you

"Commute" is an ugly word

Concerned about rail crossing safety?

Discover how easy it is to get from place to place without a car

Do we have the transportation solutions of the future?

Driving is an economical way to travel

Enjoy the most comfortable ride of your life

For dignified, reliable transportation

For many, it's the only way to go

From now on, I'm carpooling

From the rear-view mirror

Get in the express lane!

Got a transportation gripe?

Here's a ride worth taking

Here's a vote for public transportation

Here's how to avoid the headaches and hassles of traffic

High-speed rail offers a better way

Highway and transit infrastructure

Hop on and take a ride

How do we get from here to there?

If time is money, why spend it in traffic?

If you look at the cost of transportation, bikes and buses make a lot more sense

If you lose your way, follow our tracks

If you want to get there without the aggravation, try walking

Imagine a world with no traffic jams

Innovation in transportation is essential to the world's future

It's a great way of getting around

It's a great way to get there

It's basic transportation for people on the go!

It's cheaper to take a taxi

It's definitely the way to go

It's easily accessible by car, train or plane

It's not about how fast you get there. It's about getting there!

It's so nice not to have to drive

It's time to stop and ask for directions

Let's put more dollars into public transportation!

Life in the insane lane

Life is short. So is the commute!

Transportation

Live a little... ride a scooter

Looking for basic transportation?

Looking to escape traffic?

Make your rush hour easier with...

Meet me at the oasis

More roads! More cars! More congestion!

Next time take a bus!

Park and ride

Public transportation is the most economical way to get around

Put the brakes on road rage

Ride the friendly rails

Say goodbye to bumper-to-bumper traffic

Set your wheels in motion

Share the drive

Take a joy ride with us!

Take a ride on our time machine

Take the "A" train

Thanks, I'd rather walk!

The bus stops here!

The early bird catches the bus

The focus is on transportation safety

The last 10 miles are on us!

The quickest way home is to take a train

The realities of tomorrow's transportation needs

The ride's on us

The shortest distance between two points is always under construction

The smart way to go

The three R's... roads, railroads and runways

The train is a great way to get to the airport

The workhorse of transportation

There is an alternative, like public transportation

This is the only way to travel

Tired of that pesky commute?

Traffic is the life blood of transportation

Trafficologically speaking...

Trains definitely are the way to go!

Transportation is more than concrete, asphalt and steel

Transportation's on the move

Traveling to and from work can be fun

Walk, don't drive!

Walking is still considered a major form of transportation

We drive the drives

We get you rolling

We offer valet parking!

We'll get you there by wings, wheels or water

We've got old railroad cars for sale!

Welcome to traffic jams

What are today's transportation alternatives?

What is the transportation of the future?

What is wrong with taking public transportation?

What's a traffic problem?

When driving beats flying

When was the last time you rode a train?

Why allow drive time to cut into your free time?

Why do so many people endure endless commutes?

Why don't you take public transportation?

Why not a monorail?

Why not commute by bike?

Why not just tune in to traffic radio?

Why walk when you can fly?

Will it be a new era in transportation?

You can start relaxing even before you arrive, if you take the train

Your family's transportation center

Travel / Vacation

850 ways to spend leisurely days, exciting nights and little of anything else!

A dream vacation is within reach

A good travel agent is a blessing

A place where comfort is a way of life

A romantic getaway is just what the doctor ordered

A summer vacation hit list

A vacation experience you will never forget

A vacation with total relaxation in mind

A weekend with the wife, buys you everything

A whole new way to enjoy your vacation

A yen for Japan?

Affordably priced and expertly planned, it's the best way to get away more often

After a hard day of rest, it's good to have the evening to relax

All the world's a stage. Act now and you can go see some of its better props

All vacations now on sale!

Anti-freeze fares to warm your body

Before you pack your bags, consider this offer!

Biggest vacation sale ever!

Board the ship of your dreams for the...

Bon Voyage Sale now in progress

Break the monotony of everyday life and discover the new you!

Can you trust your travel agent?

Catch the urge to travel

Come to Nashville for a song

Come with us and escape!

Deal yourself in on a great vacation deal!

Dedicated to making every vacation a success

Discover the new charm of old Hawaii!

Do more than think about travel; do it!

Do we have a vacation for you!

Do you need a blast of pure escapism?

Don't blow your vacation budget for the next century

Don't hem and haw, get away!

Don't just book a vacation... book an adventure!

Don't blow your vacation on a bad choice

Dying to do something that doesn't cost an arm and a leg

Estimated time of arrival is 3 weeks, 8 days and 9 hours

Even in the middle of nowhere, you're somewhere special

Everybody has an excuse not to take a vacation

Everywhere... for everyone!

Experience the vacation of a lifetime

Fed up with the high price of travel?

For a fascinating and exotic adventure

For people who are going places

For the wild, for the warm, for the weekend, for the wallet

Free VIP travel service gets you where you want to go!

Get ready to sail this holiday season!

Getting away from it all couldn't be easier

Give us ten minutes and we'll take you to places you've never been before!

Go where you'll be happy!

Going somewhere? Maybe you should!

Grab onto an exciting vacation... Answer to nobody

Great vacation values!

Have we got a vacation for you!

Have you ever been on a dream vacation?

Head for a sun-drenched island on your vacation

Here is a vacation that will light your fire!

How badly do you need a vacation?

How could you even consider not going?

If you can't find time for a vacation, you need one

If you can't relax here, you can't relax

If you have nothing better to do... take a vacation!

If your vacation has just been a far off dream, bring it a little closer to reality

In a vacation mode?

Instead of reading a book tonight, take a vacation

Is England your cup of tea?

It is a trip of a lifetime!

It's a big country. Why don't you see some of it this weekend?

It's a great place to get away and still be in the middle of it all

It's a vacation, it's an adventure!

It's an easy way to a free getaway!

It's easy to arrange a trip to suit your needs and style

It's going to be a show-stopping weekend!

It's great to have a vacation from a vacation

It's like a ticket to nowhere

It's more than a vacation, if it's in...

It's the best way to make a quick getaway

It's time to book for holiday travel... now!

It's time to put space between you and the bitter cold

It's your gateway to getting where you want to go

Itching to go???

Join us for a vacation experience made just for you!

Kick up your heels and head out of town

Lack motivation! Need a vacation?

Let us help get your vacation off to a great start!

Let us take you on vacation!

Let us take you where you want to go!

Let us transport you to another place and time

Let's get away from it all

Let's talk vacation

Long stretches of white sand await you

Looking for a terrific weekend getaway?

Looking for an exciting vacation?

Looking for something to do this weekend? Here are a few thousand options!

Make it a weekend to go for it!

Make your getaway plans now!

Making vacation plans? Look at ours!

Memorable vacations start here!

Million-dollar luggage sale going on now!

More mileage for your vacation dollar

More vacation than you can imagine

Need a break from life's hectic pace?

Need a change of scenery?

Need a quick getaway?

No one knows the ins and outs like we do

Nobody shows you the world like we do

Now it's time to do something nice for yourself

Now when you say you're going away for the weekend and can't be reached, you'll mean it

Now you can reward hard work without being hard on yourself

Now's the time to take a well-deserved perk

Offering the great escape

Once you go with us, you'll never go with anyone else

Packed with vacation values!

Plan a vacation with the love of your life

Plan now to take advantage of this terrific vacation!

Priced to send you packing

Priceless memories, now at substantial savings!

Ready to escape the cold and snow?

Recharge! Refuel! Renew! Bounce back!

Refreshing! Exciting! Adventurous!

Relax with a good vacation

Say yes to travel!

See it all without spending it all

Skip town! Make tracks! Fly the coop!

So spoil yourself a little

So what are you waiting for?

So where on earth do you want to go?

So why not go when the going is cheap?

So, why go anywhere?

Soak up the excitement at...

Some people consider flying first class a capital investment

Sometimes a change of scenery is what you need

Sometimes, the perfect destination is a place with nothing to do

Staring at the same old four walls?

Start planning now!!!

Stay next to everything. Pay next to nothing!

Sun-drenched savings!

Take a break and explore the serenity of the desert

Take a break without going broke

Take a red, white and blue vacation for very little green

Take a vacation before you really need one

Take advantage of these great vacation specials!

Take an exciting journey into fun!

Take off for a wild weekend!

Take off for the sun and save!

Tell him you want to go

That long-awaited vacation is now!

The best travel bargains are... now!

The best value in travel... anywhere!

The days are cool. The nights are hot. The savings are sizzling.

The perfect vacation, at a perfect pace and at a perfect price!

The place to go when you want to feel right at home

The tropical atmosphere does something for everyone

The vacation you want, a price you can afford

The vacation you've longed for is within easy reach

The vacations are best when you go southwest

There's a whole big world out there waiting to be explored

There's never a better time to vacation than now!

Think getaway!

This is one vacation you won't forget

This is your vacation, after all

This summer, take a vacation that will change your life

This summer's best vacation values!

Time to take a late summer vacation

Travel is what we do

Travel the world with someone who knows their way around

Travel the world with us!

Travel to the ice country and it will melt your heart

Two weeks with us and you'll be talking like a sailor

Unbelievable vacation values!

Vacations are us!

Vacations don't just happen

Visit here before you go anywhere else

Want to get away from the same-old-same-old?

Warning! Exposure to a vacation may lead to complete serenity

Was your last vacation an escape?

We are the travel pros

We can take you there!

We go where others only dream

We handle spur-of-the-moment vacations

We make you feel like you're somewhere you're not

We will customize your vacation for you

We will make you feel like you're on vacation

We'd be delighted to take you there

We'll get you there cheap

We'll put you in a vacation mood

We'll show you the best vacation in the world

We're a traveler's best friend

We're not afraid to tell you where to go

We're the difference between a great vacation and just going places

We've got a great summer vacation for you!

We've got the weekend covered for you

We've thought of everything so you don't have to

Weekend rates all week long

What a way to get away!

What could be better than beachcombing in...

What you need to know to go where you want to get

What's better than a vacation that offers a bit of both fun and relaxation?

Whatever happened to getting away from it all?

When in America, do as the locals do

When you go on vacation, we go to work

When you gotta get away... we gotta get you away

Where can I go for less than $500?

Where the magic lasts a lifetime

Where will you go this summer?

Where would you like to go next?

Where you won't need a vacation afterwards

Where you'll find the retreat you've been looking for

Whether you're going around the corner or around the world

Who needs a travel partner when you travel with us?

Why does summer always require a vacation?

Why pay for a room you can't afford to leave?

Winterize your vacation

Wish you were there!

With a fun pack vacation, you get the sun, the moon and the stars

With winter so close, shouldn't you be here? Or here? Or here? Or here?

You can take a fabulous vacation even if you aren't loaded

You can travel around the world, but you always end up back in the same place

You don't have to go far to get away from it all

You'll never find a better time to visit...

Your first class ticket to...

Your money has never gone this far

Your passport to the...

Your ticket to the comfort zone

Zip-A-Dee-Do-It-All Vacations!

T-Shirt

Ain't too proud to beg

All this body does is eat, drink and sleep

Ask me if I care

Be flexible. Stuff happens!

Been there... done that!

Believe in me and I'll believe in you

Big hat... no cattle!

Build a bridge and get over it

Cell phone users are a jittery bunch

Censored! Me and my foul mouth

Change is good... deal with it!

Common sense makes you uncommon

Count me among those who couldn't care less

Count your blessings and move on

Do something nice for someone else

Do you have someone to talk to?

Don't buy a treadmill if you don't like to walk!

Don't mess with Mr. Zero

Don't panic. I'm organic

Education is a good thing. So are bobblehead dolls!

Everybody's a skeptic

Flying is what helped me get my life off the ground!

Frogs live in this shirt

Get in touch with reality... today!

Get off my cloud!

Get out of the way of this avalanche!

Get over yourself. Get a sense of humor

Get real. That's it!

Get used to it. I change every day!

Give me a hug to cheer me up

Good fences make good neighbors, if properly maintained

Good morning loser

Guess what? It's not a perfect world!

Happiness is having alternatives

Have it your way... go somewhere else!

Hey, I'm doing what I'm told to do!

How can the free market be hit by regulations?

I always wanted to be a somebody

I can be counted on not to be counted on!

I don't hate nobody

I get satisfaction out of doing nothing

I have me to worry about, and that's a lot

I let my t-shirt do the talking

I need all the help I can get

I thrive on adversity

I wanna be a big shot

I was born healthy

I work for the weekends

I'll have what he's stealing

I'm a big loser!

I'm a chronic procastinator!

I'm a diet dropout!

I'm a nauseating do-gooder

I'm a professional whiner

I'm already larger than life

I'm an example of what not to be!

I'm not retiring... I'm just taking a hiatus

I'm ready for that last roundup

I'm sensitive!

I'm with stupid

T-Shirt

If dogs could speak, we wouldn't understand them

If I need advice, I can buy it!

If I'm the real thing, what is left for the unreal?

If life's a gas... fill me up!

In real life, I do nothing

In tennis, love means nothing... in life, it means everything

Is it Friday yet?

Is your husband in another man's arms?

It's a free country and you have the right to be stupid

It's big to think small

Let me be frank: I just don't care

Life is crazy... Get sane!

Life is just a day at the beach

Life is what you make it

Life's a bird. Pluck it!

Life's not always a picnic

Live with it... you can't do anything about it!

Living the American saying... "Go for it!"

Make like a shock absorber and bounce over me

Mother Earth... we love you, man

My cups runneth over

My motto is "No problem!"

Never steam clean your body!

Never trust anybody who says, "Trust me!"

Nobody understands me!

Nobody's goin' to argue with me!

Nothing compares to the real thing

Oh, get real!

Only one thing's certain. Nothing's certain!

Playing God is a very difficult role

Please talk to me!

Relax, it only looks expensive

Rely on me? Are you kiddin'?

Remember, there are no stupid questions, only stupid people!

Screw the golden years

Shopping is a holiday from life!

So if you like what you see, grab it now!

Sometimes life is fair

Start me up

Stop being a pessimist... life's too short!

The days of the Lone Ranger are gone

The meaning of life is to live it

The only thing I care about is the "W"

The paranoids are after me

This bird is going to party

This body goes where it's needed!

This body is for educational and research purposes only!

This is me! Can you deal with this?

This lady ain't afraid to sweat

This space for rent

Times Square is just a theme park!

To call me overrated is an understatement!

To live free is my motto

Today, if you're lucky, you'll be totally ignored!

Warning: contents under pressure

We know who "they" are!

Well, twang my guitar

What's the point of being the same?

When things get tough, I stop!

When you get older, it takes a lot longer to do nothing

Wherever the buck stops, so do we

Who you see is what you get

You are my wake-up call

Valentine's Day

A chocolate valentine that's fit for a queen

A dozen roses are a romantic way to say...

A gift says you're special to me

A great gift for your funny valentine

A great place for Valentine's Day!

A healthy valentine for the one you love

A perfect gift for the one you love

A perfect treat for your valentine

A perfect Valentine's Day getaway!

A romantic gift for Valentine's Day!

A special gift from the heart

A sweet and sexy gift for romantics who celebrate Valentine's all year long

A sweet deal for your favorite valentine!

A sweetheart of a deal and a cupid of a sale!

A treat for your valentine, one for yourself too!

A valentine they'll never forget

A Valentine's Day extravaganza!

A Valentine's gift that's simply bizarre

A warm and touching Valentine's gift

Aim for the heart with a deal for lovers!

All types of gifts for all types of valentines

All you need is love for a romantic Valentine's Day celebration!

An appealing choice for Valentine's Day!

An e-mail valentine right online

Are you free for Valentine's Day? We are!

Are you tired of giving a box of chocolates or flowers?

Bake a heart-shaped cake for your valentine

Be a sweetheart, call someone you love and say Happy Valentine's Day!

Calling all cupid-type dudes

Can you pass the test of love this Valentine's Day?

Candies and flowers are a time-honored way to say I love you!

Candy is dandy, but flowers are sweeter

Candy's nice, but a romantic valentine could be a lot sweeter

Capture the magic of love with roses

Celebrate love with us!

Celebrate Valentine's Day all week long

Charm her with a gift of love

Coupon "Good for one hug"

Cupid values! Lovable prices! Sweet savings!

Declare your affection with...

Do something special for that person in your life

Does your heart remember Valentine's Day?

Don't give her flowers again, give a gift from...

Don't let this Valentine's Day pass without someone special!

Don't overlook that special man in your life

Don't pretend you don't remember

Don't wait until next year to be a sweetheart again

Easy ways to make someone feel special

Enjoy the magic of Valentine's Day!

Every day is Valentine's Day at...

Everything for your honey is on sale!

Express your feelings with a gift of love

Express yourself with absolute style

Fill every hour of Valentine's Day with love!

For a girl with a big heart

For a special Valentine's Day!

For last-minute lovers!

For sweethearts and sweet tooths!

For that one perfect someone on Valentine's Day!

For the one you love, Happy Valentine's Day!

From a romantic past comes the perfect present

From a secret admirer

From the heart! From a kiss! From a friend!

Get bullish on love this Valentine's Day!

Get in the mood and smell the roses

Get in the mood early for a lovable Valentine's Day!

Get ready to swoon your sweetie

Gifts from the heart

Gifts to warm your sweetheart's heart

Give her something that will make her eyes sparkle

Give your valentine more than a hug

Give your valentine the gift of gold

Give yourself something special this Valentine's Day!

Great ways to have a great Valentine's Day!

Happy Value-tine's Day!

Have a big heart this Valentine's Day!

Heart to beat savings!

Heartfelt gifts for your valentine

Hearts and flowers, everyone's valentine gift

Hearts will skip a beat at our Valentine's Day sale!

Here are the sweetest ways to say, "I love you"

Here's where to woo your sweetheart this Valentine's Day!

How many ways can you say... I love you?

How to handle your sweetie on Valentine's Day!

How to make her gasp on Valentine's Day!

If it comes from the heart, shouldn't it come from you?

If you're sweet on someone, create a someone

Is your valentine virtuous? Vivacious? Voluptuous? Valiant? Voluble?

It's a great time to make someone feel special

It's a holiday for love!

It's easier to get close to your valentine with...

It's everything you love best about your valentine

It's never to late for a Valentine's Day gift!

It's never too late to say I love you!

It's not the gift, it's the thought that counts

It's time to romance your special someone

Just make someone happy!

Keep her guessing this Valentine's Day!

Learn the language of love this Valentine's Day!

Let love triumph this Valentine's Day!

Let romance linger by giving a special Valentine gift!

Light a fire with the gifts of love

Love comes in a red heart-shaped box

Love lasts forever, but this sale won't!

Make a Valentine's greeting call to your best friend tonight!

Make every day a Valentine Day!

Make her smile this Valentine's Day!

Make it a Valentine's Day you'll both enjoy

Make someone special very happy

Make this Valentine's Day sizzle!

Make this Valentine's Day... a special holiday!

Make Valentine's Day an affair to remember

Make your valentine glow with...

Melt someone's heart... today!

No one has more ways to say I love you... than we do!

Our Valentine gifts, prices that won't break your heart!

Plan to make her heart skip a beat

Put your heart into Valentine's Day!

Remember someone you love this Valentine's Day!

Romance your valentine with...

Savings that will capture your heart

Say "I love you" to all your sweethearts

Say you love her with the sweetest Valentine's gift

Scent-sational gifts for your valentine!

Send a smile on Valentine's Day!

Share your cupid with someone you love

Show a little heart this Valentine's Day!

Show her how much she means to you

Show your sweet side... this Valentine's Day!

So how does your valentine rate in the romance department?

Start a Valentine's Day romance with our...

Straight from one heart to another heart

Surprise a loved one with a very special gift

Surprise your sweetheart this Valentine's Day!

Sweet savings from the heart!

Sweet-talk your customers this Valentine's Day!

Sweet valentine savings!

Sweeten her day with...

Sweetheart specials!

Sweethearts deserve sweet hearts

The heartthrob of your life deserves a...

The perfect way to express your love

The pursuit of love. The proof of love. The gift of love.

The smart way to say... I love you!

The Valentine gift that keeps on loving

These sweet deals won't last the day!

Things you can buy a "real man" for Valentine's Day!

This year say Happy Valentine's Day with...

Treat your sweetie with our sweets

Tug at her heartstrings with the gift of love

Twice as nice for lovebird savings!

Valentine's Day headquarters

Valentine's Day is a fabulous time to say, "I love you!"

Valentine's gifts at a price you'll fall in love with!

Ways to surprise your valentine

We have everything to sweep her off her feet

We have what you want for everyone you love!

We've got a sweet deal for your valentine sweetheart!

What every woman wants to receive on Valentine's Day!

What to get your loved one for Valentine's Day!

Whatcha givin' your sweetie for Valentine's Day?

When it comes to your heartstrings, don't lose sight of your purse strings

Whisk your valentine away for a romantic night!

You don't need a sweetheart to celebrate Valentine's Day!

Your confection connection to all our sweethearts... Happy Valentine's Day Sale!

Value

A classic value

A dollar value pay back

A fantastic value!

A garden of value$

A great place to find exceptional value every day!

A great value every day!

A heritage of value

A name that's synonymous with value

A real clean deal... sweep up these values!

A really honest value

A sale loaded with pure shock value!

A terrific value, too!

A value you can't refuse

Absolutely our very best value!

Added value to the shopping experience

Affordable is the most fitting word to describe the exceptional value!

Amazing values!

America's best values!

An excellent value for the money

An exceptional value made better

An extraordinary good value

An incomparable value

An outrageous value

Appreciate the value

As long as you can create value, you can grow the business

At extra value pricing for you!

At superb price value!

Bargain basement values!

Below blue book value

Best overall value

Best value! Best price!

Best values of the season

Best values rise to the top!

Better values every day!

Better values for your buck, no matter the price!

Big incentives! Big excitement! Big value!

Biggest values of the week

Bonus Value Days!

Cashing in on value

Catch the value

Check out our special value pack

Check out our values for yourself

Choose value over price

Clean up with these terrific values!

Compare the value, compare the quality!

Creating value for our customers

Curtain going up on incredible values!

Customers look for value

Damn, What a Value Sales Event!

Delivering value for customers

Discover the value for yourself

Do you appreciate value as much as we do?

Do-it-now values!

Dollar for dollar, there's no better value!

Dollars and sense values

Don't gamble with values like this

Double Value Days!

Down to earth values

Down with high prices, up with great values!

Emphasize value, not just service

Enjoy even more values online

Even if you get a fraction of the value, it's cheap!

Even when money is no object, value is

Exceptional value and excellent results

Exceptional value for the whole family!

Extra value for you

Extraordinary values

Fair prices and exceptional values!

Fall Harvest of Values!

Family Value Days!

Fantastic value for your money

Fantastic values!

Farm field value to your table

Five valuable words: Value, value, value, value and value!

Five-star value!

For an excellent family value

For the best value anywhere

Fresh value prices!

Genuine value

Get a great value on the best selection...

Get more value for your dollar at...

Get rolling with these great values!

Get savings! Get value!

Getting your value's worth

Go with the value you can trust

Good luck finding a better value

Grand Slam Values!

Great items + low prices = value

Great prices! Best values!

Great values and unbelievable variety

Great values available at...

Great values by the truckload!

Great values worth screaming about

Have a picnic with our great values

I definitely got my money's worth

I want value for my money

Incredible prices... amazing value!

Incredible values for you!

Incredible values... never on sale for less!

Instant values! Instant savings!

It all adds up to the best values in America!

It all comes down to value

It's an amazing value at incredible prices!

It's one extraordinary value

It's the mother lode of values

It's too good of a value to pass up!

It's value-added

It's worth every penny!

It's worth the extra money

Just step up to a great value

Kick-off values

Let's talk quality and value

Lifetime customer value guaranteed

Look at these exceptional values

Looking for value?

Low prices... great values!

More bonus values inside

More choices! More savings! More value!

More total value

More value for your money

More value in a trusted name

Must be of equal or greater value!

No better value anywhere

No tricks... just value!

Now is the time to get fantastic values!

Once upon a special value

One of the best domestic values!

Open your eyes to a new dimension of value

Our aisles are piled high... with values!

Our best value ever!

Our first word is value

Our fresh values can't be beat

333

Our values will knock you out with fabulous savings!

Our year's best value!

Outrageous values!

Outstanding values from the word go

Parade of values

Plenty of value for the buck

Pocket the values at...

Price and value are two different things

Providing value to our customers

Quality + Price = Value

Race in for exceptional values

Raining values

Real savings... real values!

Real value! Real quality! Real service!

Real values can be yours...

Red tag value

Remarkable values every day!

Sensational values on...

Service vs. price vs. value

Service! Selection! Value!

Shop early! Our limited-time values end on...

Sneak preview values

Special high value offer!

Special Value Days... this weekend only!

Step into our sale, walk away with big values!

Step up to a great value!

Stock up with savings and exceptional values!

Style. Quality. Value.

Super hot values!

Super value! Super quality! Super service!

Surprising low prices, striking good values!

Surprising savings! Incredible values!

Take advantage of a world of value

Terrific values!

That adds up to even more value

That's our great idea of a great value

That's value-added service

The best overall value of the year

The best value ever

The best value on the planet

The best values in America can be found at...

The best variety and value

The extra cost is worth it

The great news is value

The pricing is competitive and the value is there

The search for value is over during our sale celebration!

The topic of the day is value

The value is in the competitive advantage

The value is priceless... the cost is free!

The value is unbeatable

The value of adding value

The value perceived by our customers is outstanding

The values are electric

There is value here

There's no better value than...

There's no better value... dollar for dollar!

There's only one way to real value

These are all winter values!

Think value not price

This is an added-value savings event!

This is the best value in town

This is where American value starts rolling

This special value won't last forever!

This week's best values

Tips for squeezing more value out of value

Treasure hunt of values

Turn on the value... turn on the savings!

Twice the savings! Twice the value!

Unbeatable value! Unbelievable value! Unsurpassed value!

Unbelievable values... unbeatable savings!

Uncompromised performance and value

Unsurpassed value with unbeatable deals!

Value and variety!

Value beyond the expectation

Value certified

Value Days Sale!

Value for your money

Value guarantee

Value is like fine wine

Value is our golden rule

Value means different things to different customers

Value meets savings

Value never sounded so good

Value-priced

Value that can't be beat

Value you can bank on

Value you can measure

Value, all the way around

Value, value, who's got the best value?

Value. Quality. Price.

Value-added incentives!

Values that make the difference

Values that pass the test

Values to jump on during our Storewide Clearance Days!

Values too good to pass up

Wake up and smell the value

We believe you won't find a better value anywhere!

We bring home great values

We get an "A-plus" for value!

We offer you a notable value

We put the value in value-added

We say, if you value it, you pay for it

We're bustin' with values!

We're creating outrageous values for you!

We're naming it our best value

We're talking value here

We've unleashed a flurry of unbeatable values!

When it comes to value...

Where great value never ends!

While everyone shouts about value, we deliver

With an unbelievable value!

With values like this, you can't go wrong

X-treme value buys!

You can't go wrong with great values like these

You don't have to wait for a sale to get outstanding values!

You get more total value when you shop at...

You get what you pay for

You make the difference in value

You sure know a great value when you see one

You want to see value for your money

You will appreciate these fantastic values!

You won't find a better value anywhere!

You'll get your money's worth with these values!

You'll go bananas over these great values

You'll know you're getting an exceptional value

You're buying this year's best value!

You're getting a sound value

Your road map to exciting values!

Your wait for extra value is over

A day of patriotism and honor

A day to remember the defenders of freedom

A living salute to pride and valor

A salute to all veterans who are living and those who are dead

A salute to those who fought to defend liberty

A thrilling tribute to those who served

Be proud to share this Veterans' Day

Dedicated to all veterans of foreign wars

Dedicated to mourning and memory rather than to victory

Every day is Veterans' Day at...

For the men who served their country with honor

Have we taken our veterans for granted?

In a Blaze of Glory Veterans' Day Sale!

In honor of all who served so gallantly in all wars

In remembrance of America's bravest heroes

It honors the men and women who won us peace

It's time once again to let our veterans know we appreciate them

Let's hear your thanks now!

Make this Veterans' Day a special day for some veteran

May the whole world never forget the tragedy of wars

Never forgotten the sacrifices of those who went

On Veterans' Day, every American who answered the call to arms has a place in our hearts

Pay homage to the past by honoring those who helped keep it alive

Remember America's veterans from the heart

Say thanks to a veteran today!

The 11th month... The 11th day... At 11 a.m.

The freedoms we enjoy were upheld by our veterans

The Home of the Brave Sale Event!

The sacrifices you made for me, and for other Americans

Their acts of heroism and compassion won't be forgotten

They deserve to be remembered

They died for peace and freedom

This is a salute to all veterans

Those who have served, and especially those who have fallen

Today we honor those who gave their all!

Today, and each day, remember our vets

Understanding those who served and sacrificed for our country

Veterans' Day Parade of Savings!

We are grateful to those who showed their patriotism

We can never repay our valiant vets for their sacrifices

We celebrate what Veterans gave to our country

We now honor all of these people on Veterans' Day

We pause and remember all those who fought for our freedom

We salute you and honor you for your sacrifice and commitment

We would like to thank you for what you did for our country

Who risked life and limbs to defend our country?

Volunteer

A great way to give something to your community

A little volunteering can help you live longer

A rewarding sense of accomplishment

A small gesture of compassion brings enormous rewards

Acts of kindness are not just for the holidays

Aiding the needy

An opportunity to give back

Be a good Samaritan

Be generous with your time

Become part of the family... volunteer!

Being a volunteer is showing that you care

Being around people who get things done

Best of all, volunteer work builds self-esteem

Caring. Compassion. Dedication.

Catch the volunteer spirit!

Community responsibility is everyone's business

Contribute to the human experience

Do you have a little time to spare?

Do you have what it takes to be a volunteer?

Doing nice things for others

Doing something to help people less fortunate takes less time than you'd think

Donating your time and talents to make a difference

Don't be afraid to stick your neck out... volunteer

Don't let the lack of experience keep you from volunteering

Find out how you can get involved

Fit community work into your schedule

Generosity of your time is the water that will make a love seed grow

Get involved! Make a difference!

Give a little something of yourself

Give a little time to your favorite charity

Give it a try!

Give your time! Give your love! Give of yourself!

Giving back to your community

Here's a chance for you to actually do something personally

I will volunteer my free time!

If you don't do it, who will?

If you want happiness for a lifetime, help somebody

If you'd like to do something really great... be a volunteer!

Is that asking too much?

It can enrich your life... be a volunteer!

It is really rewarding to help someone

It would mean the world to them... volunteer!

It's a good feeling to know you're doing something for someone else

It's a very caring thing to do

It's a way to show someone that you care

It's a wonderful thing, volunteering

It's good guys doing good things

It's just a nice thing to do

It's your responsibility to give something back to somebody else

Just get involved

Leave a rich legacy... volunteer!

Let's give them a hand

Life is great when you volunteer!

Volunteer

Life only means something if you do something for other people

Make time for volunteering!

Never underestimate the value of giving back to the community

Now it is time to give something back!

Once you start volunteering, you want to keep going

People with big hearts are needed!

Put the volunteer spirit to work

Reach in... reach out!

Real live human beings helping real live human beings

Respectful act of giving and receiving

Share your love and abilities with your community

So, just mosey on over and see what you can do to help

Somebody's got to do it!

Sometimes you can only do so much

Take pride in contributing to your fellow man

Take responsibility for volunteerism!

Take time out of your life and give to others

The cost to volunteer is your time!

The most precious gift that anyone can give is their time

The need for a helping hand!

There is no charge; all volunteers are free!

There is nothing more rewarding than knowing you are making a difference

This is a great way to give back!

To relieve stress in your life, consider becoming a volunteer

Too busy to care?

Use your free time to benefit others

Volunteer and make the world a better place

Volunteer once a week or once a month

Volunteering for the homeless warms the heart

Volunteering is a way to transfer your experience to someone else

Volunteering knows no age limit

Volunteering: a gift of time and talent

Volunteers of all ages are welcomed!

Volunteers, we need you!

Wanna be a good Samaritan?

We all have something to share and to give each other

We don't have a lot of meetings, but we get a lot done!

We encourage you to get involved

We need volunteers to roll up their sleeves to...

We need your body... not your money!

We'll make it easy for you to be involved

We're begging for volunteers!

What can I do to make a difference?

When deeds can say so much more

When you give your time to them, you're giving to everyone

When you make a gift of time, it's a major gift of yourself

When you volunteer, a whole new world opens up

Why not get involved?

Why should I even care?

Won't you come and lend a hand?

Working to make someone else's life a little nicer

You can make a big difference!

You need do nothing other than open your heart

You won't regret being a volunteer

You'll be a happier person for it

You'll thank yourself for doing so!

Your time could be a wonderful gift

Welcome

A familiar face and a warm smile welcome

A hearty "Welcome back"

A warm hand of welcome awaits you

A warm welcome... a friendly welcome

A welcome mat to brighten your doorstep

A welcoming atmosphere that will make you feel at home

All ages are welcome!

Aloooooha!

Always greet them with a generous heart

Always welcome here

Are you ready for a warm southwest welcome?

As always, it's a pleasure

As long as you have nowhere to go, you are welcome here!

Be our special guest!

Bearing you our warmest welcome

Before you walk through the front door, you know you're welcome

C'mon in, the coffee's on!

Come home to a warm welcome

Come in and be yourself

Come on in and stay awhile

Doors are always open here!

Drop by and check us out

Eight ways to say welcome

Every voice is welcome at the table

Everyone is welcome, and bring a guest

Everyone who walks through the door is a celebrity

Everyone's welcome... everyone!

Feel free to stop by. Our door's always open!

Freeloaders are not welcomed!

Give them a Southern welcome

Hang out the welcome sign

Here comes the welcome wagon!

Here's how to get a $25 welcome bonus in the mail!

Hospitality beams from every smile

Hospitality has your name on it!

It is in the spirit of togetherness that we welcome you

It's a great spot to hang your hat

It's a joy to have you here

It's a welcome treat

It's hospitality at its finest

It's nice to be treated so well

It's our way of saying hello

It's our way of saying welcome

Just relax, trust us and enjoy

Kids are welcome

My dears, you will be treated like royalty at our...

My home is your home

No one will be turned away!

Our door is open year 'round

Our traditional approach to hospitality

Please stop by and say hello

Ready to welcome you with open arms

So welcoming and warm

So won't you come in and let our home become yours?

Spread the aloha

Stay as long or as short as you like

Stop in and stay awhile

Take off your coat and stay a while

The door is open... and you're welcome! **339**

Welcome

The hospitality starts here!

The key is under the welcome mat

The moment you step through the door, you sense that it's a very special place

The perfect place to end your journey

The red carpet is out!

The welcome mat is out for you!

There are no strangers here, just friends!

There's always a place for you

There's room for all!

To you, we say make yourself comfortable, and welcome, there's room for everyone

Tonight is hospitality night!

Touched by your warmth and hospitality

Walk-ins welcome

We always make you feel welcome

We are honored to have you here

We are pleased to welcome you as our guest!

We greet newcomers with plenty of warmth

We have only one thing to say... welcome!

We know how to make a guest feel welcome

We look forward to having you as our guest in the very near future

We look forward to saying, "welcome back"

We look forward to seeing you walk through our door

We make our guests feel totally relaxed

We make you feel... right at home!

We roll out the green carpet for you

We treat our guests like Hollywood stars

We welcome everyone!

We welcome our guests to walk all over us

We welcome you with great pleasure

We welcome your comments, criticisms, questions and suggestions

We'll give you the royal treatment

We'll greet you with open arms!

We'll make you feel like you're at home

We'll treat you like a favorite aunt

We're always happy to see you!

We're always ready to welcome you!

We're so delighted that you are here

We've got one word for tough guests... welcome!

Welcome back to the world of...

Welcome family, friends and guests

Welcome friends... new and old

Welcome has your name on it!

Welcome is about the only word we can say

Welcome is the key to our door!

Welcome to America's friendliest city

Welcome to big savings!

Welcome to our Website

Welcome to the past

Welcomed, whether you're wearing a tuxedo or tennis shorts

What a difference a front door makes

When you walk through the front door, you know you're welcome

Where strangers are always welcome!

Where you are always welcomed and appreciated!

Y'all come back, y'hear?

You are a glowing welcome!

You are welcomed from doorbell to dessert

You deserve a star-spangled welcome!

You know you're welcome anytime

You're invited to be our guest!

You've come to the right place!

Win

365 winners! 365 days!

A big time win with big time savings!

A Good Guy Winner Sales Event!

A lot of winners... a lot of savings!

A sale that's clearly the winner!

A win is a win... a deal is a deal!

A winner every day with bargain prices

A winning combination of savings!

And now, the winners!

Be a real winner!

Be ready to win...

Be the winner... be the champion... during our Winner Take All Savings Days Celebration!

Can you spot the winner?

Catch that winning feeling

Dot to dot to dot, and you win...

Dreams of winning the lottery?

Enter to win one of...

Everybody Loves a Winner Sales Event!

Everybody wins with these deals!

Everybody's a winner at...

Fill out official entry form to win

Get on the winner's list

Go with a winner... take the deal!

Good judgment wins... during our sales event of the year!

Great prizes for all winning winners!

Head directly for the winner's circle with super savings!

Here's to the winners!

Here's a winning combination... amazing deals, incredible bargains!

Honey, I won!

How to pick a winner

How winners win...

It pays to play... it pays to win!

It's a deal... it's a winner!

It's all about winning the deal!

It's an absolute winner...

It's in the bag... savings!

It's time to tally up your wins and losses

It's Winner Time Savings Days!

It's your last chance to win

It's what makes you a winner

Just win, baby! Win!!!

Keep the winning spirit

Let the winning begin!

Looking like real winners

Make the winning move!

Match any of the numbers and win!

May the best deal win!

More opportunities to win, more opportunities to save!

More prizes! More winners!

Now you can be a winner with...

One winner and no losers

Our Loss is Your Gain Sales Event!

Reel in a winner during our Unreal Bargain Days!

Scratch off and win

See yourself in the winner's circle

Shop with us and finish a winner!

Stake your claim early to win

Start a winning streak of your own

Stop and see how you can win

Take advantage of these great buys... and you'll be a winner!

Take the win with terrific savings!

Win

The best-dressed person wins a...

The last man standing wins

The one with the most toys wins!

The savings can make you a winner!

The thrill of winning! The thrill of savings!

The winner-takes-all phenomenon

The winning equation...
bargains + values = big savings!

The winning ticket is in your hand

There are no winners, only great savings!

There's nothing like winning

Think small, win big!

This is a Win-Win Situation Sales Event!

This month's winner is you!

Today only! Starting at noon! One winner per hour!

Today... everyone's a winner

Two prizes for the price of none

We do whatever it takes for you to win on these terrific deals!

We'd like to see you win...

We'll divvy the winnings on all sale items!

We'll make you feel like a winner... with big savings!

We've hatched a winner of phenomenal savings!

When it comes to winning, any time is the right time for a deal!

Win $1,000,000... Take a chance!

Win a $5,000 U.S. savings bond

Win a free trip to...

Win a holiday get-away

Win a night out at...

Win a retirement home

Win a shopping spree at...

Win cash for the holidays

Win dinner for two

Win hundreds! Win thousands! Win millions!

Win instantly!!!

Win mad money

Win prize money instantly!

Win some holiday magic

Win the grand prize and we'll...

Winner time, sales time!

Winners win more at...

Winner-take-all!

Winning is the icing on the savings!

Winning is the name of the sale!

Wrap your arms around the winner

Yeah! We won!

You are a winner already

You are the grand prize winner!

You can pick your nose... you can pick your seat... but can you pick a winner?

You could be the million-dollar winner!

You could win fabulous prizes!

You gotta do what you gotta do to win

You have never been closer to winning than you are right now!

You have the winning formula

You Have the Winning Touch Sales Event!

You may be a winner! Rub off here first!

You must register to win!

You'll be walking away a winner with fabulous buys throughout the store!

You'll need a calculator to count your winnings

You're a winner with these awesome buys!

You're always a winner with...

Your winning formula... Best buys! Super savings! Terrific values!

Winter

12 quick fixes for winter discontent

A blanket sale you'll warm up to!

A Blizzard Of Bucks... Sale Event!

A flurry of winter values!

A freezer full of savings!

A nice mid-winter sale!

A sale all winter long, so you don't get left out in the cold!

A sale for winter enthusiasts!

A snowblower beats shoveling snow

A warm-up for winter weather

A winter sale you'll warm up to!

A winter service reminder

After the winter comes repairs

All Wrapped Up In Winter Sales Event!

All your cold-weather needs are on sale!

Already-reduced prices during our Winter Clearance

An avalanche of savings!

Arctic price blast!

Are you a victim of the January blahs?

Are you really ready for another winter?

As long as your feet are covered, you'll stay warm during our boots on Sale Event!

As the temperature drops, so do our prices!

At our January sidewalk sale, great savings are just around the corner!

Baby, It's Cold Outside Sales Event!

Be warm this winter, call...

Be wise, winterize!

Beat Old Man Winter Sale!

Beat the Winter Blahs Sales Event!

Because it's been so cold, we're turning up the heat on...

Before they melt away, catch our low winter fares!

Bitter cold... hot deals!

Blizzard Blowout Sale!

Blizzard of bucks savings!

Bold in the Cold Sales Event!

Breeze through the freeze with...

Bring in your old snow shovel and receive...

Bring On the Cold... Sales Event!

Bundle up and save a bundle... Winter Sale Event!

Button Up Your Overcoat Savings Event!

Cabin Fever Sale!

Call now for winter savings!

Can you get out of your driveway?

Cast Old Man Winter to the Wind Sales Event!

Catch the savings before they thaw out!

Chase Away Winter's Chill... Sale Event!

Chill-out buys!

Cold facts about getting started in the winter

Cold front alert... be ready!

Cold Man Winter is here and so are the savings!

Cold weather alert... Cold Weather Savings!

Cold-weather savings with out cost-saving alternatives

Combat winter's chill with...

Come in out of the cold for sizzling sale bargains!

Come inside and warm up with...

Cool savings for people who hate winter, even if you love it!

Count on us to make your winter wonderful

Cuddle up with these savings!

Cut your energy bills without freezing

Despite the cold, it's time to think cool

Discover the wonder of winter

Does cabin fever have your kids climbing the walls?

Don't Be Left Out In The Cold... Sales Event!

Don't get snowed in, get a snow blower!

Don't get snowed under by high prices!

Don't let your heating dollars blow out of your home this winter

Don't miss our Winter Clearance Sale Event!

Don't wait and be left out in the cold

Dynamite Winter Clearance Sale!

El Niño Special Winter Sale!

Escape the Boredom Sale!

Escape the humdrum of winter, take a sunshine vacation!

Final Winter Blast Sale!

Five-Day Winter Write-Down Sale!

For a dash of spring this winter, call...

For a winter warm-up...

For those times when you feel like hibernating

Free snow. You haul it!

Freezer full of values!

Friday night cabin fever special!

Gear up for winter with sales on everything from...

Get a jump on this winter with a furnace inspection

Get prepared now... for frosty winter weather

Get ready for chilly days, hot buys!

Gigantic January sale!

Give Jack Frost the cold shoulder with these hot savings!

Give someone you care about a little warmth this winter

Give the winter the cold shoulder

Give your home a winter tune-up

Got The Winter Blues Sales Event!

Great values on our winter favorites

Guaranteed to take the chill out of the coldest days ahead

Hail And Ice Sale Alert!

Have we got a winter for your kids

Here's how to avoid frostbite this year

Here's some winter relief...

Here's the best way to warm your buns

Hot deals to warm up your winter!

Hot idea for cold days

Hot mid-winter specials!

Hot savings for the cold winter season!

Hot, hot, hot winter sale!!!

House-warming bargains!

How to fool Old Man Winter

How you feel about winter depends on where you spend it

I'm Not Ready For Winter Sale Event!

Ice Buster Sale!

If it doesn't snow, we'll return your dough!

If you can't beat the winter, join it!

If you're not sick of winter... what's wrong with you?

Introducing the cure for the common winter

It's a snowstorm of savings!

It's a winter wonderland spectacular!

It's freezing outside, but the "Frees" are red hot inside!

It's never too cold for a hot drink

It's not too early to get ready for winter

It's our Annual Ice Cold Sale Event!

It's our service that will keep you warm

It's snowing savings!

It's time to start dreaming about that winter getaway!

January Blizzard of Savings Blitz!

January price freeze!

January Savings – Bonus Event!

January White Sale!

Jazz up winter with...

Join the winter fun at...

Jumpin' January sale!

Just blast the blahs out of the winter blues

Keep drafts out and heating bills down

Keep the home fires burning with these hot buys!

Keep the warmth in and the cold out with...

Keep your buns warm with Uncle John's long johns

Kiss Winter Goodbye Sales Event!

Let old man winter blow you into...

Looking for a winter getaway?

Looking for ways to beat the winter blahs?

Make us your own winter relief

Make winter less hair-raising... be prepared

Mid-winter housewarming sale!

Mid-winter meltdown sale!

Nothing warms up a cold winter day like...

Old Man Winter Sale!

On a stormy winter evening, what could be more fun than...

Our "Winter Is Coming" Bargain Days!

Our annual winter sale event!

Our winter forecast is lots of... savings!

Our Winter Wonderland Sales Event!

Overwhelmed by winter heating bills?

Pre-Freezin' Season Sale!

Pre-season price freeze!

Pre-Winter Energy Sale!

Pre-Winter Sale Is On Now!

Put a little summer into your winter with...

Put some spring into your winter at...

Save big this winter with our...

Savings as fresh as new snow!

Savings that are nothing to sniff at!

Savings that will turn winter into a wonderland!

Savings to bring you out of hibernation!

Savings to warm up your wallet and your body!

Say goodbye to winter with great buys on...

Sled, ski or skate in for more savings!

Snow Foolin' Savings!

Snowbird specials!

Snowman for hire

So Don't Get Left Out In The Cold Sales Event

Stay warm... be comfortable... save money

Stock up for the long cold winter ahead

Stop the big chill with big savings!

Stop winter cold from entering your house

Take a winter break; it will do you good

Take the chill out of winter and save!

Thaw out with... phenomenal buys!

The best sale of what winter has to offer!

The best winter for savings!

The colder it gets, the better the deal!

The hottest deals can be found in winter at...

The Icy Winds Of Winter Sales Event!

The Last Cruel Days Of Winter Sale!

The snow is falling and so are our prices!

345

The weather outside is frightful, but the savings inside are delightful!

The winter is alive with some outrageous deals!

The Winter Shoe and Boot Sale!

There's no business like snow business

There's nothing like a windy winter sale to cure a case of cabin fever!

Things get pretty lively in the dead of winter at...

Think fun in the snow

This sale is the perfect remedy for winter's doldrums!

This winter you can really go places!

Turn a snowfall into a windfall of savings!

Turn on the heat on cool winter prices!

Ultimate Winter Fur Sale!

Warm up to big savings!

Warm up to our winter prices!

Warm up to the hottest savings...

Warm up to these hot, hot, hot buys!

Warm up with our prices!

Warm up your winter with hot savings throughout the store!

Warm winter savings!

We can't stop winter, but these savings will make it easier for you!

We interrupt winter for a few words about...

We Wouldn't Snow You Sales Event!

We'll help you forget the long, hard winter

We'll help you th-th-thaw out the savings!

We've frozen our prices at their lowest point ever!

We've got savings to get you started this winter

We've got the cure for the common sale

We've thawed out some great prices!

When the snow melts, so do our prices!

When warmth counts most, count on us!

Why weather the winter?

Will your furnace survive another bitter cold winter?

Winter Blizzard Sale!

Winter Comfort Sale!

Winter End Sell-A-Bration!!!

Winter favorites all on sale!

Winter Festival of Savings!

Winter fitness fever... Catch it!

Winter health tips

Winter is in full swing and the savings are heating up!

Winter Madness Marches On Sale!

Winter Meltdown Sale!

Winter price thaw!

Winter rates are now in effect

Winter sales event of the season!

Winter service special!

Winter Snow Sale!

Winter Survival Sale!

Winter warmth on sale!

Winter warm-up sale!

Winter wonderland of savings!

Winter write-down sale!

Winterize with these great buys!

Winterizing now... can save you money later!

Wintertime money savers!

Wiping out the winter blues sale!

Wondering what to do this winter?

Would you believe it's our Annual Winter Sale?

You don't have to freeze to cut your heating bills

Your boiler could be heating you out of house and home

Your prescription for a healthy winter

Yes - No

A simple yes or no will do

A sure-fire yes

Ah, yes! Of course

Cash yes, advice no!

Definitely and enthusiastically, yes!

Expensive, yes! Financially, no!

Got 'em! Yes! Yes! Yes!

He says oh, no. She says, oh, yes!

Heck, yeah!

How can we say no to that?

If I say yes, do I get a discount?

Is that a yes or no?

It is safe to say yes

It takes a few "no's" to get a "yes"

It's a nice way to say "no"

It's nice to be able to say "yes!"

Just a simple yes/no response is required

Just answer yes or no

Let's say yes to more of everything!

No, I can't take a minute to answer your survey!

No, it's too much!

No, no, no, I can't decide now!

No, not today!

No, you can't! Yes, I can! No, you can't! Yes, I can!

No! Nope! No way! Certainly not! Nooooo!

Now is the time to say yes to...

Oh yeah! All right! Yes!

Oh yes, definitely

Oh, yeah. Absolutely!

On one hand, yes, on the other hand no

Place yes sticker here!

Push the yes button!

Refusing to take no for an answer

Say yes to our best offer!

Say yes to unbelievable savings!

Saying no is not the end

Saying yes is the most important qualification

The answer is always "yes"

This is your day to say yes!

We know how to say yes!

We're not going to take no for an answer!

We're not ready to say yes, but we're definitely not saying no

When in doubt, just say yes!

When you say no, we say yes

Yeah baby!

Yep, this is it

Yes sir, and how soon?

Yes! It was worth it!

Yes! Send me more information

Yes! Sign me up!

Yes, and here's why

Yes, folks, there's still time to...

Yes, it can be done

Yes, it's that simple

Yes, of course, even if it's raining

Yes, we're open!

Yes, we've got it!

Yes, you can have it all!

Yes. You read that correctly

Yes... we have what you're looking for!

You can always tell us "No, thanks!"

Your gut will insist yes, yes, yes

Yup, it's time to get it!

Zoo

A little zoo with a big heart!

A place with so much fun, even the animals are happy!

A zoo is a great place for animal lovers

Acquainting city dwellers with nature

Adopt an animal... and help the zoo!

Adopt-a-duck and take a quack at...

An inside look at animals

Animals live here!

Be a silly goose and come and see our...

Can't afford to go to Africa? No problem... just drop into the zoo!

Come and experience what makes us different!

Come and explore the zoo

Come see our chain gang!

Come to the zoo and rattle their cages!

Do the zoo!

Do you believe in love at first sight?

Don't feed the animals junk food, it may make them sick!

Escape for a day where nobody escapes!

Even our animals will be celebrating the holiday season!

Every day is a party at the zoo!

Family membership is a great value!

For animal lovers only!

From your world into their world

Get in touch with the animal kingdom

Get your paws on our Zoo Night Celebration!

Going to the zoo can make your weekend

Hear me roar at the zoo

How to feed a hungry tiger...

In our zoo, you're in your own little world

It really is just a wild time!

It takes animals to make a zoo

It won't cost you an arm and a leg, if you keep your hands and feet out of the cage

It'll make you go ape!

It's a big world in a zoo

It's a different way of looking at life

It's a jungle in here... dress accordingly!

It's easy to be swept away by their charm

It's fun being lost in the zoo

It's jammin' at the zoo time!

It's never a tough day at the zoo with our animals

It's nice to enjoy a day rubbing elbows with your friends

It's panda-monium at the zoo!

It's ready-to-rumble party time at the zoo!

It's tranquil! It's escape! It's paradise!

Join the zoo and save on admission and special events!

Join the zoo and see the world

Join us in the lion's den for winter fun at the zoo

Join your friends from around the world

Just zoo it!

Kids are thrilled! Parents are thrilled! Animals are thrilled!

Leave your worries at the zoo

Let us show you our family

Let us tell you what's going on in our society

Make plans to meet our family

Meet our new poster boy

Monkey around with our elephants

No one could love their animals more than we do!

Nothing puts you in a tropical mood like a visit to the zoo!

One of the most unique places on earth

Open your mind to the magic of our world

Our animals always have their act together

Our animals don't play on Broadway, but they'll put on a show for you!

Our animals show up just for you!

Our animals turn off their cell phones too!

Our animals will knock themselves out for you!

Our apes will drive you bananas

Our bears don't hibernate

Our elephants will remember you!

Our wildlife will be honored by your presence

Please don't feed the humans!

Please: do monkey around with the animals!

See what our animals do for a living

Show your loyalty to the animals... visit the zoo!

Sign up for our 10k walk-a-thon for the animals!

Spend a day of fun, adventure and discovery at the zoo!

Spend the summer in our yard!

Support Your Local Zoo Day!

Take a first hand look at the wildlife world

Take an elephant to breakfast

Take your wild bunch to where the wild things are

The happiest place on earth

The home of magnificent animals

The most democratic and child-friendly place in town

The only wildlife at our zoo is human

The zoo doesn't close 'til the big lion roars!

There are no other creatures quite like our creatures

There's nothing like a zoo to calm and comfort us

There's something about the zoo that's magic

There's still a lot of animal in our animals

This is where the deer and the antelope play. But why let them have all the fun?

Trust us, you'll flip over our seals!

We bring out the animal in you

We have one word to describe our zoo... entertaining!

We have tons of talent to entertain you!

We love to brag about our family

We put on our Sunday best, every day!

We wish our animals could say thanks... so we will say, "Thank You!"

We're proud of the company we keep

Welcome to the wild, wild, wildlife!

Why not hibernate at our place?

Wouldn't you like to be our friend?

You are now entering a stress-free environment

You don't need a passport to travel throughout our world!

You'll be hobnobbing with the high and mighty

You'll get your money's worth of enjoyment and entertainment

You'll have a whale of a good time!

You'll have more fun than a barrel of monkeys!

You're invited to a Celebration of Holiday Lights at the zoo

You're invited to our animal house!

You're invited to the Moose Is On The Loose zoo party!

Zoos are for people too!

My Own Clips